THE USUAL CHANNELS

INSIDE THE MYSTERIOUS WORLD OF POLITICAL WHIPS

SEBASTIAN WHALE

Biteback Publishing

First published in Great Britain in 2025 by
Biteback Publishing Ltd, London
Copyright © Sebastian Whale 2025

Sebastian Whale has asserted his right under the Copyright, Designs and Patents Act 1988 to be identified as the author of this work.

All rights reserved. No part of this publication may be reproduced, stored in a retrieval system or transmitted, in any form or by any means, without the publisher's prior permission in writing.

This book is sold subject to the condition that it shall not, by way of trade or otherwise, be lent, resold, hired out or otherwise circulated without the publisher's prior consent in any form of binding or cover other than that in which it is published and without a similar condition, including this condition, being imposed on the subsequent purchaser.

Every reasonable effort has been made to trace copyright holders of material reproduced in this book, but if any have been inadvertently overlooked the publisher would be glad to hear from them.

ISBN 978-1-78590-854-5

10 9 8 7 6 5 4 3 2 1

A CIP catalogue record for this book is available from the British Library.

Set in Minion Pro and Sabon

Printed and bound in Great Britain by
CPI Group (UK) Ltd, Croydon CR0 4YY

For Ioana

CONTENTS

History in Brief   ix
Preface   xiii

PART I   THE OFFICE
Chapter 1   The *Good* Old Days   3
Chapter 2   A Changing Tradition   7
Chapter 3   The Chief   15
Chapter 4   A Royal Office   25

PART II   1974–79
Chapter 5   Always the Bridesmaid   39
Chapter 6   Walter   49
Chapter 7   Playing Tribune   59
Chapter 8   The Fuck-Up Squad   71
Chapter 9   Communication Breakdown   81
Chapter 10   Life Support   93
Chapter 11   Cockle   99
Chapter 12   Men of Steel   105
Chapter 13   End Game   111
Chapter 14   Lacking Confidence   115
Chapter 15   Aftershocks   125

PART III   THE THATCHER YEARS
Chapter 16   The Iron Lady   135

Chapter 17	Characters	143
Chapter 18	A Man's World	151
Chapter 19	The Black Book	157
Chapter 20	Caregivers	165
Chapter 21	Social Animals	175
Chapter 22	F. U.	181
Chapter 23	Stalked	189

PART IV   MAASTRICHT, MAJOR, MAYHEM

Chapter 24	Setting the Tone	205
Chapter 25	The Caring Whip	211
Chapter 26	Maastricht	219
Chapter 27	Major Crisis	233
Chapter 28	Chapter and Verse	239
Chapter 29	Back to Basics	245
Chapter 30	Jacqui	255
Chapter 31	Labour, Anew	259

PART V   NEW LABOUR

Chapter 32	Rude Awakenings	271
Chapter 33	A New Dawn	283
Chapter 34	Hilary	289
Chapter 35	The 'Usual Suspects'	299
Chapter 36	Paul's Gospel	311
Chapter 37	Iraq	319
Chapter 38	Fallout	329
Chapter 39	Transition	337
Chapter 40	Tommy	345
Chapter 41	Crises	353
Chapter 42	P. M.	365

PART VI   UNNATURAL COALITIONS

Chapter 43	Posture to Power	377
Chapter 44	Plebiscites	391
Chapter 45	Westminster's Secret Service	403
Chapter 46	Culture Clash	411
Chapter 47	The R Group	419
Chapter 48	Doing a Walter	425
Chapter 49	The Meaning of Strife	439

PART VII   THE FINAL THROES

Chapter 50	Big Farmer	455
Chapter 51	Feeling the Pinch	467
Chapter 52	Truss Issues	479
Chapter 53	The Last Word	489

Acknowledgements	505
Notes	507
Index	519

HISTORY IN BRIEF

A COLLECTION OF INTERESTING, NOTABLE AND POIGNANT DATES IN WHIPPING

1621: Sir George Calvert, one of James I's Secretaries of State, issues what some believe to be the first recorded whip, asking for an MP's attendance in Parliament.[1]

1769: The first reference to 'whipping them in' features in a parliamentary debate.[2]

1832: With the 1832 Reform Act, the role of Parliamentary Secretary to the Treasury as Government Chief Whip 'effectively starts', says an author and former Chief Whip.[3]

1836: MPs vote in Aye and No lobbies, counted by tellers. Previously, one side remained in the chamber while the other side went into the lobby and were counted on their return.[4]

1867: The Reform Act of the same year gives more than 1.3 million men the vote. 'It was the first sweep of the democratic wave,' notes a former Liberal Party Chief Whip.[5]

1880–81: Treasury 'Blue Notes' reveal that the Chief Whip administers the King's 'Secret Service Fund' of £10,000 per year,[6] until its abolishment in 1886.

1900: The *Western Daily Press* reports the government are accepting pairs 'without demur'.[7]

1905: In reply to a parliamentary question, Prime Minister Arthur Balfour asks an MP to communicate with a colleague 'through the usual channels'.[8]

1911: Conservative peer Hugh Cecil says Liberal MPs 'vote as the party whips tell them', since whips decide whether their expenses are paid at the election. 'In a large measure, it is a corrupt assembly,' he says. Senior Liberal Winston Churchill fumes: 'That is a gross libel.'[9]

1918: The Representation of the People Act gives some women the right to vote. The Parliament (Qualification of Women Act) also allows women to stand for Parliament.

1919: Charles Harris, the holder of a clerical post in the government whips' office from October 1917,[10] becomes the first principal private secretary to the Government Chief Whip.

1926: Anonymous teetotal MP writes that the House of Commons is a 'tipsy' assembly.[11]

1931: Conservative politician David Margesson is appointed Government Chief Whip, beginning a nine-year tenure. 'If one politician of the twentieth century deserves to be remembered for his work as Chief Whip, it is Margesson,' writes an author and ex-Chief.[12]

1939: The role of principal private secretary to the Government Chief Whip formally becomes part of the civil service.

1951: Government whip Walter Bromley-Davenport mistakenly kicks the Belgian ambassador, believing him to be a Tory MP. Ted Heath replaces him in the whips' office and in 1955 becomes Chief, credited for his handling of the Conservatives during the Suez Crisis.

1961: Freddie Warren replaces Charles Harris as principal private secretary to the Government Chief Whip.

1964: Labour MP Harriet Slater becomes the first woman appointed to serve as a government whip.

1970: Ted Heath is elected Prime Minister, five years after becoming Tory Party leader.

February 1974: Harold Wilson's Labour Party secures four more seats than Ted Heath's Conservatives in the general election, but not enough to secure a majority in the Commons.

October 1974: Labour secures a narrow majority victory at another general election, beginning one of the most notorious parliaments for whipping in British political history…

PREFACE

'Sorry,' she said. 'You're writing a book about…?'

The magazine editor scanned the crowded room as though searching for a place of refuge in case she'd heard me right.

'Um, whips,' I repeated.

'Oh,' she said, prosecco nearing the edge of her glass. 'You're writing a book about whips.'

Cornered into small talk at a book launch on London's Savile Row, I realised, spiritually at least, that we were a long way from Westminster. 'Yeah,' I said. 'Political whips.'

She dropped her shoulders and wiped faux sweat from her brow. 'Ah! Political whips!' Her relief morphed into another frown.

'Do you know *House of Cards*?'

'Right,' she said, her eyes bulging with memories of Francis Urquhart. 'Those kinds of "whips".'

We sipped prosecco as though grateful for the distraction. She waved at no one in particular and left with: 'Well, good luck with it.'

Many whips would be pleased that their work had gone unnoticed. Even for some MPs, what whips *really* get up to around the parliamentary estate remains a mystery. By design, they operate in the shadows, away from the revealing glares of camera lights and journalists' cutting questions, their silence filled by others, their motivations and practices often ascribed.

In September 2012, Jeffrey Archer, author, peer and former Conservative MP, watched the opening night of *This House*, James Graham's magnificent play on the exploits of whips during the 1974–79 parliament. While leaving the National Theatre with Patrick McLoughlin, the Conservative Chief Whip until just a few weeks earlier, Archer fielded questions from reporters on what he had made of the show.

'Patrick stood there, and nobody asked him a question because nobody knew who he was,' Archer told me. 'He said it was his proudest moment.'

The secrets of the whips' office have attracted many a curious soul. Even former whips, breaching an unwritten code, have penned tomes, diaries, and articles on its history. Among them is Tim Renton, Margaret Thatcher's last Chief Whip, who, to the dismay of his whipping contemporaries, published a part-memoir, part-study of 'The Office'.

'Chief Whips should never write memoirs nor give detailed interviews about their work or their flock,' says one of Renton's successors, who, while declining an interview, sent over musings he was happy to see published, some of which also feature in our first chapter. The man, a former Conservative Party Chief Whip, argues that holders of the position act as a 'father confessor' in addition to other duties. In his time, he handled 'one coming out, three marriage problems and other personal difficulties'.

'I would go to jail for contempt of court rather than reveal any secret of The Office or what colleagues said,' he adds. 'If Conservative MPs thought that whips would be writing books or giving detailed interviews, then no one would talk to us again on anything.'

For writing his book, Renton was banned from attending whips' functions, 'just like Peter de la Billière was banned from the SAS because he wrote a book about them', says the former Chief.

OK, I am not comparing us to the ultra-brave men of the SAS, but the rule of trust is the same. I suppose if Chief Whips of all parties wrote detailed books, then we could outsell [former Conservative Cabinet minister and bestselling author] Nadine Dorries, Jilly Cooper and God knows how many Shades of Grey – but we don't and should never do so.

Several months after this email landed in my inbox, Simon Hart, Conservative Chief Whip under Prime Minister Rishi Sunak, announced that he would publish his diaries.

Though a brave few have spilled the beans, many people who pass through The Office subscribe to its code of omertà, confidently deeming The Office a near-impregnable world.

'Ex-whips don't discuss The Office, so you will have to look elsewhere, I am afraid,' said one, when I requested an interview for this book. A former Deputy Chief Whip said: 'I have a policy of not discussing matters which occurred during the period in which I served as a government whip. Indeed, I believe that whipping, like stripping, is best done in private.'

Another Conservative whip wrote a one-word reply. 'No.'

While it's true that *some* who passed through The Office still adhere to a lifelong vow of silence, shaking their heads at those who don't, it's also true that times are changing. Liberated by trailblazers – and wanting to put the record straight – certain whips have, to varying degrees, opened up about their time in The Office.

Some 157 people contributed to this project, including more than sixty who passed through the whips' office across generations; among them, eighteen Chief Whips (nineteen if you count the Lords). For what it's worth, and despite reputations, most contributors hailed from the Conservative Party, including several Chiefs. From the outset, I contacted scores of current and former MPs, all of whom have dealt with whips to varying degrees. Anecdotes and observations about The Office poured in as though a long-closed valve had been opened.

Naturally, some needed convincing of my motives.

'It sounds a bit like you're going to rehash all the clichés about whipping that *House of Cards* was particularly responsible for,' said a former Labour Chief Whip, seizing on my assertion that I wanted to make the book 'fun'. 'There's this whole sort of trope about whipping that is logged into most journalists' computers. In the modern age, frankly, it's completely wrong.'

This particular Chief eased up and offered a generous hour of his time.

The Usual Channels charts the past fifty years of British politics, beginning (after a run-through of the whips' office and how it works) with the notorious 1974–79 parliament. In a sense, I pick up from where Tim Renton left off in *Chief Whip: People, Power and Patronage in Westminster*, which brought the story up to the 1960s.

Before we begin, some housekeeping.

Contributors' words are in the present tense, and their roles are as they were at the time, even if the person in question went on to hold a more significant position for which they are better known (Labour Party grandee Neil Kinnock, for instance, joins our story as the MP for Bedwellty). Though many of the whips' routines remain unchanged, some, including their hours of work, evolve throughout the book, often at odds with the practices of today's whips as set out in the opening chapters. Rather than notifying you of every difference, the changes unfold as we progress.

Some interviewees requested anonymity to speak freely, so they are referred to by their job titles unless doing so might reveal their identity, in which case the description is more generic or obscured. Where possible, I have tried to check anecdotes or allegations with the individual concerned and put their version or rebuttal accordingly. Occasionally, this has not been feasible, whether because the person is dead, refused to comment or declined an interview. To repurpose a phrase used by members of the royal family during recent controversies: 'Recollections may vary.'

PREFACE

I started this project in September 2023, although I had contemplated it ever since writing about whips for *The House* magazine three years earlier. Whipping, I concluded midway through the process, is politics as it really is rather than as you might want it to be. The Office gives us a window into politicians' lives and how Parliament works. To that extent, I've learned more about Westminster and its occupants in the past twenty-four months than in nearly ten years of reporting.

This is *The Usual Channels*. Please enjoy.

PART I

THE OFFICE

CHAPTER 1

THE GOOD OLD DAYS

People often say that whipping isn't what it used to be.

For many politicians brought up on vivid tales of twisted genitalia, foul-mouthed tirades and hoisted lapels, this is a blessed relief. For others, not least ex-whips casting a judging eye over the eroding powers left in their successors' hands, it is a matter of regret.

'What sort of whinging namby-pambies are some MPs these days?' asks a former Conservative Party Chief Whip.

> They complain of bullying because a whip or the Chief Whip shouted at them. Big deal… dry your eyes. I saw a Conservative MP hurled ten feet down the Committee Corridor when he had lied to his whip about voting in a committee. I thought he got off lightly.
>
> I saw a wonderful Labour Deputy Chief Whip push one of his people against a wall, take hold of his most sensitive bits and tell him that if he ever voted with the Tories again, then he would find them in a jam jar, and a small jam jar at that.

The Chief hastens to add that he doesn't condone violence and insists, in a typical whip's fashion, that such behaviour never happened while *he* oversaw The Office. For the sake of their constituents, 'some colleagues from all parties', the Chief concludes, 'should empty that jam jar and stitch them back on'.

Whipping is like other pastimes that suffer from the lament of it being *different in my day*. Documenters of Westminster have long written wistfully of a whipping regime from a bygone era, yearning for a time that may never have lived up to the mythology or, in the aspects where it did, was not revered by those who lived through it.

'Some of us old romantics pine for a return of the good old days when the rule of law and the lynchmen reigned supreme in the Members' Lobby – and whips were whips,' wrote renowned Press Association journalist Chris Moncrieff in... 1986, when the Conservatives under Margaret Thatcher enjoyed a three-figure majority in the Commons. MPs from the period might be surprised to learn that whips were, in Moncrieff's words, 'too nice'.[1]

Sentimentalism aside, it is undoubtedly the case that over the past fifty years, much of the powers, methods and composition of the whips' office *have* changed dramatically, illustrated in a frank conversation between two Conservative MPs who served in different eras.

Charles Walker, a popular, heart-on-sleeve-wearing backbencher, sat down with his constituency chairman, Cecil Parkinson,* who served in the whips' office in the 1970s. That week, Walker, first elected in 2005 and into his second term as an MP, had seen the Government Chief Whip admonish a colleague on the fringes of the House of Commons chamber. Shocked not only at the flagrant nature of the public bollocking but also at the Chief's colourful language and reddening cheeks, Walker, himself not afraid of an impassioned word or two, felt compelled to share his experience.

'Cecil, he called him every word,' Walker said. 'He used the f-word and the c-word.'

'Did he really do that?' asked Parkinson. 'Oh, dear. I don't think he should have done that, Charles.'

The two men said nothing for a short time.

'Of course, in our day, we never did that,' Parkinson said. 'We *ruined* people's careers, but we never swore at them.'

---

* Cecil Parkinson passed away in 2016.

'It was done without a twinkle,' Walker says now, recalling the conversation. 'It was just like, bloody hell!"

Though there was an element of 'pantomime' in Parkinson's remark, 'at times, it did go way over the top', Walker says. 'There was far less scrutiny, and I suspect some pretty unpleasant things probably never saw the light of day that you wouldn't get away with now.'

Everything from how whips communicate to the patronage at their disposal to the location of their office on Downing Street is *not what it used to be*. But a key fundamental – the goal that has long underpinned the entire operation of the whips' office – has remained the same.

'I always describe it as being a bit like air traffic control,' says Bridget Prentice, a Labour whip under Prime Minister Tony Blair. 'It's not your job to decide the worthiness of the plane; your job is to get it in the air or on the ground safely. That's basically the role of the whips, to ensure that the government's business gets through as close to intact as possible.'

CHAPTER 2

A CHANGING TRADITION

What is a whip? And what do they do?

Whips oversee discipline, manage the day-to-day business in Parliament and, insofar as they can, ensure their colleagues vote in line with party policy. From political enforcers to parliamentary lubricators, whips have accrued a variety of synonyms, compared over the years by both their detractors and their advocates to the Stasi, the Broederbond and the Gestapo.

THE WHIP

The term 'whip' originates in hunting, where the whipper-in, a huntsman's assistant, 'would keep the hounds from straying by driving them back with the whip into the main body of the pack'.[1] The government and opposition parties in the Commons and the Lords have a team of whips, often patrolling Westminster's corridors and watering holes, hoovering up intel.

Historians differ over when whips and whipping came into being. In his study of Chief Whips, Tim Renton cited a 1621 letter from one of James I's Secretaries of State requesting an MP's attendance in Parliament as the first recorded whip. The emergence of political groupings such as the Whigs and the Tories in the late seventeenth century

arguably solidified the need for a coordinating force in Parliament.*
By the middle of the eighteenth century, the Parliamentary Secretary
to the Treasury (a position held today by the Chief Whip) sent letters
urging MPs to support the government of the day.[2]

For all the different aspects of the job, including suggesting names
for promotions or demotions at reshuffles, the whips' driving force is to
deliver the government's business. How whips encourage MPs to vote
accordingly is subjective and often tailored to the individual. Some opt
for gentle persuasion… others draw on personal appeals… a few might
lay out the implications of a potential rebellion.

Whether MPs follow the whips' encouragement is up to them.

'I've always been very impatient with anybody who says, "The whips
made me do it,"' says former Labour Cabinet minister Harriet Harman.
'You are the decision-maker about what you do. The whips are not
your boss.'

Each Thursday afternoon, The Office distributes a circular known
as 'The Whip' outlining the upcoming parliamentary business and expectations for attendance and votes, underlined up to three times to
denote importance. A one-line whip means MPs are requested but not
required to attend a vote. A two-line whip means MPs should attend
unless they have a pre-approved reason for not doing so. Death may
be a valid reason for missing a three-line whip, but even then, it will
be on a case-by-case basis. MPs receive email invitations that update
their calendars with the week ahead, giving them fewer excuses for any
memory lapses or missed fine print. 'MPs can have a reading age of
about five when it suits them,' jokes a government whips' office insider.

Unless the issue is a free vote† – meaning they can make their own
decisions without fear of repercussions – MPs are expected to follow
the voting instruction as set out in The Whip. Going against the leader's

---

* For his deft handling of the Commons as party manager for the Whigs, some academics argue Thomas Pelham-Holles (1693–1768), the Duke of Newcastle and former Prime Minister, was the first whip.

† The line of a whip relates to attendance. In June 2025, ahead of a division on decriminalising abortion – an issue of conscience – the whips issued a three-line whip to attend but gave MPs a free vote.

wishes is to rebel, an act considered most egregious when done on a three-line whip, especially if not communicated to The Office beforehand. The whips, who must know how to count, do not like surprises. Neither does their party leader.

Rebel on a three-line whip and an MP could lose the right to represent the party, sitting instead as an independent in the Commons. MPs may also abstain by not voting for or against a motion,* viewed as a lesser evil in the whips' eyes.

When a vote is called, the whips fan out to their positions, some lingering by the entrance to the division lobbies, others taking the opportunity to put one last arm around wavering backbenchers. A whip from the government and a whip from the opposition stand at the top of both the Aye and the No lobbies, counting MPs as they pass through to vote. After cross-referencing the numbers, the four tellers head to the Commons chamber to announce the result, the two from the victorious side standing on the right facing the Speaker's chair.

With tired MPs prone to slinking off the parliamentary estate, whips also guard various portals in the Palace of Westminster. Walter Bromley-Davenport, a Conservative whip from 1948 to 1951, stood at one exit when he saw a man leaving before the vote at 10 p.m. Believing the person in question to be a Tory backbencher, Bromley-Davenport ordered him to stay, but the man refused, so he kicked him. Soon, the whip would be made aware that the person was not an MP but the Belgian ambassador. Fellow Conservative MP Ted Heath, who would regale future generations with this encounter, replaced him in the whips' office.

Voting alongside members of the Cabinet and the Prime Minister offers a chance for MPs to raise issues or concerns with seniors. It also allows whips to look MPs in the whites of their eyes before they cast their votes. 'It does have more of an impact than you just making a

---

* MPs can also vote in both division lobbies to register an abstention.

telephone call when they're in the safety of their home,' says an ex-Tory whip.

Like journalists curating sources, whips can draw on relationships in times of need. When a Tory backbencher told their whip, whom they'd known for several years, that they planned to vote against a motion put forward by the Liberal Democrat–Conservative coalition government, the whip replied: 'Could you not just go home – for me?'

Out of deference to their friendship, the backbencher did just that.

The odd principled stand might not damage an MP's career. British politics has seen its fair share of high achievers who have not abided by a three-line whip. Just ask David Cameron, Boris Johnson and George Osborne, who, in 2002, opted to abstain rather than vote against allowing unmarried and gay couples to adopt as ordered by the then Tory Party leader, Iain Duncan Smith.

What's for certain is that repeat offenders aren't likely to secure preferment of much quality, if at all. The 'recalcitrants' – MPs who can never be relied on to support the party line – whips largely leave alone.

Pivotal for The Office is avoiding an otherwise loyal MP becoming a persistent rebel. A few politicians have even shed tears after rebelling on an issue they couldn't countenance supporting. But once the Rubicon is crossed, rebellions become easier, sometimes habitual.

A WHIP'S CORE

What sets whips apart from other Members of Parliament is that they take an effective vow of silence on joining The Office.

Government whips in the Commons do not speak from the despatch box or offer their views on policy in public, save for when they hold multiple roles or a minister commits what The Office considers to be a sin against the Holy Ghost and fails to turn up to the chamber.[3]

In such a rare scenario, whips may have to take the minister's place at the despatch box.

Even the slightest hint of a minister being missing-in-action gets the whips all hot and bothered. In the first parliament of the New Labour government, Helen Liddell told a senior whip she was going to rest in her office near the Commons before leading the adjournment debate at around 3 a.m. The minister couldn't sleep, so she showered and returned to the chamber. With the previous debate nearing an end and the whips unable to locate Liddell in her office, they turned the building upside down looking for her. Hurrying back into the chamber with instructions for the minister speaking to buy more time, the whips saw Liddell in her place on the frontbench, sitting, as she recalls, 'like a little angel'.

Whips still serve their constituents and can write in their local paper, but they must avoid being the subject of journalists' interests; being caught up in controversy is a cardinal sin.

There are sixteen government whips, one of whom – usually the latest entry-level addition – doesn't receive a ministerial salary on top of their pay as an MP. The junior rank is an Assistant Government Whip, followed by Lord Commissioners, before we get to the top four: the Vice-Chamberlain, Comptroller, Deputy Chief Whip (or Treasurer) and the Chief Whip.[*]

In modern times, though not always, the Comptroller oversees pairing, an informal arrangement between whips' offices that allows parties to offset absentees. Back in the day, MPs from rival parties could agree to be each other's pair, negotiating absences before running it past their respective whips' offices. One person will also have the unenviable role of Accommodation Whip, fielding requests from disgruntled MPs for a better workspace.

After the 1997 general election, Tory whip Peter Ainsworth and

---

[*] More on these roles and the source of their grandiose titles soon.

Desmond Swayne, the MP for New Forest West, were surprised to find that the newcomer had been given a 'perfectly acceptable', albeit windowless, office on his arrival at Westminster.

'Oh, there's probably been a mistake,' Ainsworth said. 'Anyway, this is your room.'

The next day, Ainsworth paid Swayne a visit. 'Desmond, there was a mistake. We need that room for [former Prime Minister] John Major's staff. I've got a better one for you.'

Ainsworth took Swayne to a room on a higher floor that he remembers as being 'literally a cupboard'.

'You said this would be a better one?' Swayne asked.

'Well,' Ainsworth replied, 'it's got a window.'

Whips speak fondly of being part of a team, of the comradeship born of a shared cynical humour, itself a byproduct of dealing with difficult MPs and the stresses of working at the heart of British politics. One person even acts as the Social Whip (or Entertainment Whip), arranging dinners and other opportunities to kick back after pulling all manner of parliamentary strings (whips of a certain vintage were also sent abroad on so-called Whips' Trips, often to smaller countries ungraced by visits from British Foreign Office ministers). Though departmental ministers theoretically work together, often, they do so in competition or without much by way of collaboration. 'In politics, the whips' office is the only team you'll ever work in,' says a former Tory Deputy Chief.

The government and opposition parties also have a whips' office in the House of Lords, responsible for managing (or responding to) the legislative programme in the upper chamber. With far fewer goodies or leverage to motivate their colleagues – who don't face elections, whose ambitions have waned and attendance varies – whips in the Lords, known as baronesses or lords in waiting, draw on relationships to encourage peers to turn up and vote.

'In the Commons, the whips pin you against the wall and tell you how you're going to vote,' jokes a Labour peer. 'In the Lords, they come up and say, "Can I buy you a glass of wine?"'

A WHIP'S FLOCK

Each whip is assigned a 'flock', a group of people with whom they keep in regular contact, and whose attendance they are accountable for at key votes.* Depending on how many MPs or peers the party has, a whip will oversee up to thirty people in their flock.

Robert Hughes, a whip under John Major, resents the term 'flock', arguing that MPs are 'not sheep'. His colleague in The Office Sydney Chapman was fond of advising new whips about MPs: 'Not everybody needs to have their way, but everybody needs to have their say.'

Ahead of a three-line whip, Steve Bassam, then the Labour Chief Whip in the Lords, asked his team to provide an update on their flock. When one whip said they'd been trying to locate a peer for weeks, Bassam remarked: 'Well, if you do get through to him, I'd really appreciate you letting me know. After all, he's been dead for six months.'[4]

Whips are an essential two-way communication channel between the Prime Minister (or leader) and their MPs. They explain government policy to their flock, report MPs' concerns to higher-ups and, if required, arrange meetings with ministers and other senior folk for further convincing or assuaging. They also provide guidance, support and an outlet for MPs under heavy strain.

Bring together hundreds of people at random and, at any one time, some will be experiencing illness, bereavement, marriage breakdowns, financial concerns, mental ill health or any other life-related detour, and it's the whips' job to monitor, regulate and look out for MPs under

---

* Flocks were often divided by region, but modern whips' offices have opted for more of a mix, ensuring the team shares MPs from different generations, political backgrounds and personality types. An effective whips' team will also mirror its parliamentary party, with appointees from different ideological wings. This way, whips can gain access to different factions and understand the mood of backbenchers.

strain. As such, whips have a voracious appetite for, and are privy to, all manner of intelligence and information. They see, in the words of a Tory whip from the 1990s, 'the underbelly of human life', from dealing with the chancers who visit The Office to spread bile about their colleagues to identifying the lifeless bodies of MPs who have drunk themselves to death.

Each whip is also allocated one or more government departments, attending internal meetings with the relevant ministers and officials and helping to take legislation through its parliamentary stages. As part of this work, whips oversee committees that scrutinise bills in minute detail, ensuring their MPs turn up and, where possible, toe the line.

'Part of the trick with bill committees* was not putting rebellious MPs on them,' says an ex-Tory whip, who didn't want their friend, a fellow MP and expert on mesothelioma – a type of cancer – on a related committee 'because I couldn't guarantee she would support the government'. The ex-whip adds: 'You end up doing these ridiculous things of not putting people who really know a load of stuff on a committee because you need to get it through.'

News of a defeat on Committee Corridor often reaches The Office before the whip returns to their desk. There, they'll have to answer to higher-ups, not least one of the most feared political figures stalking the Palace of Westminster.

---

* Bill committees were known as standing committees until 2006. MPs selected to serve on bill committees, in addition to their support of the party line, often represent different regions and viewpoints on the matter at hand.

CHAPTER 3

THE CHIEF

Even for newcomers arriving in Westminster today, the Chief Whip – known within their parliamentary party as 'Chief' – is among the most revered individuals in British politics.

It's not just thanks to Michael Dobbs's *House of Cards* that the Chief has accrued a reputation for *putting a bit of stick about*. Often a brooding, aloof figure who sits above the fray, several stern disciplinarians (some prefer the phrase 'quietly menacing') have acted as Chief Whip, not least Conservative MP David Margesson, appointed to the role in late 1931.

Considered by many to be the quintessential Chief, Margesson was tasked with keeping together successive multi-party national governments, drawing on a firm, even-handed approach that historian Eliot Wilson characterised as 'strict but not universally bullying'.[1]

For his part in a rebellion that helped bring down Prime Minister Neville Chamberlain in May 1940, Margesson wrote to John Profumo, a young Conservative MP, and said: 'I can tell you this, you utterly contemptible little shit. On every morning that you wake up for the rest of your life you will be ashamed of what you did last night.'

With a nine-year tenure, Margesson remains the longest-serving Chief Whip in government.

The Chief, whose work is rarely seen by an untrained eye despite being felt across Parliament, is now issued a black folder inscribed with their job title. (Chiefs can, if they wish, also take home a black, rather than red, ministerial box.) A close confidant to the Prime Minister and

MPs seeking counsel or a shoulder to cry on, the Chief, who attends Cabinet, has key legislative, parliamentary and disciplinary responsibilities. At their zenith, in addition to a ringside seat at government reshuffles, Chiefs had a significant say in awarding honours, positions on quangos and appointing peers.

'We got a big map of the British Isles, put it on the floor, and we tried to allocate [honours] around the country,' remembered Edward Short, Labour Chief Whip from 1964 to 1966.[2] Short would send his list to the Prime Minister, Harold Wilson, who 'nearly always' took his recommendation.

This power is now centralised in No. 10, although, in theory, there remains the opportunity for input. Regardless of what they've lost, the Chief – also known as the Patronage Secretary – retains considerable goodies at their disposal.

A former Government Chief Whip explains:

> Because the Chief plays a really important role in advising the Prime Minister on people issues, promotions and demotions, you are treated with a great deal of care by MPs. Rightly so. Not particularly because you deserve it, but because you can cause them problems. That will probably be ever thus.

No Chief would be effective without a team of officials behind them, led by a civil servant whose contribution to parliamentary life cannot be understated, despite often going unsaid.

THE USUAL CHANNELS

When it comes to setting the parliamentary agenda, the government holds the initiative. However, given the scale of business to get through, a degree of cross-party cooperation is required to agree on a sensible timetable for bills, debates and more. And yet, before 1919, there was no *official* mechanism for political parties to negotiate. That all changed with the arrival of the most important civil servant you've never heard of.

The role of principal private secretary (PrPS) to the Government Chief Whip* is multifaceted, influential and powerful. A report for the Hansard Society argued the PrPS and their office are 'the sewers of the system'. 'No one talks about them, but without them, the system would collapse.'[3]

The PrPS supports the Government Chief Whip in securing the government's legislative programme, advises ministers and departments on procedures and bills, monitors proceedings in the Commons and runs a team of civil servants, including in the opposition whips' office.

'The holder needs to be totally across everything that's happening in government and know everything there is to know about how laws are made,' says a parliamentary expert who worked in the whips' office.

Most eye-catching from our perspective, the PrPS acts as a pivotal interlocutor, helping to facilitate discussions in what's known as the Usual Channels. A catch-all term for negotiations between the government and the opposition, the Usual Channels feature senior members of the whips' office, the Leader of the Commons and equivalent opposition spokespeople. From weekly meetings on the upcoming business to daily talks over arrangements for pairing, the system ensures that neither side is blindsided, creating a 'gentlemanly' state of competition rather than war, says a former whips' office adviser.

The Usual Channels can also pertain to backroom interactions between party leaders. Ian Blackford, the Scottish National Party's leader in Westminster from 2017 to 2022, had a 'straightforward' relationship with Prime Minister Theresa May, whose team would let him know in advance if she planned to speak in the Commons the following

---

* Not to be confused with MPs who serve as aides to government ministers, known as parliamentary private secretaries.

Monday, so that he could return from his constituency of Ross, Skye and Lochaber in time to question her in Westminster. In March 2018, Blackford also received national security briefings in the aftermath of the Salisbury poisonings, which allowed him to prepare his party's response.

With Boris Johnson, things were different. In the summer of 2021, according to Blackford, the then Prime Minister led a debate on reducing overseas aid from 0.7 per cent to 0.5 per cent of GDP without first informing opposition leaders, who would otherwise respond on their party's behalf, that he was due to speak in the Commons. 'The first time I knew that Boris Johnson was speaking was when I was watching the television in my office, and he was on his feet,' Blackford says. In August 2021, as the UK withdrew its forces from Afghanistan, No. 10 initially offered just one question each for opposition leaders to ask the national security adviser ahead of a statement from the Prime Minister in the Commons.

Blackford would say to the Chief Whip Mark Spencer, with whom he got on well, 'Look, Mark, this is just intolerable.' Spencer, he says, 'wouldn't disagree'.

As an honest, nonpartisan and trusted broker, the PrPS straddles a fine line, working for the government while being available to opposition parties. 'It requires unique skills. You have to maintain the confidence of two parties that are opposed to each other and negotiate,' says an ex-Government Chief Whip. Another says their PrPS told them: 'I work for you 51 per cent of the time and the other parties 49 per cent of the time.'

A fount of knowledge for whips across generations, PrPSs are known for their remarkable longevity. In more than a century, just a handful of people have served in the role. The first to hold the position, Charles Harris, retired in 1961, forty-two years after taking office. Earlier this decade, Victoria Warren became the first woman and fifth person overall to serve as PrPS to the Government Chief Whip. 'From the most humdrum, "What are the travel arrangements for X?" to "What is the hold-up on this bit of a bill?", she can pretty much find out anything within an hour,' says a colleague of Warren's.

As with other senior civil servants, the PrPS is chosen after an appointment process involving the Civil Service Commission, with the candidates also run past the Prime Minister. Outlasting whole governments, premierships and Whitehall departments, the PrPS is often called upon for all sorts of things outside their remit due to their expertise. 'It is absolutely not an exaggeration to say that the PrPS is the single most plugged-in person in the whole of government,' says a person who worked in The Office.

OFFICE BREAKDOWN

The whips have an office on Downing Street and another just off Parliament's Members' Lobby, a restored hallway damaged during the Blitz which separates the Commons chamber and Central Lobby. Guarded by fading statues and busts of British political titans, Members' Lobby also houses the opposition whips' office, now occupied by the Conservative Party.

The government whips' office in Parliament, taken up by the Labour Party, is split between an upper and lower section, with the latter down a short flight of stairs. Though traditionally this arrangement reflected The Office hierarchy, with desk space assigned on seniority, Sir Keir Starmer's government opted to seat junior members of the team with senior whips in the upper office, evoking the configuration used the last time the party was in power. Lord Commissioners take up the lower office.

The Chief Whip's parliamentary workspace is accessed through the upper office. The scene of tense conversations about the future of Prime Ministers, its meagre size belies its role in British political history. Inside, above a door that's no longer used, is a ticker tape that harnessed the same technology as those seen on stock exchanges from the late nineteenth century, which, when functioning, would reveal things like who was speaking in the Commons.

We often think of the whips' office as one entity, but it has different components, consisting of civil servants and aides who help support the whips in carrying out their duties.

The Government Chief Whip's Office (GCWO) came into force with the creation of the PrPS. The Cabinet Office administers the GCWO, but it essentially runs as a small government department. It includes the PrPS, a de facto deputy PrPS and other private secretaries, from legislative experts to those who manage diaries and other key administrative tasks.

Chief Whips today appoint up to three special advisers (SpAds), who work closely with whips, MPs, departments and civil servants.* From managing spreadsheets of MPs' voting intentions to writing questions for whips to ask their flock, SpAds have only increased in importance. They also get involved with some of The Office's cunning ploys.

In late 2020, Boris Johnson's government leaked like a sieve. 'You need to do something about this,' a senior No. 10 staffer told Mark Spencer, the Chief Whip. Suspecting that the leaks to the media were coming from one of the MPs serving as a ministerial aide, his SpAds devised a ruse. A letter was sent to each of the MPs reminding them that they were subject to the ministerial code and, therefore, couldn't leak government business. The SpAds made very slight adjustments to each correspondence sent out in the Chief's name, tweaking an 'and' here or an 'of' there. Soon, one of the letters emerged on the political website Guido Fawkes. The aides studied their lists and cross-referenced the

---

* Whips and SpAds, for example, collaborate with departments to develop the strategy for a government bill, including potential concessions and engagement plans. SpAds also confer with their equivalents in the Lords to understand views on the red benches and where peers might push back. (MPs seeking to amend legislation often coordinate with like-minded peers who can return a bill to the Commons with proposed changes.)

letter with those they'd distributed. Tory MP Andrew Lewer, a ministerial aide in the Home Office, lost his job.

'In nearly twenty years of elected office, I have never leaked to the press,' he told *POLITICO*. He also suggested the leak might have come from a member of staff.

The GCWO sits adjacent to the Government Whips' Admin Unit (GWAU), which oversees the whips' office's activities, from working with the Pairing Whip on MPs' absences to ensuring committees and debates are attended.

Among the legislative wonks in the whips' office is a 'fixer' who undertakes assignments such as solving computer issues and distributing papers. A former colleague explains: 'You tell him this is the mission, this is what we need from the mission, and he'll make it happen.'

THE DAY-TO-DAY

For SpAds, the day begins around 6.30 a.m. with a strong coffee and BBC Radio 4's *Today* programme. Perusing the newspapers, they try to consume as much information as possible before leaving their homes, reading the order paper while on the Tube to Westminster.

At 8 a.m., they attend a twenty-minute meeting of the Chief Whip's office on Downing Street. Civil servants, led by the PrPS, first run through the business in the Commons and any items the Chief should know. The SpAds will then discuss political issues, such as an MP overnight writing an article critical of the government – an act viewed by The Office as a transgression – and what to do about it. Only if the matter is 'dicey' will the (politically neutral) civil servants be asked to leave the meeting, says a person in the room.

The briefing prepares the Chief Whip for the daily 8.30 a.m. meeting in No. 10, where he updates the Prime Minister on any potential stumbling blocks in Parliament or political noise that he should be aware of. The Chief and the PM also speak one-on-one before a meeting of the Cabinet at 9.30 on Tuesday mornings. Whenever the Prime Minister addresses the Commons, the Chief Whip will be in or around the chamber, sitting next to the gangway. An insider says the relationship between the whips' office and No. 10 is essential in keeping the government across the sentiment in Parliament. 'It's half a mile away, but it might as well be 100 miles away sometimes in terms of where the focus is,' they say of 10 Downing Street.

Fifteen to thirty minutes before the House sits, government whips gather in the upper office for a meeting chaired by the Deputy Chief Whip, who acts as first mate, overseeing the running of The Office while the captain – the Chief – plots the route. The whips account for their flocks if there's a big vote ahead. Otherwise, the Deputy will run through the order paper, appoint tellers and reflect instructions prepared by the GWAU for the person on bench duty to follow.* The Chief will provide an update should they have one. On Wednesdays from 9 a.m., the whips and SpAds gather at their Downing Street abode for a longer meeting to discuss departments, flocks and the business.

'The main job of the whips is to make sure that business begins on time, business finishes on time, and in between, it runs as smoothly as possible,' says former Tory whip Liam Fox. 'It's the essential lubricant of Parliament. It is the oil that keeps the gears of Parliament running.'

THE OTHER VIEW

Not everyone sees The Office in a positive light.

In 2010, then Tory MP Peter Bone proposed a bill to effectively outlaw whips, arguing that Parliament needed its teeth back. Another critic is Douglas Carswell, a former Tory MP who defected to UKIP

---

* Whips rotate responsibility for sitting on the frontbench in the chamber. More on this in later pages.

in 2014. 'If you wonder why we govern 60 million people and yet the people who get to the top of politics are so dreadful, they always screen out talent,' he argues. '[Whips] encourage obsequiousness, they encourage mediocrity. People sometimes describe them as Machiavellian – Machiavelli had a philosophy and a competence… These people couldn't run a bath. They're appallingly incompetent.'

Advocates say that, far from being undemocratic – an occasional charge among critics – whips help ensure that the British people's will is enforced through implementing election manifesto pledges. 'You cannot run a programme of government, with all the moving parts that that requires, without a whipping operation,' says a parliamentary expert who worked in the whips' office.

Some also stress that MPs owe a degree of loyalty to their party and leader. A Cabinet minister under Margaret Thatcher recalled the Prime Minister following a backbencher, who had narrowly won at a by-election, out of the chamber after swearing in as an MP. The man thanked her for coming up to his constituency during the campaign and said she had earned him the last votes he needed to secure victory. Thatcher looked at the MP and said: 'No, no, no. You've got it entirely wrong. You won the 150 votes. I got you the other 25,000.'

The Thatcher-era minister adds: 'In a sense, it's absolutely true. The individual candidate makes a difference at the margins. The popularity or success of the Prime Minister is what wins or loses the actual election itself.'

Though the Chief is the most senior in The Office, three government whips have duties that, now and then, take them away from Parliament to the other key component of Britain's constitutional monarchy.

CHAPTER 4

A ROYAL OFFICE

The whips' office, not unlike the country, can pivot to moments of great pageantry at the flick of a ceremonial white stave.

The Office's second, third and fourth in command – known respectively as the Treasurer, Comptroller and Vice-Chamberlain – are part of the royal household, an organisation that supports members of the royal family. Appointed by the Prime Minister rather than the sovereign, the roles, which long predate the creation of The Office as we know it today, have coalesced over time around these three senior whips, having been held for centuries by a mixture of courtiers, noblemen, Members of Parliament and peers in the House of Lords.*

Tasked with duties of historical significance, these whips play a symbolic role in Britain's constitutional monarchy, where the sovereign is head of state but the elected Parliament makes and passes laws. From being held hostage to securing the monarch's signature, whips help bridge the mile-long stretch between the Palace of Westminster and Buckingham Palace.

WANDS, PARTIES AND BUTTERFLIES

Stage-managed between ever-grander rooms by Palace officials while

---

* The Treasurer and Vice-Chamberlain date back to the reign of Edward III and the Comptroller to Edward IV.

waiting for an audience with the sovereign at Buckingham Palace, each royal whip receives a ceremonial white stave on appointment.

'The Palace know how to make you appreciate every moment of it,' says a former whip, who received their white stave from Queen Elizabeth II. 'You feel that you are physically getting closer and closer to the Queen. I can tell you it does cause the butterflies to start fluttering.'

The 'wand of office', which unscrews into two parts, symbolises its holder's prestigious position as an officer of the royal household. Whips used to keep their staves free of charge after leaving their post before successive leaders installed a revolving door in The Office.

'It's just a bit too expensive [for the Palace] to keep giving these things away,' the former whip explains. Another says they considered buying the stave – which they priced at 'about a thousand quid' – but thought it would collect dust in their umbrella stand.

In addition to greater responsibility in The Office at Westminster, the three senior whips perform several royal-adjacent functions, including attending garden parties at Buckingham Palace dressed in morning suits or formal daywear, staves in hand. With support from royal equerries,* they introduce the monarch and other senior royals to assembled guests.

During her events – she attended nine – Anne Milton, a former Tory Deputy Chief Whip, followed Queen Elizabeth II around the Buckingham Palace grounds. 'Your feet are aching, and you look at this woman who's thirty, forty years older than you, and think, "My God, how is she still going?"' With no prior warning about wearing stiletto heels, Milton spent most of her first garden party trying not to sink into the grass across from the royal tea tent.

On another occasion, she stood before 'quite a small man' when Prince Charles entered the marquee.

---

* An officer of the royal household who attends to members of the royal family.

'Oh, I'm so sorry. I'm standing in your sight line,' Milton said to the man.

'No, no,' he replied. 'Stay exactly where you are.'

'Don't you want to see?'

'I do not want to be seen,' the man said. 'I am the head of the Supreme Court, and I've just agreed that Prince Charles's private correspondence should go into the public domain.'*

THE KING'S SPEECH

Outside of garden parties, diplomatic receptions and rarer occasions like a coronation or funeral, the three royal whips also gather for the state opening of Parliament. Here, they are involved in a ceremonial act that captures the constitutional function of the royal whips.

Known as the King or Queen's Speech, the state opening represents the formal commencement of the parliamentary year, during which the monarch sets out the government's legislative agenda on its behalf. Before proceedings begin, the Treasurer and Comptroller accompany the Vice-Chamberlain to Buckingham Palace, where they enjoy coffee and a tour of the crown jewels and wave off the royal party en route for Westminster.

In a practice dating back to the reign of Charles I, the last king to enter the House of Commons who had a contentious relationship with Parliament, the Vice-Chamberlain is then left with the Lord Chamberlain, the most senior officer of the royal household, who keeps them 'hostage' until the monarch's safe return.

With the royal party on the way and the Vice-Chamberlain in safe hands, the Treasurer and Comptroller head back to Parliament in a horse-drawn carriage supplied by the monarch.

---

* Prince Charles's so-called black spider memos were released in 2015 after a long legal battle.

Travelling down the Mall, Milton heard calls of 'Anne!' from the crowds. 'Gosh, how do they know it's me?' she thought, forgetting about the Queen's only daughter by the same name.

Back at Buckingham Palace, the Vice-Chamberlain prepares to watch the state opening on a television in a small drawing room.

A former senior Buckingham Palace official says that when offered a beverage, the Vice-Chamberlain 'sometimes wanted a stronger drink than a cup of coffee!' Sir Desmond Swayne, Vice-Chamberlain from 2013 to 2014, recalls an equerry asking whether they should open a bottle of sherry or champagne. 'Well, let's have both!' he replied. Later in the day, the Queen hosted a drinks reception in an equerry's office to thank those who had helped with the event, serving 'very stiff' gin and tonics. 'You're crammed almost like a sardine up to the Duke of Edinburgh and chatting away and all the rest, knocking back the gin. It was a frightfully enjoyable excursion,' Swayne says.

During his first state opening in late 2019, an equerry offered then Vice-Chamberlain Stuart Andrew a hot drink before saying, 'You look like you'd like something a bit stronger!' and returning with a bottle of champagne. Andrew was 'a bit swiffy' when the Queen arrived back at Buckingham Palace.

At his next state opening, the Queen turned to him at the bottom of the stairs and said: 'You have a good time again, won't you?'

THE MESSAGE

Insofar as royal responsibilities are concerned, which are secondary to the whips' primary focus of securing the government's business, one person carries the largest burden.

The Vice-Chamberlain writes a report for the monarch on events in the Commons every day it sits, except on Fridays. The process involves a degree of choreography: the Government Whips' Admin Unit puts together a draft featuring some of the salient moments of the day and passes it to the Vice-Chamberlain. The Vice-Chamberlain then makes changes, additions, flourishes or rewrites before it's given a final scan and sent to Buckingham Palace.

The report, known as the 'Message' and now sent via email, keeps the monarch abreast of their government's activities in the Commons. Usually around 600–800 words, in old money it was one or two sides of A4 paper, which a State Messenger would deliver to the Palace at 6 p.m. The letters are headed with the Vice-Chamberlain's name, followed by 'with humble duty reports' and the greeting to 'Your Majesty'.[1]

In January 2025, the King hosted a reception at Buckingham Palace for MPs first elected at the previous year's general election. The whips' office suspected there might be votes in the Commons that day, so they managed the business to ensure that any divisions would take place later in the afternoon, allowing the cohort of more than 200 new Labour MPs to return from the reception. Labour minister Nic Dakin, wrapping up the second reading debate on the Arbitration Bill, gave what an eyewitness describes as one of the most boring parliamentary speeches in recent memory to buy the whips more time.

'I will, if I may, indulge in sharing some of the supportive quotes from the sector...' Dakin said at one point, to which Conservative frontbencher Dr Kieran Mullan, apparently desperate for the laborious speech to end, shouted from his seat: 'No!'

A person in the Labour whips' office says the King was amused to read of the filibuster in the Message from Vice-Chamberlain Samantha Dixon later that day.

Some Vice-Chamberlains have underestimated the report's importance to its recipient. During Mark Spencer's tenure in 2018, an IT issue meant the Message didn't reach the Queen for two days. The Palace wrote to ask: 'Where are the updates?'

'It came as a bit of a shock that she was actually reading them,' Spencer says. 'Then you're thinking, "Shit, I've got to get this right."'

Vice-Chamberlains vary in their approach and how much they contribute to the Message. In his pre-political life, Donald Coleman, Vice-Chamberlain from 1978 to 1979, used to have a weekly column in a national newspaper. 'You can say that my daily message to the Queen … is not unlike what I used to write for *The Guardian*,' he said.[2] Spencer Le Marchant, a colourful whip and racehorse owner, would slip racing tips into his report. 'His summary was particularly appreciated at Buckingham Palace,' wrote a fellow Conservative.[3]

When Labour's Jim Fitzpatrick met the Queen for the first time as Vice-Chamberlain in 2003, he asked what she would like to read. 'Her answer was something along the lines of, "That which doesn't reach the papers is always very interesting,"' he recalls. 'In other words, give me the gossip; give me what's not fit to print.'

Richard Luce, an ex-Tory whip who served as Lord Chamberlain from 2000 to 2006, confirms: 'The fact is that the Queen enjoyed receiving these daily reports, but only if they were – I'm exaggerating slightly – spicy!' Luce once asked the Queen if she would like a similar readthrough of events in the House of Lords. 'Certainly not!' she replied.

Luce explains: 'She didn't really want any more reports, but she enjoyed the liveliness of the Commons and just knowing a bit about the personal side, not about the dreary side of what one said in the debate, because all that's recorded in Hansard.'

The Queen would raise details and observations in Vice-Chamberlains' reports during private audiences at Buckingham Palace, which take place every few months. After the 2019 general election, Stuart Andrew reflected in a letter on the 'ambitious' new intake of Conservative MPs. A few months later, the Queen asked in person if the new intake was 'still as ambitious'.

Before his first audience with the Queen, officials told Desmond Swayne that he should refer to her initially as 'Your Majesty' and then as 'ma'am'. At the end of the briefing, a courtier told him that on no account was he to follow the tradition of walking backwards on taking his leave. 'We've abandoned that,' they said.

With the meeting over, the Queen asked Swayne, a well-turned-out and eccentric MP, if he planned to walk backwards.

'Well, I was told not to,' he said. 'Do you want me to?'

'It's entirely up to you. You just struck me as a man who likes traditions, but this is entirely up to you.'

'Well, if it's all the same with you, ma'am, I will walk backwards.'

'Oh, for heaven's sake make sure you don't trip up,' the Queen said, 'or I'll be in terrible trouble with the suits!'

HUMBLE WHIPS

As part of their constitutional role, the Vice-Chamberlain must also take to Buckingham Palace a 'humble address' – a communication from Parliament to the sovereign – for the monarch to sign.

More than one Vice-Chamberlain recalls the Queen signing a document and then waving it in the air, unable to find a blotter. Timothy Kirkhope, on seeing the Queen with her arms in the air, feared that security might smash through the window and shoot him.

At Easter 2004, Jim Fitzpatrick needed the Queen's signature on a new tax treaty with Canada. His team contacted Buckingham Palace and asked what time would be convenient.

'Well, she's at Windsor. She spends six weeks up there at Easter,' an official responded.

With Fitzpatrick travelling from Westminster, the Queen asked via her officials whether he would like to stay for lunch. Driven to Windsor in a government-assigned Toyota Prius, Fitzpatrick wondered how many people the Queen hosts for lunch on a Monday. Around the table were just the Queen's private secretary, three equerries, Fitzpatrick and Her Majesty, who identified planes from their liveries as they flew overhead en route to Heathrow Airport.

'I was born on the Gorbals in Glasgow, spent most of my London life in the East End, and was the Labour MP for Poplar. Here I am, having lunch with the Queen,' he says.

To complete the constitutional circle, once the monarch has signed a humble address, the Vice-Chamberlain reports back to the Commons, standing at the Bar of the House in formal attire.

'I have a message from the King,' the Vice-Chamberlain says, clutching their wand of office. They walk forward six paces, bow and walk six paces more, handing over the message for a clerk to pass onto the Speaker before repeating the process while walking backwards. Failing to account for the challenge of wearing heels, Janet Anderson, the first woman appointed Vice-Chamberlain, once 'almost fell into the lap' of another Labour MP.[4]

Dennis Skinner, a long-serving Labour backbencher, would seize the opportunity to send up the Vice-Chamberlain. 'Not bad for a lad from Bradford!' he would say to Gerry Sutcliffe, Vice-Chamberlain from 2001 to 2003. When Tory Vice-Chamberlain Tristan Garel-Jones carried out his duty in the Commons, Skinner took out a packet of polos and pretended to chalk the end of his stave.[5]

Through their daily reports and occasional private audiences with the monarch, Vice-Chamberlains are rare among many of their political counterparts in building up something of an intimate relationship, however fleeting, with the King or Queen.

During their interactions, Timothy Kirkhope mentioned in passing to the Queen about his son, a veterinary surgeon interested in racehorses. 'She'd then remember to say, "How is your son?" which I thought was wonderful. I was very touched by that.'

LORD COMMISSIONERS OF HIS MAJESTY'S TREASURY

A government whip under John Major, serving in the mid-1990s, was walking through his local train station when a staff member waved him over.

'You've got a parcel here,' the staff member said. 'It stinks a bit.'

The whip, who had just been promoted to Lord Commissioner,[*] hadn't expected a delivery. 'I didn't know there was anything there for me. I do apologise. Can I get it on my way back?'

When the whip returned from London, he took the package home, opened it and found a haunch of venison staring back at him. 'It stunk to high heaven; I can still smell it now.' His family, who are 'more Nando's folk', had a 'good laugh' that Christmas trying to cook it.

The whip was among the last to receive a haunch of venison from the royal estate after being appointed Lord Commissioner before the practice ended under New Labour. That is, until a future Tory Deputy Chief Whip restored the tradition independently years later.

'John Randall would acquire the haunches of venison and give them out,' says a Conservative whip who served during the coalition government of 2010–15. Though a joint of game is no more, Lord Commissioners do continue to receive certificates on appointment.

While the Vice-Chamberlain has the most royal-adjacent responsibilities, whips serving as Lord Commissioners of His Majesty's Treasury, on top of everything required of them in the House of Commons, have to countersign royal warrants for the funding of the Exchequer. 'People would never believe it from the outside, but how does a department get its money? Where does it come from? The answer is it comes from *His Majesty's* Treasury,' explains an ex-whip. 'He has to sign the cheque, and then it's countersigned by the Lord Commissioner.'

One government whip under Tony Blair remembers countersigning

---

[*] Whips took on this sinecure post towards the end of the nineteenth century, in part so they could be paid for their work.

a cheque for £19 billion. 'You sit in the whips' office, and a guy brings a big pile of cheques and bankers' drafts.'

The whip said to the official: 'What happens if I refuse to sign it?'

'The Prime Minister sacks you,' the official said, 'and we appoint somebody else to sign it.'

Michael Fabricant, a Conservative MP and former whip, says he countersigned a cheque worth hundreds of billions of pounds, which he has photocopied and framed at home. Jim Fitzpatrick's wife likes to remind him that his first big contribution as Lord Commissioner was to authorise the Treasury 'to take income tax off the whole population'.

In the 1980s, a joke went around The Office that Tim Sainsbury, a Lord Commissioner whose great-grandparents founded a grocer that would become the supermarket giant Sainsbury's, was the only person who could 'sign a cheque for £300 million without feeling it's difficult'. (When Sainsbury joined the Ministry of Defence, a colleague said he'd got the job overseeing naval procurement because he was the only MP who could afford his own frigate.)

Sir Desmond Swayne, meanwhile, had to sign off on the personal pension of Sir Keir Starmer, then Director of Public Prosecutions and now the Prime Minister. Sometimes he would stop and question what he was authorising, such as when he saw two cottages on a royal estate being sold for 'knock-down' prices.

'I remember just spotting that the prices were not what you would expect to pay if you wanted to go and live on a lovely royal estate,' he says. Swayne asked for more details. 'I don't think they ever came back. The transaction clearly was discontinued, at least for a while.'

PEER REVIEW

Whips in the Lords aren't safe from royal responsibilities.

Government whips in the upper chamber who are also members

of the royal household meet the monarch on their appointment and departure from the role. As part of their endeavours, lords and baronesses in waiting have to collect visiting dignitaries on behalf of the monarch.

'I got told off when I was being driven to the airport. I was gently told, "No, you do not sit in the front with the driver,"' says an ex-whip. 'I just like chatting to the driver!'

* * *

The whips' office navigates its ancient traditions amid changing tastes and expectations, at once brandishing white staves while acting as an unofficial human resources department, tending to the wounds of MPs and writing messages to the monarch. While many smile at ceremonial hostages, enormous cheques and garden parties, others ponder how compatible it is with a modern Parliament – indeed, a modern country.

But that is, perhaps, to overemphasise the royal elements of the whips' job, whose primary purpose remains amid the rubble of its past.

For better or worse, whipping is *not what it used to be* – but to understand why, we must go back fifty years to a parliament renowned for the exploits of whips on all sides. From there, we will follow the story of The Office's many characters: its heroes, villains and foot soldiers who, via the Usual Channels, had an unseen hand in much of British political history.

PART II

1974–79

CHAPTER 5

ALWAYS THE BRIDESMAID

FEBRUARY 1974

Bob Mellish didn't have the words 'Please Don't Make Me Chief Whip Again' tattooed on his forehead, but he may as well have done. The Labour Chief Whip had been typically upfront with anyone who cared to enquire about his career aspirations, including prying members of the media and his party leader, Harold Wilson.

Even if Mellish, a proud south-east Londoner with a penchant for Millwall Football Club, amateur boxing and Catholicism, had inked up below his neatly combed side parting, it wouldn't have made a blind bit of difference. The result of the February 1974 election put paid to that, to say nothing of the uncertainty it brought to the country.

The Labour Party had secured 301 seats at the snap poll. Prime Minister Ted Heath's Conservatives, despite marginally winning the popular vote, trailed by four on 297. With neither side able to command a majority of the House of Commons' 635 MPs, Britain, a country facing myriad crises, had its first hung parliament since 1929. Outside Westminster, powerful trade unions resisted government-imposed wage controls; an oil embargo turbocharged inflation; and violence surged in Northern Ireland, with Britain still reeling from the M62 coach bombing, the deadliest mainland terror attack of the Troubles.

Unable to strike a deal with the Liberal Party and the Ulster Unionists, Heath vacated 10 Downing Street, with Wilson taking over on 4 March. While no longer Prime Minister, Heath remained Tory leader, though the sharks – frenzied, multiplying – would soon circle.

Wilson, Britain's erstwhile Prime Minister from 1964 to 1970, needed an experienced hand to man the troops and somehow conjure a parliamentary majority. He called Mellish to No. 10 and asked how he saw the future of the minority government and the tactics it should pursue; so impressive was the response that Wilson told him: 'You have talked yourself into a job.'[1]

'Always the bridesmaid and never the bride,' Mellish told political reporters.[2]

Mellish, who had just celebrated his sixty-first birthday, sighed as he entered the Government Chief Whip's office in 12 Downing Street, an interconnecting corridor away from Wilson two doors down. He looked out the window at the No. 10 garden to the east and the sprawling Horse Guards Parade near St James's Park to the west. He placed his black ministerial box on the desk used by William Gladstone and Benjamin Disraeli and sank into a tattered imitation leather chair rumoured to have received, among others, the buttocks of Sir Winston Churchill.

Mellish was no stranger to his grand surroundings, nor the Chief's poky office near the Commons chamber, which he would frequent in the afternoons and evenings. Wilson had sent him to The Office in 1969 while preparing for a showdown with Labour backbenchers over plans to curb unofficial strikes by trade unions. 'Bob's appointment was taken as a signal that Mr Wilson ... intended to get tough with his MPs,' noted a journalist.[3]

Three months later, Mellish told Wilson he couldn't get the legislation through Parliament without Labour MPs resigning from the party. Wilson, on Mellish's encouragement, dropped the proposals in return for a 'solemn and binding pledge' from the Trades Union Congress, a federation of trade unions, 'to do what they could'.[4]

'You'll not get the bill through, and that's that, and that's final. I'm telling you as Chief Whip, cut the bloody thing out,' Mellish told Wilson.[5]

Mellish 'wrapped around him a reputation of being a real hard man, a sledgehammer', says Neil Kinnock, then MP for Bedwellty. 'Bob was no softy, but he actually was a kind man, a good whip, in that he brought information down and he took information up, which is crucial.'

Mellish, like many parliamentarians and senior whips of his day, had served in the Second World War. A major in the Royal Engineers, Mellish served in south-east Asia, having signed up as a sapper, a combat engineer. The war imbued an *esprit de corps* between rival whips' offices, profound shared experiences tempering animosity. 'Danger together on the battlefield mellows criticism of others with whom one disagrees politically,' noted a Labour contemporary of Mellish.[6] Though from parties strategically at loggerheads in a working environment prone to bouts of disorder and even violence, these men had, together, fought a common enemy.

Not that shared participation in global conflict is a prerequisite for relationships to flourish; on the contrary, this takes place without shots being fired. The *entente cordiale* is often a by-product of the job itself, with whips handling their MPs amid gruelling hours with few bells and whistles to compensate. When relations break down, its effect on the functioning of Parliament is self-evident, laying bare how whips, through the Usual Channels, shape so much of Westminster life – a fact that leaves some cold and others in pragmatic admiration.

But don't be fooled; though there was respect between whips, both sides were seeking to outwit the other, to expose vulnerabilities, pushing the often-undefined boundaries to the limit.

* * *

Mellish was elected in 1946, a year after the war ended, as Labour MP for Rotherhithe. He stood as the candidate of the Transport and General Workers' Union (TGWU), for whom he had first worked as an office boy at the age of fifteen in Stratford, east London, when Ernest

Bevin, the future Foreign Secretary and one of his political heroes, was TGWU leader.[7] The thirteenth of fourteen children – eight passed away – Mellish was the son of a docker. 'I haven't a complaint about the conditions of my childhood,' he told friends. 'I lived in a slum, I suppose, but it didn't seem like it then.'[8]

One contemporary describes his whipping style as a 'mixture of shift manager and shop steward'. His hardnosed reputation belied an enduring interest in new MPs and no shortage of guile, a by-product of his early years in Parliament, when he 'felt a bit lost'. 'He took a lot of trouble to be kind to new members,' said Labour MP Tam Dalyell.[9]

Mellish would invite MPs to have lunch with him at the Chief Whip's table in the Members' Dining Room – a place to avoid or the best seat in the house depending on the occupant's disposition, interpersonal skills and approachability.

Mellish was in the *Good Company* category of Chiefs, with admirers across the usual political dividing lines. Conservative MP Jeffrey Archer, elected in 1969, says he approached the Labour Chief Whip in pursuit of a pair for the evening so he could watch a boxing match at Wembley, knowing he wouldn't have much sympathy from his own party's whips' office.

'Quite right, my boy. I'd like to go as well,' Mellish told Archer. 'I can't get [Labour MP] Jack Ashley in, so you can pair with him for the night.'

Mellish and those around him weren't always across the details. John Horam, MP for Gateshead West, recalls being invited to the Labour whips' office about eighteen months after his election in 1970.

'I'd like you to be the whip for the north-west,' Mellish said.

'OK, thank you, I'm very honoured,' replied Horam. 'But wouldn't you want someone from the north-west?'

Mellish frowned, believing he was speaking to the MP for Farnworth. 'You're John Roper, aren't you?'

'No,' Horam said. 'I'm John Horam, and I'm from the north-east!'

Mellish rescinded the offer.

Government whips would spend their mornings in 12 Downing Street, which faces towards Whitehall. Though only blessed with a few offices, a hall and a loo, the team had access to an airy L-shaped meeting room (known unimaginatively as the whips' room) with a vast table around which they'd gather every Wednesday for a longer strategic meeting.

The *pièce de résistance* of 12 Downing Street lay in its secret passages that kept whips' movements out of the public eye. A ground floor corridor ran through to No. 11, the home of the Chancellor, and on to No. 10. The Chief Whip could also go up the stairs in No. 11 and emerge on the first floor of No. 10, near a room used as a study by some Prime Ministers.

The whips' respective headquarters, within a curt word of No. 10 and the House of Commons chamber – the two key power centres of British democracy – reflected The Office's role, function and position in Westminster. The Prime Minister's eyes, ears and enforcers while also the guardians, adjudicators and, where necessary, facilitators of MPs and their views; the whips' primary and ultimate purpose: to deliver the government's business.

* * *

It was across Members' Lobby, in the opposition whips' office, where Mellish helped mastermind his party's approach to the vexed issue of Britain's entry to the European Economic Community (EEC).

In 1971, the Commons voted 356 to 244 in favour of joining the EEC, with sixty-nine Labour MPs following Heath into the Aye lobby. Mellish, who was pro-membership while other senior whips, including his deputy, were opposed, had been 'the cement that prevented the Labour Party from being split asunder', said a colleague.[10]

There had been 'many' occasions in his time as Chief when Mellish's views conflicted with the party line, he explained in an interview.[11]

'But my job takes precedence,' he said. 'The Chief Whip never makes a public speech on the policies of the day. I'm happy to follow that.'

As Chief, he could stomach rebellions – to a point. After all, Mellish, a Catholic sympathetic to the idea of a united Ireland, was sacked as a parliamentary private secretary for rebelling on the Ireland Bill, the UK government's legislative response to Dublin's Republic of Ireland Act 1948, which had ended Ireland's status as a British dominion.[12]

What Mellish couldn't abide, according to a future rebel of some repute, was the 'bleedin' bastards' who voted against the party line without warning or for 'self-advantage'.[13]

Even without the uncertainty of the February 1974 election result, Mellish, as Chief Whip, held one of the most arduous jobs in politics.[14] He would rarely leave Westminster before one or two in the morning.[15] Never would he speak of work when he arrived home to his wife, Anne – who, in fairness, was probably asleep – with whom he had five sons.

But as an experienced hand, Mellish knew this hung parliament would not last long – how could it, without a stable majority for the government to work with? – and that an election could throw up another tight result. Trapped by his own indispensability, Mellish's long-coveted career change was on hold; for how long, he couldn't know.

Meanwhile, his Conservative counterpart's career was heading in a different direction.

* * *

Conservative Chief Whip Humphrey Atkins, a rather grand and smooth operator, who was just three years old when his Kenyan farmer father was tragically gored by a rhinoceros, gathered new Tory MPs in his office after the general election.

Among the young guns attending his informal talk were Malcolm Rifkind, MP for Edinburgh Pentlands, and Jonathan Aitken, MP for

Thanet East, who, on arriving at Westminster, had been shocked by the scale and eagerness of Conservative backbenchers' disdain for Ted Heath, whom his family knew outside politics. 'It was a very edgy time,' he says.

Atkins, with his Royal Navy background and overpowering sense of good manners,[16] informed the MPs of his responsibilities as Chief Whip, a role he had held for a year. He then turned to the weekly issuing of the whip.

'Under the name of the business, there will either be one line, two lines or three lines, meaning one-line whip, two-line whip or three-line whip,' Atkins said. 'Now, one-line whip means we don't care what you do. You don't even need to be in the chamber. That's your decision.'

For a two-line whip, he said: 'You're expected to be there when the vote takes place and to support the party unless you are paired with a Labour member and you both agree to abstain.'

Rifkind felt rather smug; he had already paired with Labour's Robin Cook, a constituency neighbour.

Then came a three-line whip. Another new Tory MP, Roger Sims, recalled Atkins saying: 'A three-line whip … means you are either there or you are dead.'[17]

The Chief Whip surveyed the room. 'Any questions?'

Rifkind raised his hand. 'Chief, just one question, if I may? Thank you very much for explaining the significance of a three-line whip. What is the proper policy if one wishes to vote *against* a three-line whip?'

His colleagues' uncomfortable shuffling and throat-clearing was all that broke the deathly silence that had befallen the office of the opposition Chief Whip.

Atkins smiled as though pleased for the opportunity of a polite put-down.

'Thank you, Malcolm,' he said. 'That's a very important question. I can give you a very straightforward answer. If you're contemplating voting against the party on a three-line whip, you will inform us first and we will ensure that you do vote with the party.'

Rifkind's political career, he jokes, 'almost came to an end on the first day'.

* * *

Mellish's fears of a dysfunctional parliament liable to descend into chaos were well-founded and quickly proven. Rumours of an early election abounded, with smaller parties, emboldened by the parliamentary arithmetic, throwing their weight around.

In recognition of Mellish's enhanced importance, Wilson made him a full member of his Cabinet, which Chief Whips had previously only attended. Mellish, now an equal, saw his salary rise from £9,500 to £13,000 a year,[18] but even a pay bump couldn't assuage his frustration as the government suffered consecutive defeats over its nationalisation policy. 'This parliament is no longer feasible,' he declared.[19]

The papers speculated, rightly as it turned out, on an October election. Whether Mellish would make it there as Chief Whip was another story.

At the beginning of the summer recess – which ran from late July until early October – he told reporters that he planned to 'make up for all the hours and hours and hours of lost sleep'.

'Assuming there is a general election in the recess, and we are returned again, and the Prime Minister asks me if I will be Chief Whip, my answer is, "I pray he does not".'[20]

His remarkable candour did not go rewarded.

The Labour Party won 319 seats at the general election, providing a slender majority of three in the Commons. For all he wished otherwise, Mellish, with his range of expertise, was no less crucial in his role as Chief Whip. 'He will need every ounce of experience and agility to steer the [government's legislative] programme through Parliament,' a journalist noted.[21]

Never had truer words been said, though Mellish would need his whole team of whips and officials at the peak of their powers to keep the government and its business afloat for a full parliamentary term. Not least the boundless skills of his notorious deputy, a man synonymous with whipping and all its constituent parts.

The good, the bad and the downright brilliant.

CHAPTER 6

WALTER

MAY 1968

Walter Harrison rushed along Committee Corridor, his rolling gait and broad shoulders knocking him into passers-by. Whipping two bills concurrently left him vulnerable should the opposition, either by fluke or design, coordinate their actions so that two votes were held simultaneously. Surely not even the great Walter Harrison could be in two places at once.

The standing committees were composed to ensure a government majority – he had also done his due diligence, as a good whip should, to ensure that Labour MPs selected to participate weren't likely to spring too many surprises and rebel – but it was tight. On this late May morning in 1968, every vote, including his, would count.

He could see the lower door of the committee room start to close, signifying the end of the voting period. Harrison grimaced, stuck out his foot and braced for impact. Those inside turned in unison as Harrison, most of him anyway, spilled onto the floor.

Shadow Chancellor Iain Macleod addressed the chairman of the standing committee.

'Would you be good enough to enquire from the policeman at the lower door whether or not the Government Whip, Mr Walter Harrison, whom we greatly respect, did or did not enter this room after the doors had been shut?' he asked fellow Conservative MP John Jennings.[1]

Dusting himself down, Harrison, with an etched grin and taut, proud posture, gave his defence. 'The greater proportion of my body was actually through the door,' he said. 'Unfortunately, below my left knee was not quite through, and not getting my knee through made me fall onto the floor.'

The room erupted in laughter.

'I can announce the result now,' said Jennings, rising to the occasion. 'It was 22¾ votes to 22. The position is that Mr Harrison was in the process of coming through the door, and I rule his vote valid.'

The government won the division – by a fraction of an MP.

Four years into his parliamentary career, Harrison had garnered a reputation for intelligence gathering, wily tactics and sheer nous. Within minutes of jamming his leg in the door, he was called upon again to deploy more of his whipping arsenal.

As the whip on duty covering the most renowned legislation for long-winded, often all-night sessions, Harrison was responsible for ensuring the Finance Bill went through its committee stage unamended. But a vote in the House of Commons dragged Finance Minister Harold Lever and other Labour MPs away midway through discussing an opposition amendment.

As Harrison doubtless would have done in their position, the Conservatives called a vote, seeking to inflict a government defeat. Spotting the danger, Harrison sought to buy time by arguing that not enough MPs were present for a division to occur. 'With regard to the amount of people in the room, I was of the opinion there was no quorum,' he said.

Macleod, believing Harrison had ordered the few remaining Labour MPs out of the room in a bid to strengthen his case, grew angry.

The intervention, though unsuccessful, allowed Lever to return from the division lobbies. 'When I was on my way here in the lift, the lift instead of moving upwards moved downwards,' he explained. 'When we arrived on the floor below, we found the lift refused to move at all.'[2]

Lever resumed his speech, either oblivious to or purposefully ignoring that a division was under way. Macleod protested that the vote had already started, but the committee chairman agreed with the minister that, in retrospect, Lever had a right to finish his speech before a division.

Macleod, by now seething with an exaggerated rage so often the wont of an opposition member seeking to highlight alleged government mistreatment of Parliament, accused Harrison and Lever of playing for time.

'That is disgraceful treatment of an opposition,' he said.[3]

The opposition amendment, when the vote finally took place, was defeated.

* * *

Walter Harrison, one of ten children, was born in Dewsbury, a market town in West Yorkshire, on 2 January 1921. His parents Henry and Ada were committed socialists.[*] 'They were the real people of the Labour movement,' Harrison said. 'It is easy to define; they were the salt of the earth.'[4]

In 1940, Harrison, only just nineteen, signed up for the Royal Air Force. His service during the Second World War took Harrison to twenty countries, including much of the Middle East. The poverty he saw stirred his social conscience to the extent that, alongside his career as an electrician and a foreman, he became a political activist.[5] In October 1964, he was elected to Parliament with a majority of 11,930 in the constituency of Wakefield.

'Walter was a character in his own right,' recalls Dafydd Wigley, a Plaid Cymru MP with whom Harrison would soon have many dealings. 'A gruff Yorkshireman with an etched smile on his face and, if necessary, no doubt a dagger in his hand. He was a great character.'

A mover and shaker across his pre-political life, including in the

---

[*] So committed was his mum to the Labour cause – a movement to which she regularly offered up some of her limited financial resources – that she would ask would-be suitors of her five daughters to show their party cards in return for her approval to take them out.

Electrical Trades Union, for which he was Yorkshire president, Harrison arrived in Westminster curious about how Parliament operated, making the whips' office a natural home-from-home. 'It's like working in a power station; it's no good if you don't know how it works,' he said of Parliament.[6]

After the snap election of 1966, Harrison was one of eight new appointments to the government whips' office, including the Chief, John Silkin.[7] Several promotions and retirements had stripped out half The Office, with Harriet Slater, who in 1964 had become the first ever female whip, standing down as an MP. Within two years, Harrison, recently promoted to Lord Commissioner, was made Pairing Whip and Accommodation Whip.

'Whips have a bad name, it's true; but it depends how you operate it,' a Labour MP summarised of Harrison's attitude to whipping. 'The whips' function is to help their colleagues: it's like being a contracting foreman… you can't get the best out of the men if you are just flogging them; you've got to have a good working relationship.'[8]

Tensions were high throughout Harrison's first parliament in opposition. Appointed Deputy Chief Whip in July 1970, he was involved in a great row with Conservative Chief Francis Pym over the government's controversial Industrial Relations Bill, which sought to impose a requirement on trade unions to register officially as legal entities.

Labour MPs, playing up to the role of mistreated opposition, cried 'fascists', 'swine', 'dictator' and 'resign' as Cabinet minister Willie Whitelaw announced plans to introduce a guillotine motion, restricting the number of hours spent debating the bill. A watching journalist saw Pym and Harrison 'arguing bitterly' and jabbing each other in the chest.[9]

Labour Chief Bob Mellish was told of the guillotine motion less than an hour before Whitelaw's announcement, a move that would otherwise have been discussed in good time through the Usual Channels. Pym said he had left that morning's Cabinet meeting, where the guillotine was agreed, to find Mellish. Unable to locate him, Pym had tried to track down Harrison, but – by apocryphal Westminster rumour or not – was told that he was having lunch off the estate after being overcharged for a prawn salad in the Commons canteen.[10]

The suggestion may have rankled Harrison. 'I am a down-to-earth man,' he said of his eating habits. 'I don't want any fancy dishes. I want my roast beef and Yorkshire pudding.'[11]

Whether a prawn salad constitutes a fancy dish is not for these pages.

Labour declared all-out war, vowing to end pairing for the remaining stages of the bill. Pym and Mellish, the former hoping to smooth things over, shared a beer a week later, in what one commentator described as the 'most remarkable act of fraternisation since British troops played football with the Germans between the trenches at Christmas 1914'.[12]

Despite the cordial pint, the bitterness didn't end there. During the final night of voting on the bill, Labour MPs staged a walkout, prompting some Conservative MPs to shuffle across the Commons to act as a mock opposition.

In the corridors, Labour spied deceit. Harold Wilson was asleep at his London home, believing he'd been paired with Prime Minister Ted Heath (the Usual Channels were up and running again, albeit tentatively). Heath, a renowned sailor who had just captained Great Britain to victory in the Admiral's Cup, had returned from Cowes in the Isle of Wight to vote in the divisions. Harrison, brandishing a list with all the pre-agreed pairs for the evening, approached the Prime Minister, who 'brusquely' told him there was no pairing arrangement.*

'The Prime Minister will never get another pair from us,' Harrison told his Tory counterparts.[13]

In December 1973, police arrested Harrison after a dispute over how he intended to pay for fuel at a petrol station in Victoria, London.

---

* The Conservatives argued Wilson had refused to pair with Heath for weeks and insisted no approach had been made.

Harrison, whose car plate on his Jaguar was KHE 2L – or 'Kick Harrison's Enemies to Hell'[14] – was released without charge later that day.

All three incidents speak to Harrison's stubborn, confrontational style and propensity to be in the thick of the action, an aspect of his personality and approach that, for some, is a cause of regret.

* * *

Frank Field* joined the Commons as Labour MP for Birkenhead in 1979. 'He was always threatening to hit me,' he says of Harrison, who, along with other senior whips, had earmarked him as a potential troublemaker. 'He'd rush up to me with his fists and stop there,' Field explains, holding his fist just short of his face.

Field had approached the whips' office when he first arrived to ask about securing a work area. 'We've been waiting for you,' a senior whip replied. The whips gave Field the furthest cubicle away from the chamber. He explains: 'I had criticised the Labour government before coming in, and whether [the whips] thought, "This is to be punished," I don't know.'

Field went into rebellion mode early, disputing the whips' appointment of a select committee chair. 'I hadn't realised they used all these positions as rewards and punishments,' he says.

In one incident, Field and Harrison encountered each other on a staircase at around two in the morning. Field 'disagreed with something', so Harrison 'dived' at him. 'I jumped up the stairs to miss him. He fell on the stairs, and I was away,' Field recalls.

Despite these encounters, Field says he liked Harrison, whom he recalls procuring bacon sandwiches for MPs serving on a committee which went through the night. 'But he didn't like people disagreeing with him,' he says.

---

* Frank Field passed away a few months after giving an interview to the author.

Jack Straw, another of Labour's 1979 intake, was a rising star in the party's shadow Treasury team. In his own words, he was getting 'a bit cocky' – until Harrison 'took me in hand'.

Spotting Straw as he walked past the opposition whips' office, Harrison, who disagreed with his tactics on the government's Finance Bill, grabbed him for a word. Harrison relayed his views, only for Straw to push back. Harrison fixed his eyes on Straw, and as he did so, the Labour MP felt a 'pain between my legs I'd not experienced since the school rugby field'.[15]

'His grip tightened. I rose on tiptoes as he pushed up as well. My mouth came open; only a little screech came out.'

Harrison said: 'Now, lad. Have you got the point, or do you want some more?'

His antics earned him the nickname 'Mr Mafia'.[16]

'Walter had a reputation of being a bit of a thug,' says Dennis Canavan, Labour MP for Falkirk West.

A former aide to a constituency neighbour of Harrison's said the MP they worked for 'really hated him and thought that he was brutal, rude, crude, lazy in the constituency … They had a very bad relationship.'

Plenty have nothing but positive things to say about Harrison, whose behaviour nonetheless speaks to the highly charged political environment. A fellow whip and deep admirer of Harrison said he regarded his colleagues with a mixture of 'sorrowful cynicism and threatening menace'.[17]

'Walter was such a lovely man. He was tough; he was tough with everybody,' recalls Helene Hayman, who served as a Labour MP alongside Harrison from 1974 to 1979.

Bar a protesting John Prescott, Labour's James Johnson sat alone in the Commons while MPs filed through to watch Her Majesty deliver the Queen's Speech in the House of Lords. Recovering from surgery, Johnson had mistakenly left his walking stick on the roof of his car as he drove into Parliament. 'We can't have you walking around with no visible means of support,' Harrison said, procuring Johnson a spare walking stick from a senior colleague.[18]

Neil Kinnock says of Harrison: 'This guy was brilliant... a real tough nut.' Harrison was 'pristine fair', which meant that 'if he was after you, he told you, usually in the corridor, unless it were something personal, then he'd take you to the office'.

'He never bollocked me, but he didn't give a damn who was around – policemen, servants of the House, guardians, Tory MPs – you got it, straight in the face. But if he could help people in difficulty, he would go to the ends of the earth. He was a real diamond.'

Labour MP Barry Sheerman, walking down a corridor one day, bumped into Harrison, who asked him: 'You know that House of Commons china?'

'Yes,' Sheerman replied.

'Would you like some?'

Harrison took Sheerman to a windowless room in the depths of Parliament where staff kept the crockery. 'With the House of Commons logo, all the Americans are stealing it, so we're changing it all and getting rid of it,' Harrison explained.

Whenever the Sheermans use one of their eight sets of plates, wall plates, cups or saucers, they think of Harrison. 'I paid for it, but it was the sort of thing he did,' Sheerman says.

David Clark, MP for Colne Valley in West Yorkshire, says Harrison helped him a 'great deal'. MPs always voted at 10 p.m. on Thursdays, with the last train to Yorkshire departing at 11.30 from King's Cross Station. The whips, including Harrison, would make sure MPs could leave once the important votes had passed so they could make it back to their constituencies.

Harrison would also make an impression on opposition MPs. Matthew Parris, a Conservative backbencher, recalls Harrison approaching him after he'd spoken about gay rights during a debate in Parliament. 'Just a bit of advice from the other side of the House, lad,' he told Parris.

'Just steer clear of this issue. It's not going to do you any good in politics at all.'

Perhaps most people wouldn't view this exchange in a positive light today. But Parris says it's an illustration of a whip looking out for another MP, given the treatment of gay people, including gay politicians, at the time. Parris would receive similar interventions from Conservative whips.

In another noteworthy Harrison story – which has likely taken on additional flourishes – he joined two Conservative MPs on a parliamentary trip to New Zealand. One, former whip Jasper More, had to double up with his Tory colleague while Harrison took the single room. When More complained about his bedfellow's snoring, Harrison volunteered to take his place. The next day, Harrison, refreshed, grinning and whistling, appeared well-rested.

'How did you manage that?' asked More.

'It was simple,' replied Harrison. 'Just as he put out the light, I said: "Give us a kiss, love," and he sat bolt upright all night.'[19]

Michael Meadowcroft, who served as the Liberal Party's Deputy Chief Whip, remembers Harrison saying warmly: 'The only thing I want from you, Michael, is trouble.'

It was his skills as a whip that garnered Harrison's formidable reputation. A drinker of some repute, he would stake out Parliament's many bars to keep track of backbenchers' views. He also had a network of ministerial drivers and other shrewd intelligence sources, including well-honed relations with MPs from rival parties, making him arguably Westminster's most plugged-in occupant.

Among his haunts was Annie's Bar, where 'he declared that he would never mix London tap water with his spirits'.[20] Sheerman remembers: 'He must have had an amazing constitution because he did like to drink. He knew everyone's strengths and weaknesses.'

It was a constitution that would endure. Then BBC Parliament journalist Mark D'Arcy recalls having lunch with Harrison at his local pub in 2004, where the former whip asked for an orange juice and was duly poured a double whisky.

What's for certain is that Harrison's intelligence-gathering capabilities would prove crucial in the parliament he's best remembered for, one in which he did as much as anyone to keep a struggling government afloat.

And yet it almost didn't happen; after eight years in the whips' office, Harold Wilson was considering Ernest Armstrong for the role of Government Deputy Chief Whip, before a change of heart that would prove crucial to much of what followed.[21]

As a colleague of Harrison's says: 'He was the great unsung hero of that period.'

CHAPTER 7

PLAYING TRIBUNE

DECEMBER 1974

Bob Mellish hovered near the division lobbies, his arms folded, watching in disbelief as fifty-four of his Labour colleagues voted against the government's defence statement in breach of a three-line whip; among them, nine parliamentary private secretaries.

The rebels felt the series of planned cuts, which would see defence spending reduced as a percentage of gross national product from 5.5 per cent to 4.5 per cent over the next decade, didn't go far enough. Such ill-discipline was anathema to Mellish, who, though unafraid to take a stand, couldn't imagine a world in which Labour MPs so nakedly breached an instruction of this nature, let alone those working for government ministers, with a majority as fragile and in such volume. Not to mention that the motion before the House was only to 'take note' of the government's defence statement and not to approve the proposals formally.[1]

He would not be the first Chief Whip, nor the last, to conclude that something had gone very awry.

The government had started the parliament two months earlier, in October 1974, with a majority of three; this had already been reduced by one after the mysterious disappearance of a Labour MP, who was missing, presumed dead.

Betty Boothroyd, who had joined Mellish's team after the election, was the whip for Walsall North MP John Stonehouse and other members from the West Midlands. She had returned from a whips' meeting in mid to late November to find a note on her desk that read to the effect of:

Dear Betty,
   Thank you very much for allowing me to pair for the next few days.
   It's very good of you, see you soon.
   John Stonehouse.[2]

With such a slender majority, no whip of any repute would have sanctioned an absence of this kind. Boothroyd's seniors in the whips' office had even asked her to keep tabs on New Palace Yard, a key portal to Parliament, to ensure no MP left the estate without approval.

Not two months into the job, Boothroyd, aware it was her responsibility to be across her flock, knew this would take explaining. 'Well, I mean, I almost fainted,' Boothroyd said of Stonehouse's note. 'Nobody was allowed to leave the House. Bob Mellish… he went berserk.'[3]

Stonehouse had attended Harold Wilson's Cabinet as a minister in the late 1960s, but claims that he was spying for the Czech security service, which he denied and weren't made public at the time, curtailed his political career. Files later revealed he had regular meetings with intelligence operatives from the Czech embassy in London for more than ten years.[4]

After losing his ministerial salary, he set up various companies to supplement his income as an MP. When the firms ran into financial difficulty, Stonehouse resorted to deceptive creative accounting, becoming the subject of interest from the Department of Trade and Industry. He stole the identities of two deceased men from his constituency, flew to Miami, left a pile of clothes on the beach after checking into the Fontainebleau Hotel, and, seemingly, went for a swim. He then disappeared.

Boothroyd called Stonehouse's young secretary, Sheila Buckley, into her office.

'I can get you a job with another Member of Parliament,' she said.

'No,' Buckley replied. 'I was only valuable to John.'[5]

Buckley and Stonehouse, who was married with three children, were having an affair. Stonehouse would soon surface in Australia, thirty-four days after his disappearance, having faked his own death.[6]

Mellish, still digesting the defeat from the night before, already had enough on his plate. With a majority of two, he had to think pragmatically of how he could get the government's business over the line – save for tracking down a man believed to have drowned or been eaten by sharks, a task beyond even the capabilities of his finest whips – especially given the rebellious nature of Labour MPs. In a series of conversations and negotiations that would continue throughout the parliament, Mellish, along with Walter Harrison, had already approached MPs from smaller parties, whose importance always grows exponentially in a tightly composed House of Commons. Among them were the three Plaid Cymru MPs, Dafydd Wigley, Dafydd Elis-Thomas and Gwynfor Evans.

Harrison had taken to calling on Sundays to enquire about the Welsh MPs' health and whether the government would have the pleasure of their company for the coming week. 'The government needed our support from time to time,' says Wigley. 'Being in a party which hadn't existed previously, we needed to get ourselves established.'

For the first months of the parliament, the Plaid Cymru MPs didn't have an office, working out of the flat of the Clerk of the House, the top official in the Commons. One evening, Mellish spotted Wigley and Elis-Thomas having dinner together in the Members' Dining Room.

'What are you two boys doing tonight?'

The pair told him they were thinking of having an early night. Mellish said he was a few votes short for a division on the London docks and needed a favour. Plaid Cymru MPs wouldn't usually interfere with local issues pertaining to England, but, short of an office, they looked to capitalise.

'You two boys look after me tonight,' Mellish said, 'and I'll look after you with a decent office.'

Gambling that Mellish, a straightforward and honourable man, would be true to his word, they voted with the government. 'It was no skin off our nose,' says Wigley, a glint in his eye. The move proved profitable, securing a suite of offices assigned to the party on the fourth floor of the Norman Shaw North building on Whitehall, overlooking the River Thames. 'That was the wheeling-dealing,' says Wigley. 'Bob Mellish was a rough diamond.'

When a senior Conservative whip, John Stradling Thomas, sent a 'curt note' some years later asking them to vacate the office, with plans afoot to reassign it to sacked and sulking Tory frontbenchers, the Plaid Cymru MPs were furious. They replied warning that if he carried on in that vein, they would barricade themselves in the office, put a placard out the window that overlooked the embankment saying Tory landlords were throwing out defenceless tenants, and phone every newspaper and broadcaster in London. They heard no more about the proposed eviction.

On Wednesday 18 December 1974, two days after the defence statement rebellion, Mellish, realising that Downing Street had no plans to punish the parliamentary private secretaries (PPSs) who had defied a three-line whip, and with rebel MPs boasting of their untouchability, handed in his resignation to the Prime Minister.

'When I issue a three-line whip, I expect it to be obeyed. This is not being done at the moment and I cannot carry on like this,' he told journalists.[7]

Mellish informed his whips at the weekly meeting in 12 Downing Street, several of whom said they too would walk away if Wilson accepted his resignation. 'I am sure my own [resignation] and others will follow,' Harrison said.[8]

Wilson broke off a lunch with the Prime Minister of Mauritius to meet Mellish for a twenty-minute conversation, urging him to rethink. Mellish, who had succumbed to Wilson's advances before, wouldn't budge, but a second meeting that evening swung him round. Downing Street released a statement saying he had agreed to withdraw his resignation.[9]

* * *

From defiant rebels to a missing MP in John Stonehouse, to one of his team, Walter Johnson, quitting after finding being a whip and a constituency representative 'too much to bear',[10] Mellish had endured a rough start to the parliament. But he was still confident of the government seeing through a full term.[11]

While there are challenges with a slender majority, he said in an interview, the government could rely on two Northern Ireland politicians: a 'staunch' ally in the shape of Social Democratic and Labour Party (SDLP) founder and leader Gerry Fitt and independent MP Frank Maguire. 'The situation isn't as bad as it seems,' he said.

The whips would deploy senior Cabinet ministers to meet Fitt to ensure his support ahead of crucial divisions. Fitt was initially amenable, saying that while he couldn't formally accept the Labour whip, he could not 'foresee any situation in which I would lend my support to the defeat of the present government'.[12]

Ensuring the presence of the ever-elusive Maguire, who ran a pub in his constituency of Fermanagh and South Tyrone, was more challenging. In their Wednesday morning meetings, whips would discuss when best to hold crucial votes in the parliamentary weeks ahead. Mellish and Harrison were often against running three-line whips on Mondays or Thursdays, as it would be harder to ensure MPs, some of whom had to travel several hours to get to Westminster, were present. Typically, it would be a toss-up between Tuesday or Wednesday evenings, often hinging on one man's availability.

Harrison would call Maguire's wife to enquire about his movements. 'Is that you, Philomena? It's Walter.'

'Oh, Frank can't come Tuesday – it's dance night,' Philomena would explain.

'What about Wednesday?'

'Oh, he'd probably come on Wednesday,' Philomena would reply.

'The business of the government literally depended on dance night at a pub in Fermanagh,' says Labour whip Peter Snape.

A member of the whips' office would be deputed to pick up Maguire from Heathrow Airport, fearing he couldn't manage the journey to Westminster alone. In disparaging Maguire's intellectual prowess, Fitt would recount a joke of Maguire queuing for a train ticket. When the person in front said, 'Maida Vale, return,' Maguire walked up and said, 'Frank Maguire, single.'

For security reasons, the whip responsible for picking up Maguire couldn't take a government car and would have to drive their own vehicle to Heathrow Terminal 1. During his turn to collect Maguire, Snape would hide behind a pillar so that arriving Northern Ireland unionist MPs wouldn't see him; the government would try to face both ways insofar as unionist and nationalist MPs were concerned, a permutation that would prove unsustainable.

'Frank was always the last off the plane out of complete bewilderment,' says Snape.

Finally in the car, Maguire would ask Snape to make various stops along the way, including the Golden Eagle pub in west London, where regulars greeted him with a knowing cheer. On to Westminster, where Snape would hand him over to a fellow whip, Albert 'Jock' Stallard, with whom Maguire got on well. Stallard would take Maguire straight to a bar, 'where he'd get quietly pissed until ten o'clock, and then he'd vote for us', says Snape.

'After we got his vote, it didn't matter if he slept on the Thames as far as we were concerned!' he jokes.

These light-hearted moments helped temper the stress and travails of Mellish's job, which, nevertheless, were hitting home. He suffered a minor heart attack in early 1975, attributing the episode to his hours of work. 'A routine like this, day after day, week after week, eventually takes its toll,' he said.[13] He took a two-week holiday with his wife at their bungalow in Sussex to recuperate.

The hours were catching up with everybody; not least MPs' spouses, some of whom lamented their partners returning home in the middle of the night, often due to filibustering opposition MPs – spurred on by the Conservative whips – who took advantage of the government's reluctance to guillotine debates by making long-winded speeches.

To timetable proceedings and thereby limit the length of a debate was always a controversial move likely to draw the ire of the opposition and media alike, seen as a means of stifling opposition and, in more over-the-top interpretations, closing down democracy.

Mellish, where possible, wanted to facilitate MPs. During a debate on the budget in late 1974, thirty Conservative MPs rose, signalling their interest in speaking. With the debate still going on at 1.30 a.m., rather than introduce a guillotine motion, he adjourned the debate for the day, resuming the following afternoon. 'We gave the opposition eight hours to make their points,' he said. 'I didn't need to do that, but I'd think myself a very poor parliamentarian otherwise.'[14]

With the Labour whips needing their MPs to remain on the premises to counteract any opposition moves – always favouring caution over vulnerability – both frontbenchers and backbenchers bore the brunt. 'You'd have Cabinet ministers in the tearoom at three in the morning because every vote was absolutely essential,' says a Labour backbencher.

Labour MP Robert Hughes, who lived in Hampstead while away from his Scottish constituency, would always take his dog for a walk when he arrived home. Returning from a walk at half past three one morning, he found his wife waiting for him at the front door.

'Where the hell have you been?' she asked.

'Walking the dog.'

'You walked the dog's lead,' his wife said. 'You left the dog at home!'[15]

One spouse eventually drew a line.

Lisanne Radice, the wife of Labour MP Giles Radice, organised a letter to Mellish protesting the 'hours which our husbands sit every week' – longer, she claimed, than any other legislature. As a result, MPs were 'less efficient' and more 'ineffective', while parliamentary families 'lead deprived lives'. 'Wives are lonely and children fatherless,' she wrote.[16]

She proposed that Parliament finish by eight in the evening, with question time and government statements commencing in the morning. The letter, signed by other partners, triggered debate about whether political lives are conducive to successful marriages.

The suggestions caught Mellish's eye, who met Radice and proposed that the Commons conclude business at ten each night. A welcome relief to one Tory MP, Charles Irving, who had complained: 'Quite frankly many of us are sex-starved.'[17]

Despite Mellish's best intentions, working conditions in Parliament would only deteriorate. Labour MP William Hamling's death, with Conservative candidate Peter Bottomley securing the subsequent by-election, reduced the government's majority to one. Crucial committees that discussed legislation in detail would have to reflect the parliamentary arithmetic, meaning the government's right to maintain a majority was hanging by a thread.

And a group of Labour backbenchers was starting to get organised.

* * *

A photocopied document, which had fallen into the hands of the press, gave the game away.

Distributed to the eighty Labour MPs inside the left-wing Tribune Group, the document advised how to vote on amendments tabled to the government's anti-inflation policy, instructions often at odds with the official line put out by the Labour whips' office. In July 1975, with inflation at around 25 per cent, the government proposed limiting wage increases for millions of British workers to £6 a week. The authors of the Tribune Group document sought to play it down, but to the media, it was clear: there was a party within a party.

Bob Mellish knew early on that something was afoot. The Office was already 'getting sick and tired' of unofficial whips wandering around the Commons urging Labour MPs to rebel.[18]

Loyal MPs were outraged. Facing local pushback for voting *with* the government, Labour MP Paul Rose threatened to resign as a PPS in protest at the lack of action against the dissenters. 'One has now reached the absurd position where a Labour MP is likely to be censured or dismissed because he supports the Labour whip,' he observed.[19]

Among the Tribune Group members who met weekly were Geoff Edge and Neil Kinnock, two PPSs who rebelled over the defence statement in December 1974, and Dennis Canavan. 'We relied on each other's expertise,' says Edge, who took an interest in the south-east Asian nation of East Timor, which was fighting for independence from Portugal. 'If I said we should vote against something in relation to this, then we would.'

The group's unofficial whips were Kinnock and fellow Tribune Group member Ian Mikardo. 'You always need a bit of organisation,' Kinnock explains. '[We would] whip them sometimes into opposition votes, abstentions or support when things were tight.'

While outwardly angry at the indiscipline of MPs, Mellish 'knew that if it ever came to a confidence vote' – a crunch division called to ensure the government still has the confidence of the House of Commons to continue – 'then he could count on our vote', says Canavan.

Edge and Bruce Grocott did most of their rebelling over issues related to the European Economic Community – yet they also kept their PPS jobs. 'It didn't necessarily mean political death,' Grocott says of rebelling.

Europe continued to divide the Labour Party and its whips' office;[*] Walter Harrison was among nine whips to vote against the government's bill to introduce direct elections to the EEC. The issue was made a free vote to avoid widescale resignations and sackings.[20]

The Labour Party had pledged to renegotiate the terms of EEC accession in its election manifesto, with Harold Wilson, following talks in Paris and Dublin, calling a referendum on Britain's continued membership for June 1975. But Eurosceptic Labour MPs weren't happy with his efforts. Harrison had an 'astonishing row' in the Commons with his close friend Foreign Secretary James 'Jim' Callaghan, who warned that he would be 'finished' if he voted against the Prime Minister's renegotiation. Other MPs were furious that Wilson had imposed a 'parliamentary gag' on ministers who wanted to speak against continued EEC membership in the Commons. Eric Heffer was sacked as Industry Minister for doing just that.[21]

The Commons, in the end, endorsed the renegotiation, and Britain voted by 67 per cent to 33 to remain in the EEC at the referendum.

Unleashed from collective responsibility, Heffer became an instigator, organising a walkout of left-wing MPs from a committee considering the government's Industry Bill over fears ministers wouldn't allow enough time to debate amendments.[22] He was also involved in another extraordinary flashpoint in the Commons chamber.

In March 1976, thirty-seven Labour MPs abstained on Chancellor Denis Healey's public expenditure white paper, a countermove organised by Kinnock in protest at the sheer depth of the proposed spending cuts in areas such as education, set out in the months before the International Monetary Fund issued Britain – 'the sick man of Europe' – a loan.

Discussing the move at a Tribune Group meeting on the Monday

---

[*] For more than a year, Labour refused to send representatives to the European Parliament or pair Conservative MPs who split their time between London and Brussels.

night before the vote, Dennis Skinner, the MP for Bolsover, noted: 'We'll defeat the government if we abstain.'

'Yeah, that's simple arithmetic, and if you don't want to defeat the government, vote with them,' Kinnock said. 'If you think the government should be defeated, abstain.'

'Well, if you put it like that,' said Skinner.

'Well, there's no other way to put it. The maths is very, very simple.'

'What would happen then?' asked another member of the group.

'We'll have a confidence vote, and we'll vote with the government and win,' Kinnock said.

Healey returned from the division lobbies and 'just about went ballistic', Canavan recalls. 'He started cursing and swearing; he was almost literally foaming at the mouth. He used the f-word several times at me. I thought at one stage he was going to hit me.'

Members of the lobby* watched the confrontation from the Press Gallery above the Commons chamber, but Canavan declined the opportunity to reveal what Healey had said. A journalist reported that Labour MP Russell Kerr had waved two fingers at Healey before leaving the chamber, while another bellowed: 'Stalinist! Stalinist!'[23]

Despite the fractures, Labour MPs voted in favour of the government at the confidence vote, preventing a general election.

* * *

Neil Kinnock, notably, led the rebellion against the government's flagship plans for devolved assemblies in Scotland and Wales. Though the Tribune Group, like much of the Labour Party, was split on the issue, Kinnock and a band of dissenters held significant sway. The whips would encourage him to pair on devolution votes and 'take the night off'. Unless he couldn't defend staying away, Kinnock took the whips

---

* The collective term for journalists who report from Parliament.

up on their offer. 'Maybe it was eight or ten times, but it meant that I saw the kids eight or ten times more than I would have.'

The battle over devolution would play a key role in the government's fate.

Kinnock and Canavan turned down jobs during the parliament, with the latter asked to join the whips' office. Kinnock's fundamental disagreements over policy, not least on devolution and government spending, meant taking on a ministerial post would have been 'bloody dishonest', he says.

Despite their political differences, Canavan had a decent working relationship with Jimmy Hamilton, the Labour Scottish whip, who was 'very considerate' in granting him time off after the death of his youngest son.

Though unafraid of carrying out major rebellions – a whopping ninety Labour MPs voted against increasing the Queen's income – several factors reduced the Tribune Group's potency.

First, the group's support of the government at no-confidence votes. Second, the fact that its members didn't always agree internally on major issues. And third, rival parties' inability to rally around a collective position.

The Conservative Party whips, after all, had enough on their plate.

CHAPTER 8

THE FUCK-UP SQUAD

Each day at 2.30 p.m., the order would come. 'Stand by your beds!' The Conservative Party whips would dutifully follow Bernard 'Jack' Weatherill's quasi-military instructions, taking position by their desks ahead of the daily meeting that he, as Deputy Chief Whip, would facilitate. 'There were a lot of chuckles going on,' says a whip.

A man of a different style but very much the equal of his government counterpart, Walter Harrison, Weatherill was respected by the Labour whips, who kept tabs on his whereabouts and movements. If he disappeared, they knew that the Tories were planning an attack.

'Find Weatherill!' senior whips would cry out.

Weatherill, a twin, was born on 25 November 1920, in Guildford, Surrey. After attending Malvern College, Weatherill took an apprenticeship at the family business, an eponymous tailoring firm which would find a home on London's prestigious Savile Row.

As war broke out in 1939, he enlisted in the Oxfordshire and Buckinghamshire Light Infantry. A year later, he was commissioned into the Dragoon Guards, reaching the rank of captain, before serving with the Indian Army in the 19th King George's Own Lancers, where he learned to speak Urdu, took up meditation and, in response to the 1943 Bengal famine, became a vegetarian. His military service also took him to Burma and Malaya.

After the war, he returned to the family business, working as a director, managing director and chairman. Despite the lofty titles, his father had made sure he earned his tailoring stripes, refusing to release him from the workroom, where he sat cross-legged until he had made a pair of breeches for King George VI.[1] On his mother's advice, he carried a silver tailoring thimble to keep him grounded in his family origins.

Elected an MP for Croydon North East in 1964, Weatherill, overawed by his surroundings and finding his feet, would recall catching onto a conversation about himself between two Conservative colleagues in the Commons toilets while hiding in a nearby cubicle. 'I don't know what this place is coming to... they've got my tailor in here now!' an MP said.[2]

Appointed to the Conservative Party whips' office in 1967, he quickly rose through the ranks, becoming a Lord Commissioner in 1970, Vice-Chamberlain the following year, Comptroller in 1972 and finally Deputy Chief Whip in December 1973.

A stickler for timekeeping, Weatherill was displeased to find a Tory whip enter the office after the daily call to 'stand by your beds'. Before he could rebuke him, the whip explained that his tailor – a colleague of Weatherill's – had been late and held him up.[3]

In the cross-party world of the Usual Channels, Weatherill was renowned as a man of his word. 'If something were agreed, then he would stick by it,' says a Labour whip.

Tories would equally respond with righteous indignation to any breach of a pre-agreed deal. 'Whips are a much-misunderstood breed of man,' Weatherill said. 'However, they have in common an understanding of the procedures of the House and the importance of mutual confidence and trust, without which the Usual Channels would break down.'[4]

A kindly man with bushy eyebrows, a restrained, sympathetic smile and a brisk, military manner, Weatherill, despite his measured disposition, was nonetheless a man *au fait* with practices known as the dark arts.

* * *

Fresh from reporting on the Watergate scandal in Washington, a young political adviser by the name of Michael Dobbs arrived in Westminster to begin work at the Conservative Research Department (CRD). A breeding ground for rising stars, the CRD counted Iain Macleod, Rab Butler and Enoch Powell among its alumni.

Dobbs entered the CRD building on Old Queen Street, overlooking St James's Park, half a mile from the Tories' Central Office at 32 Smith Square. Led by Chris Patten, the CRD then included in its ranks the likes of Michael Portillo and David Nicholson, all future MPs.

Soon after arriving, Dobbs was handed the job of 'Special Duties' in the CRD's political section. He didn't know what this meant, only that the person who had passed over the job seemed desperately relieved.

The position, it transpired, involved working out of the Conservative Party leader's parliamentary office. As part of this role, he acted as secretary for a committee known as the 'Fuck-Up Squad'.

The Fuck-Up Squad gathered one evening a week to discuss ways of putting pressure on the government in Parliament. 'Now, how do you do that as backbenchers? You ask the awkward questions, you back each other up,' Dobbs explains.

With the Fuck-Up Squad's encouragement, Tory MPs would work together to drain the government benches of energy long into the night, filibustering in the Commons and employing other forms of skulduggery. They also considered ways of exposing Labour Party vulnerabilities, such as the growth outside Parliament of the Militant Tendency, a Trotskyist group.

'It met on a weekly basis to decide what are our best issues and what are our best tactics to expose that the government is rocking,' Dobbs explains. While nominally overseen by Sir Jasper More, a long-serving MP and former whip, a senior member of The Office really administered the Fuck-Up Squad: Jack Weatherill.

A Conservative whip says the long hours had more of an effect on younger MPs than on the battle-hardened older hands. He remembers his colleague Spencer Le Marchant, whose personality was as large as his six-foot-six frame, ringing his wife, who was asleep in the Isle of Wight, at five in the morning to say: 'I've been up all night and it's time you woke up!'

Through the Fuck-Up Squad, Dobbs got to know members of The Office. After a drink with a whip in Parliament, he soon realised they weren't like other MPs.

Sitting in Strangers' Bar about three drinks in, the whip began pointing at people in the room, identifying not only their names but also their personal and sexual predilections. It was a formative exchange Dobbs wouldn't soon forget.

'My goodness me, as a young, naive Westminster-goer, I was deeply shocked and deeply impressed.'

* * *

Jack Weatherill's tough but fair approach married well with the suave charms of fellow Second World War veteran Humphrey Atkins, the Conservative Party Chief Whip.

Joining the whips' office in the same year as Weatherill, Atkins's rise was even more meteoric, becoming Chief Whip in 1973, in partial recognition of his performance while Deputy Chief Whip, predicting the Conservative vote on Britain's entry to the EEC by one. 'And the one I got wrong', he said later, 'was an awkward bugger anyway.'[5]

Atkins had a propensity to take a restrained approach to reprimands, knowing that what went unspoken could have greater impact.

Conservative MP Roger Sims was sitting at his office in Dean's Yard by Westminster Abbey when the division bell rang. He had eight minutes to vote after walking through Parliament Square onto the estate. Usually, on such occasions, a police officer would stop the passing traffic to allow MPs to cross safely, but this evening, no officers were present.

'I just got to the division lobbies, and the door was shut in my face,' he said.[6]

The Labour government won the division by one. Seeking to preempt the bollocking to come, Sims wrote a contrite letter to the Chief Whip, informing him what had happened. The Chief replied:

Dear Roger,
   Thank you for your letter explaining why you missed the vote … Not to worry. It's the sort of thing that happens to us all – just once.

Atkins underlined 'just once' three times.[7]

Weatherill and Atkins ran the Conservative Party whips' office in a manner commensurate with their experience. 'Almost everybody had been in the army. The whole tone of the thing was very much like the officers' mess,' says Conservative MP Christopher Tugendhat.

Carol Mather, a decorated veteran, joined the whips' office in November 1975. His twenty-two years with the Welsh Guards saw him partake in the first Special Air Service operations, land in Normandy on D-Day plus one, walk around 600 miles through the Apennine Mountains after escaping from an Italian prisoner of war camp and act as a liaison officer for Field Marshal Bernard 'Monty' Montgomery, one of the outstanding Allied commanders in the Second World War. He left the military after rising to lieutenant colonel.

Monty recommended Mather for a Military Cross following a successful reconnaissance mission to the occupied Dutch city of Nijmegen in September 1944, during the second day of Operation Market Garden. The following January, Mather was attacked by enemy fighters while in an Auster plane, with the pilot dead and slumped in his seat. Mather, who had been struck by four bullets, applied the flaps while a fellow soldier seized the controls.

Monty visited Mather at his hospital bedside in Eindhoven.

'How many holes in him?' he asked the army doctor.

'Counting the shrapnel, thirteen,' came the reply.

'Thirteen, thirteen! Excellent, excellent,' Monty said, before leaving.[8]

Such military prestige in the whips' office induced respect and deference among many newer MPs. 'People fitted neatly into it if they had been outstanding heroes in the last world war,' says David Hunt, MP for Wirral. 'The whips were, therefore, people everyone respected.'

The Conservatives had begun to fine-tune the composition of the whips' office between those who would remain indefinitely and newbies destined for ministerial office who were, in the words of one, 'greenhousing'. 'It was extremely valuable because you got to know about individual MPs and the character of the party,' says ex-whip Richard Luce. 'You got to know how government worked.'

The clear ideological dividing line between the Conservatives and Labour helped whips to keep MPs onside. A challenge for The Office, however, was to ensure the attendance of backbenchers, some of whom – known as knights of the shires – were content with holding jobs outside Parliament while not harbouring ambitions at Westminster. In these cases, the whips had to lean on MPs' sense of loyalty rather than dangle ministerial carrots.

George Young, who joined The Office midway through the parliament, says instilling discipline was relatively easy. 'Most Tory MPs had done national service. So, obedience, loyalty, unity were in the genes – and they didn't all want to be ministers.' He adds: 'We were ahead in the polls; not a lot to rebel about.'

* * *

The Conservative whips' immediate priority following the October 1974 general election centred on the party leadership. Tory backbenchers, among the most ruthless of parliamentary groupings anywhere, wanted a change at the top. The scale and virulence of ill-feeling towards Ted Heath shocked the whips. 'There certainly was [disquiet],' says one whip. 'We had a lot of discussion on that.'

The whip was among those who'd had a bad experience with Heath. The ex-Prime Minister had grown more insular following two election losses. After the whip shared his views on a prominent political issue, the Tory leader was in 'such a bad condition that he couldn't even talk. He just grunted.'

Under severe pressure, Heath consented to a review of internal elections by his predecessor, Sir Alec Douglas-Home, who recommended that the party leader be elected annually and that, to win on the first ballot, the candidate with the most votes must have a margin over their nearest rival equivalent to 15 per cent of all Tory MPs.

In January 1975, Heath called a leadership election for 4 February to firm up his position. Atkins, to Heath's considerable dismay, opted for a strategy of strict neutrality in the contest. 'I appointed you all!' Heath protested.[9] The senior whips decided Weatherill would be 'sacrificed' and required to update Heath on how The Office thought MPs would vote.[10]

Subsequent Chiefs would follow Atkins's approach to varying approval levels among their MPs, who believe they owe their loyalty to the leader. Chiefs often disagree, suggesting that if they show their hand, they cannot be seen as neutral henceforth, undermining their role in facilitating communication between the party rank and file and the upper echelons.

Though initially expected to win easily, Heath found himself placed second in the first ballot, by a margin of eleven votes. Bristling with resentment at the challenge lodged by the outsider, someone he had appointed to his Cabinet, Heath resigned as leader.

Margaret Thatcher firmed up her victory in the second ballot, securing 52.9 per cent of the vote, becoming the first woman to lead a major political party in the United Kingdom. Atkins, perhaps in reward for his rigid neutrality, remained as Chief Whip.

Thatcher didn't blend well with all the whips' office hierarchy. Despite giving Tory MPs a free vote on the issue of proportional representation (PR) for European elections, Thatcher, who was opposed, stood outside the division lobby, taking the names of those who had supported PR. Among them was Weatherill.

'Jack, what are you doing in that lobby?' she said.

'It's a free vote, Margaret.'

'Yes,' Thatcher said. 'But there are free votes and free votes.'

With a disgruntled Heath taking up his pew on the front row below the gangway of the Conservative benches, scarcely concealing his transparent contempt for the party's new leader, Thatcher endured a challenging time as the new frontwoman of the opposition.

'Having a woman leader was a revolution in those days. If you put that into context, then everyone had doubts about her,' says a Conservative MP.

The government's precarious standing, if anything, only placed Thatcher under more pressure, akin to a sports team going up against an opponent who has had a player sent off. Everyone involved expects the team to win and win comfortably, but to her contemporaries, Thatcher wasn't landing the punches nor extracting a poll lead befitting the state of play.

'Maggie Thatcher had been treated, even by much of her own side, as a "silly woman" with nothing expected of her,' says Michael Dobbs.

Still to find her feet in the Commons as leader, Thatcher was guilty of lacklustre displays when it mattered most. Labour MPs would squeak when she rose to speak in the chamber to mimic her 'shrill' voice, Dobbs recalls. She also had to deal with internal splits over issues such as Europe and devolution, suffering frontbench resignations on the latter.

Alick Buchanan-Smith, shadow Secretary of State for Scotland, and Malcolm Rifkind, one of his junior shadow ministers, both quit after Thatcher ordered that her MPs vote against the Labour government's plans for a Scottish Assembly, both having argued the party should abstain.

Thatcher asked to see Rifkind in her parliamentary office. 'If you are willing to continue on the frontbench without resigning,' she said, 'I will look the other way if you abstain rather than vote with the party when the vote comes up.'

'That was a very good gesture of hers,' Rifkind says. He declined her offer, ended up voting in favour of a Scottish Assembly and returned to the frontbench a year later. 'There was no bitterness about it.'

* * *

The Conservative whips were known to some backbenchers as 'the Praetorian Guard'. To the Labour government, they were the opposition, although relations between the whips' offices were strong. Whips would negotiate when to finish a committee session, with one side (the Tories) hoping to go late and the other (the government) to wrap up as reasonably early as possible, while Pairing Whips would meet daily to discuss who would be off that evening.

Senior figures would also meet in the government whips' office, with great care and attention given to where opposition whips would be seated,[11] to negotiate over issues like extra supply days or the dreaded introduction of a guillotine motion, depending on their party's needs.

The natural pace and requirements of Westminster life rely on the smooth running of these relationships, but at several junctures during the 1974–79 parliament, the Usual Channels malfunctioned.

CHAPTER 9

COMMUNICATION BREAKDOWN

JULY 1975

Walter Harrison gathered a group of Labour whips early on a Tuesday morning in July 1975. Frustrated that Conservative MPs had taken to calling divisions and then not voting – part of the opposition whips' guerrilla tactics for wearing down an embattled government – he wanted to counter what he deemed to be delaying and unconstitutional manoeuvres.

For this division, he told his colleagues, we'll ask Labour MPs to vote twice, once in the Aye lobby, once in the No.

'It was a joke I knew could not misfire,' Harrison said.[1]

Three Labour MPs voted in each lobby; two others said they had refused Harrison's request.

Despite Harrison providing disguises – doubtless the punchline of the joke he sought to play on the opposition – the Tories cottoned on. 'I saw it happening, and I made representations at the time,' said a Conservative MP.[2] The government motion was carried by twenty-five votes to three, not enough to constitute a quorum. The Tories demanded answers and an apology from Harrison, describing the move as a culmination of 'ineptitude and cheating'.[3]

With Harrison on the frontbench, Bob Mellish made a rare statement to the Commons, defusing the situation by saying: 'I spend all my time trying to get as many MPs as I can to go in one lobby. I'm overwhelmed at the enthusiasm of those who voted in two.'

This was not the first time the volatile House of Commons had pivoted from exaggerated dissent to brief reconciliation. Nigel Lawson was seen laughing at the entrance to the chamber with Stanley Clinton-Davis soon after the Tory MP's order paper had struck the Labour minister's face during a fiery row over guillotines and government honesty.[4]

The stresses of the time, with continued union unrest, high unemployment and persistent inflation, placed added emphasis on parliamentary debate and the policies chosen by the government to help stem the tide. In January 1976, demonstrators threw leaflets from the public gallery as the government survived a challenge on its plans for dealing with unemployment. Nine protesters were taken to the Commons cells to cool down.[5]

With late nights, drink and a predominantly male House of Commons thrown into the mix, the chamber could quickly descend into chaos.

'People forget that in that parliament, the House was suspended quite often because of disorder – people fighting, brawling,' says a Tory whip. Labour whip Joe Ashton said: '[MPs] came from tough backgrounds, coal miners and many, many more manual workers, and very few women.'[6]

Against such a backdrop, and despite their mutual respect, the government and opposition whips' offices would nonetheless have cause for grievance.

* * *

On 16 March 1976, Harold Wilson stunned the nation by announcing his resignation as Prime Minister. 'In March 1974 I decided that I would remain in office for no more than two years,' he said. 'I have not wavered in this decision, and it is irrevocable.'[7]

A Labour MP said Bob Mellish 'wept at the news'.[8]

Before Wilson's shock resignation, Mellish had spent much of his time trying to track down errant Labour MPs. In one famous incident, he encouraged Peter Snape, a new addition to The Office, to visit Coventry North West MP Maurice Edelman, who had been off sick for some time. Snape called in at Edelman's Westminster flat, where they had a courteous conversation, and Edelman agreed to vote in the Commons the following Monday.

Over the weekend, Snape settled down to watch the early evening news. During the headlines, the newsreader announced the death of 'long-serving Labour MP Maurice Edelman'. Within minutes, Snape's phone rang. It was the Pairing Whip, Michael Cocks, who barked, 'For fuck's sake, Snape, overkill!' before slamming the phone down.

Mellish appointed Snape as a minder for the Labour candidate in the subsequent by-election, with the warning: 'If we don't hold the seat, don't effing come back.' Fortunately for Snape, the people of Coventry North West elected Labour's Geoffrey Robinson.

With a key vote in the offing, the Chief Whip made an unprecedented appeal on BBC Radio to John Ryman, a barrister and MP for Blyth, who, unsanctioned by the whips, hadn't been seen in the Commons for two months.

'I hope you are listening, John … I need your vote very badly,' he said.[9]

Ryman, who faced court proceedings for alleged irregularities in the declaration of his election expenses and said he had been advised to avoid votes in Westminster, was furious at the public reprimand. He also claimed he had been in Parliament when Mellish made his remarks.

Mellish insisted he should have replied to his many letters and telegrams. 'I have phoned him time after time with no response,' he told BBC Radio. Mellish amusingly summarised the situation: 'It's just another heartache. I have got to live with it.'[10]

The government was desperate and unafraid of showing it. John Stonehouse, who had returned from Australia and was facing trial at the Old Bailey charged with theft, fraud and conspiracy, was still technically a Labour MP, with the party in turmoil over whether to strip him of the whip despite the frankly unbelievable set of allegations hanging over him.

In an extraordinary appearance on bail from Brixton Prison, during which the Speaker interrupted him several times to ensure he didn't deviate from a pre-agreed speech, Stonehouse spoke of his 'complete mental breakdown' leading towards his 'psychiatric suicide' and the death of what he called 'an idealist'. He delivered the monologue from the Conservative benches, a move he insisted reflected the fact that the opposition side of the chamber was where he had begun his political career rather than being a statement of intent.

After causing Labour considerable embarrassment, he repaid the favour of retaining the whip and voting in the Commons by leaving the party in early April 1976, which, combined with the death of Health and Social Security Minister Brian O'Malley, stripped the government of its majority.

Humphrey Atkins immediately called for the Committee of Selection, which appoints MPs to standing committees, to take account of the new parliamentary arithmetic. Liberal Chief Whip Alan Beith also urged Mellish to begin talks on altering the government's legislative programme to make it more palatable 'to majority opinion in the country'.[11]

Mellish was already teetering on the edge. As thirty-seven members of the Tribune Group abstained on Denis Healey's white paper, Mellish, said to be 'disgusted', threatened to resign once more.[12]

In just a few days, such a move would no longer be necessary.

Foreign Secretary Jim Callaghan emerged as the frontrunner to replace Harold Wilson, winning the deciding round for the party leadership on 5 April. A few days later, Snape walked into the whips' office to find Mellish, who had backed Michael Foot's bid to be leader, in tears.

'What's wrong?' Snape asked.

Mellish looked up from his desk. 'Oh, I've just been to see Callaghan, and he's given me the sack.'

Like anyone who had paid attention, Snape knew Mellish had been angling for a move.

'Yeah,' Mellish said, 'but I thought I'd move on to something else!'

It came as a surprise to some that Callaghan threw the hospital pass of Chief Whip to Michael Cocks, a former geography teacher, and not to his friend Walter Harrison. Though a significant promotion, and his first time attending Cabinet, Cocks had little chance to celebrate.

* * *

The Labour whips hurried back to The Office with a printout of the first vote, a tie, 303 to 303.

The Speaker, George Thomas, had voted with the Noes against the Tory amendment to block the government's bill to nationalise the shipbuilding and aircraft industries, adhering to precedents established more than a century earlier. However, the whips knew that if the next vote turned out to be another tie, as expected, then the Speaker would likely follow similar precedents that would see him vote *against* the substantive government motion, too.

The legislation, on the evening of 27 May 1976, hung in the balance.

Labour whip Tom Pendry had taken the bill through its record-breaking committee stage, which saw fifty-eight sittings across 140 hours. Despite this, Jack Dormand, the new Pairing Whip, had told him to sit out the first vote at 10 p.m., certain the government was going to secure the narrowest of wins. 'You know the score, Tom,' he said, having negotiated pairs with his opposite number, John Stradling Thomas.[13]

With another tie in the offing, the whips, along with their civil servant manager, Bert Green, scoured the division lists. Michael Cocks urged a Labour MP to make a point of order in the Commons to buy more time before the next vote.

'Where's Fred Peart?' a whip asked. The agriculture minister, who had been eligible to vote that morning, hadn't done so. Instead, he was in Copenhagen for a fisheries meeting.

The division bells rang for the government motion. Pendry, having sat out the first vote, and confident he could now take part in Peart's absence, rushed to the division lobbies. He encountered Stradling Thomas, the Tories' Pairing Whip, who asked why he had voted. Pendry, not feeling obliged to go into details, hurried to his office 'somewhat flustered'.[14]

MPs awaited the result in the chamber, certain of another draw. But the two government tellers facing the Speaker's chair moved to the right, signalling a victory.

The result: 304–303.

Tory MPs, incredulous that the government had magicked up an extra vote, yelled accusations of cheating.[15] Their anger was further entrenched when jubilant Labour MPs, led by members of the Tribune Group, broke out into a rendition of the Labour anthem 'The Red Flag', defying usual parliamentary decorum.

> The people's flag is deepest red,
> It shrouded oft our martyred dead…

It wasn't the first time members of the Tribune Group had burst into song during the parliament, though this time they made it beyond the first verse or two.

> And ere their limbs grew stiff and cold,
> Their hearts' blood dyed its ev'ry fold…

Michael Heseltine, the shadow Secretary of State for Industry, who had led the debate for the opposition, simmered on the Conservative frontbench.

COMMUNICATION BREAKDOWN

…We'll keep the red flag flying—

Heseltine strode forward, seized the five-foot-long, ten-kilogram mace from its place on the table that divides the Commons and held it aloft as though to strike the government frontbench.

Shocked, Margaret Thatcher nudged a senior colleague, who leapt up to restrain and catch the mace as it came over Heseltine's shoulder. 'I swear to this day, he lifted Jim Prior off his feet,' says Tory MP David Hunt.

The Commons descended into chaos. A skirmish developed near the Tory frontbench, with Geoffrey Rippon appearing to be in 'full physical conflict' with Dennis Canavan,[16] while another watching journalist felt Rippon had thrown a punch at Canavan, who was restrained by Peter Snape before he could retaliate.[17]

The Deputy Speaker, Myer Galpern, suspended the House for twenty minutes after Prior returned the mace – a historical symbol of royal authority that must be placed correctly for the Commons to sit – to its rack the wrong way around.

The fracas continued at the entrance to the chamber, with Tom Swain, a miners' MP from Derbyshire, 'taking a poke' at Tory MP Michael Spicer, who too was grabbed before he could respond in kind.[18] Spicer said Swain had hit him in the stomach, while the Labour MP insisted that Spicer had come at him with arms flailing 'like a windmill'.

Labour MP William Hamilton had a furious row with the Serjeant-at-Arms,* accusing Rear Admiral Alexander Gordon-Lennox of using 'the most foul language' as he tried to restore order.[19] Snape and Nigel Lawson were also said to be locked in a tussle at one point.[20]

Pendry learned that the House had been suspended from the annunciator in his office. Jack Cunningham, Jim Callaghan's MP aide,

---

* The Serjeant-at-Arms maintains order and security within the Commons wing of the parliamentary estate.

soon entered and urged him to come and see 'the boss'. 'And I warn you he is not well pleased.'[21]

In the Prime Minister's office behind the Speaker's chair, Pendry fielded questions on whether he was paired. He insisted he wasn't, but 'it was a question of the arithmetic by the pairing whips'.[22] Callaghan then demanded that George Grant, PPS to the missing agriculture minister Fred Peart, be tracked down. Worse for wear in Strangers' Bar, Grant, misreading the room, arrived and encouraged Callaghan to join in on the celebrations. The Prime Minister eventually got hold of Peart – also somewhat inebriated on his trip to Copenhagen – who, when told he was speaking to the Prime Minister, asked if it was Harold Wilson. Peart said that he *thought* he was paired.

Beyond the Prime Minister's study, the Tories upped their war of words. Thatcher called on Callaghan to set aside the result and hold another vote.[23] The usually composed Humphrey Atkins declared all-out parliamentary war, bringing an end to pairing for the rest of the session. 'There will be no cooperation in any way whatsoever from now on. No more meetings will take place between business managers.'[24] The hostilities even extended to the all-party football team, where MPs would only pass to members of the same party. 'We went to heavy defeat against the press gallery,' says Tory whip George Young.

Heseltine, already nicknamed Tarzan for his long locks by newspaper cartoonists, tried to apologise to the House, but the Deputy Speaker cut him short: 'There have been grave scenes of disorder here tonight and I adjourn the House ... until tomorrow.'

'I should not have done it,' Heseltine said the next day.[25]

Scottish National Party MP Douglas Henderson went so far as to compare the night's events to the German parliament of the 1930s. 'The scenes were reminiscent of the Reichstag,' he said. 'There were so many similarities ... The Nazis would sing hymns and then beat up the opposition.'[26]

Meanwhile, on the Greek island of Corfu, Peter Fry shuffled

uncomfortably as the news reached his sunbed. Having departed for a holiday the evening of the vote, the Conservative MP, who thought he was paired, realised he might have cost the opposition a crucial victory.

'He shouldn't have gone,' Atkins was reported as saying. 'I don't care who knows it.'[27]

* * *

The fallout from the remarkable evening in the Commons was twofold.

Firstly, it drew outside attention to the notion of pairing, with long-time opponent of the practice Labour's Eddie Loyden expressing his strongly held views. 'I believe pairing arrangements only exist to cover up when people want to leave,' he said.[28]

Of far greater consequence in Westminster was the suspension of relations through the Usual Channels between the Conservatives and Labour – despite a series of overtures and soothing letters from leading whipping lights in the latter party.[29]

Conservative MP Jill Knight came out of Kruger National Park in South Africa to find Humphrey Atkins wanted her back at the Commons urgently, her pair no longer in service.[30] Ministers put the government's bill on nationalising the shipbuilding and aircraft industries on ice, with the Tories angling for a rerun and even complete abandonment of the legislation.

Labour MP Helene Hayman had been paired ahead of a Labour Friends of Israel trip after the Whitsun recess. Elected aged twenty-five in October 1974, Hayman was a few months pregnant with her first child.

Knowing a pregnant MP would be a foreign notion to many of her contemporaries, to say nothing of broader British society, which had never known of such a phenomenon, she had largely kept the news quiet. In early 1976, Bob Mellish had invited her into his office and asked if she'd like to become a whip. Hayman told him she was pregnant and couldn't imagine how she could be a whip – with the gruelling late hours and demands – concurrently.

'I thought he was going to have a heart attack when I told him,' she says. A shocked Mellish agreed that there was 'no way' she could take up the offer.

The trip to Israel was due to be her last before giving birth later in the year. She saw her pair, Conservative MP Norman Lamont, also due for an overseas visit, in Members' Lobby before departing the next day.

'You're not coming back, are you?'

'No, absolutely not. This is done, this is the arrangement; we're paired,' he reassured.

Hayman flew to Israel. She was wrapping up the visit when a man from the Israeli Labour Party approached her and said: 'Who is Michael Cocks, and why can he say I have to put you on the next plane home?'

The first person Hayman saw that evening back in Parliament was Lamont, whom the Tory whips had also ordered to return home. 'That was the power of the whips in that parliament; you didn't quibble,' she says.

Seeking to bridge the parliamentary divide, Jim Callaghan wrote to Margaret Thatcher suggesting they have an investigation into the events of 27 May. Tory fingers had been quick to point at Tom Pendry, who was having none of it. 'I feel it is very unjust and I am extremely angry that I should be accused of cheating because the opposite is true,' he said.[31]

Nearly a month after Heseltine swung the mace, Jim Callaghan and Margaret Thatcher gathered for a half-hour meeting; before them, a report compiled by Cocks and Atkins over what had taken place.[32] In a somewhat self-explanatory statement to the Commons, Callaghan said the inquiry had clarified there was an 'undoubted misunderstanding' over pairing arrangements for absent MPs. The Prime Minister also consented to Thatcher's request for a rerun of the vote.

For his part, the investigation exonerated Pendry for voting in the second division. 'I should like to make it quite clear that the inquiry found no personal blame attached to [Pendry],' Thatcher told MPs. Twenty-four years later, Pendry sued Heseltine for libel, after he suggested in his autobiography, *Life in the Jungle*, that Pendry had cheated by voting.

* * *

Though the Usual Channels eased back into life within a few months, the Conservatives, under Margaret Thatcher's instructions, were more discerning with pairing, meaning the government needed every vote the whips could muster.

Former Prime Minister Harold Wilson accused the Conservatives of a 'deliberate insult' to the World Zionist Congress after they withdrew his pair hours before he was due to attend an event and receive an international gold medal.[33] Ted Heath grew further embittered towards Thatcher after he had to return from sailing to vote in the Commons.[34] Government whips cabled Labour MP Walter Johnson to fly back from India.[35] Within thirty minutes of winning a by-election in Walsall North, Conservative candidate Robin Hodgson received a call from Atkins to say he urgently required his vote in the Commons the following Monday.[36]

Strained backroom relations coincided with the long, hot summer of 1976, which swept across Europe and caused a severe drought in the UK. Still at Parliament at one in the morning, Hayman, six months pregnant, was lying on the floor in the ladies' members' room, trying to cool down. Upon seeing Hayman, Barbara Castle, a former Cabinet minister of considerable stature, declared: 'This is not what the suffragettes died for.'

Castle marched off to bollock Conservative Chief Whip Atkins. Soon after, Thatcher entered the ladies' members' room. 'I have a sore throat; you are pregnant. We are both going home,' she told Hayman.

Hayman was still 'reeling' from her first exchange with the Conservative Party leader when she saw the Labour Chief Whip making a beeline for her, 'f-ing and blinding'. 'I've got to send you home. I'm keeping the Prime Minister here... And Barbara says I've got to send you in my car!' Michael Cocks said.

Hayman gave birth at the end of October, but with the government in desperate need of bodies, as a defiant House of Lords sent legislation back to the Commons, she considered her options. Hayman wrote to Thatcher asking if they could resume their brief pairing arrangement but received a message back from Atkins saying, 'It's up to your side.'

'There was no way I was going to say, "Send [sick Labour MP] Doc Broughton in instead of me." That was how I ended up taking the baby in for that terrible two weeks.'

The media gave Hayman a kicking after news travelled that she was breastfeeding her newborn on the parliamentary estate. The only saving grace was a cartoon of Jim Callaghan walking across New Palace Yard holding a carrycot, saying, 'Majority of One'.

Hayman, through neither design nor aspiration, became a hero to equality campaigners and a villain to puritanical observers who believed her breastfeeding in Parliament to be a political act.

Labour MP Shirley Williams occasionally let Hayman use her room for privacy. The chief doorkeeper to the Commons told Hayman that the Serjeant-at-Arms had advised him how much force he could use if she tried to enter the chamber with her baby, which she never attempted to do. According to Alan Beith, Liberal MP for Berwick-upon-Tweed, when an MP enquired why Hayman, a relatively new MP, had eventually been given her own room, Walter Harrison responded thriftily: 'Breastfeeding.'

Labour whips, as demonstrated by Hayman's experience, were forced to go to extraordinary lengths to get the government's business through the House.

Lengths that may have been responsible for people's deaths.

CHAPTER 10

LIFE SUPPORT

With the Usual Channels faltering, the ambulances started to arrive.

The ill had been on the scene since the end of pairing, with one infectious Conservative MP forced to stay in a car while on the parliamentary estate.[1] Following an inspection by whips, the sick would be nodded through after ambulances parked up at New Palace Yard, at least spared the ordeal of voting in the division lobbies.

'Every day, you had an emergency crisis,' said Labour whip Joe Ashton.[2]

The government whips would meet and check their lists. 'How's [X MP] getting on?' a senior whip would ask.

'Oh, he's in a bad way. He's had an operation,' would come the reply.

'Bring him in,' the whip would insist. 'Ring the surgeon and say, "Can he come in?"'

With the government's shipbuilding bill back before the Commons, Margaret Thatcher refused to pair her MPs with sick Labour members, believing it was wrong to deny any of her side the chance to vote against the controversial legislation, particularly considering events in May. Three Labour MPs – Scottish Minister Frank McElhone, Welsh Minister Alec Jones and backbencher Alex Lyon – travelled by ambulance to Westminster. Only William Molloy, in hospital after a major kidney operation, was spared the ordeal.[3]

The government won the vote by three.

Harold Wilson was among those to sponsor a motion calling for tellers to accept medical certificates for sick MPs as a substitute for personal attendance.[4] There was precedent for forcing them to vote in person, however, as the former Prime Minister knew all too well. With Labour clinging on to a tight majority between 1964 and 1966, both a Tory and Labour MP had been brought onto the parliamentary estate in ambulances after recent heart attacks.

'For all intents and purposes, we pushed them through [death's] door,' said a Labour whip.[5] 'I think we killed three members towards the end of that first period.'

In a famous case during the 1974–79 parliament, retold with apocryphal details on its travels around political dinner parties, St Helens MP Leslie Spriggs was brought in to vote after a severe heart attack. That evening Labour whip Joe Harper, a former miner and MP for Pontefract and Castleford, had the job of inspecting the sick along with Tory whip John Stradling Thomas, known as Dick because of, well, 'John Thomas'.

'It was not a sophisticated place,' notes a Labour whip.

The two whips entered the ambulance and saw Spriggs lying on a gurney. Stradling Thomas said to Harper: 'How do we know he is alive?'

Harper leaned forward, turned the knob on the heart monitor and saw the green light flash to indicate a heartbeat. 'There, you've lost – it's 311.'

Barbara Castle, who had arrived by ambulance after recovering from a congestive disease, walked through the division lobbies with tubes coming out of her body. Labour MP Bruce Grocott jokes that the media, all too aware of the government's precarious position, became 'stupendously interested in one's health'.

He went into Burton Hospital with peritonitis. He'd only been there ten minutes when his wife started getting phone calls from journalists. 'There was no interest in me; it's just that I was the number that might make the difference between winning and losing,' he says.

From a combination of postponed operations to those rushed in soon after surgeries, Ashton said the whips' office effectively killed six people, including Labour MPs Alex Wilson, Millie Miller and Frank Hatton. Among those who may have died because of the demands of the time was Labour whip Joe Harper, an angina sufferer who had been putting off an operation while carrying out his job. He died in office aged sixty-four.

* * *

Decisions regarding the sick would be considered at length within an internal group of senior whips and Cabinet ministers established by Michael Cocks to discuss tight votes, factoring in the views of medical professionals and the willingness of ill MPs to participate.

Primitive and staggering though it seems, whips would argue that this was nonetheless part of the efforts required to keep the government afloat – and, by definition, to keep the Conservatives from power, a task they believed was in the national interest and thereby worth the (human) sacrifices – along with other sordid endeavours.

With Labour MPs prone to missing votes, whether through cars breaking down, extended family members taken ill or upset stomachs, Harrison decided to 'get professional' and type up a regular whips' duty roster, pinned to the noticeboard.[6] To prevent a recurrence of an incident where a Labour MP missed a vote due to being locked in the toilet, a new duty appeared: 'Flusher – lower deck.'

Each evening, one of the Labour whips would be deployed as a 'bog trotter', a person who would check the bars and toilets on the ground floor after the division bell rang to see if anyone – whether drunk, asleep, hiding or a combination of all three – was locked in a cubicle.

Whips had to look under the cubicle door for any signs of feet. If any were spotted, they had to clamber over the top to check who they belonged to. If the person wasn't one of theirs, they left them alone, but if they were, then they got them out, often by using a screwdriver to remove the door.

The 'upper deck' whip on duty would scour locations on other floors, including the Commons library, where 'some of the more elderly members dozed after dinner', said a Labour whip. 'These were not the most glamorous or sought-after duties.'[7]

A former aide to Jim Callaghan says one male MP was found in the ladies' retiring room, 'absolutely drunk to the world'. The whips carried him through the lobby to vote. Northern Ireland Ministers, meanwhile, would be hastily helicoptered back to the mainland.

During the eight-minute voting period, two or three of the 635 MPs would get trapped in a lift, fall asleep, be delayed on a train or get locked out of the lobbies. 'Fortunately the accidents happen on both sides and so the majority is maintained,' Ashton explained.[8]

Whips, in control of various forms of patronage, would even try to encourage biddable opposition MPs to take overseas trips. A Conservative backbencher known to be interested in defence matters was whisked away on a navy exercise very far from Parliament, an aide to Callaghan says.

Alongside trying to win votes, the Labour hierarchy always had one eye on a potential general election, with several MPs needing face time in their constituencies to try to preserve a marginal lead. Persistent absence from the local area would not aid a re-election bid, as business managers knew all too well. But as time progressed, and the number of government MPs continued to dwindle through deaths, defections and more, few would consider an unapproved absence from the Commons, such was the pull and authority of the whips' office.

Or would they?

* * *

Labour MPs sat semi-comatose in the Commons tearoom while awaiting another late-night, knife-edge vote. Prime Minister Jim Callaghan had elevated a dastardly Conservative motion to halve Chancellor

Denis Healey's salary into a confidence issue, meaning a loss would lead to a general election.

Walter Harrison, the party's omnipresent Deputy Chief Whip, entered the tearoom and squinted as though searching for someone.

'Anybody seen Litterick?'

Tom Litterick, a left-wing Labour backbencher from the West Midlands, had been through the wringer of late. He'd had a heart attack a year earlier, which his wife, Jane, attributed to Parliament's demanding hours and rushing home from Westminster after his family received death threats. Colleagues of Litterick suggest a 'stormy' marriage had also played a role.

Michael Cocks sent his whip Peter Snape by train with instructions to persuade Litterick to return as soon as possible, though Jane was policing his bedside. Seeing the press gathered outside the hospital, Snape, with the help of a bread-van driver, found another entrance and spoke to Litterick's doctor, who told him that he was not to be moved. On returning to London, he was denounced by the Chief Whip as a 'softie'.[9]

Litterick had grown close to a journalist from the *Times* newspaper, which he revealed to Jane before leaving the hospital to stay at the reporter's home in West Kensington. 'I have been advised by a doctor to live away from my wife because of stress,' he, extraordinarily, told the press.[10] 'I have to get peace and quiet or I will end up dead.'

Not all MPs were that understanding of Litterick's plight on his return to Westminster, with one mercilessly calling out in the Commons: 'Go away and have another heart attack!'[11]

Jane, later that year, set the woman's home ablaze. In a statement, Jane told a court: 'I don't really know what happened next because the whole lot went up in flames. I didn't even strike a match.'[12] Thankfully, no one was inside. She was placed on probation for two years after admitting to the crime, which caused at least £13,000 of damage, on the condition that she continue psychiatric treatment. Litterick suffered a relapse after the ordeal and was admitted to hospital. The *Times* journalist took him abroad as part of his gradual recovery.

With Harrison seeking an answer to Litterick's whereabouts, Jeff Rooker, a constituency neighbour, filled in the gaps. 'Oh, he's away.'

Harrison frowned. 'He's away? He's not on any bloody list as being away.'

'I think he's in Crete with his girlfriend,' Rooker explained.

Harrison glared, his face contorting through anger. 'Crete? He'll be in bloody concrete when he gets back!'

Everyone roared with laughter except for Harrison.

'He was purple with rage,' says Neil Kinnock, who was sitting next to Rooker. 'It was a real betrayal. The guy had been ill, he just had to tell Walter he was going away for recuperation, and he would have been paired.'

The Labour Party told inquisitive journalists that Litterick was away on the Greek island on 'semi-official business'. His name even flashed on Cretan television screens as the whips' office made desperate efforts to get him on the first flight home.[13]

Though unsuccessful in tracking down Litterick, the government won the confidence motion by five votes. A rare boon for the new Chief Whip, who, from the moment of his appointment, had been battling wildfires.

CHAPTER 11

COCKLE

Peter Snape and Arthur Davidson listened from the government frontbench as a Tory MP spoke during an annual debate in the House of Commons on the Royal Air Force.

'This guy is making a lot of sense,' Davidson said to Snape. 'What would the whips' office say if I accepted his amendment?'

'Cut your balls off, probably.'

Snape checked his watch: nearly 9 p.m. He looked towards the Speaker's chair and saw the Prime Minister enter the chamber.

'Here's your chance now, Arthur,' he said.

Davidson, a good friend of Snape's, whispered: 'Shut the fuck up.'

Callaghan took a seat next to Snape. 'Where are we on this, Peter?'

Snape filled him in. They sat and listened to the MP.

Callaghan shuffled further along the bench. 'How old are you?' he asked Snape, who offered up his age. 'Have you ever thought of emigrating?' Callaghan enquired.

'Well, not really, Prime Minister,' said Snape, taken aback. 'Why would I?'

Callaghan paused. 'I think this country's finished.'

Snape absorbed the Prime Minister's words. 'I thought subsequently I could have sold that story and made lots of money,' Snape says now. 'I obviously wouldn't do that because I had a lot of time for Callaghan. He was in a very depressed mood.'

Snape told Michael Cocks about the conversation the next day. 'He'll get over it,' replied the Chief Whip, who met regularly with Callaghan during the parliamentary week. 'He gets up and down, a bit like that.'

Cocks, who was always keen to convey that his name was spelled like the organ, not the apple,[1] joined the whips' office in March 1974, rising to Lord Commissioner and Pairing Whip before his surprising appointment as Chief under Callaghan.

Along with Deputy Chief Whip Walter Harrison; the new Pairing Whip, Jack Dormand; and the Leader of the House, Michael Foot, Cocks was part of the 'Fix It Four', known individually as Harassment, Dormant, Footing It and Cockle.[2]

A moustached man with an imposing, stocky frame and little patience for the left of his party, Cocks was still, for some, a person 'for whom the word urbane was invented'. 'Nothing ever seriously fazed Michael, although he was a man of some brutality in some ways,' says Snape.

Born in Leeds and educated in Edinburgh and Wakefield, Cocks taught geography after national service in the Royal Navy. He was elected as the Labour MP for Bristol South in 1970, a constituency neighbour of Cabinet minister and left-wing pin-up Tony Benn, his bête noire, a picture of whom he would throw darts at in his office.

Labour MP Oonagh McDonald says Cocks was undervalued. 'People may not have liked his political stance, but he was a very faithful servant of the party and did everything he could to get legislation passed without a majority. That takes a lot of doing.'

Another Labour MP, who went to school with Cocks in Wakefield, remembers him as an old-fashioned Chief Whip who spoke 'the language of Walter Harrison', prone to saying to errant backbenchers: 'What the fuck do you think you're doing? You'll go nowhere.'

David Clark, a former flatmate, says he was a 'much-underrated individual'. 'He was one of these people who tried to act as if he didn't know very much, but he was one of the brightest people I ever knew.' On his period as Chief, Clark adds: 'It wasn't the easiest time, but he carried it off with great aplomb.'

Cocks had a cynicism befitting the challenge before him. In January 1976, before his appointment as Chief, a civil servant bustled into the whips' office and pinned up a news report revealing that two Labour MPs had quit and were setting up a breakaway Scottish Labour Party. Underneath the story was the result of the 2.30 horse race at Sandown Park Racecourse. Cocks looked at the board and said: 'I had my suspicions that that nag would finish second.' In inviting friends for a tour of Westminster after taking over from Bob Mellish, he stressed: 'Don't leave it too late. My job is liable to be very short-lived.'[3]

The whips' office was a mixture of tension and humour, which Cocks, as 'the ultimate cynic', was 'ideally suited to', says Snape. Cocks laughed rather than fired Snape when he stuck a note to his door, saying: 'The Chief Whip's indecision is final.'

The routine challenge for Labour whips was ensuring their MPs continued to stay on the premises – as they had done night after night, month after month, year after gruelling year. At midnight, some MPs would drift away, prompting a defeat. Cocks would then give his team a bollocking and say: 'You're taking your eye off the ball!'

As Pairing Whip, Jack Dormand bore the brunt. Facing down requests to leave, Dormand would tell MPs ahead of a vote: 'Go and do your duty.'[4]

Ensuring people's attendance was a matter of playing the man or woman. Confronting Education Minister Gerry Fowler about his 'crap' division record, Snape would say: 'Unless you buck your ideas up, I'll see it's relayed to your constituency party, and we'll see what they've got to say.' While Snape says he wouldn't have followed through on this threat, it's about 'carrots and sticks'. 'By and large, I preferred the carrot approach.'

Snape was driving home from a garden party when he heard Labour MP Gwilym Roberts, a member of his flock, on the radio. Roberts, Snape says, was not averse to securing time off, perusing the weekly business and deciding to submit a pairing slip for anything less than a three-line whip or 'what he regarded as a soft three-line'. As such,

Snape was surprised to hear Roberts say over the radio: 'I'd love to do much more in the constituency, but the demands at Westminster are such that I have to be away for five days.'

'Well, he was never away for more than three,' Snape says. 'I seized upon this and reminded him of it on quite a few occasions afterwards.'

Labour whips' intelligence gathering would also prove crucial in tracking down missing MPs. Unable to get hold of a Labour minister, the whips rang someone they knew he'd been spending time with away from Parliament. The person said they didn't know where the minister was, so the whip responded: 'I'd better ring his missus then.' Shortly after, the minister took hold of the phone, and the whips instructed him 'to return forthwith'.[5]

On another occasion, a policeman working on the parliamentary estate rang the whips' office to say he'd heard on his radio that a Labour MP had been breathalysed and arrested after driving the wrong way up a one-way street. Knowing the MP was regularly in the company of a female Labour backbencher, the whips worried they would be two votes short for the division at 10 p.m. A member of The Office put in a call to a senior police officer while the Chief Whip's driver was despatched to Paddington Green police station. 'Both of them were allowed to vote before the formalities were completed and the inevitable disqualification followed,' wrote a whip decades later.[6]

An acquaintance of Cocks said: 'He knows more of the extramarital affairs of Labour MPs than anyone else; his parliamentary life is that of the barefoot walker whose path is strewn with broken glass.'[7]

* * *

Whereas his predecessor Bob Mellish enjoyed widespread respect, if not universal popularity, Cocks was more of a divisive figure. Among his detractors – and perhaps the strongest of the lot – is Neil Kinnock, who describes Cocks as a '22-carat bastard'.

Kinnock often visited Commons Leader Michael Foot in his office for a glass of whisky and a chat. Cocks would sometimes blast through the door, usually effing and blinding. The Chief Whip would then sit on a chair, put his feet on the radiator and, according to Kinnock, 'very deliberately, fart loudly'.

'Now, once or twice, that's funny,' Kinnock says. 'When it happens repeatedly, it's just plain bloody pig ignorance.'

After this sequence played out five or six times over a period of months, Kinnock finally snapped.

'You're an ignorant bastard, but you're very lucky,' he told Cocks.

'Why?'

'That you didn't encounter my mother.'

'Oh,' Cocks said. 'Why is that?'

'My mother came from a family that was so poor that she had to leave grammar school when she was sixteen and, instead of becoming a doctor, became a nurse. She was a district nurse in one of the toughest, roughest areas in our country… She'd have dealt with you in ten seconds, you ignorant bastard.'

Cocks 'got up, and actually, he took a stance', says Kinnock.

'He was a big guy, a big soft dickhead, really, and I thought, "Please throw a punch," but he didn't. It was that ridiculous, but it was probably one o'clock in the morning, very tense. He would have had some drink, so. But he's the only one that I never, never could have got on with.'

Cocks was nonetheless crucial to Callaghan, who was brokering a deal that would help sustain the government's survival. From bringing in ambulances to scouring the Commons toilets, the Labour Party finally hit the nuclear option on the scale of political desperation.

The Liberals.

CHAPTER 12

MEN OF STEEL

Alan Beith only had a dozen MPs to keep on top of – but then again, whipping free-thinking Liberals is rarely an easy thing.

'I had a party, several of whom were prima donnas of various kinds and who either were in the position – or believed they were in the position – that only they could win the seat for the Liberal Party,' he explains. 'So, these are not easy people to discipline or regiment.'

His tenure as Liberal Chief Whip had begun amid inauspicious circumstances.

In March 1976, Beith's predecessor Cyril Smith had resigned on medical advice from his hospital bedside, where he had been holding court with reporters. Party leader Jeremy Thorpe, mired in scandal over claims about his prior relationship with Norman Scott, a former model whose Great Dane had just been shot as part of a botched assassination attempt, then picked up the phone.

Thorpe, under serious threat, asked if Beith would take over as Chief Whip. Beith said he would take on the job but would not follow Smith in acting as his defender or advocate. 'I was prepared to manage the parliamentary party but not get involved in trying to explain what I knew next to [nothing] about,' he explains.

With pressure over his dealings with Scott mounting, Thorpe stood down as leader two months later.* Former leader Jo Grimond stepped

---

* Thorpe would be charged with conspiracy and incitement to murder, charges for which he was acquitted before disappearing from public life.

in on an interim basis before David Steel, a former Chief Whip, took over.

'It was a nightmare, really. I just got on with the job,' says Beith. 'We made the parliamentary party as effective as we could and demonstrated that we were still in business.'

Being a party of thirteen MPs, Beith was the only active whip, with his fellow Liberals taking up various frontbench spokesperson roles. Thankfully for Beith, a Liberal Chief carries different expectations than those of the two larger, more disciplinarian parties. 'We try to proceed by agreement, so that people have ownership of the decision,' he explains.

In the engine room of the Usual Channels, Beith dealt mainly with Walter Harrison, whom Michael Cocks had deputed to look after minority parties – or, more specifically, the 'Odds and Sods' – so they could try to lobby their votes. 'I had a natural rapport with them,' says Beith, though Harrison and Cocks's 'approach to life was not mine'.

'They were there to get Labour's business through whatever it was.'

Before the Labour whip passed away, Beith also got on well with Joe Harper, the MP for Pontefract and Castleford and a proud Yorkshireman, whom he recalls approaching him at a Buckingham Palace garden party, saying: 'Come over here, Alan, 'av a word wit' t'prince.'

The Usual Channels was also the space to address members' misdemeanours.

'I used to say it was a bit like a wartime film of a prisoner of war camp,' says Beith. 'If one of the Dutch internments did something, you went to the senior Dutch officer and sorted it out with them, or the senior British or American officer. This place was run like that.'

In the days before committees to monitor and maintain standards, whips would police the goings-on in Parliament. Beith gives the example of a member misusing parliamentary stationery, perhaps corresponding with Commons letterheaded paper in inappropriate circumstances. Beith would go to the MP's Chief Whip and ask them to do something about it – while conscious that one day, a Liberal MP could be accused of the same wrongdoing.

'In some ways, it was not ideal as an enforcement system, because each party had an interest in doing it the quiet, covered-up way,' he says, before stressing that 'on no occasion' did he see an issue dealt with in this way when it would have been 'seriously inappropriate' to do so. 'It was minor infractions,' he continues, such as 'not paying your catering bill', which two or three people in every party were notorious for failing to do.

Beith enjoyed a good rapport with Cocks and Harrison, but he was conscious that they weren't afraid of pulling a stunt or two. For a bill to have a third reading debate, six MPs had to put their names down on a motion. On one occasion, two minutes before the House rose for the day, Cocks, apparently wanting to avoid a debate, asked officials to remove his name, which was one of the six, from the motion. 'That took everybody by surprise,' says Beith.

* * *

By March 1977, the Labour government, facing yet another vote of no confidence, teetered on the edge. Could it enter a pact with a rival party to survive?

The Liberals were cautious of doing a deal with the government. 'We were suspicious of Labour's agenda and lack of commitment on issues that mattered to us,' says Alan Beith. The party had a list of demands in return for lending their support to the government at crunch votes, including codifying any agreement in a written document.

The Prime Minister met David Steel in No. 10 to iron out the details. After a Cabinet meeting lasting an hour and twenty minutes, Callaghan's top team signed off on a Lib–Lab pact.

In a joint statement, the two parties agreed to set up a joint consultative committee, which would consider government policy and Liberal policy proposals though not commit either side to accepting the other's views.[1] The Chancellor and the Liberal Party's economic spokesman would meet regularly, with Steel and Callaghan meeting as necessary. Among other commitments, the government agreed to bring forward legislation for direct elections to the European Assembly – which would be given a free vote – and to allow parliamentary time to secure the passage of the Housing Bill.

Cumulatively, Callaghan, following talks with other parties, including the Ulster Unionists, ahead of the confidence vote, had also agreed to no more nationalisation, a new bid to ensure devolution in Scotland and Wales, and a consultation on increasing the number of Northern Ireland MPs.[2]

He won the confidence vote by twenty-four.

The backlash was swift. Dozens of Labour MPs wrote a letter to Cocks warning him that they were not party to the Lib–Lab pact nor did they feel bound by it.[3] Margaret Thatcher, who had otherwise been hopeful of securing a general election, was incandescent. 'When socialism is sustained by Liberal MPs, it must surely be a bad day for the United Kingdom,' she said.[4]

Labour whips, on a surer footing than at any point during the parliament, had breathing space. Even so, the rebellions kept piling in. 'Either this government governs or it goes,' Callaghan warned as his MPs listened in silence in a packed Commons committee room.[5]

One of the most consequential rebellions of the 1974–79 parliament came thanks to a rare slip-up from the whips' office. Audrey Wise, the MP for Coventry South West, was known as 'something of a left-wing nuisance', recalled a lobby journalist, a state of affairs that 'she viewed as necessary and desirable'.[6] Nonetheless, Wise and fellow backbencher Jeff Rooker slipped through the net and found their way onto the committee considering the Finance Bill, where they lodged an amendment to link personal tax allowances to the rate of inflation. With Tory support, the Callaghan government suffered an embarrassing defeat.

The Lib–Lab pact saw Beith earn a civil servant to help with the running of the Liberal whips' office. More than ever, he had to ensure his colleagues turned up and remained on the estate. When he struggled to track down Liberal MP Russell Johnston, who was notorious for being out of the country, Beith rang around every hotel within easy reach of Heathrow Airport, thinking he may be on an early flight the next morning. 'And I found him,' he says proudly.

Beith also worked out a system to allow Emlyn Hooson, a practising barrister, to be in court all day in Preston before coming down in the late afternoon to vote, returning on the sleeper train for the next day's hearings.

He compiled a rota to ensure he had enough MPs present during the early hours. By ten o'clock, Liberal MP Richard Wainwright would be in his coat on his way out of Parliament.

'OK, could you come back at five or half past five and take over?' Beith would ask.

'That's fine. I really must go to bed now,' Wainwright would reply.

The Lib–Lab pact worked 'quite well', says Labour whip Peter Snape. The Liberals had 'better access' to senior ministers than some Labour backbenchers did, but they held no government posts, Snape argues. 'We thought they'd sold their souls somewhat cheaply.'

It was a point also felt among the party faithful, with Liberal president Basil Goldstone warning that unrest would only grow without the government consenting to more Liberal measures. Cyril Smith, who called for a renegotiation at the party's annual conference that September, was also a vocal critic, with Liberals languishing at by-elections after the pact came into force.[7]

With Gladstone's fears well-founded, and the pact running longer than foreseen, Steel told Callaghan in December 1977 that the Lib–Lab arrangement could not go on beyond the summer. With the brief respite near its end, all signs pointed to an autumn election in 1978.

'There was a growing rapport between myself and the Prime Minister,' says Steel. 'What started out as a temporary measure became a permanent measure. Then he rather blew it.'

CHAPTER 13

END GAME

On 7 September 1978, with a prime ministerial broadcast scheduled for 5.55 p.m., Jim Callaghan had a nation on tenterhooks.

His Cabinet had just met for two hours and thirty-five minutes, during which the Prime Minister had confirmed his choice after a summer filled with speculation of an autumn general election. The government had recovered in the polls, and the economy was going through a rare window of comfort. Many in No. 10 thought he would go to the country.[1]

The Lib–Lab pact had come to an end in July. Some MPs due to stand down were so confident that Callaghan would call an election that they cleared out their filing cabinets and held farewell parties.[2] But the Labour whips, led by Michael Cocks, had tapped up MPs in marginal seats as to whether they would retain their constituencies.

'It was the only time I was ever asked by the whips my opinion about anything,' says Helene Hayman, who had a majority of 520 in Welwyn and Hatfield. While Hayman said Callaghan should go for October, other MPs such as Bruce Grocott, who had a majority of 331 in Lichfield and Tamworth, warned they wouldn't win.

Following their conversations, the whips believed Labour's seats in Scotland and Wales were safe but English marginals were vulnerable, with few gains likely in the north. They voted by a 'clear majority' against holding an autumn election.[3]

In the weeks before Callaghan's broadcast, Labour figures had also been speaking with minority parties. Plaid Cymru MPs saw Michael

Foot in Cardiff, a meeting facilitated by the new principal private secretary to the Government Chief Whip, Murdo Maclean. They also met Parliamentary Labour Party chair Cledwyn Hughes in Menai Bridge.

In return for their support, Plaid Cymru MPs had a list of six demands for the Queen's Speech – due when Parliament returned – including compensation for slate quarrymen suffering industrial lung diseases.

Privately, Chief Whip Cocks and Commons Leader Michael Foot, filtering feedback to Callaghan from MPs who believed they would lose, counselled against an early election.

In what onlookers described as 'the biggest gamble of his political life', Callaghan, in a five-minute television address, said he would not be calling a general election.[4] Hoping that the economy would recover further in the interim, Callaghan had also seen new polling that suggested the Tories held a lead over Labour, with the Liberals on just 5 per cent. He would need Steel's party to perform well to reinstate the Lib–Lab pact or even enter a coalition should Labour fall short of commanding an overall majority, as seemed likely.

Steel was flabbergasted. The announcement, he said, was 'truly astounding'.[5]

Callaghan was banking on the eleven Scottish National Party and three Plaid Cymru MPs supporting the government's Queen's Speech in November, which included a commitment to start preparations for a referendum on devolution for Scotland and Wales. This was far from guaranteed, as the SNP was still reeling from a successful amendment by Labour MP George Cunningham, with 40 per cent of the *overall* Scottish electorate now required to vote in favour of devolution for a Scottish Assembly to be approved.

Eight Labour MPs' deaths so far in 1978 only served to amplify Callaghan's desperation, bringing the total to thirteen Labour MPs who had passed away during the parliament.

But goodwill among sympathisers had worn thin.

The government introduced its Queen's Speech, including all six of Plaid Cymru's requests. As expected, the Conservatives put forward an amendment which, if passed, would lead to a general election. The usually reliable Gerry Fitt, leader of the SDLP, was furious at the decision to introduce more MPs for Northern Ireland, a policy choice that had led Jock Stallard to quit the whips' office.*

Northern Ireland Secretary Roy Mason's approach to the role further compounded Fitt's displeasure, to the point where he decided he could not support the government at the confidence vote (as did the SNP; however, two of the party's MPs abstained). 'In his speeches, on his television appearances, he made himself out to be totally in support of the unionist case to the total exclusion of any other form of political opinion and that created tremendous difficulties for me,' Fitt said of Mason.[6]

With the Ulster Unionists not voting, Callaghan and his government scraped through. But it was outside Westminster that the Prime Minister was most vulnerable.

* * *

Despite ministers pushing for a 5 per cent pay rise cap to help tackle inflation as part of Jim Callaghan's incomes policy, car giant Ford awarded its striking workers a 17 per cent increase, facing down the threat of government sanctions, which duly followed.

The Conservatives, deftly driving a wedge in the heart of the Labour Party, forced a vote on the sanctions and, with the help of abstaining Tribune Group MPs, whom they knew disagreed with the 5 per cent pay threshold, inflicted a 285–279 defeat on the government.

The government withdrew financial penalties against Ford.

The Ford strike and subsequent pay increase helped precipitate a

---

* Stallard said the move may 'consolidate still further the polarisation' of nationalist and unionist communities in Northern Ireland.

wave of industrial action. Britain entered what would become known as the Winter of Discontent.

Not everyone agrees that Labour might have won if the Prime Minister had called an October election, but a bitterly cold winter – the coldest for sixteen years – coincided with a prolonged period of industrial unrest and perceived indifference at the top of government.

Coffins, awaiting the return of striking gravediggers, filled up disused Liverpool warehouses. NHS workers created blockades around hospitals. Tourists posed for pictures on benches by piles of rubbish in London's Leicester Square.

Callaghan, returning from a summit in the West Indies lightly bronzed, told the press: 'I don't think that other people in the world would share the view that there is mounting chaos.' His remarks prompted a journalist at *The Sun* to write the headline: 'Crisis? What Crisis?'[7]

On 1 March 1979, Scotland and Wales held a referendum on devolution. Scotland voted by 51.6 to 48.4 per cent in favour, but only 32.9 per cent of the overall electorate had joined the majority, so the result was nullified, as per the terms of the Scotland Act. In Wales it was a resounding no. Later that month, the SNP and the Conservatives tabled a motion of no confidence in the government, with the support of the Liberals and the Ulster Unionists.

The scent of political death wafted through Parliament's thin glass windows.

CHAPTER 14

LACKING CONFIDENCE

28 MARCH 1979

Margaret Thatcher, wearing a blue checked blazer and white pussybow blouse, waved for photographers outside her constituency home in Finchley, north London.

'How do you think it's going to go tonight?' asked one of the journalists, who clutched microphones and notepads while policemen in open-faced helmets kept order.

'I'm not prophesising,' Thatcher said as she opened the gate and walked onto the street. 'We will know in about thirteen and a half hours, and I'm prepared to wait.' The Conservative Party leader, flanked by her husband Denis, paused slightly before offering: 'I'm looking forward to it being over.' She smiled and blushed as though she had overshared.

Thatcher had, to no avail, called several votes of no confidence in the four years since she became leader. Today had to be different.

'Do you think it's going to be a successful result?' asked the journalist.

'We're hopeful,' Thatcher said. 'I think it's an even chance.'

The Labour whips, under Michael Cocks's instruction, were already meeting at 12 Downing Street, accounting for their flocks. 'A very short roll call was made of those who weren't immediately in the vicinity of Westminster,' said Labour whip Bryan Davies.[1]

They, too, had been here before – and had successfully faced down every effort to oust the government since October 1974 – but this evening's vote of confidence felt different, with support from minority parties ebbing away. 'The mood was very sombre. We knew what the stakes were. We knew the government could lose,' said Labour whip Ted Graham.[2]

A strike by House of Commons catering staff provided an unwelcome additional hurdle, with parched MPs likely to disperse to bars and pubs around Westminster, off the estate.

Cocks's strategy team of senior whips and Cabinet ministers had met to discuss their approach to the confidence vote, with top figures assigned to different target groups. One of the main topics for discussion was what to do about Doc Broughton.

Alfred Broughton, known as Doc, a GP, former whip, and MP for Batley and Morley, had suffered a heart attack just a week earlier and had been in bed for three months. Battling with bronchitis, Broughton was among the sick MPs brought in to vote by ambulance during the parliament, recuperating in a Labour minister's office between divisions. Jack Weatherill had even taken to instructing members of the Batley and Morley Conservative Association to keep an eye on Broughton's home so that the Tory whips knew whether he was heading to Westminster.

Broughton had contemplated resigning his seat due to ill health, but his fear that the government might lose the subsequent by-election – a sense of party loyalty that garnered tremendous respect and admiration from his contemporaries, not least Walter Harrison – saw him cling on.

Now, aged seventy-six, he was gravely ill.

Senior Labour figures had discussed what would happen if Broughton died on his way to London; government whip Ann Taylor was among those eager that he be brought down, offering to accompany him from Yorkshire. Rumours abounded that if he made it to the Commons, he would not be pronounced legally dead until he had been transported off the premises to the nearest hospital, supposedly due to Parliament's status as a royal palace. But then what if he died as a result of voting, only for the government to lose another confidence vote soon after?

There were other targets to consider too, not least independent MPs and minority parties, who might be persuaded without anyone's lives being put at risk. 'We weren't sure if Doc Broughton would be the crucial vote,' says an aide in No. 10.

With journalists camped outside their home, the Broughtons left calls and their doorbell unanswered. Earlier in the week, Harrison, keen for the latest medical prognosis, had sent his wife and daughter to push a note through the Broughtons' letterbox asking for an update.[3]

The Conservative Party whips, while cautiously optimistic, knew they couldn't afford to fire and miss again. Humphrey Atkins addressed his team and asked for an update on their flock. Peter Morrison looked down at his list and hovered over the name of Peter Bottomley.

The backbench MP had joined a delegation to Washington at the start of the week along with Labour MP Bruce Grocott, to the shock and indignation of their respective whips' offices. Morrison had rung Bottomley and urged him to come back. 'I will be back in time, and if I'm not, I won't be back in time with Bruce Grocott,' Bottomley pointed out, meaning his lack of vote would be offset by the Labour MP's absence.

Jack Dormand, the Labour Pairing Whip, couldn't believe Grocott was abroad. 'Where's Grocott? Why isn't he back here?' he asked his fellow whips.

Two of Callaghan's close aides had approached the Prime Minister during the week with a list of potential deals he could pursue with minority parties. But Callaghan had responded as though the aides were 'corrupt politicians' carrying out grubby backroom deals, despite such arrangements having been a prominent feature of the government's survival to date.[4]

Roy Hattersley, one of his Cabinet ministers, had also spoken to Callaghan about an option to win over some of the eight Ulster Unionists MPs, to whom the whips had assigned him. Hattersley had a deal on the table with Harold McCusker and John Carson over a price index for Northern Ireland. But the two Ulster Unionists said they could bring over more MPs if the government would commit to building a pipeline between Great Britain and Northern Ireland.

Passing Enoch Powell, the former Conservative MP and now Ulster Unionist, in the corridors, Hattersley said: 'I think we ought to talk.' Hattersley subsequently met Callaghan in No. 10, but the Prime Minister turned down the idea out of hand. 'This government is not for sale.'[5]

For all this might suggest otherwise, Callaghan hadn't been afraid of trying to charm old allies. On the Monday before the vote, he invited Gerry Fitt to Downing Street. Fitt stressed that he couldn't support the government while Northern Ireland Secretary Roy Mason remained in place. Callaghan pulled out a piece of paper from his inside jacket pocket and said that as it currently stood, the result would be 311–310 against the government. The Prime Minister then nodded at someone behind Fitt's shoulder. A staff member walked in and placed a bottle of gin on the table. 'And I didn't like that one bit,' Fitt said.[6]

Hattersley met McCusker and Carson at 10 a.m. to thrash out the final details of a special price index and sought to put pen to paper after lunch. His aide typed out a statement on a portable typewriter. Hattersley signed in a green biro, which the unionist MPs didn't like. Another statement was produced and re-signed. 'It was a day of considerable farce,' said Hattersley.[7]

Independent Northern Ireland MP Frank Maguire had just arrived at Heathrow Airport, where a whip waited outside, ready to bring him to Westminster. A reporter flanked Maguire at Arrivals, his blood-orange shirt matching the stain on his lips and flushing cheeks. Blinking quickly, Maguire said he'd had talks with 'some of the Labour folk' over the weekend and hadn't yet made his mind up about how to vote. 'No decision at all at the moment,' he said, angling to get away. 'Late afternoon we'll decide. I'll make my decision.'[8]

Labour MPs knew there was a chance that Maguire was coming over to Westminster under strict instructions from republicans not to vote with the government. SDLP leader Fitt, who felt Maguire wasn't across the political situation in Northern Ireland, had confronted him over his failure to condemn terrorist atrocities in his constituency.

'Gerry,' Maguire replied. 'If I start condemning the IRA, they'll blow up my pub.'[9]

The last time the government had required his vote, the Home Secretary Merlyn Rees had rung Maguire early in the morning while he was still in bed to say: 'Frank, if you don't come and vote with us, we're fucked.'[10] A minister had taken Maguire to lunch in the town of Lisnaskea, Northern Ireland, but the republican had yet to see movement on one particular issue that occupied his mind: the state of prisons housing paramilitary prisoners.[11] Jock Stallard, despite having quit the whips' office over the increase in the number of Northern Ireland MPs, was assigned to look after Maguire once more, moving from bar to bar.[12] Labour whip Bryan Davies said: '[He] deployed every conceivable strategy in the book.'[13]

The whips reported the state of play to Downing Street every few hours, ranging from predicting the government would win by one to, at worst, a loss by three votes.[14]

Though the hours ticked by, still no final decision had been made regarding Broughton. Cocks was reluctant to act without sanction from the Prime Minister. In a meeting with Callaghan facilitated by Cocks, Broughton's whip said the MP wanted to come down to save the government. His consultant said it was up to Broughton, but his view was that doing so could kill him. The consultant said he was prepared to talk to the Prime Minister.

Callaghan called the consultant, who 'confirmed everything', said Labour whip Frank White. 'Please pass on my kind regards to Doc Broughton, thank him for his loyalty, but tell him it won't be necessary,' Callaghan told the consultant.[15] Harrison, too, had concluded that it would be 'morally wrong' to risk Broughton's life in this way. The time was 1.20 p.m.[16]

* * *

Liberal Chief Whip Alan Beith arrived at Westminster with his mind elsewhere.

The Liverpool Edge Hill by-election was due the next day, caused by the death of Labour's Arthur Irvine in December, with young Liberal candidate David Alton standing a good chance of becoming the party's latest MP.

Weeks earlier, Beith had hosted Cocks in his office to explain why he should hold a by-election to replace Irvine – even though the government would likely lose the seat. Plying him with whisky, Beith argued it would be more in Cocks's interest for the Liberals to succeed at a by-election than for him to gain another left-wing 'headbanger from Merseyside' at a general election, which was more likely to happen without the former taking place.

'He bought it,' Beith says.

* * *

Just after 3.30 p.m., with MPs stuffed like preserved anchovy fillets in the undersized chamber, Speaker George Thomas rose from his seat. The vote would take place at ten o'clock, he told the House. If the division bells or lifts failed in any part of the premises, he would be 'most unlikely' to rerun the vote. 'It is the responsibility of [MPs] to make sure that they are present, or near the chamber, in advance of the time for the division.'

He called on the Leader of the Opposition. Thatcher moved the motion: 'That this House has no confidence in Her Majesty's Government.'

Philomena Maguire watched from the public gallery above the Commons chamber as Gerry Fitt stood up to speak just before 6.30 p.m. In devastating remarks, Fitt said there were 'despicable' rumours circulating that Maguire, who had yet to make his maiden speech in the Commons, was in the building talking with a whip. If Maguire votes with the government, he said, 'it will be in opposition to everything that his constituents sent him here to do'.

'Such an action would be completely dishonest, and he has not given us the benefit of his opinion or his vote on any of the issues that affect Northern Ireland,' he said. 'If this government have to depend on such a representative to get support tonight, it is a very sad day for the Labour Party and the Labour government.'

Philomena left the public gallery to find her husband. There's no way you can support the government now, she would tell Maguire privately before he appeared by the Speaker's chair, surrounded by ministers and MPs pleading for his vote.

Jack Weatherill knew the writing was on the wall. He went to see Walter Harrison, his opposite number, for a quiet word away from the chamber.

'Well, Walter, I'm afraid this is it,' the Conservative Deputy Chief Whip said.[17]

'Not at all,' Harrison said defiantly.

'Well, you've lost Frank Maguire.'

'No,' he said. 'We've got Doc Broughton.'

Weatherill frowned. 'You can't bring him in. You haven't got time to bring him in anyway; it's seven o'clock, he won't be here in time.'

Harrison straightened his jacket, adjusted his posture and fixed his gaze on Weatherill's. 'I am now formally asking you to honour your word.'

'What on earth are you on about?' replied Weatherill.

'We've always had an agreement to pair sick with sick and I'm formally asking for a pair to cover Broughton.'

Weatherill raised his eyebrow. 'Walter, I haven't got a pair on a motion of no confidence.'

'Nevertheless,' Harrison said, seeking to pull out one last rabbit. 'I'm formally asking you to honour your word on this.'

Weatherill paused. He and Harrison had always had a close and honourable arrangement as deputies. Both had done so much for the running of Parliament, including serving together on a committee considering security on the estate.[18] They had spent their time as whips, Harrison for thirteen years and Weatherill for twelve, hoping to outfox the other, but never had they lost respect for or underestimated their opponent.

Harrison had pulled at Weatherill's sense of honour and duty.

'Walter, I must tell you, I agree we've always had this gentleman's agreement,' he said. 'I haven't got a pair. But I will keep my word, and I shall stand down tonight. I won't vote.'[19]

Harrison's eyes widened in surprise. He considered the offer – an offer that would likely jeopardise Weatherill's career and standing in his party the very instant it became known – and shook his head. 'I'm not going to put you in that position.'

The two men left the conversation vowing never to repeat a word.*

A former aide to Jim Callaghan says: 'If we had known that, we would have done it.'

At 9.28 p.m., Commons Leader Michael Foot rose to conclude the debate.

With Commons catering staff on strike, Janet Fookes and a group of Tory MPs retired to Charles Irving's nearby flat to eat smoked salmon sandwiches. Before a drinks reception at his home on Great College Street, Tory MP Tim Sainsbury had taken the precaution of stocking his fridge with bottles of Pol Roger, the favourite champagne of Sir Winston Churchill.

Cocks deployed his whips to do a final trawl of the outbuildings at Westminster. By 9.50 p.m., Davies had only one pub left to check, St Stephen's Tavern, where he found a Labour MP drinking whisky and bitter at the encouragement of two lobby correspondents who wrote

---

* In 2004, Jack Weatherill revealed this conversation to the political journalist Mark D'Arcy for BBC Parliament.

for newspapers unsympathetic to the government's cause. 'I was worried where his judgement was at that stage, so I decided he'd got to come with me there and then,' Davies said.[20]

Just after 10 p.m., the motion was put to the House.

The Prime Minister took his seat at 10.15, seen fiddling with a piece of paper and looking relaxed. Two minutes later Labour whip Jimmy Hamilton, one of the two government tellers for the vote, entered the Commons chamber 'flushed with fallacious triumph'.[21] Labour MPs and ministers cheered in a 'great roar of relief' after he appeared to give the thumbs-up.[22]

Roy Hattersley, sitting on the government frontbench, watched Thatcher's reaction. 'I don't believe it,' the disconsolate Conservative leader said.

Michael Dobbs and Gordon Reece were joined by a handful of other advisers in Thatcher's parliamentary office, listening to proceedings unfold over the radio. When news came through of Hamilton's thumb raise, Reece exclaimed: 'Fuck, fuck, fuck, fuck, fuck it!'

Not even a minute later, the long, stocky frame of Tory whip Spencer Le Marchant appeared, beaming a very different kind of message. 'It was quite obvious the original report had been premature,' says Conservative minister Malcolm Rifkind.

The four tellers, including Le Marchant, lined up in front of the Speaker's chair, with the two Conservatives pivoting to the right-hand side.

Tory MPs sprang to their feet. Thatcher hugged Willie Whitelaw while backbencher Elaine Kellett-Bowman jumped on the spot. Without realising, Richard Luce found himself standing up, waving an order paper in the air.

'It was so overwhelming because, instinctively, you knew this was the end of an era,' he says. 'If you looked at Prime Minister Jim Callaghan's face, you could see he knew that as well.'

The Ayes to the right, 311. The Noes to the left, 310.

CHAPTER 15

AFTERSHOCKS

In the event, Frank Maguire, like his fellow Northern Irishman Gerry Fitt, had not voted at all. 'I have come over here to abstain in person,' he explained to journalists.

Walter Harrison had tried one last attempt to get Maguire in his desired division lobby, knowing which strings to pull. 'Come on in, Frank, and I'll buy thee a pint.'[1] Plaid Cymru MP Dafydd Wigley, who had seen Maguire during the day drinking beer after beer, recalls that Maguire finished with the famous line: 'And who said anything about voting!'

All thirteen Liberals and eleven SNP MPs had voted against the government, while two Ulster Unionists and the three Plaid Cymru MPs had supported Jim Callaghan's administration. Ultimately, Doc Broughton's absence secured the Conservatives' victory.

'We could have won tonight,' Walter Harrison told the press.[2]

Alfred 'Doc' Broughton passed away the following Monday, on 2 April.

Despite the vote loss, Michael Foot made good on his pledge to Plaid Cymru MPs regarding the Quarrymen's Compensation Bill, which went through Parliament in double-quick time. Reflecting on what his party managed to extract from the government in return for their support, Wigley says: 'There were lessons to be learned in the wheeling-dealing stakes.'

With Jim Callaghan announcing a general election for 3 May, David Alton faced the prospect of being an MP for only a handful of weeks following his by-election success on 29 March. David Steel and Alan Beith welcomed him to Westminster, but the atmosphere was mournful, on edge, after terrorism struck at the heart of British democracy.

Airey Neave, the shadow Northern Ireland Secretary, who had helped run Margaret Thatcher's insurgent leadership campaign, drove his light blue Vauxhall Cavalier out of the underground car park in New Palace Yard on Friday 30 March. At 2.58 p.m. an explosion rattled and smashed a pane of glass in nearby offices. George Jones, political correspondent at *The Scotsman*, peered out of the Press Gallery window to the source of the commotion.

A pall of black smoke rose from the car park entrance, with a badly wrecked vehicle contorted halfway up the ramp, its windows and lights smashed and the roof bent upwards. Neave was still inside, lying across the front seats. 'Bloodstained papers and documents were scattered around the car, blowing in a cold March wind,' Jones wrote.[3]

A doctor and nurse, quickly on the scene, clambered through the windscreen to tend to Neave. The Serjeant-at-Arms and Harrison went down to the car. Harrison confirmed that it was an MP inside, though he couldn't identify the victim.

In a breaking voice, Michael Cocks told the Commons: 'It is with the deepest regret that I have to inform the House that an explosion has occurred on the precincts of Parliament, involving a car and a person as yet unidentified.'[4]

Neave was driven to hospital, where he later died. The Irish National Liberation Army claimed responsibility for his assassination.

* * *

Winning 339 seats, the Conservatives secured a majority victory at the general election.

New MPs arrived at Westminster with tales of the previous parliament still reverberating around the estate, as they would for political generations to come. 'That spilled over for a long time and didn't dissipate,' says George Foulkes, Labour MP for South Ayrshire.

Even for those who lost their seats, there was a sense of relief that the parliament was no more. When Labour MP and minister Frank Judd fell short at the election, he shocked friends by singing with joy. 'It was somehow a feeling of relief that an impossible situation had gone,' he explained.[5]

The Conservative whips' office largely broke up after the election. Humphrey Atkins was made Northern Ireland Secretary, with former junior whip Michael Jopling filling his boots as Chief. John Stradling Thomas was promoted to Deputy, later becoming a Welsh Office minister. 'This is not promotion; it is demotion from the whips' office,' heckled Walter Harrison when MPs congratulated Stradling Thomas for his new position.

Without a government job, Jack Weatherill pivoted in a new direction.

Even though the Conservatives had a workable majority, the Labour whips' office acted as though they were still fighting the war, whereas politics, tastes and expectations were evolving around them.

'We had a very rigid whipping system,' says Foulkes, whom Cocks gave a 'dressing down' early in the parliament. 'I'm not small and I'm not too reticent, but… I must say, it was scary.'

Other newbies struggled to embrace Cocks's style. 'I never regarded him warmly because he was a bully. He was unpleasant to me personally,' says Tony Lloyd, first elected in 1983 and speaking before he passed in 2024. 'He regarded anybody who was younger than sixty as being a potential dissident. There was just a generational shift that didn't suit his own way of thinking.'

Harriet Harman, elected MP for Peckham at a by-election in 1982, says: 'The idea that Michael Cocks could do pastoral support is like putting Dracula in charge of a blood bank.'

Harman, who had just had a baby and was suffering from mastitis, an inflammation of breast tissue, swore never again to confide anything in the whips after they revealed her private medical information to the press 'to undermine and humiliate me'. She says: 'I felt very much that their approach was to break me, that they would get compliance by making your life miserable.'

Conservative MP Robert Hayward, a constituency neighbour of Cocks, with whom he got on well, says there's no doubt he was a 'complete bruiser'. Cocks once forwarded to Hayward a seven-page letter written in green ink from a member of the public. He attached a note, saying: 'Yours, I think – thank God!'

Cocks, whose distaste for the left would eventually lead to his 1989 book, *Labour and the Benn Factor*, was 'not my favourite person', says Alf Dubs, elected MP for Battersea South in 1979.

After Dubs's local constituency party organised a seminar on the Middle East featuring Israeli and Palestinian speakers, Cocks told the MP: 'You had a real Palestinian propaganda mill in your party offices. How dare you.' He then threatened: 'There's an old people's home in your constituency. I'll make sure you're not allowed to canvass there.'

Dubs, who had a majority of around 300, defended the seminar, which he attended but did not chair. 'Anyway, he never did stop me, but it was an awful threat,' he says.

There was time for nostalgia as Walter Harrison and a dozen other MPs attended the premiere of *Majority of One*, a play at Oldham's Coliseum theatre written by former Labour whip Joe Ashton, inspired by the 1974–79 parliament. By the play's premiere in February 1981, the Labour Party, under the leadership of Michael Foot and on a leftward turn, was beginning to split. A month later, four breakaway Labour MPs formed the Social Democratic Party.

The role of Harrison and co. was known to those at Westminster but hadn't fully trickled through to the public consciousness. One person who was always grateful was Jim Callaghan, who inscribed a copy of his memoirs to Harrison: 'Walter, who made it all possible.'[6] The whips, in conjunction with Commons Leader Michael Foot, 'performed heroically', Callaghan wrote.[7]

Harrison was still a key fixer on the estate, helping to escort MPs such as Dennis Skinner off the premises after the Speaker suspended him from Parliament for refusing to sit down.

'You get the impression with Walter that there's not a sparrow that fell in Westminster that he didn't get a full, detailed account of its political significance,' says political journalist Mark D'Arcy, who, in a 2004 BBC Parliament documentary on the vote of no confidence, revealed Jack Weatherill's sensational offer to pair with Doc Broughton.

Harman says the whipping regime at the time was 'small-c corrupt, really'. She remembers sitting in a 'ginormous' room that had been assigned to a new MP. After she admired the room, the MP replied: 'Yeah, I'm a mate of Walter's.'

* * *

Neil Kinnock took over as Labour leader following the party's disastrous performance under Michael Foot at the 1983 general election. He got rid of Michael Cocks as Chief Whip by offering him a seat in the House of Lords. In 1985, Cocks faced a challenge from Tony Benn's former constituency secretary, Dawn Primarolo, to run as the Labour candidate in Bristol South, which he lost. He left the Commons at the 1987 election, joining the Lords the same year. He passed away in 2001.

Walter Harrison returned to the backbenches in 1983 and stood down in 1987. A place in the Lords didn't beckon for Harrison, but Kinnock categorically denies that this omission was due to a falling out. 'Walter never asked either Michael Foot (as far as I know) nor me and frankly, I never thought of asking him,' Kinnock says. 'I would certainly have listed him if I had received any indication of his desire to be a peer and he was held in such high regard by the government whips that they would have supported his claim.'

The surviving Labour whips of the 1974–79 Parliament last met for a reunion dinner in 2009, thirty years after the vote of no confidence. By now, a young playwright named James Graham had become captivated by the events of that extraordinary period. He wrote to journalists, MPs and whips from the era with a view to writing what would become the play *This House*. While meeting another former MP, he came across Ann Taylor, a government whip from 1977 to 1979, who hadn't responded to his request to speak. 'It was a pretty intimidating, impenetrable world and then because I'd met her briefly and I'd looked her in the white of the eyes, she agreed to have a conversation.' Securing Taylor's guidance proved crucial. I 'probably wouldn't have been able to write the play without her', he says.

Next, and still top of the list, was Walter Harrison. But a press announcement of the play, which referred to Harrison before he'd managed to get in touch, put Graham on the back foot. He called Harrison's old Wakefield constituency office and asked for his number.

'Hello,' answered Harrison.

'Oh, hi, it's James, that guy writing the play.'

There was a pause, before Harrison said: 'You took your time.'

When Graham visited Harrison at his home in West Yorkshire, the former whip was around ninety years old, but the steely core was still evident, mixed with a 'paradoxical mischievous twinkle and warmth'. Harrison showed Graham papers from his time in The Office, including his tattered notebooks and correspondence with Jack Weatherill, his enduring friend.

Harrison died on 19 October 2012, a month after the first performance of *This House* at the National Theatre, which he never got to see. Peter Snape, Taylor, Murdo Maclean and Joe Ashton were pallbearers at his funeral. 'I remember how heavy he was,' says Snape, who asked on the day: 'Have you filled this coffin with Hansards as well as Walter?'

Harrison, according to Graham, still felt conflicted about turning down Weatherill's offer to pair with Doc Broughton. 'Maybe Thatcher would have eventually got in anyway,' Graham says, 'but it's tempting to imagine: what if?'

PART III

THE THATCHER YEARS

CHAPTER 16

THE IRON LADY

The Chief would call his team into the upper whips' office for a debrief following the ten o'clock vote on a Thursday evening. Tory whips, fatigued after a long week, would gather and swap stories from the day, careful not to be too indiscreet should a grateful Cabinet figure make an unscheduled appearance armed with a celebratory bottle.

The Chief would sit resting his legs on a table, unless the Prime Minister was due to visit, in which case he would vacate his captain's chair. Margaret Thatcher would enter, kick off her shoes and sit with her feet up. Archie Hamilton, one of her whips, would pour whisky in a large tumbler glass and hand it over to the Prime Minister. The rest of those present, especially in the aftermath of a notable Commons victory, would opt for champagne.

'So,' Thatcher would begin, her whips eagerly seated around her. 'What's happening?'

The Prime Minister would stay for around half an hour. 'She was really interested in how the machine worked,' says Glasgow-born Gerry Malone, a Conservative whip.

Thatcher, no fan of small talk, opinionless sycophants or fence-sitting equivocators, would seek the unvarnished views of individual whips. 'Gerry,' she would say. 'What's happening in Scotland? I hear there's a problem with…'

'You'd be put on the spot,' explains Malone, who admired her 'granular attention to detail'.

Her semi-regular presence in the whips' two headquarters – a special bottle of whisky also awaited the Prime Minister in 12 Downing Street – would catch some visitors off guard.

One evening, Bertram 'Bertie' Bowyer, otherwise known as Lord Denham, the Conservative Party's Chief Whip in the Lords and long-serving peer of multiple Tory leaders, burst into The Office worse for wear.

'Deputy, I'm afraid I've got to report yet another defeat in the House of Lords!'

Standing in the centre of the room, Denham failed to notice that the Prime Minister was sitting behind him. An eyewitness remembers Thatcher saying: 'Well, Bertie, what are you going to do about it?'

Denham turned on his heel and said: 'Prime Minister, I'm going to catch the first plane to South America!'

It wasn't that the Prime Minister was overly involved in the running of the whips' office – she was more than happy to delegate that responsibility – but she trusted and relied upon her whips. 'Margaret found great comfort in just sitting down with people who knew what the party thought,' says a senior whip.

This, in itself, had been a learning process.

* * *

In a continuation of her four years as Leader of the Opposition, Margaret Thatcher's first term in office had been beset with challenges, doubters and internal Tory unrest.

Her economic policy, moulded by Thatcher and her first Chancellor, Geoffrey Howe, had split the party between two groupings, anointed by the Prime Minister as 'Wets' and 'Dries'. The government's efforts had yet to bear much fruit, with unemployment running in the millions and interest rates in double figures to combat inflation. Palpable social unrest fed onto Britain's divided streets, with widespread race riots taking place across the country, from Brixton to Leeds. A defining showdown with trade unions fermented.

All the while Thatcher remained belligerent, urging others to U-turn if they wanted to, as her personal poll rating plummeted. 'Thatcher was feeling her way at that stage and didn't feel that she was strong enough to completely impose her will on everybody and get a Cabinet that would support her,' remembers Archie Hamilton.

Her new Conservative intake – including the Blue Chip Dining Group founded by Watford MP Tristan Garel-Jones, which first met in William Waldegrave's kitchen and included eight future Cabinet ministers – were free-spirited, forthright and, in the case of the Blue Chips, of a contrasting political disposition to Thatcher.

The government, with a comfortable majority, could take a rebellion or two, although dissent wouldn't aid MPs hoping to climb the ministerial ladder quickly.

Blue Chip member Robert Atkins abstained early on as Thatcher sought to withdraw the automatic right of entry for husbands or fiancés of women settled in Britain. He had written to the Prime Minister after his election saying he would not be able to support the measures as he had a large immigrant community in his constituency of Preston North.

Despite Home Secretary Willie Whitelaw offering compromises to his white paper, nineteen Tory MPs abstained in this, Thatcher's first big rebellion as Prime Minister, late in 1979.

'Right, every one of those people, I want them on a list, and they are not to get any preferment of any description,' Thatcher said to her whips, making an exception only for Atkins.

As with the rest of her frontbench, Thatcher's whips' office had an eclectic range of views. When Ian Twinn arrived in Westminster, he had as his first whip Tim Sainsbury. After Twinn rebelled unannounced on a cut to overseas aid, Sainsbury accosted him in the corridors.

'Look, Ian. I'm going to have to tell you off. You didn't tell us what you were going to do beforehand. It's very confusing when you do that.'

But he continued: 'A lot of us in the whips' office feel very strongly about this issue, and we really admire what you did. So, you can take this as a very strong telling off.'

Bloody hell, Twinn thought. 'It was the right way to whip – I didn't do it again,' he says.

Lethargic economic progress only served to entrench divides in the Tories between those who wanted a change of heart – Wets – and those who did not – Dries. In November 1981, amid speculation that more Conservative MPs would follow Christopher Brocklebank-Fowler in defecting to the breakaway Social Democratic Party, twenty-five Tory backbenchers signed a letter to Chief Whip Michael Jopling warning they would oppose any further 'anti-deflationary' economic measures in the Chancellor's upcoming Autumn Statement.

Stephen Dorrell, Tristan Garel-Jones and Chris Patten – among the so-called 'Gang of 25' – were invited to bridge-building drinks in Thatcher's office in the House of Commons. But in December, Jopling wrote to Thatcher that another twenty MPs were planning to join a mass abstention in a vote on the important financial statement, thus jeopardising the government's majority. 'We are facing a very serious situation which we must discuss,' he told her.[1]

Ian Gow, Thatcher's PPS, brought in Chancellor Howe and his senior minister Leon Brittan to talk with potential rebels, but later sent a note accusing Jopling of overplaying the stakes. 'Michael, though an outstanding Chief Whip, does not share our conviction,' he wrote.[2]

Fourteen Conservative MPs, including eleven of the Gang of 25, abstained in the vote.

The tide turned for Thatcher after Friday 2 April 1982, when Argentinian forces landed on the Falkland Islands, a remote archipelago and British territory in the South Atlantic. The next day, Parliament sat on a Saturday for the first time since the Suez crisis more than a quarter of a century earlier.

MPs weren't due to vote on going to war with Argentina – the government would respond unilaterally, despatching a naval task force to the South Atlantic without ever formally declaring war – but the sitting was nonetheless a major event. Whips had been sounding out their flocks about military conflict in the weeks before the invasion, as well as each other.

'What is your view?' a senior whip asked of The Office. One whip says they replied: 'I don't think there is an alternative.'

Thatcher echoed similar words in her address to MPs. 'We are here because, for the first time for many years, British sovereign territory has been invaded by a foreign power.'

The House, however, needed convincing.

MPs' criticisms centred on two main areas: Britain's apparent unpreparedness for the invasion and comparisons with a separate incident in 1977, when Britain, under Jim Callaghan's leadership and in response to heightened tensions, assembled deterrence ships around 400 miles off the Falklands, leading to diplomatic talks. Though said talks were inconclusive, MPs wondered why similar measures hadn't taken place when a small Argentinian ship had landed without sanction on South Georgia on 19 March, refusing to leave.

Defence Secretary John Nott wrapped up the debate, but Tory MPs were unimpressed with the Cabinet minister's performance. On the advice of a fellow MP, Robert Atkins went to Chief Whip Jopling, proposing to hold a further meeting of backbenchers in Committee Room 10. 'My dear fellow, your every wish is my command,' Jopling replied.

Foreign Secretary Peter Carrington resigned after the invasion, along with two of his ministers, former Chief Whip Humphrey Atkins and another ex-whip Richard Luce, as the public demanded answers.

The Prime Minister was in the whips' office the night of 10 May 1982.

An aide entered and handed Thatcher a note with news that HMS *Sheffield* had sunk after receiving heavy damage from an Argentine missile. Twenty crew members perished in the attack, the first Royal Navy vessel sunk in action since the Second World War.

'I shall never forget how she cried,' says a senior whip.

Thatcher wiped away her tears. 'We must go on for their sake,' she said before leaving.

David Hunt says the Prime Minister was a 'very brave lady but with real compassion', which is why her whips 'were proud of the fact we were her Praetorian Guard'.

Luce dined with Atkins and their partners in Parliament that evening. 'Now, look, this will be the first of several tragedies. You fight a war, you will have big setbacks and disasters. This is one; you just have to accept it,' Atkins said, drawing on his Second World War experience.

After a ten-week war, the UK reclaimed the Falkland Islands. Thatcher rode a wave all the way to a whopping 144-seat majority victory at a general election the following year. 'Thatcher was no Iron Lady that day,' recounted a journalist who watched the 3 April Saturday sitting from the Press Gallery. 'But after the Falklands were recaptured, she was.'[3]

* * *

It wasn't war but the much more benign issue of choosing the next Speaker of the Commons that prompted Thatcher to redress how she approached her whips.

No fan of Jack Weatherill for reasons largely known only to herself, Thatcher had concluded that the former whip, now a Deputy Speaker, would not be a viable replacement for the outgoing George Thomas. Her whips, many of whom held Weatherill in the highest possible regard, disagreed.

MPs nominally voted for the Speakership, but rarely was a nominee who had been put forward via the Usual Channels and backbench committees contested on the floor of the House. By and large, the whips' choice prevailed.

A Conservative was due to replace Thomas, a Labour MP before he renounced party affiliation to become the Speaker, but with three days to go, there was no clear frontrunner. Thatcher was openly supporting Francis Pym, a former Conservative Party Chief Whip, but with her opposition to Weatherill holding things up, a few other names entered the fray. Among them, says a senior whip, was Humphrey Atkins.

But the whips, who felt certain commitments had been given to Weatherill, went out of their way to persuade Thatcher to back him. The Prime Minister eventually relented.

Atkins moved the motion calling for Weatherill's election as Speaker, seconded by Jack Dormand, the former Labour Party Pairing Whip. Weatherill became chair of Commons proceedings uncontested on 16 June 1983.

The episode entrenched Thatcher's view that she had to get close to the whips' office, who didn't do her bidding on the speakership. Fortunately for the Prime Minister, they were an entertaining bunch.

CHAPTER 17

CHARACTERS

Matthew Parris, the Conservative MP for West Derbyshire, greeted constituents in Parliament's bustling Central Lobby, a focal meeting point for visitors and politicians.

'Darling,' boomed a familiar voice from across the octagonal hallway. 'Why are you such a cunt?'

In his inimitable way, Conservative whip Spencer Le Marchant was merely drawing attention to a member of his flock's failure to vote in a division – granted, in a very public, inappropriate manner. Parris, for what it's worth, took the reprimand well.

'Because Spencer was like that,' he explains, 'and the "darling" helped to soften the "cunt".'

Le Marchant was perhaps the most gregarious of the Conservative Party whips' office's many characters. Elected in 1970, his penchant for half-pint tankards of champagne, combined with his fantastic capacity for rudeness and expansive swearing, yet without much by way of malice, made him a man of all colours and creeds, albeit in a combination that would cause his early demise.

'His goal in life was to spread bubbling bonhomie to whomever he met: this pushed up the collective bill for the whips to alarming proportions,' said John Major, who became a junior whip in 1983.[1]

Le Marchant would insist he was 'entertaining for England', with champagne proceedings beginning around 10 a.m. 'Your health,' he would toast his fellow whips, before asking: 'Can I pour you one?'

A whip who served with Le Marchant in the 1970s says he was a 'larger-than-life character'.

'I wasn't a strong drinker, but he used to put on all our desks a glass of champagne and we'd go right into the middle of the night.'

Le Marchant didn't feel bound by social norms or rules. An Old Etonian racehorse owner and stockbroker, he devised a plan to race young Tory MPs around the perimeter of the members' Smoking Room without touching the floor, intending to dress Parris in yellow and green racing colours – a plan jeopardised when the *Evening Standard* caught wind of it.[2]

Strikingly tall at six-foot-six, Le Marchant would refer to his friend Don Concannon, the six-foot-five-inch Labour MP and fellow whip, as 'the short one'.[3] He facilitated a £20 bet between MPs to lose a stone after two months of personal training from ex-military instructor Dave Leach in Parliament's gym. The participants had one last blowout lunch at Le Marchant's Westminster home, cooked by his wife Lucinda.[4]

Though he was married, Le Marchant had an open mind. After a rebellion, he summoned Michael Brown to his flat 'for a dressing down over a bottle of champagne'. 'I learnt a whole new meaning to this phrase as he tried, unsuccessfully, to seduce me,' the MP later wrote. 'But it was an effective way of ensuring that I voted with the government thereafter.'[5]

In another incident, Brown wrote of being frogmarched into the Commons Smoking Room after rebelling. 'Punishment would be meted out according to my ability to consume the champagne,' he said.[6] 'On one occasion I escaped, but was summoned for a dressing down over breakfast and a jug of Bloody Mary the next morning.' Le Marchant also helped to 'kill any trouble' heading Brown's way through his relations with press barons on Fleet Street.

Le Marchant subpoenaed another member of his flock, Tory minister Cecil Parkinson, to a Westminster bar for similar treatment. After two large Bloody Marys, a wary Parkinson said he wouldn't have a third as he found tomato juice too acidic in the morning. 'Quite right,' said Le Marchant, before ordering: 'Two large Bloody Marys, without the tomato juice.'[7]

There are many more such anecdotes, which otherwise make light of Le Marchant's relationship with alcohol. A joke went around Westminster that he had to be sent home on a train with a placard around his neck, saying: 'Please put this MP out at Buxton.'[8]

In addition to his excessive drinking, Le Marchant was known for his curt handling of Tory rebels, including an esteemed former Prime Minister with whom he was otherwise friendly.

'You ****,'* Spencer shouted at Ted Heath, whom he had pinned to the wall. 'You and your scrofulous yachting friends use my house on the Isle of Wight like a ******* hotel, all times of day and night. Now what do you do? You betray us.'

'Calm down, Spencer, I only abstained,' replied Heath.[9]

A Tory MP and future whip says Le Marchant had been seen bellowing across the lobby, 'screaming abuse at various unfortunate young MPs in a way that just wouldn't be tolerated any more and should not have been tolerated then'. He once locked a rebel MP in the division lobby, holding up to the glass a piece of paper full of expletives and obscenities.[10]

Appointed to the number three position in the whips' office, Le Marchant's lifestyle eventually caught up with him. In his memoir, Parris recalled Le Marchant, by now knighted and no longer a member of the whips' office, having dinner in the Members' Dining Room with his skin yellow, face sagging and liver all but gone. 'He had drunk only water, but ordered "melon with port" for dessert,' he wrote.[11] Le Marchant stood down in 1983 and died in 1986 aged fifty-five.

Le Marchant's antics did not detract from a whips' office whose military credentials continued to elicit respect from Tory MPs.

---

* The newspaper that reported this encounter opted to spare Le Marchant's blushes and concealed his words.

Along with Carol Mather, Robert 'Bob' Boscawen became the second recipient of a Military Cross (MC) to serve in the Conservative whips' office under Margaret Thatcher on his appointment in 1979. Landing in France shortly after D-Day, Boscawen was involved in liberating Brussels from the German Army. His tanks withstood a night of intense bombardment south of Arnhem, Holland, after which Boscawen was awarded the MC. While attempting to capture a bridge near Enschede towards the end of the war, four hidden German guns targeted his position, bullets and shrapnel igniting petrol in his Sherman Firefly tank. 'There was a whoof and the turret was engulfed from below in a whirlwind of flame,' he wrote in his diary. 'I eventually broke free from the flames and stumbled back for some 200 yards to safety.'[12]

Severely disfigured from his burns, Boscawen, one of pioneering surgeon Sir Archibald McIndoe's so-called guinea pigs, underwent months of treatment.[13] Still carrying the scars of his military service, Boscawen was a respected, if restrained, character in Parliament, like Mather, with hardline views on issues pertaining to law and order.

'He was a very nice man but dull as dishwater,' says one of his flock.

When a whip turned up dressed in an olive-green Loden overcoat, Mather looked him up and down in horror, glanced at Boscawen as though for confirmation they were thinking the same thing, and said: 'The last time I saw someone wearing a coat like that – I shot him.'[14]

The whips' office was reminiscent of an officers' mess.

'It's not that they gave you orders and expected you to agree with them,' says an MP who later became a whip. 'It's much more around the male clubbiness of an officers' mess. These days – crikey, it was a bit out of time in the 1980s – but it's extremely out of time now.'

*   *   *

The whips gathered late at night in the upper whips' office, awaiting an update from the Chief, John Wakeham.

It was the height of the Westland crisis of 1985–86. Defence Secretary Michael Heseltine was pushing for a European-led consortium to take over Britain's last helicopter company, as opposed to US company Sikorsky, as he believed Margaret Thatcher and Trade and Industry Secretary Leon Brittan supported.

Brittan authorised the leak of legal advice suggesting there were material inaccuracies in some of Heseltine's claims about the bid. When Thatcher told her senior ministers that future statements about the issue should be cleared with the Cabinet Office, Heseltine, believing he'd been silenced, resigned.

'Heseltine was on a mission, and Leon was the fall guy. That's the beginning and the end of the Westland affair,' says Gerry Malone, who served as Brittan's parliamentary private secretary.

With Brittan facing questions about persuading companies to withdraw from Heseltine's European consortium, he appeared before backbench Conservative MPs at the 1922 Committee. One called for Brittan, who was Jewish, to be replaced by a 'red-blooded Englishman'.[15]

After the meeting, Malone, who had liaised with whips throughout the scandal, says he told Brittan: 'I'm sorry, you do not have backbench support. You just don't. There are enough idiots out there who are being vociferous – and some of them were very nasty.'

Brittan resigned a day later.

A week or two passed before Malone received a call. 'You got a minute, old boy?' Wakeham said. 'For you, Chief, always a minute,' Malone replied.

Wakeham, who took over from Michael Jopling in 1983, was smoking a cigar in the Chief Whip's office when Malone arrived for their meeting. 'Come on in, sit down. I won't beat about the bush. There's a vacancy in the government, it's in this office. Do you want it?'

'Yes,' Malone said.

'Well. That's that then. You're a member of the government.'

Malone flew to Aberdeen that Friday morning wondering how his constituents would receive his great news to find it merited just two lines in the *Press and Journal*. 'I thought, "Well, that's that. I understand where I am."'

Wakeham had made an emotional return to the Commons earlier in the parliament. His wife, Roberta, was one of five people killed by an IRA bomb planted under the bathtub of room 629 in Brighton's Grand Hotel during the Conservative Party conference. Also killed by the 2.54 a.m. blast on 12 October 1984 was former Deputy Chief Whip, Sir Anthony Berry. The bomb, purposely placed to compromise the hotel's large Victorian chimney stack, caused masonry to rip through several floors, demolishing Thatcher's bathroom in the hotel's Napoleon Suite two minutes after she had left it. Wakeham and fellow Cabinet minister Norman Tebbit were trapped in the rubble for around four hours and seven hours respectively.[16]

Arriving at hospital, Wakeham, who had suffered serious injuries to his legs, said to the doctor: 'I'll give you this telephone number, it's the switchboard at 10 Downing Street, tell them that I'm OK.'[17]

Returning to Parliament that December, the House of Commons – bar some left-wing Labour MPs, including Eric Heffer and Dennis Skinner, who stayed seated[18] – roared and waved order papers as Wakeham entered the Commons.

For some time, Wakeham carried the emotional and physical scars of the ordeal.

The whips had encouraged Tory MP Robert Hayward, who had just found out he had multiple sclerosis, not to go public with his diagnosis. Coming across each other in a division lobby, Wakeham spoke to Hayward about the condition, which appeared to trigger memories related to the bombing. 'He burst into floods of tears,' says Hayward.

By the time of the Westland affair, Wakeham was back in the chair.

While he met the Prime Minister to discuss how to handle the crisis, his whips waited in The Office. Passing time, they gathered around Carol Mather, who was standing on a chair performing an 'innocently obscene' routine called the One-Armed Flautist, performed by the character Major Tickeridge in Evelyn Waugh's *Sword of Honour* trilogy.

'The only thing I remember about it is Carol Mather standing on a chair, with a finger coming out through his flies, holding a pencil representing a flute,' says a whip.

The dozen other people in the whips' office had 'tears of laughter running down their faces', at which point an ashen-faced John Wakeham entered the room, still 'very, very lame because this was only eighteen months after the Brighton bomb', the whip continues.

'He must have looked around at the whips' office and thought, "What on earth is going on here?"'

The Office, self-evidently, had a distinctly male feel, a macho culture its occupants had been keen to protect.

CHAPTER 18

A MAN'S WORLD

Of all the myriad ways whips held sway – be it through appointments to newly created select committees, the distribution of highly coveted offices or deployment on overseas trips – the Prime Minister's reshuffles offered perhaps their greatest source of power.

'We would draw up the lists of ministers who should be promoted, ministers who should be sacked,' says David Hunt. 'Privately, that was real power, but actually, there's a huge responsibility.'

Margaret Thatcher would ultimately be the person wielding the axe or dishing out the goodies, but the whips' views on lower-rung posts especially would help fill in the gaps for a Prime Minister who, as with others before and since, needed a helping hand. The Chief Whip, meanwhile, would play an integral role in shaping the Cabinet, regularly navigating the corridor between 10 and 12 Downing Street to hold late-night meetings with the Prime Minister about her top team.

'Thatcher was a very inspired leader who had clear ideas about what she wanted, but networking with the party wasn't her strong point at any stage,' says Archie Hamilton. 'I don't think she really understood what the whips were about at all, but she took a lot of guidance from the whips' office about junior appointments and that sort of thing.'

The whips, who cover every sinew of parliamentary activity and, between them, develop relationships with all MPs from their party, are well-placed to provide counsel on such matters. Bench duty, where a whip observes proceedings in the Commons chamber, documenting the session in a notebook, has always been a key point of reference, alongside reports on ministers' performances at the unheralded but essential standing committees.

Another whip explains: 'Her reshuffles were very heavily influenced by the whips' office.' Conservative MPs were well aware of this dynamic: whips' 'narks' would spend a lot of their day in and out of The Office stirring the pot about their colleagues or self-aggrandising about their achievements, hoping, usually in vain, for some kind of promotion.

One Tory MP says that he sent a bottle of whisky to a whip he had heard was responsible for backbenchers' preferment. 'Heaven knows whether it was true or not because you never knew what went on in the whips' office,' the MP says. The MP did go on to hold ministerial office, despite sending whisky to the renowned teetotaller Tristan Garel-Jones.

Knowledge of the whips' role in reshuffles served to infuriate ambitious politicians.

'Alan Clark* hated me with a passion,' says Hunt. 'He regarded me as one of the nastiest people he'd ever met ... because I had kept telling the Prime Minister that he was drunk again.' Once, when Clark was speaking in the Commons, Labour's Clare Short asked for the House to be adjourned so the government could find a minister who was sober enough to lead the debate.

The whips, famously, also chose their own.

'If there were a vacancy in the whips' office, the whips would have a meeting where we would talk over the candidates,' says a Tory whip. During the meeting, a consensus would generally emerge, and the Chief Whip would then sort it with the Prime Minister.

While Thatcher would need to sign off on the appointments, this was largely a formality. 'It was basically a self-electing body,' says Hamilton.

Each whip was assured they had an effective veto, or black ball, on an appointment to The Office should a colleague put forward an

---

* A junior minister, author and renowned diarist.

unagreeable name. 'In my time, it was never put to the test,' says a whip who served in the late '80s.

Even though the party had broken the mould in electing Thatcher as leader and now Prime Minister, the Conservatives, unlike the Labour Party, had yet to appoint a woman to the whips' office.

And there were plenty of willing applicants.

'I was very keen to work in the whips' office,' says Edwina Currie, MP for South Derbyshire, as was Ann Widdecombe, MP for Maidstone. A Tory MP says their female colleague also wanted to be a whip, but 'she was told she was barred from service: wrong chromosomes'.

The thwarted MP had military veteran Carol Mather as her whip, who had previously never had a woman in his flock. While walking to a meeting in Parliament, Mather would insist on being in front of her to open the door before letting her through. He would then overtake her again before the next door, repeating the process many times until the MP finally said: 'Look, Carol, you know where you're going – I don't – I'm perfectly happy to follow you!'

As to why women were *persona non grata*, one whip is none the wiser. 'It was just a very male environment – a lot of bad language,' he says. 'There would have been a sense that the regimental mess flavour would have been changed, but honestly, I don't remember the way in which it was discussed. It was pretty glaring as an omission.'

A regular visitor says the British adult comic magazine *Viz* was 'very much the reading material' in The Office. 'There was a cartoon stuck on the wall where they changed [*Viz* character] Johnny Fartpants to various members of the government or backbenchers.'

Female Conservative MPs hoping to challenge the male whip orthodoxy made approaches, but they were brushed aside with excuses such as the use of bad language or hard drinking. 'It was a prejudice. And the whips' office – of all places – should have tackled that and said, "We will have women in the whips' office,"' says Currie.

Both Currie and Widdecombe respected the authority of the whips' office and had each found it useful while settling in at Parliament. Soon after her election in 1983, Currie told her whip, David Hunt, that she wanted to speak in the Commons as soon as possible. Hunt came back and said: 'Right, you're on tomorrow.' By tomorrow, he meant in front of a packed chamber on the day of the Queen's Speech.

'That's right,' he said to an aghast Currie. 'There will be a speech welcoming from an established backbencher and then there will be a speech from the opposition and then it's you.'

He advised: 'Eight minutes, no more. Say nice things about your constituency and your predecessor, a couple of sentences on something that you're interested in and sit down.'

Widdecombe had done the whips' bidding in lining up outside a parliamentary office at seven o'clock on a Tuesday morning, ready to submit for a Ten-Minute Rule Bill, a legislative proposal put forward by backbenchers. Concerned that Labour had secured too many of these motions – despite such bills rarely ever becoming law – Tory whips encouraged Widdecombe to queue ahead of time. 'It got to the stage where we were there at midnight,' she says. 'Then we were queuing during the day on Monday, and I had to organise a rota so that people could go to the loo.' Eventually, Widdecombe told Tony Durant, the whip in charge of the endeavour: 'This is getting silly – we've got to come to some sort of agreement with Labour.'

Widdecombe says: 'And so we did, in the end.'

Thatcher and her Chief Whips considered a spell in the whips' office as an 'apprenticeship to better things', including Cabinet roles or key ministerial positions.[1] 'I could have told you, even if I didn't know, which ministers were ex-whips and which weren't, because they understood how the system worked,' says a whip. Among those trusted to take on a significant portfolio was Hunt, who became Minister for Coal midway through the miners' strike and later the minister responsible for introducing the controversial community charge, known as the poll tax.

Other recognisable names to have served in Thatcher's whips' office include Michael Portillo, Francis Maude and John Major. 'There's an argument that actually all government ministers should be promoted from the whips' office,' says Hamilton. The Tory Party, he argues, is divided into people who are loyal under all circumstances, those who are persuadable and mavericks who represent nobody but themselves. 'It's rather important to know that before you become a minister.'

Female Conservative MPs felt they were handicapped without the opportunity to serve in the whips' office. 'Why would that have been useful? Because it's a preparation for being a government minister,' says Currie. 'It's a Broederbond. It means that from there onwards, whoever's been in the whips' office, the others would look after them.'

Each whip was responsible for at least one government department, regularly attending prayer meetings – departmental gatherings of the Secretary of State, ministers and civil servants – as well as other engagements. Whips would also oversee the passage of any legislation pertaining to the department.

'They would make quite clear: "We can get this through", "This is best done late at night", "Maybe we could do this as a statutory instrument", that sort of thing,' says Currie, who served as a Health Minister. 'I regarded the whips' office as being absolutely essential.'

But Currie believes her ministerial career, which ended after her controversial warnings about salmonella in British eggs, might have gone differently had she had the backing of would-be former colleagues in the whips' office. 'The effect on the women ministers was that we were not as well-known when we were appointed and we were not as well supported once we were,' she argues. 'That applied to [Tory minister] Marion Roe, who only lasted a year in office. It certainly applied to me.'

Currie also believes that had she been in the whips' office, she would have counselled against appointing John Moore as Health Secretary, believing he was not up to the job. '[The whips' office] would have been my first port of call,' she says.

But a colleague, perhaps evoking the controversy around salmonella in eggs, says Currie had fallen foul of the 'worst thing to happen to you in parliamentary politics', which was to garner a reputation 'as someone who is always looking for a headline, always speaking out, always making trouble'. 'Edwina Currie: a supremely intelligent and wise person, but once she'd acquired that reputation, she was finished – completely finished,' they argue.

Of course, one person could have insisted the whips take on women, but no instruction, seemingly, was forthcoming. Nor did Thatcher ever appoint a woman from the House of Commons to the Cabinet.

Currie, who says female Tory MPs 'adored' the Prime Minister, believes Thatcher 'had a kind of imposter syndrome'. 'I think she felt she was a bit of a fraud or there was some element of her that did not deserve to be where she was and that another woman would know it.'

Women's exclusion extended well beyond the whips' office. While a Health Minister, Currie discussed the appointment of a new breast cancer advisory committee with a senior executive of the National Health Service, who handed her a list of names.

'You've only got two women on this list?' Currie said.

'Well, there aren't many women,' Len, the executive, replied.

'They're our breasts, Len!'

She concludes: 'It was an unconscious, all-pervasive, unspoken, very powerful prejudice. And it was there all the time. And the Prime Minister practised it more than anyone else. It was astonishing.'

Perhaps Conservative whips were reluctant to open their world of traditions, quirks and occasional skulduggery to those of a different perspective. 'Accepting one excessive and stupid tradition means that they were a little bit too ready to accept others,' says Currie.

CHAPTER 19

THE BLACK BOOK

As the Speaker's Chaplain begins prayers, which precede every day's sitting, MPs stand facing the perimeter wall, their backs to the Commons chamber. One day, in the middle of prayers, a Labour MP caused an interruption.

A Conservative backbencher turned around and saw the whip on the government frontbench reach forward and press a button under the lip of the table in front of the Speaker's chair. Less than a minute later, the Chief Whip and several of his team stood at the entrance, surveying as events unfolded in the Commons.

The bell, which hitherto the MP didn't know existed, connected to the whips' office on Members' Lobby, alerting colleagues to any potential danger or points of interest in the chamber. One of many eccentric appendages in the whips' office, the bell garnered far less attention than another mainstay, the whips' fabled Black Book.

Or, as some evasive whips still like to say: 'What Black Book?'

'I knew there was going to come a time in this conversation when I was going to say, "I can't discuss it,"' says one Tory whip, whose commitment to The Office's code of omertà endures.

The Black Book acted as a key intelligence-gathering mechanism for note-taking whips seeking to be across every possible political or personal permutation. Its rumoured but unconfirmed existence also vicariously, and perhaps purposefully, served to heighten the mystique around The Office's activities.

'There was always a bit of chatter about "They've got a little Black Book and if you step out of line, you get into their little Black Book,"' says a Tory MP.

It did the whips no harm for murmurs of their practices to swirl. The extent to which whips capitalised on the information jotted down during patrols is hotly debated and a point forcefully contested by those in The Office.

'I never saw it used as leverage,' says a whip who served in the early 1980s. The same whip says they could imagine the information being used to remind an MP about potential hypocrisy, such as speaking out about the importance of promoting marriage. 'It might be true that the Deputy Chief Whip might just have reminded him that it didn't quite chime with the two mistresses he kept down the road. That would be a proper activity of the whip.'

Tory whips insist note-taking was integral to forming the overall picture, meaning they could make allowances where necessary, pre-empt looming disasters and look out for their flock.

A note suggesting an MP was going through a divorce or family illness, for example, might prompt whips to make a concerted effort to look out for the politician, or to encourage a senior – even the Prime Minister – to write a letter or offer a kind word.

Gerry Malone neatly summarises: 'If there was a Black Book, do you know what it would be like? It would look like [long-running British radio soap opera] *The Archers*. An everyday story of House of Commons folk.' He adds: 'You never know where the trivial story is going to develop into a front-page story line. We were there to see the tremors of the earthquake so that we weren't just dealing with aftershocks.'

Reference to the Black Book, whether figurative or literal, can be found in historical newspaper clippings. In 1902, the *Greenock Telegraph and Clyde Shipping Gazette* reported that around a dozen Irish MPs 'are said to be in the Black Books of the whips' due to poor attendance. In 1911, Liberal MP Joseph Martin discussed how once a member rebelled, he got into the Black Books of the government, who were 'not slow in letting him know that'.[1]

In a 1941 profile of David Margesson, a journalist reported on suspicions that the legendary Conservative Chief Whip maintained a Black Book and that it took 'years of good conduct to compensate for one offence'.[2]

Talk of a Black Book continued throughout the latter half of the twentieth century, adding to the whips' reputation across all parties. But Peter Snape, who served in the Labour whips' office from 1975 to 1979, insists they didn't keep things on record. 'Everything was done verbally. I can't remember anybody ever putting anything on paper. There was no book. We all knew who had a mistress and who didn't,' Snape says.

Among the Conservatives – a party with a proclivity for upholding and protecting tradition, at least historically speaking – things were different, but many whips still plead the fifth. Their obfuscation about the Black Book is not wholly cynical; the Black Book didn't exist in a completely *literal* sense – some dispute that it was black, others that it constituted a book – allowing them to play dumb when nosy journalists with a deadline raise the subject.

'Put it this way: we exchanged information in a wide variety of ways, which may or may not have included the existence of a black or many-coloured book at some time or another,' says Malone.

Another whip stresses that those who say there wasn't a Black Book are correct. 'There was a system of notes that allowed intelligence to be shared.'

Notes would be read out at the daily 2.30 p.m. meeting in the upper whips' office, a perpetually cluttered space filled with paperwork, overflowing ashtrays, unwashed wine glasses and newspapers.[3] Naturally, the meeting had its traditions and emphasis on hierarchy.

Senior whips were at desks around the perimeter of the room, with others on sofas in the centre. The most junior whip took up a low armchair out of sight of the Deputy behind, who led proceedings for the first half of the meeting. The Chief joined twenty minutes in, assuming his chair opposite the Deputy, before reading out the whips' notes.[4]

Two notebooks were stored in a huge, old-fashioned safe in the corner of the upper whips' office, the password of which was usually the Prime Minister's date of birth. 'Whips are expected to use them to record any "intelligence" that may be of interest as concisely as possible,' explained a Tory whip years later.[5] 'There's a top copy which is torn out for the Chief to read out. The carbon remains in the notebook.'

The Black Book wasn't *exclusively* for potentially compromising material, as captured in press clippings and Commons whispers, but rather a collection of *all* intelligence gathered daily by the whips, much of it inconsequential and, on the surface, superfluous. Personal information featured but was not the focus or sole purpose of the book itself.

Or was there more to it?

Whips from previous eras spoke of the Black Book – or 'Dirt Book', as some referred to it – in a slightly different tone, suggesting a lot of the emphasis *was* on personal information.

'The Dirt Book was just a little book in which you had to write down various things that you knew or heard about people,' said Willie Whitelaw, Tory Chief Whip from 1964 to 1970.[6] Asked by a senior journalist to expand on what it would include, he said: 'I don't think I shall go any further than saying you could take a very good guess of all the sorts of things that happen in life.' He added: 'You would have a good spread of them that would be happening to varying people that you had heard about, or knew about, or may be true.'

Tim Fortescue, a Conservative whip from 1970 to 1973, said the Black Book would include 'scandalous stories, I suppose, which possibly are not at all accurate'. The purpose of the book, he said, was 'so that we knew everything about everybody'.

As to why, Fortescue said: 'Because we were a very efficient organisation ... and when you are trying to persuade a member that he should vote the way he didn't want to vote ... it is possible that you suggest that perhaps it would be not in his interests if people knew something or other – very mildly.'[7]

These accounts portray a different side of the Black Book and its purpose, while those who served under Thatcher stress it also held other objectives.

During the Falklands War, a group of Conservative MPs led by backbencher David Crouch said they would support the naval taskforce en route to the South Atlantic, but if blood was shed, their support could drain away. Whips' notes would help keep abreast of sentiment and foresee any threat to Thatcher's leadership. 'Every time the Chief Whip went in to see Margaret Thatcher, I had to make sure he was up to date with the latest views,' a senior whip explains.

Alongside visiting different corners, dining areas and outposts in Westminster, whips attended and documented regular meetings of the 1922 Committee of backbench Conservative MPs, all-party committees and other events to pulse-check MPs' views. 'As a whip, you'd spend quite some time in the tearoom, hanging around and picking up the tag end of conversations. It's just building up a picture. You have to do it,' says a whip.

The party's annual conference was also a useful information hunting ground. 'You were always on information-gathering mode,' says Malone, who was responsible for taking an energy bill through the Commons and would stake out events pertaining to the subject at Tory Party conference.

Such practices could lead to a change in government approach if the whips concluded that a bill wouldn't get through without ministers adapting certain aspects. Backbenchers, therefore, would often encourage whips to pass information up the food chain. Note-taking 'was a means of keeping the flow going in both directions. It genuinely does work in that way,' said Fred Silvester, who worked in the Tory whips' office in the 1970s.[8]

Government whips would meet on Wednesdays in 12 Downing Street for a longer meeting, usually from 10.30 a.m., to talk about the week ahead. But the Conservatives, of course, would do things a little differently.

At 11.30 a.m., the most junior whip, holding the role of refreshment officer, would pour champagne into individually engraved silver goblets and hand them out to those who wanted to partake. Meanwhile, a former Labour whip jokes, 'We had a cup of tea if we were lucky.'

While whips alerted the meeting to potential rebellions, Hunt, as Deputy Chief Whip, would 'scribble alongside the issues and we would also have a document recording who had voted against the government or abstained', storing the analysis in a safe, he says.

Every day, Hunt would meet Chief Whip David Waddington, who had succeeded John Wakeham in 1987, at 8 a.m. in 12 Downing Street to brief him on the 'views'. 'No way did it have "So-and-so is sleeping with so-and-so or has done this, that or the other,"' he stresses.

Not every whip agrees on this, though Hunt may have been describing a different record.

Whips were told to be indiscriminate but to the point with what they wrote down. Notes could include an MP's views on a particular bill, a development in someone's private life, be it illness, an extramarital affair or otherwise, and information related to the opposition. That way, whips could get ahead of a potential rebellion, understand why an MP might be behaving in a certain way, or pre-empt manoeuvres.

'What would be in [the Black Book]? If we were sitting in the tearoom and we heard someone saying, "This bill is going through and I have the greatest possible reservation about X, Y and Z that it's trying to achieve," we'd write that down,' explains Archie Hamilton. 'If we heard that you were having an affair with somebody, we would write that down. Absolutely anything that might have some influence over what happened in the future. That was why it had to be completely confidential.' It was 'critical' that whips wrote everything down so that others could verify the intelligence, he adds.

Trying to locate a Conservative backbencher at around 3 a.m., The Office broke into laughter as the whips realised they had twenty-seven phone numbers for a 'very happily married' politician, who was notorious for having extramarital affairs. 'That didn't matter as long as we knew where to find him,' says a senior whip. When passing on their personal details, 'quite a number' of MPs highlighted the contact they wanted the whips to use – and the one they didn't.

Whips stress that they didn't go out looking for information about people's private lives. Instead, it was mainly if someone was unhappy with a speech, or thought the party line on an issue was misguided, or perhaps they didn't like the whipping instruction ahead of a vote. 'But if somebody told us about their private life – and it was relevant – then we would take that on board,' says George Young.

Hamilton insists that if the information was potentially serious or pertained to a criminal activity, it would be escalated to the Chief or Deputy. 'They'd probably call somebody in if they thought it was a serious matter of one sort or another,' he says.

Equally, if the whips had caught wind that one of their MPs was on the verge of defecting to another party, 'all the alarm bells would start ringing and the machine would grind into action to try and head it off', he says.

Given there were some 'baddies' in Westminster, whips had to be on their toes. It was known, an ex-whip says, that two Members of Parliament – including Tory MP Burnaby Drayson – 'had very close relationships with the Soviet Union'. Having that knowledge allowed whips to ensure the MPs 'didn't get themselves onto committees which might get information which would be useful'.

Whips, Malone explains, were there primarily to get the government's business through and ensure this wasn't interrupted by anything that might come out about an MP, which could impede their ability to carry out their duties.

'There are three categories,' he says. 'Sex, money and alcohol.'

CHAPTER 20

CAREGIVERS

On their travels, whips encountered MPs on the verge of bankruptcy, suicide, marriage breakdowns and alcoholism. With few other parliamentary means of care available, whips were the primary outlet for MPs needing support. 'There was a lot of genuine pastoral care,' says a whip.

A whip would be assigned responsibility for pastoral matters, facilitating MPs' time away at discreet facilities offering an assortment of recovery programmes. However, every member of The Office would contribute by looking out for their flock. 'They really did look after you if you were straight with them,' says a whip.

This care for MPs had a blend of empathy, camaraderie, on occasion altruism, and undoubtedly, if not predominantly, a good dose of considered pragmatism. It was not in the party's or the leader's interest – let alone the individual's – for scandals to hit the press. MPs also couldn't continue in office if declared bankrupt, forcing a by-election.

'In my time, there were half a dozen colleagues who got into serious financial difficulties,' says Archie Hamilton, including one MP who nearly went bankrupt after his chain of care homes 'went belly up'. The whips rallied round and sourced help to straighten his finances out enough to see him through to the next general election. 'Or more to the point, [so that he] wouldn't find himself in potentially suicidal difficulties.'

The whips would turn to wealthy MPs willing to dig into their pockets to help a colleague. Among them was Tim Sainsbury, a former whip whose great-grandparents had founded a grocer in 1869, which later became the British supermarket giant Sainsbury's. 'Yes,' Sainsbury confirms of helping MPs in need. 'I'd rather not go into detail.'

A whip's act that still moves the recipient to tears involves Tristan Garel-Jones, whose Machiavellian instincts and contrasting politics, on the surface at least, make him perhaps an unlikely candidate to help a right-wing Conservative in the shape of Harvey Proctor.

What made Garel-Jones's gesture even more notable was how the two MPs had gotten off to a bad start. Proctor, MP for Basildon and then Billericay, encountered Garel-Jones ahead of a vote on immigration, a subject on which the backbencher held strident views. Though a committed attendee and a staunch Thatcher supporter, Proctor was preparing to vote against the government on an immigration issue in favour of a harder line. Garel-Jones sought to steer him in another direction.

'He threatened that he and the whips' office would be dead against me for ever more if I didn't support the government,' says Proctor. If he rebelled, Garel-Jones said he would put Proctor on unwanted committees, ban him from going on overseas visits ('not that I was a great traveller, so that didn't hold much sway') and inform his constituency party.

'If you do any of those things,' Proctor replied, 'then I won't just vote against the government on this particular measure; I will abstain from voting with the government on all matters until you unblock me.'

Proctor also had a run-in with John Stradling Thomas late one night in the Commons chamber after voting with the Ulster Unionists on an issue relating to Northern Ireland. 'He came in, swaying, saw me and charged up to me to complain about what I'd done,' says Proctor. 'He had to be physically restrained by other whips from hitting me. The reason for that was he was drunk.'

In 1986, *The People* newspaper reported allegations that Proctor had been involved with male prostitutes aged between seventeen and twenty-one. The legal age of consent for gay men at the time was twenty-one. The following year, with a general election looming, Proctor was arrested and charged with gross indecency. The night of his arrest, the MP went to Parliament and sat in his usual place in the House of Commons chamber. 'I wanted to do that as a matter of principle,' he says.

Seeing Proctor alone, whips encouraged him to sit with them on the government frontbench. 'Sorry if I get emotional,' says Proctor, who broke down in tears recounting the memory. 'I've always remembered that and was grateful to them for doing that – very grateful.'

Proctor resigned as an MP before his trial, where he was fined £1,450. 'Those charges, I have to say, are no longer offences.'

Knowing his difficulties in finding employment, and despite Proctor no longer being an MP, Garel-Jones raised money from Tory donors so that Proctor could start a clothing company selling shirts and ties at a shop in Richmond, London. Those who contributed include Garel-Jones, Jeffrey Archer, Michael Heseltine and members of The Office. 'A chap like Garel-Jones, who might have been regarded to be on the left of the party, still helped… helped me when I was at my lowest ebb,' says Proctor, becoming emotional once more.

The whips also looked out for what they believed to be MPs' best interests.

Matthew Parris had been an MP for two years when he agreed to speak at the Oxford Union proposing the motion that 'this House is glad to be gay'. Parris, who had yet to come out but intended to do so gradually, felt he ought to tell the Chief Whip, Michael Jopling, about his plans. Jopling called him into his office and offered him a glass of whisky.

'I'm going to tell you something that I've told very few people,' the Chief Whip told Parris. 'I don't think I've even told my wife. I certainly haven't told the constituency chairman, and it doesn't appear on any of my election leaflets: I don't believe in God.'

Jopling continued: 'But I don't feel the need to go to church, as I do, and stand up in the pew and shout, "I don't believe in God!" I don't need to occasion a local newspaper headline saying, "I don't believe in God!" It's just something between me and God.'

That was the end of the conversation.

'Some people think when I tell this story that I'm being unkind to Michael, but I'm not actually,' says Parris. 'I think it was a friendly thing to do, and I think he meant it.'

Regardless, Parris went ahead with the Oxford Union debate. 'I took no notice.'

Shortly after, Health and Social Security Secretary Patrick Jenkin asked Parris to be his parliamentary private secretary. 'I was absolutely delighted, and I said I would,' says Parris. But Jenkin then spoke to him and said the post couldn't go ahead. 'I didn't ask him why, but I think I knew why,' Parris says. 'Because the Chief Whip had had a word with him.'

Those were the times, Parris reflects. 'The Chief Whip, one of his principal functions, is to try to guard against any bad publicity or embarrassment for the party or any kind of a fuss or anything that would cause the leader of the party difficulty, and he was doing his job.'

The whips, plainly, took great care to avoid negative headlines. An MP who is now dead once crashed a car while over the limit with a woman who was not his wife in the front seat. Police were called to the scene, where he was breathalysed. With the offender due in Horseferry Road Magistrates' Court in Westminster, the whips exercised the 'only power they did have', says a fellow MP. 'His case was heard at the unusual time of nine in the morning before the press had arrived. It normally opens at ten. It was never in the newspapers.'

Despite these examples, the whips' relationship with journalists in the lobby had long been a source of suspicion. 'I never suffered under it, but I just was faintly aware that one of the risks of offending the whips was that you'd get roughed up in the *News of the World*,' says Michael Heseltine, who was first elected in 1966. 'When I first heard that perception, whether I was a young aspiring politician or whether I was in the House of Commons, that is all blurred in history.'

Gerry Malone says he had an 'exceptionally good relationship' with the lobby while in the Commons. He attended an annual lunch at the Garrick Club with reporters including Geoffrey Parkhouse from *The Herald*, Angela Palmer from *The Times* and Michael White from *The Guardian*. 'I would brief [members of the lobby] insofar as I could. I never broke a privacy,' he says of his time as an MP. 'But background briefing was important for these people because they treated it with great respect, and they would put stories into context. And I was happy to do that. I did that even as a whip.'

It was a two-way relationship, with Malone picking up information from journalists about the opposition and other matters. 'If you're a whip and you don't use every means at your disposal to gather information, then you're failing in your duty,' he says. A key rule of being a whip, however, was 'never appearing in the press, being recognised or noticed'.

As Chief, Jopling had a 'sort of obsession with secrecy', says Hamilton. After returning to the Commons from Cabinet, Jopling would say he had some confidential information and shut all the windows in The Office on the basis that people could be standing below listening to what was going on. Given that details of Cabinet often leaked to the media, No. 10 would pre-empt gossipy ministers by sending out a press release. 'All this "confidential information" we were given used to appear in the *Evening Standard* the same day!' Hamilton says.

Ostensibly, John Wakeham was more open, making available to any whip who wished to read them all the Cabinet papers that came his way.[1] He was categorical on one thing, however – keeping the whips' notes to himself. 'I regarded it as a key part of my job to tell Mrs Thatcher what she needed to know – but I'd never have shown her the whips' notes,' he said.[2]

A Conservative Party official says: 'As we all know, whips could be a great social service, but they could also be pretty ruthless enforcers. She didn't need to know about that; she didn't want to know about that.'

Nicholas Bennett was one of a handful of the 1987 Tory intake chosen by Garel-Jones, along with future whips David Davis and Michael Fallon, to cause mischief in the House of Commons, asking speculative points of order and filibustering to frustrate Labour MPs. 'One of my tricks was to stand up with Erskine May in my hand,' Bennett says.

On the whips' encouragement, Bennett and Roger King raised a point of order in the Commons about a report in *The Sun* regarding three Labour MPs' expenses on an overseas trip. John Prescott, one of the Labour MPs named in the report, confronted Bennett in the division lobby around midnight, poking his finger in the Tory MP's chest.

'You fucking mention me, tell me beforehand,' Prescott said.

The whips encouraged King to raise another point of order regarding the exchange the next day. 'I understand that the incident consisted of some physical and verbal abuse,' King said.

'[The whips] spun that story for a second day into *The Sun*,' says Bennett. 'They obviously had quite close links to the political reporters.'

* * *

For all their pastoral work, whips weren't afraid of the odd threat or political bribe.

If a particular MP was falling out of line through rebellions or unapproved absences, the whips would discuss whether a message should go out for the straggler to meet the Chief.

Richard Needham, a member of the Blue Chips who, by his own admission, had been rebellious in his first parliament, was invited for a 'bollocking' from Michael Jopling. Needham recalls: 'He told me that if I went on like that, I would never be offered a PPSship.' After the 1983 election, Needham decided he needed to knuckle down rather than garner an unsalvageable reputation. He approached Northern Ireland Secretary Jim Prior and asked to be his PPS.

Jonathan Aitken, whose Kent constituency would be affected by plans to construct the Channel Tunnel link to France, was offered an honour in return for his prospective support for the bill. 'What do you want?' a senior whip asked. 'A peerage? A knighthood? A junior minister?'

'He did beg me, more or less,' Aitken says. 'I was principled enough to say no.'

After Nicholas Bennett expressed his displeasure to Tristan Garel-Jones at the proposed handover of Hong Kong from the UK to China, he found himself on a trip to the British colony. 'They'd buy you off to a certain extent. They had the goodies they could offer you.'

Whips were naturally apprehensive about sending MPs away, however, in case the opposition sprang a surprise. Sizeable majorities reduced this threat considerably but made pairing more of a challenge, with fewer opposition MPs to go around.

Every few weeks, backbenchers without a pair could get permission to leave the Commons during a two-line whip via a system the Tories referred to as a 'bisque' – a term derived from croquet, where the player receives a free or extra turn.[3] The Office also had a tradition of accepting a request if the absence was based on a reason that no one else had thought of; Tim Sainsbury sanctioned a bisque to Toby Jessel so he could attend the premiere of his brother-in-law's Ninth Symphony.[4]

When securing a longer period of absence, it helped to have friends in high places. Peter Morrison was still the Tories' Pairing Whip when he was best man to Jonathan Aitken. Before the November ceremony, Morrison asked his close friend what he wanted for a wedding present. Aitken had one thing in mind.

'The day after the wedding, let me off until Christmas,' he asked. Aitken was paired for the full five weeks of his honeymoon.

Typically, the whips would have decided their strategy for the evening but would keep it closely guarded. Bennett, who didn't have a pair, remembers whips coming around the tearoom in the early hours, reiterating: 'There may be more divisions later. Please stay.'

To assist wining and dining MPs, many restaurants, hotels and pubs surrounding Parliament have division bells which ring whenever a vote is called. Robert Hayward, entertained by a company at a hotel on nearby Tothill Street, kept asking staff if the bell was working, as many votes were due that evening but no bell had rung. 'Oh yeah, it's on,' staff insisted.

When he returned to the Commons, he discovered that he'd missed a series of votes. He was so cross and embarrassed that he summoned the hotel manager to Parliament to apologise. 'They thought they'd switched it on, but they'd switched it the wrong way.'

It wasn't in the whips' interest to wear out their MPs to the point that they inadvertently fostered a new tranche of potential rebels. They would also try to bring proceedings to a close, expressing frustration with their own side for making long-winded speeches.

On bench duty, John Major once sent a note to Conservative MP Peter Bruinvels, who was speaking to an almost empty chamber.

'Do you have any children?' Major wrote.

Bruinvels shook his head and carried on speaking.

Major wrote a second note: 'Then why don't you go home and do something useful?' The MP sat down soon after.[5]

Tired and impatient MPs would closely watch the annunciator, and the second the day's proceedings moved to the adjournment debate, they'd say: 'Right, we're off!'

One evening, Roy Galley, MP for Halifax from 1983 to 1987, left the Commons at midnight and returned to his home in Islington after catching wind that the Labour Party wouldn't force a vote. Five minutes after he arrived, his wife answered the phone.

'The whips want you to go back in. There might be a vote,' she said.

'No, I'm not going to do that, dear,' he replied.

'Well, I've just passed on the message.'

Galley says: 'There wasn't a vote, and I could have got up, gone back in at two o'clock and found that it was all over.'

CHAPTER 21

SOCIAL ANIMALS

Whether it was the Christmas party, dinners at the Carlton Club or hosting drinks for MPs at 12 Downing Street, whips, who otherwise had little spare time, maintained a vibrant social calendar.

A favourite point in the schedule arrived before the summer recess, when whips would hold a black-tie dinner with Margaret Thatcher in 10 Downing Street.

Gerry Malone approached his first whips' dinner with enthusiasm ahead of the summer break and a rare chance to rest. A plane to Aberdeen tomorrow morning, nice dinner tonight, listen to what the Prime Minister has to say… life's good, Malone thought, helping himself to another sherry. Before the meal, John Wakeham took him aside.

'You are remembering it's a tradition that the Chief Whip sits on the Prime Minister's left, and the junior whip sits on the Prime Minister's right?'

Malone's face fell. 'A large glass of water was taken, and I was sitting next to her,' he says.

Thatcher engaged with her junior whip before tapping her glass. 'It's been a great year,' she said. 'We've got a couple of slots that we're looking at in the autumn, so we're interested in ideas about legislation.'

The Prime Minister turned to Malone. 'Gerry, what do you have in mind?'

Malone nearly spat out his drink. 'I came out with something about education, which she nodded sagely at, and we moved on.'

Experienced whips were better prepared for the Prime Minister's pivot to serious matters. At the previous year's dinner, taking on board Thatcher's transparent desire to leave behind small talk, Wakeham proposed that John Major, the Treasury whip, provide an update on backbenchers' views.

'They don't like some of our policies,' Major told the Prime Minister bluntly, in a manner suited, he felt, to how a whip should deliver such news. 'They're worried that capital expenditure is being sacrificed to current spending.'[1]

Thatcher wasn't amused. After some back and forth, she said: 'I'm astonished at what you're saying.'

'That's what colleagues are saying, whether you like it or not – it's my job to tell you, and that's what I'm doing,' Major, who shook with anger, replied.

'We used to have great debates,' says David Hunt. 'It was in one of those that John Major thought he'd totally lost it because he'd started telling her the economic policy was all wrong, and she got very angry.'

Thatcher stood firm despite Bob Boscawen and Carol Mather weighing in on Major's side. Heading for post-dinner drinks, Denis Thatcher sidled up to Major and said: 'She'll have enjoyed that.'[2]

With Thatcher out of the room, Ian Lang teased: 'Well, that's it, John!'

Suffice to say the episode did not impede Major's career. Thatcher sat beside him while on bench duty the next afternoon and said she'd like to discuss some ideas he had raised in a previous conversation long before. They retreated to the whips' office and settled into armchairs, with no mention of the previous night's festivities.

'As long as she felt you were loyal, she liked people who would argue with her,' says a whip.

In dinners at the Carlton Club, a favourite haunt of Conservatives, whips would choose an overall Shit of the Year, the award handed out to the most enraging, self-interested member of the Commons, whittled down by nominations put forward for Tories and opposition MPs. The practice became known as the whips' Shit Lists.

Some would compare notes with the opposition, with one meeting Labour's John Smith in the lower whips' office to swap a list of 'baddies' in the Commons, only to find they had the same names written down. 'People that my mother would say you wouldn't invite for tea,' says the whip.

Liberal Deputy Chief Whip Michael Meadowcroft says whips from across parties would play 'silly games' late at night. One of Tristan Garel-Jones's was the competition for the most obnoxious MP, with each whip having to nominate someone from their own party.

* * *

New Zealand-born Paul Beresford had garnered quite the reputation as leader of Wandsworth Council in south London, where the Conservatives, despite a majority of one, had never lost a vote – the result, in part, of the British-Kiwi's forceful whipping.

In recognition of the Conservatives' success on the council, Thatcher invited Beresford and his team for drinks in No. 10. One of his councillors, Edward 'Eddie' Lister – a familiar name in Conservative Party circles* and the best man at Beresford's wedding – was late.

'Look, we can't keep the Prime Minister waiting. Let's go up now. If and when he comes, can you bring him up?' Beresford asked a member of the No. 10 staff.

The councillors chatted with the Prime Minister while a butler served their drinks. He was about to hand the Prime Minister her 'glass bucket full of whisky' when Lister finally arrived. When Thatcher asked if he'd like a drink, Lister said, 'Oh, yes, please,' and grabbed her whisky.

'It was just wonderful,' says Beresford. 'Maggie didn't bat an eyelid. The butler almost fell on the floor.'

Though missing out on the more intimate whips' dinner, Conservative

---

* Lister, a member of the House of Lords, later served as Boris Johnson's chief of staff in Downing Street.

MPs would also be invited for Downing Street drinks, which one year corresponded with an upcoming vote on salary raises for judges, civil servants and generals, which had prompted industrial action by teachers and general uproar among public sector workers who missed out. Roy Galley, a potential rebel, was targeted the moment he arrived at Downing Street. A whip nodded to the Prime Minister, who spoke to Galley about why he must vote with the government.

'Well, what about the teachers, Prime Minister?' Galley asked.

'Don't you bother about the teachers. You leave them to me. You must vote for us tonight,' she said.

Galley did not.

Thatcher's first major defeat in the House of Commons on a piece of primary legislation – and the last time a government was defeated during the second reading of a bill – came during efforts to end regulation of Sunday trading in England and Wales. On 15 April 1986, seventy-two Tory MPs rebelled on the fated Shops Bill, killing it at source.

'The Conservative Party had a majority of 140-something in the Commons, so it was pretty astonishing to lose it at all,' says a whip. 'We were all madly rushing around trying to get people in line but with a complete lack of success.'

The defeat, which otherwise would have been significant, was drowned out by news that American warplanes – many of which had taken off from British airbases – had bombed targets in Tripoli, Libya.

'There was a bit of a view [in the whips' office] that the Foreign Office had been asked to arrange a diversion to distract attention away from the defeat on the Sunday Trading Bill and had overdone it,' the whip quoted above says.

The suggestion – however serious – that the British government, knowing a defeat was possible, had encouraged the American bombing to correspond with the vote on Sunday trading was perhaps beyond the imagination of even the most famous fictitious character associated with whips and whipping.

A character who had remained inside the mind of a close Thatcher aide until the summer of 1987, before his unceremonious departure from political life forced it out into the open.

CHAPTER 22

F. U.

SUMMER 1987

Michael Dobbs lay beside a swimming pool on the serene Maltese island of Gozo with a bottle of wine, a writing pad and a bruised ego. The 1987 general election campaign had ushered in another majority of over 100 for Margaret Thatcher but had also seen Dobbs, a veteran of the Conservatives' Fuck-Up Squad, leave his job as the party's chief of staff.

Dobbs stared into the cloudless sky and wondered where it had all gone so wrong. Thatcher had ruthlessly dressed him down a week before polling day on what became known as Wobble Thursday when, overcome with doubt, she thought she was destined to lose.

The '87 election campaign had been bitterly fought internally, with the Prime Minister even turning her fire and the No. 10 briefing machine on her party chairman Norman Tebbit, with whom Dobbs, as chief of staff, worked closely. Thatcher, Dobbs explains, suspected Tebbit of wanting her job and plotting to oust her.

'He had already told me that he was retiring from the frontbench at the next election because he had to take care of his wife,' says Dobbs, describing Thatcher's misplaced accusations over Tebbit as symptomatic of a wider problem.

'There were discussions, not in Cabinet but in corners,' Dobbs explains. 'She found that more comfortable to deal with, and essentially, in my view, she fell for it. She fell for the views, the ideas, the rumours – the lies, if you like – that were being put around.'

Dobbs got caught in the firing line, finding himself disinvited from Chequers, the Prime Minister's country house. Eventually, he wrote to the PM to acknowledge their worsening relationship. Then came the dressing down on Wobble Thursday.

'I was her sacrificial lamb in front of a few members of her Cabinet, and I knew exactly what to say to her to stand up for myself, but five seconds too late!'

After leaving his job, he retreated to Gozo and, on his wife's advice, started to write. Dobbs put just two initials on the page: F. U. – which provided both a neat insight into his feelings towards his former employer, and the initials of his protagonist, Francis Urquhart.

As a former journalist who had worked at the *Boston Globe* during the Watergate scandal that brought down US President Richard Nixon, Dobbs had the outline of his book sketched out in twenty-four hours and written up in four to five months.[1]

By the time of the 1987 Tory Party conference in Blackpool, which Dobbs, wanting to soak up the post-election fervour, had decided to attend, the story was well in the works. Ending up at a bar late one evening, he spoke with a former contact at *The Times*, who asked: 'What are you doing now?'

'Oh, well, I'm writing a book,' Dobbs said.

The journalist assumed he was writing an explosive political memoir.

'No, it's just a silly novel. I don't know when I'm going to finish it.'

'Do you have a publisher?' the journalist asked.

'No, I haven't got a publisher; I haven't sorted that out. I'm just having fun with it.'

A piece about the book appeared in *The Times* shortly after. His phone started ringing with publishers asking to meet for lunch. 'I was already at the end of the trail, with the gods saying, "Come and wine and dine with me."'

Dobbs hadn't written the tell-all memoir from his decade or so in politics but instead a work of fiction, albeit laced with the hallmarks, insider details and exaggerated characters such an experience might bequeath.

A Shakespearean story of toppled leaders, devilish deceit and murder.

House of Cards was published in 1989. It would go on to become a number one bestseller, spawn two further books and two highly successful adaptations. The novel charts the exploits of a scorned Chief Whip, whose mooted promotion is discarded by the incoming Prime Minister. Affronted by his flippant treatment and realising he must force the issue, Urquhart, with the support of his wife Elizabeth, plots, entraps and connives in a bid for full, unadulterated power, utilising on his way all the information and skills acquired from years in the whips' office.

'To me, both she and Francis were sociopaths,' says Diane Fletcher, who played Elizabeth Urquhart in the BBC adaptation of *House of Cards*, which first aired in 1990 and ran for three seasons. 'He considered himself a supreme being who wanted power, and she was going to do everything possible, while also being a sociopath, to help him, including helping to murder the odd person.' Ian Richardson, a highly regarded Shakespearean actor who had just played Richard III, took on the role of Urquhart, deploying his lines with sinister aplomb.

In February 2013, Netflix aired the first season of its adaptation of *House of Cards*, based in Washington DC. Oscar-winning actor Kevin Spacey played the role of Frank Underwood, Urquhart's American equivalent.

Dobbs's creation is part of British political folklore. He insists that Urquhart is an 'amalgam' of the many characters he met while in politics, up to and including the whip who relayed all the MPs' personal proclivities in a Westminster bar years earlier. But theories still abound about his true muse.

Though several whips were rumoured to have inspired Urquhart, one man stands above the rest. As a former colleague wrote: 'There was no staircase so twisting, no trapdoor so concealed, and no footfall so silent that Tristan didn't know of it.'[2]

* * *

Tristan Garel-Jones, a teetotal chain smoker, had an eclectic hinterland.

A collector of Spanish art and literature and a reputable linguist, the Welsh-speaking Garel-Jones was born in Swansea in 1941. His family moved to Madrid, where his father set up a language school, La Casa Inglesa.

Chris Patten, a fellow member of both the 1979 intake and Blue Chip dining group, said Garel-Jones was 'honourable, loyal, eccentric, sometimes infuriating, funny and with virtually no personal ambition save to see his friends do well'.[3]

On the left of the party and regarded by some as a 'dripping, wringing' Wet,[4] Garel-Jones was part of a group calling for a change of economic policy, producing a pamphlet in October 1981 titled: 'Changing Gear: What the Government Should Do Next'.[5] Margaret Thatcher comfortably survived a Labour vote of no confidence weeks later by 312 to 250, but Garel-Jones warned he didn't want to see the government accused of having 'cold hearts dressed up as economic logic'.[6]

Despite his disagreements with the leadership, Garel-Jones, a man with shark-like eyes, a headmasterly glare and dusty grey hair, was invited to join the whips' office in 1982. Indeed, while privately he may have maintained his reservations on both policy and personality, Garel-Jones renounced, from a professional perspective, his misgivings for the Tory leader on entering The Office. He replaced it with intense loyalty, once saying he would 'kill for Thatcher'.[7]

The unlikely duo enjoyed good relations. Garel-Jones introduced Thatcher to a Spanish minister who bowed, kissed her hand and said: 'Doña Margareta, of your high intelligence the whole world knows. But your beauty, your astonishing beauty, has taken my breath away.'

She would later ask: 'How is that charming minister you introduced me to?'[8]

Appointed the Friday whip, Garel-Jones, a 'man of dark, Satanic appearance',[9] would yell 'Object!' to Private Members' Bills (PMBs) – legislation introduced by MPs who are not members of the government – from his position on the frontbench. Labour accused him of killing no fewer than thirty-eight PMBs.

Garel-Jones's astute and quick thinking would prove valuable throughout his time in The Office. 'He was the quintessential. He was the essence of a whip,' says a colleague. 'A brilliant operator, always looked like he was conspiring, even when he wasn't.'

The whips knew that many Tory MPs resented plans to introduce dental and optical charges, and so 'carefully managed the situation so that we didn't lose', says a senior whip. The real issue was with charges for eye tests, so David Hunt, the Deputy Chief Whip, decided to hold the vote on teeth first. 'The whips' office was essentially in charge of the order paper,' he says.

The government won the first vote, with the eye tests motion to come. Garel-Jones spoke to a group of Liberal MPs, including Cyril Smith, who were eager to get home.

'Well, you won that pretty easily,' Smith observed to Garel-Jones.

'Yep,' the whip replied, before cunningly adding: 'And the next one too.'

Smith left with his fellow Liberals, and the vote was passed.

After several Wets were appointed ministers, some right-wing Tories, believing no MP was promoted without being an MoT – 'Mate of Tristan's' – viewed Garel-Jones with suspicion. The 92 Group, so called because they would meet at Patrick Wall's home at 92 Cheyne Walk in Chelsea, expressed no confidence in Garel-Jones, who was now a Lord Commissioner.

George Gardiner, chairman of the 92 Group, was instructed to pass on the views to Chief Whip John Wakeham. 'I greatly value

[Garel-Jones's] contribution to the whips' office,' Wakeham said. 'He has my full confidence.'[10]

A whip explains of the backlash: 'Tristan was not a Thatcherite but was utterly loyal to her and was always distrusted by the Thatcherites, who saw him as a kind of Fifth Columnist and had no idea of how effective he was as a political operator.'

Jonathan Aitken, a passionate opponent of the European Community, considered Garel-Jones an operator, a 'wonderful character' and very likeable. 'But he was a snake with sixteen forked tongues because he was so passionately pro-Europe,' he says, adding: 'He loved Europe as though Europe was his mother.'

A colleague in The Office says Garel-Jones 'made his distaste for the Eurosceptic right of the party very obvious', noting: 'I don't think that a whip should create gratuitous enemies.'

Whips were always cagey about revealing dates for the end of parliamentary sessions, significant political events and more, seeking to ensure enough MPs were around should plans change. But Robert Hayward, one of Garel-Jones's flock, could derive when the recess would be from when his whip was planning to fly to his palatial estate south of Madrid.

MPs also wouldn't be told the date for the state opening of Parliament. However, Hayward had insight from his lodger, who drove the number 87 London bus. 'It's up on the notice board in Stockwell bus garage that Parliament Square will be closed,' his lodger told him.

Some in the whips' office felt there were often secret discussions taking place in another room, with Garel-Jones always at the centre. Michael Dobbs, who would stay with Garel-Jones in Spain, says of rumours that he inspired Urquhart: 'I got a lot of Tristan's methods in the way he listened very carefully and acted on that. [But] I liked Tristan far too much to make him Francis Urquhart!'

In the presence of a rebel, Garel-Jones's manner could quickly turn threatening.

'I looked at his face and where his eyes should have been there were just two pits of hatred,' said an MP who encountered the whip on the Commons terrace.[11] Speaking of his colleagues, Garel-Jones once said: 'One of the boring things about being in government is that you've got to be friendly to a shit when what you want to do is spit in his eye.'[12]

To his colleagues, Garel-Jones would downplay the significance of their world. 'Lucky it's only a game,' he would say. While leaving The Office at the start of his duties for the day, he was also prone to saying: 'I've got to go off and run the country!' Tim Sainsbury says: 'He stood out as being a real character … He had all the qualities needed to be a good whip.'

Steve Norris, an MP, says Garel-Jones was extraordinarily good at doing deals and getting people back onside, while also having the ability to say: 'Well, it would be a shame if you did that because, I mean, all that stuff about you and the bank… I'd hate for that to come out.'

Norris adds: 'Was there ever an instance of that sort of thing happening? Oh God, yes. But always done with a smile.'

Perpetually hungry for information, Garel-Jones would greet passing journalists with: 'Any news?'[13] His intelligence was such that he predicted the exact outcome for a key second reading vote to a renowned journalist. 'Our Tristan has got his job in the whips' office fine-tuned to a degree that actually makes him indispensable there,' wrote Chris Moncrieff.[14]

Through these abilities he helped monitor the first challenge to Thatcher's leadership and foresaw the overthrow to come.

CHAPTER 23

STALKED

26 OCTOBER 1989

Tim Renton was driving along the Thames Embankment, the river flickering from the midnight sky and London's ceaseless glow, when his private secretary rang to say that Downing Street was hoping to speak with him.

Nigel Lawson's resignation after six years as Chancellor in protest at Margaret Thatcher's reliance on her economic adviser, Alan Walters, had triggered a Cabinet reshuffle. Beneath the explanation offered for his departure was a continued difference over sterling's prospective membership of the European exchange rate mechanism (ERM), with Thatcher increasingly sceptical of further integration with Brussels, and Lawson taking the opposite view.

John Major, only recently promoted to Foreign Secretary, replaced Lawson at the Treasury, continuing his surge from the whips' office. Douglas Hurd would take over from Major in the Foreign Office, with David Waddington, the Chief Whip, heading to the Home Office.

The position of Chief was the last unsolved piece of the reshuffle jigsaw.

Geoffrey Howe, the Deputy Prime Minister, was next to ring Renton, his former PPS and close political ally. Earlier that evening, Tory Party chairman Kenneth Baker had proposed appointing Renton as Waddington's successor, an idea Howe enthusiastically endorsed despite his friend never having served as a whip.

Renton had, in fact, turned down an opportunity to join The Office earlier in the decade, wanting to preserve his outside income. But now on the government payroll, such a calculation no longer mattered.

'There's always a certain amount of controversy about having somebody as Chief who hasn't been a whip,' says a Tory whip under Thatcher. 'You've got to understand the whole purpose of The Office and how it works.'

Howe said he'd been asked if Renton would serve as Chief. 'Cor,' Renton replied.[1]

The last Chief to serve without prior experience of the whips' office had been appointed more than sixty years earlier. Renton said he'd speak to his wife, Alice, and call Howe back.

Though this was ultimately a formality, taking on the position of Chief was a big undertaking. Successive election wins had only temporarily mollified internal Tory fractures, which were growing ever more pronounced over domestic policy and Europe.

The controversial community charge, the replacement to the ratings system for local government financing loathed by Thatcher, was put forward to make councils – especially those run by Labour, whom the Conservatives felt were profligate with spending – more accountable. But the policy, dubbed the 'poll tax', was seen as regressive, hitting the less well-off more than the rich. It already had to its name thirty-eight Tory rebels, with more rumoured in the background, as England and Wales prepared to follow Scotland in rolling out the policy.

The economy, meanwhile, was heading in a downward trend, with interest rates in double figures. Lawson's spring budget of 1988, in which he cut the top rate of income tax by 20 per cent and said couples would soon no longer be able to claim double mortgage tax relief, led to a spending spree, a housing bubble and, coupled with his decision to shadow the Deutschmark, rising inflation.

Renton, on the left of the party, had his reservations about the Prime Minister's rhetoric over Europe – as had the increasingly isolated Howe, still seething after being moved from the Foreign Office that summer – and the rollout of the community charge. And yet, he rang Howe back and said he would take the job. 'Well, that's firm then,' Howe replied.[2]

Renton's appointment was one of Thatcher's 'big mistakes', says a former whip. 'Tim had never been a whip, was not a natural whip and was not an ally either. He was very close to Geoffrey Howe. The thought was, "Keep your enemy close…"'

* * *

When, in November 1989, Anthony Meyer put forward his nomination to run for Conservative Party leader, he had anticipated that another, more likely challenger would step forward. Alas, none was forthcoming, so Meyer, a relative unknown running as a stalking horse against the incumbent, Margaret Thatcher, was left to front the charge in a leadership election that was all but lost from the beginning.

Tim Renton stated his intention for the whips to remain neutral, as Humphrey Atkins and other Tory Chiefs had done before him. However, his deputy, Tristan Garel-Jones, ran an unofficial committee organising Thatcher's support. His intelligence suggested there were forty-five 'hopeless' MPs liable to vote against Thatcher, and twenty-five doubtful.[3]

Renton invited Meyer to his office off Members' Lobby, an offer the Conservative backbencher promptly briefed to the Press Association. Renton suggested Meyer should stand down as a contest would be divisive, but he refused. The Chief asked to keep the process even-tempered. Meyer, unhelpfully for Renton, also briefed the press about their cup of tea.

'I extended a hand of moderate friendship to him, tried to persuade him to desist but did not threaten him with expulsion from the party or attempt to bully him into submission,' Renton later summarised.[4]

As per the reforms to Tory leadership contests introduced under

Ted Heath, the person with the most votes required a lead equivalent to at least 15 per cent of all Conservative MPs over the nearest rival to win in the first ballot. In this case, Thatcher would need to win by fifty-six or more to avoid a second ballot.

When the voting was completed on Tuesday 5 December, Meyer had thirty-three votes to the Prime Minister's 314, with twenty-four spoiled ballots and three abstentions. On the surface, a comprehensive first-round win – but the fact that sixty MPs, 16 per cent of the Conservative parliamentary party, had failed to support the Prime Minister was all anyone could talk about.

* * *

As poll tax protests spread in British cities, including a riot in nearby Trafalgar Square, restive Tory MPs made their mark at the start of the 1990s. Ann Widdecombe fell out of favour with The Office after she led a successful rebellion to increase allowances for those in residential care. The MP had agreed with the whips not to rebel in committee, expecting some movement, but when none was forthcoming, she took matters into her own hands.

'The whips made the fatal mistake: they assumed we would lose,' says Widdecombe. The Prime Minister 'gave [the whips] hell', Widdecombe says, joking that to cover the cost of the defeat Thatcher should surcharge all those who went out to dinner and missed the vote. Garel-Jones told Widdecombe the next morning that her antics had knocked 2 per cent off the value of sterling and had precipitated a by-election loss in Mid-Staffs. 'You won't see ministerial office this parliament,' he said. Fewer than six months later, Widdecombe was made PPS to… Garel-Jones, now a minister in the Foreign Office after eight years as a whip.

With Garel-Jones departing the whips' office in summer 1990, Alastair Goodlad took over as Deputy, while George Young, one of the poll tax rebels and a former whip, came in as The Office's number three. Thatcher also had a new PPS in the shape of Peter Morrison, a devotee, former whip and government minister.

A whip says: 'Peter, while utterly devoted to her, was, by that time, not effective.'

Though intimately involved in reshuffles and a regular attender, along with his wife, at Chequers, Renton had only a distant relationship with Thatcher. However, this was nothing compared to how far removed Thatcher had become from Geoffrey Howe, who felt cocooned from decisions as Deputy Prime Minister.

Thatcher, too, had doubts about Howe's close relationship with Renton. 'Your master's speech on Europe last week was very unhelpful,' the Prime Minister flippantly remarked to the Chief.[5] They also disagreed on reshuffles: Renton strongly pushed back on Thatcher's preference to have right-winger Norman Tebbit, whom she had once suspected of wanting her job, installed as Education Secretary, while the Prime Minister bristled at his more left-wing alternatives.

The final straw for Howe came after the Prime Minister attended a European summit in Rome, savaging the European Community's federal ambitions on her return to the Commons. 'No! No! No!' she said defiantly of European Commission President Jacques Delors's vision for institutions in Brussels.

Howe resigned two days later.

Two weeks had passed by the time Howe rose to deliver his resignation speech in the Commons, an offer afforded to departing Cabinet ministers. In a nineteen-minute statement delivered in a hushed chamber, the senior Conservative explained with devastating effect why he had left the government. Michael Heseltine, who had been biding his time since leaving the Cabinet in 1986 over the Westland affair, listened intently. When it came to acting on his well-known leadership ambitions, it was surely now or never. As he left the chamber, he came across former Chief Whip Michael Jopling.

'What the hell do I do now?' Heseltine asked.

'You do nothing; you'll be Leader of the Opposition in eighteen months,' Jopling replied.

To which Heseltine said: 'I don't want to be Leader of the Opposition.'

The next morning, on 14 November 1990, Heseltine announced he would run for the leadership.

Ted Heath made a rare visit to the whips' office with advice for the Chief on remaining neutral in the contest – a stance he had resented when Humphrey Atkins had chosen a similar path. 'He is an old hypocrite,' Jack Weatherill, the Commons Speaker, told Renton shortly after.[6] On Renton's instructions, the whips stuck to sounding out colleagues over how they would vote, rather than canvassing in favour of Thatcher.

'We continued to do the job of whips to the extent we could of telling the Prime Minister about the business of the House and what the party was [feeling],' explains George Young.

On Monday 19 November, the day before the vote, Thatcher travelled to Paris to attend a conference on security and cooperation in Europe. On Morrison's encouragement, she decided to hold a press conference after the result of the first ballot, due the next evening. Morrison visited Renton that morning to say he was off to the French capital to 'hold the Prime Minister's hand'.[7]

Voting took place among the oak panels and wall-hung tapestries of Committee Room 12, supervised by 1922 Committee chair Cranley Onslow.[8]

Renton walked along Committee Corridor undecided. He felt the Prime Minister was increasingly reliant on right-wing MPs in the No Turning Back group, formed in 1985 to reinforce and support Thatcher's free market policies. He also felt his personal disagreement with her over Europe was too profound to endorse her continuing in No. 10.

'On the other hand, having fought for her for so long, I could not vote against her,' he later confessed. Renton abstained.[9]

George Young, the whips' third in command, who voted for Michael

Heseltine, says he would have thought that around half the whips' office 'probably didn't support her'.

Voting closed at 6 p.m., after which the Labour Party tabled a motion of no confidence.

An official brought the results of the first ballot to the whips' office. Heseltine had 152 votes, Thatcher 204, with sixteen abstentions or spoiled ballots. With 55 per cent of her MPs behind her, Thatcher was just four votes shy of the majority required; Renton's abstention was now even more pronounced.

'Second ballot necessary,' the whip counting the vote had scribbled.

Renton rang Morrison, who was sitting with the Prime Minister in a third-floor suite at the British embassy in Paris. 'Not quite as good as we thought,' Morrison said, writing down the numbers and showing the Prime Minister.[10]

'Does this mean a second ballot, Tim?' Thatcher asked, taking the phone.

'Yes, I am afraid so, Prime Minister,' Renton said. 'You got a good majority of the party but not quite enough. A second ballot will be necessary.'

'I will go and talk to the press straight away,' Thatcher replied.

'Yes, but you will use the words that we agreed that you confirm it is your intention to let your name go forward to the second ballot,' he said.

'Yes. Intentions can always be withdrawn.'[11]

Foreign Secretary Douglas Hurd, staying in a neighbouring room, told her to stand in the second ballot, promising his and John Major's support, with whom he had just spoken.

Thatcher surprised reporters with her early appearance, emerging outside the Paris embassy while BBC journalist John Sergeant was midway through a broadcast.

'Naturally, I'm very pleased that I got more than half the parliamentary party, and disappointed that it's not quite enough to win on the first ballot,' she said. 'So, I confirm it is my intention to let my name go forward for the second ballot.'

Even her most ardent supporters had their doubts. Members of the No Turning Back group, including Nicholas Bennett and Cabinet minister Peter Lilley, met in a windowless committee room down in the depths of Parliament. A 'massive row' ensued as Bennett and Lilley said, given the result, there was no way Thatcher was going to win.

'You don't increase your vote; it ebbs away when you've been mortally wounded,' Bennett says.

Neil Hamilton accused them of being traitors.

Tory MPs began filtering through the whips' office to deliver their verdict. Timothy Kirkhope, who had joined The Office that summer, said there were 'discussions and a bit of shouting occasionally'.

As the most junior whip, and thereby the refreshments officer, Kirkhope had to keep the drinks cupboard well-stocked. After an MP left the Chief's office, it was his job to offer them a beverage. 'So, I learned that evening what a load of lying bastards some people are.'

He explains: 'It annoys me occasionally when books come out either saying, "I defended Margaret to the very last" or alternatively, "I was one of the first to say she should go." I know what they really thought at the time, and some of them don't quite relay it accurately.'

He also recalls a 'not terribly important member' of the 1922 Committee leaving the Chief's office 'bright red in the face'. This 'pompous chap' turned right, grabbed a handle and threw himself into the drinks cupboard, thinking it was the exit to the whips' office.

Amid the uncertainty over Thatcher's future, a handful of Tory MPs had taken to visiting a different whips' office to discuss their feelings. 'One or two Tory members used to turn up after the House had risen and pour their heart out,' says Liberal Democrat Chief Whip Jim Wallace, who facilitated the meetings with a trusty bottle of Scotch. 'They weren't sure who was on whose side. I was totally discreet.'

Several senior Conservatives, including five Cabinet ministers, went to Catherine Place in Victoria, the home of Tristan Garel-Jones. Over dinner, Norman Lamont, Malcolm Rifkind, Chris Patten, William Waldegrave, Tony Newton and others discussed next steps. Collectively, they agreed that Thatcher was done for and that if she ran again in a second ballot, Heseltine might swoop in and become Prime Minister. That, they concluded, mustn't happen. Someone else, either Major or Hurd, or both, would have to stand. The five ministers returned to Parliament to deliver their verdict to the Chief.

At midnight, as Renton prepared to head home, the senior Tories arrived in his Commons office. The Chief suggested they speak to the Prime Minister, or, if they wanted, he could mention their names to her in the morning. 'At that there was some hesitation particularly from Tony Newton,' Renton said. 'I suggested that he should think about it overnight.'[12]

Newton confirmed Renton could pass on the news the next morning.

The following day, Renton had breakfast with a former occupant of 12 Downing Street, Willie Whitelaw. Afterwards, he came across Tory MP Robert Hayward in Members' Lobby, who was making his name as an astute analyst of Conservative Party elections following his successful prediction of the stalking horse leadership challenge a year earlier.

'How many people do you think will feel they've honoured their commitment to Margaret by having voted for her on the first ballot but not on the second?' Renton asked. 'I think it will be four.'

Hayward said it would be up to twenty.

'Are you really sure?' Renton said.

'Yep.'

Thatcher flew in from Paris and met Renton and senior Cabinet ministers in Downing Street at lunchtime. The Chief, who repeated the whips' assessment about MPs switching their vote, emphasised that a number of colleagues thought she wouldn't win on the second ballot. He said the whips believed it was too close to call, but a competent campaign would make a difference. Thatcher later coolly recounted that Renton had given a 'characteristically dispiriting assessment'.[13]

Renton had already lost an argument over the timing of Thatcher's post-conference statement to the Commons, which the Chief wanted to come the next day before the no-confidence debate to allow time for the Prime Minister to meet her Cabinet. In the event, he agreed that Thatcher should meet her top team in her Commons office that evening rather than hold a special Cabinet. He departed No. 10 with the impression that Thatcher would stand, a conclusion amplified when the Prime Minister told reporters on Downing Street: 'I fight on, I fight to win.'

After Thatcher's Commons statement on the Europe meeting, an 'agitated' Murdo Maclean, the principal private secretary to the Chief Whip, greeted Renton holding a copy of the *Evening Standard*, whose front-page story suggested he had told the Prime Minister that she wouldn't win and must withdraw.[14]

The Chief told the paper's political editor and other journalists the story was incorrect, but the seed of doubt had been planted. George Gardiner, head of the right-wing 92 Group, entered his office and 'virtually accused' him of misleading the Prime Minister.[15]

Others feared the Prime Minister was being shielded from the reality that she would come up short at a second ballot. Francis Maude, a government minister, visited Morrison outside Thatcher's parliamentary office. The Prime Minister, who had just held her weekly audience with the Queen, was due back in Parliament by 7 p.m. for her meeting with Cabinet ministers.

'Look, I think this is going badly, and I think she's going to lose,' Maude told Morrison.

Thatcher appeared in the corridor. 'Ah, Prime Minister, Francis has got something he wants to tell you,' Morrison said.

Maude went into Thatcher's office and sat opposite her on a sofa. 'He left in a state of some distress; nor had he cheered me up noticeably,' Thatcher recalled.[16]

Outside, the Cabinet were lining up in the corridor. Over the next ninety minutes, senior ministers, brought in one at a time by Tory MP Ian Twinn, met with the Prime Minister, most recounting a similar theme of expressing their personal support but believing she would lose. One mentioned Robert Hayward's analysis regarding the number of MPs who would switch to Heseltine. 'I'm not interested in what Robert Hayward thinks. I want to know what you think,' the Prime Minister said.

John Wakeham, coordinating support for Thatcher, had notably struggled to assemble a campaign team, with Tristan Garel-Jones, who had played a key role mobilising support for Thatcher in the stalking horse election a year earlier, rejecting the invite out of hand. 'His view of Conservative politics had always been that the line of least resistance is the best course, and I suppose he was being consistent,' Thatcher said.[17]

On 22 November, Nicholas Bennett, a member of the No Turning Back group, rang Peter Morrison on his way to do the morning broadcast round. 'I will play a straight bat that she's going to carry on,' he said, knowing the opposite may be true. Alastair Goodlad entered Renton's office in 12 Downing Street with the news that Thatcher would announce her resignation at Cabinet.

Renton walked through to No. 10 and took his position at the far end of the Cabinet table. The Prime Minister entered looking pale and tired, pronounced rings around her eyes.

Reading from a prepared statement, Thatcher reflected the view of those around the table. 'There is a danger of the policies that I believe in not being continued, and so I have concluded that I…' she said before breaking down. David Waddington, her penultimate Chief Whip, mirrored her tears. Cecil Parkinson, her loyal defender, suggested a minister read the statement for her, but she refused. After less than a minute, she continued. '... I have concluded that I should not let my name go forward for the second ballot.'

* * *

Douglas Hurd and John Major announced they would join Heseltine in standing for the Tory leadership. With the Prime Minister's tacit endorsement, her allies helped with Major's election efforts, led from Tory MP Alan Duncan's home on Gayfere Street.

The first episode of the BBC adaptation of *House of Cards* aired the Sunday before Thatcher announced her resignation. It began with Francis Urquhart at his desk, holding a silver-framed photograph of Thatcher and saying: 'Nothing lasts for ever. Even the longest, the most glittering reign must come to an end some day.'

When he read the script earlier in the year, Dobbs, believing the Prime Minister would face a leadership challenge that November, expressed his concerns to the BBC's drama department, which were largely ignored until fiction and reality converged. Regardless of the optics, the BBC proceeded with the show as planned.

The series, broken down into four episodes, continued throughout the leadership campaign. Dobbs was told on good authority that Major's team came to a halt one Sunday evening, when they gathered to watch the latest episode.

Major emerged with the most votes at the second ballot, fifty-four more than Heseltine and well ahead of Hurd, who trailed in third. With Heseltine and Hurd dropping out, Major took over as Prime Minister.

Renton's perceived involvement in Thatcher's downfall, be it through failing to prevent it or somehow playing a hand, still leaves a bad taste for some Conservatives. 'Tim Renton was that rare thing, a very disloyal Chief Whip,' argues Jonathan Aitken. Tory MP Christopher

Chope says Renton and his whips were 'part of the great conspiracy' to destroy Thatcher.

The Conservatives had to come together after the dethroning of their party leader, whose shadow cast far, long and wide. It was a task that would stretch The Office to breaking point, as the vexed issue of Europe drove a further wedge in an already divided party.

As one MP says of Thatcher's dethroning: 'I don't think we ever really got over it.'

PART IV

MAASTRICHT, MAJOR, MAYHEM

CHAPTER 24

SETTING THE TONE

Richard Ryder, the Government Chief Whip, looked through his contact book in search of Robert Hayward's number. The backbencher had just lost his Kingswood seat at the general election – an election he had correctly predicted the Conservatives would win after analysing polling data throughout the year before the nationwide ballot in April 1992.

Following Margaret Thatcher's defenestration and after thirteen years in office, few, other than Hayward, expected the Tories would end up with a majority of twenty-one. But, armed with a soap box and an easy charm, John Major confounded the pollsters. Hayward's correct prediction spawned the phrase 'shy Tories' – an addition to the political lexicon that didn't feature anywhere in his report, which he produced at the request of Tories John Patten and Chris Patten, but nonetheless refers to voters who keep their Conservatism to themselves.

Ryder, a man with owlish spectacles and boyish features, who reminded some MPs of Christopher Robin, picked up the phone and dialled Hayward's landline at his London flat. His lodger, John, answered.

'Do you know where he is?' enquired the Chief, who, like Major, represented a seat in the east of England.

John said he had no idea.

'He did know where I'd gone, but he didn't dare tell the Chief Whip,' Hayward says.

Prior to the election, Hayward had decided to come out, regardless of whether he won or lost his seat. The Monday after the Thursday election, he found himself in Halfway to Heaven, a gay bar on Duncannon Street, just off the Strand in London. 'I'd gone there freed up of the publicity of being in a gay bar as an MP. I thought I was going to celebrate my freedom.'

A barman received a call and tapped a microphone. 'Is there a Robert from Camberwell here?'

Hayward waited to see if anyone else came forward, then went over to the bar. 'I'm Robert from Camberwell.'

The barman passed over the phone. 'The Chief Whip wants to see you,' his lodger told him.

Hayward finished his pint before heading down Whitehall to see Ryder in his office. 'He just wanted to see if I was OK,' Hayward explains.

While soothing the wounded souls of ousted MPs, Ryder's team were also busy tapping up new additions to the Conservative benches. 'I'm just ringing because when you come down, there's going to be a vote on electing the Speaker,' a government whip told a Tory MP, who had just reclaimed a seat from Labour. 'It's a free vote. Have you had any thoughts on that?'

Among those in the running to succeed the outgoing Jack Weatherill were Conservative candidate Peter Brooke and Labour's Betty Boothroyd, both veterans of their party's respective whips' offices. A Speakership election hadn't been contested since 1951, with the Tories hoping to secure another of their own in the chair.

But the MP liked the sound of Boothroyd taking on the role, and in so doing, becoming the first ever female Speaker. 'You know, Betty Boothroyd, I really like that idea,' the MP said.

'Yeah, but she's Labour!' the whip pointed out.

'Oh, right,' said the MP, his new reality sinking in. 'Yes.'

Some whips had reached out to their MPs long before the new parliament. After becoming Tory candidate for Tiverton, Angela Browning received a Christmas card from an MP who told her he would be her whip. 'It's always very encouraging for a candidate when there's certainty that you're going to be elected! And it rather endeared me to him,' she says.

Robert Hughes returned to his parliamentary office in Norman Shaw South, waiting for a different kind of call. The Tory MP for Harrow West, who had worked on Major's leadership campaign alongside Ryder, was hoping for a government job but had missed out during the first wave of ministerial announcements. He was unpacking his things when his usually placid PA, who never swore, made a startled appearance. She grabbed Hughes's phone and started frantically pressing buttons. 'The fucking divert won't come off!' she fumed. The Chief Whip was calling to offer Hughes a job in the whips' office.

After the Speakership election, which saw Boothroyd secure a historic victory, the new intake of Conservative MPs gathered at 5 p.m. in Committee Room 10 for a 'welcome' talk by government whips. The MPs sat at desks while the whips stood in a line on a platform, a motley crew of all male shapes, sizes and degrees of receding hairlines, tales of their rumoured power and influence hovering like ghosts.

'This idea that they were almost like secret policemen, they had lists of your peccadillos, they knew where your finances were coming from, and they could sort you out, was very much on my mind,' says Eric Pickles, MP for Brentwood and Ongar.

Tim Boswell, who had recently been promoted to Lord Commissioner, gave a frank induction speech, which included the line: 'And when there is a three-line whip you will be here to vote – unless you can produce a doctor's certificate… showing you are dead.'[1]

A witness remembers: '[He] basically said to us, "If you keep your noses clean, you'll be all right, but otherwise, you'll be in trouble."'

The newbies laughed nervously when they realised he wasn't joking.

'We all felt this is a fairly brusque introduction into life in Westminster,' says one. Another says it was out of character for Boswell, whom they got to know afterwards. Nonetheless, it 'got us all off onto slightly the wrong footing'.

Michael Fabricant, the incoming MP for Lichfield, says: 'It set the tone, but I remembered it! So, I'll give him that.'

The new intake looked and acted differently to many that had come before, with an approach the whips' office viewed as occasionally bumptious and entitled. Four of those elected in 1992 met the Chief Whip the following year to ask when they would be made ministers. 'Unthinkable behaviour in previous generations,' said Major judgementally.[2]

In the Prime Minister's eyes, a breed of professional politicians had replaced knights of the shires, the reliable old guard with few Westminster-based aspirations or contentions. The whips, many of whom had worked in previous incarnations of The Office, still imbued a militaristic feel, albeit without the decorated Second World War service to back it up.

'What you had was a generation of whips who, while they themselves didn't have that military background, assumed that that was how things should be, and a large intake coming in which was less inclined to be biddable, less deferential,' says David Lidington, MP for Aylesbury.

The whips were thrown by Fabricant, a former businessman known for his elaborate blond hairstyle. A few years earlier, Fabricant had approached a Conservative Party official after deciding he wanted to become an MP. 'Yes, you'll make a splendid Member of Parliament,' the official said. 'Have you tried the Liberal Democrats?'

The new MPs were hoping for guidance on life in Westminster and a degree of handholding, but the government whips, seeking to instil discipline with a small majority, were on transmit mode. 'They were there like school prefects rather than just people who were there to help,' says a new MP.

Fabricant remembers whips, including the assertive up-and-comer David Davis, asking him to come in on a Friday and keep a debate going, without explaining why.

SETTING THE TONE

'Do a speech now and make it as long as possible,' a whip would say.

'But I don't know the subject,' Fabricant would reply.

'Just make the speech now!'

After speaking for forty-five minutes, Fabricant went up to the whip on bench duty, who closed his notebook to conceal what he'd written.

'Was I all right?' Fabricant asked.

'Yes,' the whip replied quickly.

Browning had an office off the parliamentary estate in Millbank, as did a former two-time Olympic gold medal-winning runner and now Tory MP. When the division bells rang, Browning would tell others she 'slipstreamed Sebastian Coe' on the way over to vote. MPs complained about how long the journey took, prompting Boothroyd, wearing heels to replicate the experience for some female MPs, to take the route herself. She declared it was comfortably done in eight minutes, 'so that was the end of that!' says Browning.

Though their military credentials had waned, the whips' power remained undiminished.

'The whips controlled everything,' says Pickles, including who joined or chaired select committees, which scrutinise the work of government departments. 'A telephone call from the Chief Whip would have been regarded as quite a strong thing to be received by your association chairman.'

But this new tranche of free-thinking MPs was less tolerant of perceived institutional unfairness. Pickles went on a speaking tour of Conservative organisations in the West Country but was told by his whip that he had to come back every night to vote. He would be up at half four, do a full day's work and be back in time for the ten o'clock division. After two months of this pattern, Pickles discovered his whip had been letting his friends in the party off to attend the opera. 'I never took them seriously again, I have to say,' he recalls.

The whips may have had ulterior motives in their rough-and-ready approach to the new intake.

In December 1991, Major returned from negotiations in the Netherlands on the Maastricht Treaty, the foundational agreement of the European Union, which brought in the type of integration with Brussels protested by Margaret Thatcher and a band of Tory Eurosceptics. Major had secured opt-outs from the social chapter and the goal of progress towards economic and monetary union – significant amendments to the provisions that otherwise applied to all founding members. Parliament backed Major's negotiation approach and welcomed his achievements. The treaty didn't feature as a main issue in the general election, but with a healthy mixture of fresh-faced and hardened Brussels dissenters in Tory ranks, the mother of all parliamentary rows beckoned.

Major would require his whips to be on the front foot, The Office's best tacticians working hand in glove with the enforcers, not least, a 'burly bruiser' by the name of David Lightbown.

CHAPTER 25

THE CARING WHIP

Jerry Hayes, a Conservative backbencher with no background in the health sector, naturally found himself on the committee for the government's Health and Medicine Bill during Margaret Thatcher's last parliament as Prime Minister.

The legislation, if enacted, would abolish free sight tests and dental check-ups, inspections Hayes knew, despite the limitations of his medical expertise, could spot serious diseases. He dug a little deeper and, with the help of co-conspirators Jill Knight and David Davis, in the days before 'DD' joined the whips' office, organised a rebellion.

During the bill's committee stage, Hayes made a speech highlighting Cabinet ministers' dislike of the policy, set out in previous letters to constituents, including reference to correspondence penned by none other than Thatcher herself.

The government whip on the committee, David Lightbown, whom Hayes had sarcastically dubbed 'the Caring Whip', waited until the MP had finished and then bundled him outside.

'You little cunt… No more overseas trips for you, lad,' Lightbown fumed.

'Actually, I don't want any,' Hayes replied.

'Well, I'll make sure you are deselected then.'

'Well, I did call a meeting of my executive last night and they fully support me.'

'You little shit,' Lightbown said, thumping Hayes in the chest.

'Oh, fuck off, you fat twat,' Hayes replied, kicking the whip in the groin.[1]

'He lost his rag a bit,' remembers Hayes, a confessed political gossip, who documented this exchange in his memoir.

With the incident leaked to the press, MPs called for senior whips to rein in Lightbown.[2] Word of the encounter, via letters written to the Queen by the Vice-Chamberlain, even spread around the royal estates, according to Hayes.

'Oh, Mr Hayes,' Prince Charles said to the MP at an event. 'I understand you were thumped by David Lightbown. Is he really like that?'

'Yeah, he is, but it was a bit of a laugh, really,' Hayes replied.

Lightbown was renowned for his propensity to grab an MP by the lapels as much as he was for his counterintuitive warmth and teddy bear core. He was also famed for his imposing size, documented by excitable reporters as weighing anything between 17 and 25 stone, while standing at six-foot-three.

Labour whips observed Tory MPs fearful of Lightbown jumping through hoops. 'It was always said that you had a nice whip and a villainous whip,' says Tory MP John Bowis, one of Lightbown's flock. '[Lightbown] was a large personality in a large body who would stomp around and beard anybody who wasn't following the whip as he expected.'

Eric Pickles describes Lightbown as a 'giant of a man' whose loyalty to the party was unquestionable. 'You never thought he was doing it for himself.'

Michael Fabricant is in an illustrious group of MPs whom Lightbown had pushed or pinned against a wall. 'He got me off balance, actually. I remember he pushed me in the voting lobby, probably because he wanted everybody else to see,' he says. Fabricant wasn't expecting the shove, so he went 'bang against the books'. One minister recalls seeing Maureen Hicks crying in the tearoom after a 'very rough time' with Lightbown.

'He didn't mince his words, but in many ways, he wasn't a reinforcement

THE CARING WHIP

of Francis Urquhart because he didn't have that Machiavellian side to him,' Pickles says. 'He was a throwback to an earlier age.'

Lightbown was indiscriminate with whom he confronted, squaring up 'nose to nose' with Tory MP Paul Beresford, a man with a shared stature and taste for tough whipping. With Lightbown upset about newbies 'causing trouble', Beresford informed him: 'If you want us to get through the division lobbies, you've got to tell us what to do, and you've got to persuade us. If we don't agree, you're in trouble, and if we do agree, we'll obey the whip.'

Lightbown stared at him for a minute and said: 'OK.'

Journalists too would receive the Lightbown treatment.

'I will settle you some way other than you are doing now,' he told *The People*'s political editor Nigel Nelson when pressed on why he hadn't declared his shareholdings in Harvey Proctor's clothing company.[3] One lobby journalist was his told his glasses would be 'turned into contact lenses' if his attitude didn't change swiftly.[4]

Lightbown would even take on MPs from rival parties. He dismissed as 'disgraceful lies' the rumour that he had thumped a Liberal MP after a fracas during a vote on the Major government's Railways Bill.[5] Lightbown alleged that some Tory MPs had been locked in the nearby toilets to prevent them from voting and the doors of division lobbies wedged shut with old copies of Hansard, leading to a row behind the scenes.

'I never thump anyone,' Lightbown stressed. Fellow whip Robert Hughes, who said he had only seen Lightbown shout at the MP, added: 'But I do admit that when Lightbown shouts at you, you feel as though he has thumped you.'[6]

Lightbown was not afraid of deploying violent imagery. When another delay was announced to the building of a hospital in his constituency, Lightbown fumed: 'I've got my axe out, I've taken the cover off, and I'm sharpening it up while I decide who to stick it into.'[7] Above his desk in the whips' office was a poster warning MPs that this is where they are brought to 'have their legs broken'.[8]

'I think that most people I deal with understand me and understand my powers of persuasion,' Lightbown told a senior journalist. 'They're not all sticking them up against the wall and putting the knee in. I sometimes kiss them better.'[9]

* * *

David Lightbown was what you might generously call a no-nonsense Tory. In retrospect, he was more of a hard-line social conservative amenable to Europe and entrepreneurialism.

Lightbown hated 'yobs' almost as much as he hated political correctness. He believed in capital punishment, wanted IRA terrorists hanged, opposed abortion, described homosexual acts as 'not natural',[10] called for acid house music to be outlawed, found socialism 'beyond the pale' and argued that people under thirty-five shouldn't be allowed to run for Parliament. He was as forceful and resolute in these opinions as he was in seeking to convince other MPs to change their voting intentions.

Lightbown, managing director of a successful engineering firm and a former Rolls-Royce employee, was elected MP for South East Staffordshire in 1983, having made a name for himself as leader of Lichfield District Council and a member of Staffordshire County Council.

'He was a big guy in every way,' says Edwina Currie.

As with new intakes to come, Lightbown, on arrival at Parliament, was taken aback by the abrupt nature of The Office. 'The whips, I suspect, despite the rather curt way they write to and address their colleagues, are human beings who could even have parents of some form,' he wrote, 'and I realise now that all the lining on the little notes they send me regularly are shorthand for a message they wish to convey.'[11]

He initially spent a good amount of time in Westminster trying to correct the misspelling of his surname. 'I've given up. Boxes, lockers, tickets, keys, have all been inscribed "Lightbrown" in spite of all my efforts – so it looks as if I'm stuck with it,' he said.[12]

Lightbown visited Northern Ireland as part of a series of tours organised by Richard Needham in his capacity as parliamentary private secretary to the Secretary of State, James Prior. On patrol in west Belfast, the group stood behind Lightbown, peering into the darkness, 'wondering whether we were going to be shot at or not', Needham remembers.

Lightbown was involved in an altercation during a second visit to Northern Ireland through no choice of his own. After dinner at Stormont Castle on the outskirts of Belfast, demonstrators ripped up paving slabs and used them as ammunition, hurling lumps of concrete and stones at the departing vehicles as guests were driven away from the premises.

'We were unharmed and well looked after,' Lightbown said.[13]

His staunch views and confrontational nature emerged during an extraordinary public row with a constituent. A 27-year-old mother of two had visited Lightbown hoping he would help speed up an already approved claim from the Department of Health and Social Security (DHSS) for two stair gates to help protect her children at home. Her youngest, a two-year-old, had recently fallen down a flight of stairs. 'I went to see Mr Lightbown full of hope and he just shot me down,' said the woman. 'I felt degraded – as if I was a serf begging my master for something.'[14] The woman took the issue to a Labour councillor, a potential rival of Lightbown's at the next general election, who opportunistically briefed her allegations to the local paper.

The next week, Lightbown hit back, producing written evidence that he had successfully approached DHSS with the woman's request, stating that the woman had a 'shopping list' of around fifty other items for which she was seeking to claim. In his letter to DHSS, Lightbown said he was not particularly supportive during the interview, as 'she is a classical product of the welfare state'.[15]

In October 1986, a month after the toing and froing in his local paper, Lightbown was made a whip, covering DHSS and his flock in the north of England. 'He was perfectly placed in the whips' office because he was a natural bully and also a naturally very kind, shrewd and intelligent man,' Currie says.

He became the whip for the Foreign Office and then the Treasury before being promoted to Lord Commissioner in 1987, Vice-Chamberlain for six months in 1990 and then Comptroller, the number three, the same year. His flock became Welsh MPs.

By tradition, a senior whip would dress up as Father Christmas at the annual whips' Christmas party, which one year was not only attended by wives and partners to thank them for their tolerance of The Office's arduous hours but also their children too.

Lightbown was the natural choice for the role but resisted, having already fulfilled his obligation at a previous do. His colleagues opted for liquid persuasion, procuring Lightbown a bottle of whisky. 'This proved to be a mistake,' a whip later reflected, as a well-refreshed Lightbown wrapped some of the presents assigned for girls in blue and ones destined for boys in pink.[16]

Before the party, the Pairing Whip had agreed through the Usual Channels that the opposition would not oppose government business that evening. But Dennis Skinner, Labour's long-standing disrupter-in-chief, heard about the party and decided to divide the House. Lightbown turned up in the division lobbies in his Santa outfit and had to remove his hat while voting to prove that he was the MP for South East Staffordshire.[17]

When confronted with problems, or problem MPs, Lightbown opted for brute force; he even hacked his way out of his home with a chainsaw when a storm felled a tree in his garden.[18]

A fellow whip recalls walking into the upper whips' office to hear Lightbown bluntly tell a minister before slamming the phone down: 'Well, you might not be there, son, but the minister will be there: whether it's you or not is entirely up to you!'

A colleague thought there was more to Lightbown, who would often escort colleagues for a drink after a dressing down. 'He was a caring and congenial man.'[19] Lightbown would say of the Conservative parliamentary party: 'We're a family.'

'Therefore, if anybody had problems, Lightbown would sort it out,' says Ann Widdecombe. Heavily in debt, Tory MP John Heddle tragically took his own life in late 1989. 'I wish he'd told us,' Lightbown told Currie. 'We have people who could have cleared those debts for him.' After Heddle's death, Lightbown went out of his way to ensure everything possible was done to help his widow and children.[20]

Lightbown was well-known before the bill to enact the Maastricht Treaty trickled its way through the Commons. Still, his work in dealing with Tory Eurosceptics would cement his reputation. A senior minister said: 'It's time to let Lightbown off the leash.'[21]

CHAPTER 26

MAASTRICHT

Ministers and whips fanned out to their respective targets after the Speaker called a division on the night of 4 November 1992. Conservative MPs who had resolved to abstain sat firmly on the green leather benches while Cabinet minister Michael Heseltine and Tristan Garel-Jones, the Europe Minister taking through the bill to enact the Maastricht Treaty, made personal appeals. David Lightbown eagerly followed a would-be rebel out of the chamber.

A whip and a Eurosceptic were seen in full verbal confrontation. 'Keep your mouth shut… get away from me… do not give me that lip,' they were overheard saying.[1] Wild stories emerged of a mutineer being physically dragged into the 'right' lobby while others were blocked from entering the 'wrong' lobby.

The Prime Minister took a backbencher gently in hand and made his final pleas, offering a major concession. The dense Commons air teemed with rumours of the whips' tactics, as MPs passed on rehashed accusations of blackmail. A breathless Lightbown made a desperate attempt to enter the division lobbies, fearing he'd left it too late…

FIVE MONTHS EARLIER

'The Danes have saved our bacon.'[2]

Tory MP Christopher Gill, like many Eurosceptics, knew this could change everything.

On 2 June, Danish voters narrowly rejected at a referendum the Maastricht Treaty by 50.7 per cent to 49.3 per cent. With all twelve members of the European Community required to ratify the treaty by 1 January 1993, the Danes had blown up Brussels' timetable and left the future of the Maastricht plans uncertain.

In Britain, the government's European Communities (Amendment) Bill, known as the Maastricht Bill, had breezed through its second reading in May. Although twenty-two Conservative MPs had voted against it, with four abstaining,* John Major was otherwise still riding a wave for his efforts in the Netherlands six months before.

'He had gotten the best possible deal he could with the opt-out from the euro, the opt-out from the social chapter,' says a Tory MP. 'The UK, in many ways, had the best of both worlds.'

But the Danish referendum had uncertain implications for the future of Major's Maastricht Bill, which was due to have its committee stage that week. Major met Foreign Secretary Douglas Hurd, Chief Whip Richard Ryder and others to discuss what to do. 'We'll get the bill if we push it hard,' said Ryder. 'But there'll be blood all over the floor.'[3]

David Davis and Tristan Garel-Jones, respectively the whip and the minister in charge of taking the legislation through the Commons, were keen to press ahead. But Ryder and Major were uneasy, believing it would be harder to get MPs onside if the future of the bill was outside Westminster's control, in the hands of the Danes. 'Upon further consideration the whips came down against going ahead with the committee stage of the bill,' said Major.[4]

At Prime Minister's Questions, Major consented to outgoing Labour leader Neil Kinnock's request for a debate on Maastricht before paving the way for the bill to enter its committee stage, the entirety of which would take place in the House of Commons chamber. 'I might not have made the offer had I known of the political and economic neutron bomb that was primed to explode,' he later conceded.[5]

In the chamber, Major also addressed Eurosceptic calls for the UK

---

* The bill sailed through its second reading with support from opposition parties.

to emulate the Danes and hold a public vote on Maastricht. 'I am not in favour of a referendum in a parliamentary democracy,' he told MPs. Later in the year, France would approve Maastricht by 51 per cent in favour to 49 per cent against. The Danes prepared to vote again.

Bill Cash, a lawyer and the Eurosceptics' Anorak-in-Chief, had travelled to Denmark around the time of the referendum, expressing solidarity. Along with Christopher Gill, Teresa Gorman, Michael Spicer, James Cran and a couple of dozen other MPs, Cash had dined at the Carlton Club to strategise ahead of the Maastricht Bill's second reading.

Despite Major's opt-outs, the Eurosceptics felt Maastricht would drain away sovereignty and lead Britain down a very particular and undemocratic path. Gill and Cran were made the group's unofficial whips to help coordinate rebellions and shore up support.

'What we had, of course, was a whipping operation being conducted by rebel backbenchers,' says whip Robert Hughes. The Office suspected that some ministers were working with them. There were, after all, plenty of like-minded souls on the government payroll.

Ardent and long-time Eurosceptic Jonathan Aitken, a member of the Conservative European Reform Group – a 'very mild' and 'polite rebel force' within the Tories' parliamentary party – had recently been made Minister for Defence Procurement. Before joining the frontbench, he'd been involved in his fair share of rebellions on Europe. In 1988, he protested a Brussels directive seeking to harmonise lawnmower noise.* Concerned that the government was on the verge of losing, whips brought back ministers from overseas. Margaret Thatcher was forced to forgo dinner with the Prime Minister of Malta to vote. 'I hear this is your doing,' she told Aitken, as rebels imitated lawnmowers in the background.

---

* Germany had introduced a national noise limit to bolster its quieter (and lucrative) lawnmower market by locking out competition from (louder) imports. The EU directive – permitting a higher decibel level – would allow British companies to re-access the German market, which is why London hadn't contested the directive.

The Eurosceptic branch of the Conservative parliamentary party had grown in the ensuing years. 'Because I'd been a Euro rebel, I was uneasy about Maastricht myself,' says Aitken. 'Of course, if I'd been a backbencher, I'd have voted against it. But as a minister, you have to swallow quite a lot of things you don't necessarily want to swallow.'

The day after the Danish referendum, Spicer tabled an Early Day Motion (EDM), a device used by MPs to draw the House's attention to a particular issue. Rarely do EDMs garner much outside attention, but this one did.

The EDM called for the government to use the postponement of its bill to 'make a fresh start' with the 'future development' of the European Community. The motion, known as the Fresh Start Motion, received ninety-six signatures overall, more than two-thirds of whom were Tories, including new MPs John Whittingdale, Michael Fabricant and Liam Fox. 'We have a serious problem on our hands,' Richard Ryder said at a meeting in 12 Downing Street, 'and I want action.'[6]

The Chief Whip encouraged his team to speak with MPs who had signed the EDM and urge them to rethink. David Davis, the whip responsible for taking through the Maastricht Bill,* told Fox, the MP for North Somerset, he would 'have no political future as a consequence'. 'It was an interesting time to cut your teeth,' Fox says.

One brave – or naive – MP volunteered to their whip that they had signed the motion.

'Oh really?' said the whip. 'You know what EDM stands for, don't you?'

'No,' replied the MP.

'Extremely Dim Members.'[7]

David Lightbown went about his instructions in typically subtle and restrained fashion, telling an MP: 'Take your bloody name off the EDM! You have just blown your career!'[8]

---

* Robert Hughes would later assume this responsibility.

Five MPs would ultimately withdraw their support. As a parliamentary private secretary, David Evans had to do so anyway, while Olga Maitland and Hartley Booth, both new backbenchers, removed their signatures. The pair subsequently received places on select committees, while others in their intake who had not withdrawn their signatures did not. 'The one thing we did have available then, which helped us, was patronage,' says a whip.

The Eurosceptics cried foul after Nicholas Winterton, a government rebel, lost his chairmanship of the Health Select Committee. The government insisted it was due to unrelated and coincidental changes to the number of years MPs could serve in the roles. MPs demurred.

Spicer's motion spawned the dissident Fresh Start Group, featuring around twenty-five Eurosceptic ultras. They continued to dine together regularly while Cash took up offices on Great College Street in an eighteenth-century house owned by Conservative peer Alistair McAlpine, printing out briefing notes for MPs with tactics, lines to take and policy implications of Maastricht.[9]

Notable visitors included Margaret Thatcher, now in the House of Lords and a fully paid-up member of the anti-Maastricht movement, who, in a previous life, had played a leading role in the creation of the European single market. Gerald Howarth, Thatcher's one-time PPS, phoned MPs on her behalf, lobbying for them to face down the bill.[10]

'I was asked to be involved with their rebellion, but I didn't get involved with it and I did actually support Major,' says Ian Twinn, a close ally of Thatcher. 'I thought we would be completely sunk as a party if we started having these alternative groups campaigning.'

Ahead of the summer break, Major ordered his whips and ministers on a 'marketing exercise' to sell the merits of Maastricht and his opt-outs to MPs.[11] He met Ryder, Davis and other whips in the Cabinet Office briefing rooms below Downing Street before Parliament resumed, with both Davis and Ryder speculating on allowing Conservative MPs a free vote.

Major was against the move, believing it would maximise dissent and encourage 'doubters to crawl out of the woodwork'. He also thought a united government must deliver the bill.[12]

'What do you think about that?' Davis said to fellow whip James Arbuthnot as they walked back to 12 Downing Street.

'Impressive but terrifying,' Arbuthnot replied.[13]

Then came Black Wednesday.

On 16 September, after months of pressure from currency speculators, the government was forced to withdraw the pound from the European exchange rate mechanism. Major, who had been Chancellor when Britain entered the ERM, faced the biggest crisis of his short reign, with interest rates now at 12 per cent and the economy flatlining.

The Eurosceptics sought to capitalise. Spicer tabled another EDM, this time garnering seventy-one signatures, stating: 'This House welcomes the government's decision to leave the ERM; and urges a fresh start to economic policy...'

'The whips were genuinely taken aback by the turbulence in the parliamentary party, the lack of biddability,' says David Lidington, who signed Spicer's June motion. 'Most of us, we might have discontents but would support the government in the end, but you did rather want to be taken through the argument rather than just told: "This is what you need to do."'

All roads led to early November, with Major hamstrung by his commitment to a paving debate before the Maastricht Bill could move to its long-awaited and certain-to-be-painstaking committee stage.

* * *

To best understand The Office's strategy in whipping Maastricht, it is worth looking at the days around the paving vote in isolation.

Pleadings were made to MPs' party loyalty, with warnings over John Major's future if the government was defeated. Rough-and-tumble threats, flattery and bribes about people's careers and standing in the party had been dished out all through the year, with incendiary accusations over blackmail and private information to come.

Political friends, seniors, constituency associations and even family members were deployed or targeted to help ramp up the pressure. Older hands, though largely intractable, were quietly squeezed, while new, more pliable MPs received arguably the most granular attention.

Individually, each act may have been navigable, but the sheer cumulative weight of the whips' endeavours – the constant phone calls from all-comers, the quiet words, the subtle, coded warnings – ably supported by senior ministers ushered in to help where necessary proved too much for some, overbearing to a few more and unpalatable to others.

Ultimately, however, it worked.

MONDAY 2 NOVEMBER

The whips continued their intensive lobbying exercise, with senior ministers drafted in to talk with targeted backbenchers based on who would be likeliest to sway the MP in question.

'The PM will fall if we lose this one,' they collectively warned MPs. The previous week, Major had told the 1922 Committee that he examined all changes pertaining to Europe before recommending them and in that sense, he was the 'greatest Eurosceptic in the Cabinet'.

David Lightbown was seen having a stand-up row in the Commons tearoom with Welsh Tory MP Walter Sweeney, a member of his flock and, insofar as the Maastricht Bill was concerned, a potential rebel. 'I haven't been so badly barked at since my bull terrier died six months ago,' Sweeney quipped.[14]

Lightbown accused the MP of disloyalty and warned that his ministerial career would end before it had even begun if he followed through and rebelled.[15] Without directly attributing the quote to Lightbown, Sweeney told a journalist that a whip had asked him: 'How are your kneecaps?'[16]

Despite Lightbown's public remonstration, Sweeney understood his approach: 'The whips have a job to do. If I was a whip I would do exactly the same,' he said.[17]

Lightbown had also threatened Tory MP Harry Greenway, who was facing corruption charges,* that if he 'voted with the Maastricht rebels, he would get no moral or other support from the party'.

'You'll be the loneliest man in the dock,' Lightbown warned, according to David Lidington, who says understatedly: 'It could be more than pretty brutal.'

Throughout the passage of the Maastricht Bill, Timothy Kirkhope, dubbed the 'Psychological Warfare Whip', would capitalise on Lightbown's endeavours as the 'Physical Whip'.

'He used to go around people quite heavily. "You will do this, you little effing…" – this sort of stuff and leave people shivering,' says Kirkhope. Kirkhope would then emerge from The Office and say to the MP: 'Hello, any problems?'

'That man's mad. He's a maniac. Do something about him. I can't stand it,' the MP would say.

'Dear oh dear, how unfortunate,' Kirkhope would reply. 'Well, David has a lot of faults. He had a difficult upbringing. One of his faults, of course, is that he's loyal. And I wonder whether it might be a good idea to vote with the government tonight. If you do that, I will make sure that I have a word with David, and I think things will improve dramatically.'

TUESDAY 3 NOVEMBER

A senior Welsh Conservative Party agent attended unannounced a meeting in Walter Sweeney's Vale of Glamorgan constituency to discuss the MP's position on the Maastricht Bill.

'He advised them that my stated intention to vote against would put

---

* The case against Greenway later collapsed due to lack of evidence.

the Prime Minister's future at risk,' said Sweeney, who was informed of what had taken place. 'There then ensured a discussion as to what to do.'[18] Former Conservative Party chairman Norman Tebbit said the presence of the agent was unprecedented, but one of his successors in the role, Norman Fowler, insisted it was routine for area officials to attend such meetings.[19]

Bill Walker, MP for Tayside North, received a rare call at his constituency office from Lord Sanderson, chair of the Scottish Conservatives, who urged him to change his mind.[20] Walker would claim that he was warned by whips that he could be isolated and lose his chairmanship of Scottish Tory MPs in Parliament if he rebelled.[21]

Still dressed in white tie and tails after a Buckingham Palace banquet for the Sultan of Brunei, John Major spoke with Tory MP Robert Jones for half an hour – one of many potentially malleable backbenchers he had met in recent days – seeking to bring him onside.[22] Richard Ryder had earlier told the PM that the government faced defeat.

WEDNESDAY 4 NOVEMBER

The whips were still doubtful of the government's chances of victory on the morning of the vote.

Richard Ryder was a rugby fan and admirer of Willie John McBride, the legendary captain of the victorious British and Irish Lions side that toured South Africa in 1974, who instigated the 'ninety-nine call', a policy of 'one in, all in' when a member of his team retaliated against an action by a Springbok. Ryder had shared this code with the whips and he told David Lightbown that morning: 'Ninety-nine today, David.'[23]

John Whittingdale, a one-time aide to Margaret Thatcher, had taken a group of fellow Tory MPs to his former boss's office in the House of Lords to hear her case for the destruction of the Maastricht Treaty. A week later, the MP, elected in April, was in front of the Chief Whip, with Ryder saying Major's survival depended on his support.

Whittingdale visited Thatcher at her office in Chesham Place to explain that he would not be voting against the Maastricht Bill. 'It was an extremely difficult and painful decision but at no point did I cry,' he insisted amid rumours to the contrary.[24]

Anne Jenkin, a former Tory candidate at a general election, arrived at her husband Bernard's parliamentary office, which she ran on his behalf. For the past few days, she had fielded phone calls from Conservative politicians pleading for her partner to vote with the government, including an invitation from Jenkin's whip to speak on the terrace peering over the River Thames. On receipt of another call, this time from a soon-to-be-appointed whip, Andrew Mitchell, Anne felt the tears rising.

Mitchell later remembered: 'I enquired whether there was any briefing or help I could provide to assist him on this particularly difficult issue.' Anne broke down in tears: 'I can handle the nasty ones. It's the nice ones that get me going.'[25]

Walter Sweeney received a fax with the result of his constituency meeting, which had voted 15–6 in favour of him reconsidering his opposition to the Maastricht Treaty. Sweeney would later say he changed his mind after receiving a strongly worded letter from his constituency executive noting their 'displeasure' at his intention to vote against the government.[26]

Norman Tebbit, by now in the House of Lords, stalked Members' Lobby, with wavering rebels brought over by the Eurosceptics' whips for 'a little arm-twisting chat'. Ted Heath, the Europhile former Prime Minister, walked past and muttered: 'This is absolutely appalling.'[27]

The whips deployed one of their own to watch Tebbit in case the peer broke convention by taking a pew in Members' Lobby. 'If he sits down, arrest him,' a whip quipped.[28]

The debate began at 3.30 p.m., with Betty Boothroyd announcing that no fewer than ninety MPs had requested to speak. Midway through proceedings, Michael Fabricant, a one-time waverer, handed the Prime Minister a note.

John. My turn to lobby you! Whether we win or lose – and I will be voting with the government on this now – do not abandon us. We need you. Best of luck. Mike.[29]

The Prime Minister read the note, put it in his pocket, then took it out and looked at it again later.

Major left the chamber to meet MPs in his nearby parliamentary office. Michael Heseltine, the Trade and Industry Secretary, came to see him and said they were still behind. 'Probably by one,' Ryder confirmed in his office off Members' Lobby. Heseltine went to chat with Tory MPs Michael Carttiss and Gerard Vaughan. 'Let me deal,' he told Major and Ryder.[30]

On the Commons message board in Members' Lobby, MPs found pink telephone slips with messages from Gerald Howarth, acting on behalf of Margaret Thatcher, urging them to vote against the bill.

The Labour Party amendment to delay the bill until after a meeting of European leaders in Edinburgh fell short by just six votes. With the division on the main motion to come, whips feared the margin of victory on Labour's amendment was too small. Cabinet ministers and whips watched for their target MPs before the division was called, ready to pounce.

Some members of the whips' office likely had their reservations about Maastricht, not least David Heathcoat-Amory, the Deputy Chief Whip, who would leave the government later in the parliament over the single European currency. David Davis, the whip understudy to the Maastricht Bill, was also a Eurosceptic. But, like generations of whips before them, they parked their personal views for the job in hand.

The division bells sounded and the whips, ministers and rebels dispersed, the latter group keeping together, believing there was safety in numbers. Teresa Gorman and Ann Winterton, an MP and the wife of Nicholas, went through the No lobby together, with the former saying she faced calls of 'Scab' and 'Judas' while some MPs tugged at her clothing, urging her to join them in the Aye lobby.[31]

Major saw Michael Carttiss hesitating near the division lobbies, still unconvinced despite Heseltine's final pleas. The Prime Minister put his arm around Carttiss's shoulder.

'Come on, Michael. We need you tonight,' he said.

'But the Danes might vote no again,' Carttiss said.

'Michael,' Major began, 'we won't complete the bill until we know their position.'[32]

Bernard Jenkin, seeking quiet, wandered through Members' Lobby towards the House of Lords, surveying the artwork that lines the storied corridor, resigned to abstaining following days of unabating pressure.[33]

MPs swapped stories that one of their own had been sent home in a taxi after being plied with alcohol. Timothy Kirkhope, though he's not certain on which vote this took place, would carry out a similar strategy on Nicholas Fairbairn, a Scottish Tory, Maastricht sceptic and voracious drinker of whisky, spending the evening with him in Parliament's Smoking Room. 'I lived to regret all this nastiness on my part, but I must admit, when he was asking for a whisky, I was doubling it,' he says. The whip, who poured himself singles, was starting to go down, but managed to walk Fairbairn through the lobbies while talking about Scottish poet and lyricist Rabbie Burns. 'I don't think he ever quite realised that he voted with the government on that occasion,' says Kirkhope, who had to be bailed out with black coffee for hours in the whips' office. 'You may think "This is horrible, this is terrible," but the point is … we had to get the business.'

David Lightbown, exhausted after his not inconsiderable efforts, followed a Eurosceptic so enthusiastically into the Commons toilets that he left it too late to vote – with suggestions he was accidentally locked inside – arriving at the division lobbies to find the doors closed.

Ryder sat next to Major on the frontbench. David Davis peered into view behind the Speaker's chair, giving the thumbs-up and puffing out his cheeks. The government won by three, with twenty-six Tories voting against and six abstaining, Major propped up by the Liberal Democrats and other MPs from rival parties.

'Lo and behold, again, as Chief Whip, I was the one sent out to explain something that I had been against in the group,' says Jim Wallace, who, along with Charles Kennedy, had encouraged Lib Dem leader Paddy Ashdown to oppose the government. 'We both noted that those who were most vociferous in backing up Paddy couldn't be found anywhere.'

Major joined the whips in The Office for a celebratory drink. 'I did happen to share a glass of champagne with the Prime Minister afterwards, so I think he's still speaking to me,' joked Lightbown after missing the vote.[34]

Later that evening, the Prime Minister wrote back to Fabricant.

Dear Mike,
  Many thanks for your kind note and your support. It was a damn close-run thing.[35]

THURSDAY 5 AND FRIDAY 6 NOVEMBER

The recriminations over the whips' activities began in earnest the following morning, with newspapers full of stories about MPs' experiences.

'They went too far in terms of the good of the party,' said Norman Tebbit.[36] Christopher Gill, who witnessed some 'very nasty arm-twisting', said: 'It was unprincipled, unfortunate and is bound to lead to lasting resentment.'[37] John Carlisle fumed: 'There is apartheid in the Conservative Party. If you do not toe the line, they do not want to know you.'[38]

MPs had been threatened with deselection and the withholding of promotion, overseas trips and spacious offices, reporters wrote. One journalist said three backbenchers had been reduced to tears, including two new MPs.[39] And then, on 6 November, the *Daily Mirror* ran the headline: 'Blackmailed by Major's Sex Thugs'.

In the front-page story, the paper reported that a 'stunned waverer' was 'confronted [by a whip] with the name of his mistress' and told 'it may not remain a secret much longer'.

'Threats were made to some people about their personal relationships,' asserted Bill Walker.[40]

But a journalist following up on the story said Walker had provided no evidence for his claim, saying he had heard the rumour from another MP, who in turn had heard it from someone else.[41]

Regardless, the sheer scale – and ultimate success – of the whipping operation drew a harsh spotlight on an office and its various characters whose work had hitherto largely gone unseen, raising questions for the Prime Minister under whose name the whipping had been carried out.

CHAPTER 27

MAJOR CRISIS

John Major, by all accounts, was an exemplary whip. 'He was the best Chief Whip we never had,' said a colleague.

He joined The Office in early 1983, accepting the job from a public phone booth at King's Cross Station. He soon impressed with his grasp of detail. As the whip for the Department of Environment, Major had several contentious bills to steer through Parliament, including plans to abolish the Greater London Council and annual debates over local government financing.

Major would return from prayer meetings and relay any legislative pitfalls, how to navigate them and which key players would need winning over. 'He just had the whole thing at his fingertips,' says a fellow whip. 'We used to sit there in stunned admiration.'

His emollient and sympathetic style earned admirers from all corners of Parliament. After catching wind that a family member of a Liberal MP had taken ill, Major approached the party's Deputy Chief Whip, Michael Meadowcroft, during a debate on the floor of the House.

'I understand that Alan Beith's son is ill?'

'Yes, he is. He's quite ill,' Meadowcroft replied.

'Well, let's adjourn the House early then so he can go home.'

Liberal Chief Whip David Alton says Major was a 'deeply honourable man'. 'He didn't need to particularly deal with me because we didn't have the votes to make that much of a difference. He treated me as though I did.'

Major said of his time in The Office: 'We planned parliamentary business, bullied and cajoled where necessary and shared every piece of intelligence that came our way.'[1]

Before he became Prime Minister, Major had few detractors. Many supporters of Margaret Thatcher had followed her lead in backing him to succeed her as Conservative leader. 'It was only when he became Prime Minister that he made enemies,' says a former member of his flock.

Unlike other Prime Ministers, Major had a firm handle on the whips' office. '[He] interacted with us a lot because he had been a whip, so he understood what went on,' says a whip. This filtered through to the Usual Channels, with Labour leader Neil Kinnock enjoying a more fruitful and open relationship with Major than he had experienced with Margaret Thatcher. 'In Thatcher's time, either because they were conforming to her general attitude, disposition, or they were frightened of her, any Usual Channels facilitation was very, very, very limited,' he says. 'They fought the war on all fronts.'

As a former whip, Major was allowed access to the bench duty notebook and the system of notes read out by the Chief each day. Notes marked with an 'X' on the top right-hand corner would be sent privately to Major in his flat at No. 10, on request by the Prime Minister and consented to, despite whips' reservations, by Richard Ryder.

A whip who joined The Office under Major remembers being on bench duty when the Prime Minister opened a debate for the government. The whip noted: 'Started with a joke that fell flat, but the speech then got better.'

Major took his pew as the Leader of the Opposition responded to his opening remarks. He asked the whip on bench duty: 'Can I have a look at the book?'

The whip, forgetting what he'd written at the start of the debate, handed it over. He then thought to himself: 'Oh, shite!'

Major glanced at the whip's report and said before leaving: 'Yes, I think you're probably right.'

* * *

In the aftermath of 4 November 1992, once-charmed Eurosceptics had come to think differently about their party leader. '[The heavy whipping] was done in John Major's name and it is now up to him to try and heal the wounds,' said Nicholas Winterton.[2] But No. 10 briefed that no disciplinary action would be taken against his whips, whom Major felt were doing the government's bidding with aplomb. If anyone should apologise, he likely believed, it should be the rebels.

The animosity would filter through to the Maastricht Bill's turgid committee stage, as the Eurosceptics, teaming up with an increasingly dextrous opposition, deployed guerrilla warfare against the government. For several months, over 200 hours of debate took place in the House of Commons chamber, with MPs considering more than 600 amendments and new clauses to the Maastricht Bill. Many of them were lodged by Eurosceptics, who felt the prolonged scrutiny – and thereby more focused attention on the issue at hand – aided their cause.

Outside the chamber, when not in front of the TV cameras set up on College Green, the rebels were occasionally seen chatting with senior Labour whips, working out each other's position with the hope of furthering their causes by defeating the government in what many Conservatives deemed an unholy – and completely unforgivable – alliance. 'When you're elected to Parliament or even to a council, you do owe your party some loyalty,' says Tory whip Robert Hughes, who worked closely with David Davis on the Maastricht Bill. 'What you don't do is to organise against your own party.'

John Smith, the leader of the Labour Party, had to navigate his own tightrope. Labour, long divided on the issue of Europe, had its own tranche of Maastricht opponents – even more of them than the Tories in some cases – not all of whom came at it from the same angle. 'There were a lot of us who weren't happy with Maastricht,' says Lynne Jones, elected MP for Birmingham Selly Oak in 1992. Opponents were divided into two camps: pro-Europeans like Jones who didn't like the European Community's direction of travel versus those who were opposed to the common market from the start. Labour also had its fair share of MPs who wanted the party to be supportive, which Smith was insofar as the substance of the treaty was concerned, albeit while providing stubborn opposition on specific points, as he felt was his duty. Smith facilitated debates at Parliamentary Labour Party meetings to neutralise the splits, granting MPs their say. And with the help of Labour MP Geoff Hoon, a lawyer and Member of the European Parliament, he drafted enticing amendments designed to tempt Conservatives and other parties.

A frustrated John Major hoped to drive the Maastricht Bill through the Commons faster, but efforts to speed up proceedings were blocked by the Labour Party and the rebels. The glacial progress stymied the government's legislative agenda. An aide in the No. 10 Policy Unit says work was stopped for at least a fortnight because the whips feared a defeat.

MPs had to go through the night. Cabinet minister Ken Clarke was seen at 5.30 a.m. knocking back a plate of bacon and eggs, washed down with coffee and a cigar, preparing to wind up the case for the government at around 6 a.m.[3] 'It was not the nicest of times because most of your opponents were on the same side of the House,' says John Bowis.

Whips were living by the hour, unsure what progress could be made through the various amendments and clauses without assurance of victory. They met several times a day, summoned by their pagers, to see if they had the numbers to hold a vote. Richard Ryder, enduring a second agony in the shape of a cripplingly bad back, would spend meetings lying on the floor.[4]

For the whips, it was an exhausting period. Robert Hughes, a vegetarian, hadn't eaten all day ahead of a difficult evening. He went to the upper whips' office and leaned against the door. 'Pull yourself together,' David Lightbown said. 'You ought to get a good steak inside you.'

Whips would scour the bars and lavatories to ensure sufficient MPs were present should a vote be called. To win over rebels, they would dangle carrots in the shape of promotion, the lure of an honour or general flattery, while also using their more coercive techniques. Hughes still has a 'marvellous' video of when a division was called on a 'particularly difficult vote'. He says: 'You can see all of my placemen, some of them Cabinet ministers, fanning out to find their target.'

John Gummer, a minister, former whip and member of the General Synod of the Church of England, was lined up to convince Harry Greenway, a man of similar faith, to abstain. Hughes saw the two men walking out of the government's preferred lobby, arm in arm.

Hughes said to Gummer: 'That's amazing! What did you say to him?'

'I can't tell you,' Gummer replied, 'but it wasn't very Christian.'

At the end of each day, Hughes would write a briefing note for Major and drop it at Downing Street at 1 or 2 a.m. Richard Ryder and David Davis met regularly with Liberal Chief Whip Archy Kirkwood, who had taken over from Jim Wallace, to discuss his party's position. The whips also had a spy at Aldergrove Airport to see if the Ulster Unionists, who were anti-Maastricht though sometimes sympathetic enough to abstain, had made the flight over.[5]

Davis, Ryder and Tristan Garel-Jones, the Europe Minister, met with the four MPs from Plaid Cymru, including Dafydd Wigley, who had been Major's pair for over a decade. In return for Plaid Cymru's support, the government consented to three items, including a third seat for Wales on the Committee of the Regions in Europe.

The Eurosceptics were also organised, appointing a 'whip' on duty in the chamber and meeting to liaise over votes. But notes from the gatherings were often left on a desk in the whips' office. 'We never found out the identity of our informant, but it had to be someone at the very centre of the sceptic camp,' said Major.[6]

The whips' office was itself a broad church, with a wide range of views and tentacles in the Conservative backbenches. Some whips kept their back channels open to Eurosceptics. 'We would generally know what they were doing,' says Hughes.

The biggest danger to the government came from Labour's so-called ticking time bomb amendment on incorporating the social chapter, which Major had opted out of in Maastricht. Garel-Jones said he had received legal advice that this would be inadmissible, but the advice changed on review.

Labour devised the amendment so that it didn't block the bill from becoming law but would require the government to hold a vote on the social chapter before final ratification. Though the Deputy Speaker Michael Naseby controversially ruled the amendment out of order, the decision was reversed and a vote would be held after the bill's third reading.

The Maastricht Bill finally completed its committee stage in April. On 20 May, its third reading passed with a majority of 180, with forty-six Tories voting against. The conclusion of the Maastricht debates was set for 22 July, more than a year after the bill's second reading.

For the rebels, one last throw of the dice.

CHAPTER 28

CHAPTER AND VERSE

The last thing Eurosceptics wanted was for Britain to sign up to Brussels' new-fangled – and, in their eyes, overreaching and interventionist – social chapter, but that wasn't the point. This was the last opportunity to try to kill the Maastricht Bill, a factor cutely exploited by the Labour Party in dangling a carrot that would prove alluring and irresistible not only to the rebels but to the Liberal Democrats and Scottish National Party too.

In the intervening period, the rebels' ranks had been bolstered by one, after John Major sacked Trade and Industry Minister Edward Leigh, one of four ministers, including Michael Portillo, Eric Forth and Peter Lloyd, who had previously sought a meeting with Major or Richard Ryder during the Maastricht debates. 'It looked like a nascent rebellion, and could not be allowed within the government,' Major later said.[1]

David Davis was sent to see the ministers with a prepared statement. 'I am authorised to tell you all, if you want or insist on a meeting with the Prime Minister, you will get one individually, and it will be brief and to the point – and probably your last,' he said. 'Any questions?'[2]

The whips had made it to July on a steady diet of caffeine, adrenaline, liquid refreshment and cynical humour. At a Wednesday meeting, Deputy Chief Whip David Heathcoat-Amory began proceedings by highlighting that it was National No Smoking Day, before adding: 'Would anyone like a cigarette?' to which they all, even the non-smokers, obliged.[3]

Unable to rely on other parties, bar the Ulster Unionists, whose party leader Jim Molyneaux had shocked Major by pledging their support, Ryder counselled that the government would lose the vote.

John Major and his Cabinet discussed how to respond to such a result. Murdo Maclean, the principal private secretary to the Chief Whip, floated a follow-up confidence motion that would specifically approve the government's policy on the social chapter, superseding the earlier result. House of Commons officials confirmed that such a motion would be above board.

Ryder, with Major's consent, tried one last overture to the rebels, offering an assurance that the UK would not re-enter the European exchange rate mechanism in the life of the parliament. Though the diehards were resolute, some of the rebels couldn't bear to vote for the social chapter. As such, the Eurosceptics needed all the troops on the ground.

Bill Walker had been away from the Commons with illness. His whip was Timothy Kirkhope, who on a previous vote during Maastricht had struggled to locate the Scottish Tory. He walked into a designated 'family room' in Parliament, where he found Walker 'tucked behind the sofa, trying not to be seen'. 'Bill, come along now,' Kirkhope said. 'Time to vote soon.'

The rebels offered to put Walker in a helicopter, but he opted for the train. Bill Cash, collecting him at King's Cross Station, hailed a taxi for his den on Great College Street, before driving him the short distance to Parliament. Pairing Whip Greg Knight confronted Walker and said he'd been paired for the evening, which Walker denied.

'That's declaring war on your own party,' Hughes says.

The rebels weren't the only ones taking desperate measures. In echoes of the 1974–79 parliament, Cabinet minister John Patten, suffering from an intestinal illness, was brought onto the estate in an ambulance to be nodded through by whips. Michael Heseltine, who a month earlier had suffered a heart attack, also came in to vote. So too did two sick Labour MPs, Rachel Squire and Bob Parry, the latter recovering from a quadruple heart bypass.[4]

Whips had opted for a softer approach than ahead of the paving debate. A whip carrying a bottle of claret entered The Office soon after backbencher Toby Jessel sat down for a chat with Richard Ryder.[5] A shadow minister accused the Tories of offering knighthoods and channelling parliamentary consultancies through the whips' office to be issued as 'bonuses for loyalty'.[6]

Major, moving the motion that the House notes the government's policy on the adoption of the social chapter, opened the debate with helpful interventions from Michael Lord, John Carlisle and Nicholas Winterton, three rebels who signalled they would support the government. 'We're still down,' Ryder told a briefly optimistic Major after he left the chamber.[7]

The Cabinet met at 7 p.m., with Murdo Maclean in attendance, to agree on Major's proposals for a follow-up confidence motion endorsing the government's rejection of Maastricht's social chapter and allowing the bill to be ratified immediately.

Ryder chuckled at the end of the table. 'Charge of the Light Brigade,' he explained to Major's inquisitive stare. 'After Cardigan had led the Light Brigade into the guns, with massive casualties, the sergeant-major galloped up to him, saluted and said, "Same again, sir?" That's what we're going to do.'[8]

The first vote was on Labour's amendment requiring the government to delay ratifying the Maastricht Treaty until notifying the European Community that it intended to adopt the social chapter. The tellers lined up, and the Labour benches erupted as the whip announced a tie, 317 to 317.[*] Speaker Betty Boothroyd, applying precedent, gave her casting vote against the amendment.

---

[*] It emerged the next morning that there had been a missed count and the government had actually defeated the motion by one.

The substantive motion followed. The government lost by eight votes.

Major rose to announce that a motion of confidence would be debated the following morning. 'We must resolve this issue; it cannot be allowed to fester any longer,' he said.

His bold move proved decisive, with just one Tory MP, Rupert Allason, who was away and who lost the whip for his troubles, not voting. The government won by thirty-eight votes and the Maastricht Bill became law.

* * *

'Against the background of no Conservative majority for the bill, the achievement in carrying it was the finest piece of whipping I ever saw.'[9]

That was John Major's verdict on the effort of his whips, who saw that the government got its Maastricht business. David Davis, Greg Knight, Robert Hughes, David Lightbown, Timothy Kirkhope, Richard Ryder et al. 'performed heroically', the Prime Minister said.

But at what cost? The Maastricht debates left behind deep fissures within the Conservative parliamentary party, ostensibly irreparable scars that would reopen periodically. One Labour MP says a Eurosceptic claimed that, if he documented what he saw in a memoir, 'there would be an election immediately and Labour would win and go on winning'.

Kirkhope argues the whips 'handled it as well as we could'. His fellow whip Andrew Mitchell believes it is a 'reasonable proposition' that Maastricht was 'the most successful example of whipping since the end of the First World War'.[10]

The whips are certainly not exclusively to blame for residual ill-feeling. The rebels, however justified they felt in their actions, ultimately sparked a war of attrition within their own party.

'They didn't care about the whips,' says Tory MP Alistair Burt of the rebels, asserting: 'As always with the anti-Europeans, they think they're right, and they think that being right gives them the right to go against the party because this was more important than anything else. They were as arrogant and unpleasant as they became [later on].'

In dealing with anti-EU rebels, other Tory leaders would opt for placation. Major, belying his measured nature, and backed by a powerful whips' office, confronted the Eurosceptics head on. Blood – to use the vernacular of the era – would have been shed either way; how much is a contested question.

Tory divisions weren't helped by the leak of a candid moment between the Prime Minister and a senior ITV journalist, Michael Brunson. After an interview, their conversation captured by a still-live feed cable, the pair spoke about the state of the Conservative Party. Brunson said three Cabinet ministers had threatened to resign over the government's Europe policy. 'You and I can think of ex-ministers who are causing all sorts of trouble,' Major said, explaining his reasoning over whether to sack the ministers. 'Do we want three more of the bastards out there?'

Rebels seized on Major's words, wearing the moniker with pride. One, Teresa Gorman, penned a book recounting the Maastricht debates titled *The Bastards: Dirty Tricks and the Challenge to Europe*.

The intemperate clashes of the Maastricht debates would resurface during the remainder of the parliament. Ann Widdecombe witnessed a row between Tristan Garel-Jones and Edward Leigh in which the former whip accused the ex-minister of briefing against the government.

'It was not pleasant. We were all very split,' says Ian Twinn. Michael Fabricant agrees: 'I did not enjoy 1992–97 one little bit.' Burt adds: 'How much of it was still a resentment to the removal of Margaret Thatcher is difficult to say.'

Insofar as Tory infighting over Europe was concerned, the passing of the Maastricht Bill was not the beginning and end of it.

Eight Eurosceptics – Michael Carttiss, Teresa Gorman, Nicholas Budgen, Tony Marlow, John Wilkinson, Richard Shepherd, Christopher Gill and Teddy Taylor – lost the Tory whip on 28 November 1994 after abstaining on the European Community Finance Bill in defiance of a three-line whip. Richard Body resigned the whip voluntarily in support of the eight MPs. 'It certainly seemed like the right thing to do at the time,' says Robert Hughes. Other MPs had, to no avail, warned Major against removing the whip.

The fallout came amid a series of scandals, defections and by-elections that further diminished Major's already tight majority and the Conservatives' public standing.

CHAPTER 29

BACK TO BASICS

Labour MP Margaret Hodge, a new addition to Parliament after a by-election in June 1994, thought she should take her pair, the Tory backbencher Alan Howarth, out for a meal.

Green to Westminster, though not to politics, Hodge had endured a rude awakening. Invited to lunch by a journalist, Labour's newest recruit expressed her view that the role of an MP could be a job share to encourage more women to run for Parliament. Hodge was asked to visit the Labour whips' office the Monday after the *Sunday Times* ran a story on her take. There, she found whips throwing darts at a picture of her in the paper, which they had pinned to the wall.

Hodge received the guiding hand from her pair that she didn't have from her whips. When news reached her that Howarth had broken up with his wife, she turned to her assistant and said: 'I'd better take him out to lunch.'

She prepared to leave Parliament thinking she was about to get two hours' worth of ranting about women and relationships. 'Wish me luck,' Hodge told her assistant. Instead, she got two hours' worth of ranting about the Conservative Party. 'That was the start of bringing him over,' Hodge says of Howarth, who had served as a whip under Margaret Thatcher.

John Bowis, a member of his flock, recalls Howarth confronting him over a potential rebellion while serving on a bill committee. 'You will have no future in this party unless you support the government's line and hold your fire,' Howarth told him. In fact, it would be Howarth who ultimately would have no future in the party.

He defected to Labour after twelve years as a Tory MP, the first of four Conservatives to join a rival party during the parliament. He was the latest casualty in Tory ranks, with the party already losing six seats at by-elections, with two more to come.

* * *

At the Conservative Party conference in October 1993, the autumn after the Maastricht debates finally concluded, John Major, shifting gears away from Europe, promised to lead the country back to a traditional morality rooted in self-reliance, decency, family and respect. 'It is time to return to core values, time to get back to basics,' he said.[1]

While not his intention, Major's 'back to basics' campaign became a morality benchmark against which his MPs were held. And so, when backbenchers and ministers faced allegations of accepting cash to ask questions in Parliament, or their sexual activities were splashed all over the papers, Major, vicariously, took a significant hit.

The following January, Tim Yeo, who had previously railed against the rising number of single mothers in society, resigned as Environment Minister amid reports he had fathered a child outside his marriage, making him the third minister to quit, after David Mellor and Michael Mates, since the start of the parliament. And then, in early February, Stephen Milligan, a former journalist turned Conservative MP, died when an auto-erotic asphyxiation game apparently went wrong – circumstances that some, to this day, still find suspicious.*

The whips had approached a *Daily Telegraph* lobby correspondent, a friend of Milligan's, when they couldn't locate him early on the afternoon of Monday 7 February. Milligan's secretary alerted police, who

---

* In 2018, senior BBC journalist John Simpson, a friend of Milligan's, repeated a theory that Russian spies may have been involved. An inquest ruled his death as misadventure.

attended his home in Hammersmith, finding him on the kitchen table in the lurid circumstances which were promptly shared around Westminster. A member of the whips' office – Tory whips identify Tory MPs after they pass away – was sent to identify his body. Andrew MacKay, as Milligan's regional whip, had the duty on this occasion.[2]

A week after Milligan's death, Hartley Booth, a Methodist lay preacher and married father of three, resigned as PPS after newspaper reports that he was having an affair with a House of Commons researcher. Two more PPSs would follow amid the cash-for-questions affair, before ministers Tim Smith and Neil Hamilton resigned over claims that they had accepted money from businessman Mohamed Al Fayed to table parliamentary questions.

A year after Milligan's passing, Nicholas Fairbairn died from liver disease, his alcoholism catching up with him.

The scandals and deaths prompted veterans of The Office to question the whips' apparent unpreparedness. 'When people say the whips know everything, I'm not so sure,' says one.

The whips would argue they could only do so much to help an individual, relying to a degree on the MP or friends coming forward to alert them to any problems; the keeping of a Black Book, in their eyes, was fully vindicated.

Alcoholism was certainly prevalent during the 1992–97 parliament. The whips found one colleague spreadeagled on the stone floor by the members' cloakroom. They also appointed a minder to help Iain Mills, whom they were encouraging to get control of his drinking, through the division lobbies. The Tory MP soon passed away from acute alcohol intoxication.

Derek Conway, a government whip, started searching for Mills one afternoon after he had failed to turn up to a vote in the Commons two evenings before. Along with a security guard, he found the MP dead in his bed at his flat in nearby Pimlico.[3]

'They slipped up badly twice,' says an MP of the whips. Normally, they would 'welfare these people and catch them when the booze was too much'. 'They should have caught them.'

In fairness, the whips had assigned someone to look after Mills and knew of his troubles, albeit not the true extent. Speaking after the coroner's verdict, Conway said: 'We knew he was drinking, but we had no idea it was in the order found by the pathologist.'[4]

Parliament's myriad bars, late nights, high stress and tough hours, coupled with many MPs' isolated existence from their families, served as a highly potent mixture for men and women seeking respite through alcohol.

David Lidington says: 'One of the hidden strengths of the whips' office is the willingness to help people who are genuinely in need.' In turn, whips also saw the darker side of MPs seeking to capitalise on colleagues' misdeeds. 'God, you saw the underbelly of human life,' says one. MPs would visit to feed whips information that 'might do down another person' or enhance their own position.

With the cash-for-questions scandal raging, Major established the Committee for Standards in Public Life, which, in its first report and under its chair, senior judge Michael Nolan, codified seven principles. The Nolan Principles on public life, as they became known, are selflessness, integrity, objectivity, accountability, openness, honesty and leadership.

In a significant shift for the Usual Channels, in 1995, the House agreed to a Committee on Standards and Privileges, with an expanded remit to consider matters relating to MPs' conduct. This came in conjunction with the creation of a Parliamentary Commissioner for Standards. 'Before, all that kind of housekeeping was done by the whips,' says one.

Steve Norris, alleged to have had five mistresses, was almost unique among government ministers in getting caught up in the back-to-basics saga and yet keeping his job. 'A whole lot of it wasn't true,' he says of the reporting. 'It enhanced my reputation as a swordsman. However, sadly, as all the people involved would happily tell you, [the reputation was] wildly misguided!' John Major helped to neutralise the story by saying Norris and his wife's separation was well-known and that his private life was his own business. 'The whips were [also] nothing but supportive,' Norris says.

The whips were indeed accommodating of most things. That is, unless your partner was about to give birth.

* * *

David Lidington's wife was in labour at Stoke Mandeville Hospital in March 1995. With the whip removed from eight rebel Eurosceptics and one sympathiser following suit, as well as four by-elections going against the Conservatives in just under three years, the Tories' majority had fallen to single digits. Lidington, who was with his wife in hospital, was due to serve on a bill committee monitored by government whip Liam Fox the next day.

Overnight, a midwife came in every ninety minutes or so to say: 'Oh, Mr Lidington, the government whips' office is on the phone.' Each time Fox asked for an update, his voice was 'slightly more slurred' and the background music was 'slightly louder', Lidington jokes.

The whips had already exploited Fox's career as a GP in getting his assessment of the health of elderly, sick MPs, whose possible deaths could trigger by-elections. 'I used to be despatched to see people with my medical hat on,' Fox says.

The government's diminishing majority now placed greater pressure on whips. Bill committees reflected the composition of the Commons, meaning attendance by Tory MPs was essential.

'Well, we really do need you tomorrow. Can you be there by ten o'clock?' Fox asked.

'I don't know when this baby is going to be born yet,' Lidington replied, to which Dr Fox enquired: 'Well, what's the dilation?'

Later in the evening, Lidington had to say: 'I'm very sorry, Liam, but the government could bloody well fall tomorrow. I'm not leaving until this baby's born.'

The Lidingtons' baby arrived at 8.30 a.m. The phone rang again not long after.

'Are you able to come?' asked Fox.

Yes, came the reply.

'OK, there's a vote at midday.'

'Yeah, I can just about make that,' said Lidington.

He went straight to Stoke Mandeville Station, shaved and changed into a suit in a toilet on the train to London. He voted in the midday division, which the government won by one. After the vote, the committee chair, Labour's Gwyneth Dunwoody, offered her congratulations to Lidington – 'or more accurately', she said, 'to his wife'.

* * *

Alastair Goodlad, a veteran of The Office, took over as Chief Whip in the summer of 1995. The move came after he helped marshal John Major's re-election bid as Conservative Party leader, a campaign the Foreign Office Minister ran out of his London home.

In a continuation of his approach in taking on the Eurosceptics, Major had spectacularly resigned and called a 'put up or shut up' contest, amid months of wrangling over Britain's position on the European single currency and speculation over his leadership. Major beat staunch Eurosceptic and ex-Cabinet minister John Redwood – the only challenger – by 218 to 89 votes. He had decided during the campaign that he wanted to make Goodlad, a man of few, but always considered, words, his Chief Whip.

With a new-look team – David Lightbown and Sydney Chapman, now knighted, left that summer after years of service* – Goodlad had

---

* Lightbown died suddenly aged sixty-three while watching the Oxford versus Cambridge varsity rugby match at Twickenham Stadium in December 1995.

quite the in-tray. The Tories' majority hung by a thread, another uncertain by-election was due and the parliamentary party still had their fire turned inwards. He also inherited a whip scandal ready to burst out into the open.

In the same reshuffle that saw Goodlad appointed Chief, David Willetts, a talented newbie known as Two Brains because of his seismic intellect, was promoted to Lord Commissioner. A year earlier, Willetts had written two whips' notes, duplicates of which were discovered by civil servants in Downing Street,* about an ongoing Commons inquiry into the cash-for-questions affair. Former minister Neil Hamilton faced accusations of accepting money and gifts from businessman Mohamed Al Fayed – including stays at the Ritz Hotel in Paris – in return for tabling questions. Following a complaint from an MP, the Members' Interest Committee (MIC) was considering the allegations. In the meantime, Hamilton had lodged a libel claim against the *Guardian* newspaper, which had broken the story.

In his first whips' note, Willetts said the Tory MP chairing the inquiry, Geoffrey Johnson-Smith, wanted advice over the investigation. In the second note, Willetts said they had explored two possibilities: investigating the matters quickly, 'exploiting the good Tory majority' on the committee, or pushing for it to be deferred until after Hamilton's libel claim.

The following June, the MIC concluded that Hamilton was 'imprudent' not to have registered his stay at the Ritz but took no further action. Tory members of the committee had argued that the inquiry couldn't be extended because of the pending libel case.

Before the notes became public, Richard Ryder took legal advice on what he could do now that they had been discovered, amid uncertainty over whether they were state papers or his personal property. '[He] decided he could not go and collect and burn them,' said a whip.[5]

---

* The result of Major requesting to see the whips' notes, a select few of which were sent to Downing Street.

The Guardian subpoenaed the notes and when they reached the public domain in October 1996, they were interpreted as Willetts seeking to influence the result of the inquiry, an accusation both Johnson-Smith and Willetts denied.[6]

The Standards and Privileges Committee investigated the claims against Willetts. While giving evidence, Willetts, who insisted he had not tried to pressurise Johnson-Smith improperly, took a beating from his fellow Conservative, Quentin Davies. A Labour member of the committee says: 'There was obviously old malice, a division between these two men.'

In its report, the committee said MPs were 'very concerned that any member should dissemble in his account ... and believe that [Willetts's] response ... has substantially aggravated the original offence'.[7] Given the strength of the report's conclusions, Willetts resigned from the frontbench, while Tories privately seethed at Davies.

Despite the furore, Goodlad insisted that his whips continue to write notes. 'He needs the information, so does the PM,' wrote Gyles Brandreth, a broadcaster and Tory whip who, unbeknownst to his colleagues, was writing a diary throughout his first parliament as an MP. 'But, sleep easy, boys, from now on the notes will be shredded on a regular basis.'[8]

Within two months of becoming a whip in November 1995, Brandreth had – inadvertently – nearly got a government minister sacked.

In response to a speech by Margaret Thatcher, in which the former Prime Minister lamented a lack of policies for *our people*, Alistair Burt, a Work and Pensions Minister, wrote a furious letter to *The Times*. He sent it on a Saturday, with the paper running it on Monday morning.

The whips, on instruction from Downing Street, had put out a diktat that there would be no comment on Thatcher's speech. Burt's whip, Brandreth, had not passed on the message.

On Monday morning, Goodlad was raging. 'He'll have to go,' he said of Burt. The Chief then turned to Brandreth: 'You spoke to him, didn't you?'

'Yes,' Brandreth answered under pressure, 'he knows he shouldn't have sent the letter. He's full of regrets.'

'Fuck his regrets. Get him over here.'[9]

Burt had spoken with his Secretary of State, Peter Lilley, a great fan of Thatcher, who said no more about it. Then Burt got a call from the Chief Whip.

'Did you write this letter?'

'Yes, I did,' Burt replied.

'Fuck.'

Goodlad put the phone down. Not long after, Burt spoke with his whip. 'I don't want to drop you in it,' he told Brandreth. 'But somehow they have to know I didn't get the message.'

Greg Knight, the calm, steady and astute Deputy Chief Whip, arrived in the lower whips' office. 'Now tell me the truth,' he said to Brandreth. 'It's just between us. No one else will ever know. You didn't speak to him, did you?'

'No, I didn't.'

Knight said to always come to him in a situation like this. 'I'll sort it,' he said paternally.[10] Burt and Brandreth both kept their jobs, including at the following year's reshuffle, which moved the Tory whips' office in a new direction.

CHAPTER 30

JACQUI

The Conservative whips' office looked and felt a little different. David Davis, Richard Ryder, Timothy Kirkhope, Robert Hughes and others had left, replaced by the next generation of whips and would-be ministers, including Sebastian Coe and, for the first time in the party's history, a woman.

It was in July 1996 that Major suggested it was about time a woman joined The Office, to which Alastair Goodlad, after discussing it with his whips, agreed. But the real blockage appeared to have been removed a year earlier: a well-placed source reveals that the principal resistance to having a woman in the whips' office had come from none other than David Lightbown. 'He was vehemently opposed,' this person says.

Jacqui Lait, the MP for Hastings and Rye since 1992 and a PPS to rising star William Hague, became the first female Tory whip. 'The warm arm went around my neck,' she says. 'I was obviously delighted, pleased and proud to make that step forward.' However, with an MP godmother and having been involved in a campaign to get more female newsreaders, Lait was used to a degree of trailblazing.

A July thunderstorm corresponded with the day of her appointment. While giving an interview, a 'great thunderbolt' came down nearby. 'This is the whips' office deciding they don't want a woman!' she joked.

Anthony Grant, a long-serving MP, had pledged to take his whips' tie – given to every person who passes through The Office – and burn it in New Palace Yard if the tradition of an all-male whips' office was broken. But he had changed his mind by the time of Lait's appointment. 'Grant, ever the gentleman, presented the tie to her,' wrote his obituarist.[1]

Born in Paisley, Renfrewshire, in 1947, Lait worked in public relations before moving to the Government Information Service and the Department of Employment in 1974. She arrived in Parliament accustomed to late-night finishes from her days in the Privy Council Office in 1978–79, when she worked on Jim Callaghan's bill on a Scottish and Welsh Assembly. 'Night after night after night, I was not getting home until two, three and four in the morning,' she says. As such, when the House sat until the early hours during the turgid Maastricht debates, she didn't think anything of it. 'It was so similar that Maastricht didn't surprise me,' she says. 'For me, that was life, that was part of being an MP.'

By the time Lait joined The Office, flocks were no longer based on regions, with the whips handed MPs from across the map. There was a 'fair amount of "let's see what she's made of"', Lait says of her appointment, 'but in those days, you expected it'.

'Once I was appointed, that was it. I was used to working in a man's world, so I went into the whips' office and just got on with it.'

As the junior whip, Lait took on the role of refreshment officer, which also extended to hot drinks – a job she was happy to pass on when others joined The Office. 'The militaristic aspect had gone,' she says. 'The organisational hierarchy had gone.'

Prior to Lait's arrival, Conservative MP Angela Browning says the whips treated women differently. Though making no fuss of hauling men out of the gents' toilet in the division lobby, whips wouldn't dream of going into a ladies' loo and doing the same, she argues. But other female MPs did face robust treatment. Cheryl Gillan told colleagues that two whips swore at her in the lobby after she missed a vote. She told the whips in no uncertain terms: 'Don't you dare ever speak to me like that again. If you do, that will be in the newspapers!'

Lait, as with the other new joiners, spent most of her year in The Office swimming against a rip tide. By the end of the parliament, Major's notional majority had disappeared, his party destined for a generational electoral drubbing. Two months out from an election, the whips ran a sweepstake on a blackboard in The Office, with most betting on a Labour victory.

On the other side of Members' Lobby, the opposition had been revamping its whips' office, in part attempting to emulate the model long set by the Tories, as the party prepared for government.

CHAPTER 31

LABOUR, ANEW

With his arch-nemesis Michael Cocks assured of a place in the House of Lords, Neil Kinnock looked forward to working alongside Derek Foster as his new Chief Whip, a position that, for the first time, members of the Parliamentary Labour Party had elected.

It was 1985, and Norman Hogg, a Scottish Labour MP and Deputy Chief Whip, had been the clear favourite to become the next Chief. But Foster, Kinnock's choice for the role, had snatched glory, overturning a 24-vote deficit to win on the second ballot 96–95.

Kinnock instructed his whips' office as he had his personal team: nobody keeps a memoir, and tell me bad news straight away. 'The intelligence they collect is absolutely invaluable,' he says of the whips.

With just 209 MPs, there was little the Labour whips could do to bring about much influence beyond stringing out committee sessions and other delaying tactics. Foster branded a group of Labour MPs who would keep the Commons running until late the 'Fighting Forty'.

Not every MP was eager to remain on the parliamentary estate. Tony Lloyd, who joined The Office in 1986, remembers a member of his flock who had a suspicious number of grandmothers die in rapid succession. 'He was forever appealing for time off on the basis of family bereavement.'

Foster, a Salvation Army captain and reformed teetotaller, took a different approach from his forceful predecessor.

'Why did you vote that way?' Foster asked an MP who had rebelled over war widows' pensions.

'Well, I think they ought to get pensions,' the MP replied.

'Oh, fine,' Foster said.

In cahoots with Kinnock, Foster set about adjusting The Office's composition, seeking to replicate the Conservatives' approach of blending young talent with experienced veterans. 'We had a mixture of shop steward convenors, hard cases and promising young backbenchers,' Kinnock says of the whips' office.

In the eyes of some Labour MPs, the Tories were naturally more adroit at the art of whipping. 'I've always subscribed to the idea that the Tory whips are cleverer and better than our whips,' says Barry Sheerman. A future whip says: 'The Tories' operation is generally more sophisticated – at least in my time.' But one MP believes the Conservatives oversee a more sinister enterprise: 'The Tory whipping operation is far more ruthless than the Labour one.'

Dennis Skinner, the veteran and at times vituperative left-winger, had given Paul Boateng advice on how to handle the whips on his first day in the Commons in 1987. 'Whatever you do, never ask the whips for anything.'

Alan Simpson, MP for Nottingham South, says he received blunter guidance from Skinner. 'Don't trust the bastards, because they won't guard your back; they'll be looking to stab it.'

Behind the scenes, however, similar support was being offered to MPs on the verge of bankruptcy. One such MP had run up bills after overvaluing a family heirloom, living a life beyond their means. Senior Labour figures, to prevent the by-election that would follow if the MP was declared bankrupt, tapped up party supporters with deep pockets while also encouraging the reluctant MP to sell some of their more extravagant possessions. Resentful at being made to part ways with precious belongings, the MP rebelled more freely.

As Kinnock set about reforming the wider party, he also tried to instil discipline in Parliament, expelling Labour MPs Dave Nellist and Terry Fields for membership of the insurgent left-wing campaigning group Militant. 'Derek couldn't get through to them, but otherwise he ran a tight ship and, most of the time, a fairly happy ship,' says Kinnock.

Though efforts were made to balance the whips' office between future stars and lifers, not every minister in waiting would take up the opportunity to join. Ian McCartney was one MP who rejected the offer. 'I don't like the culture. I don't like the structure of it,' McCartney explained to Kinnock. McCartney says Kinnock 'called me all sorts' and highlighted that his father Hugh, a former Labour MP, had served in the whips' office. 'Well, that's my dad. He loved it, but I'm not my dad, and I see it differently from how he sees it.' It wouldn't be the last time McCartney faced down his party leader.

Number one on the list at Prime Minister's Questions, McCartney headed to the leader's parliamentary office on request by Kinnock's team, who wanted to give him a probe to ask Margaret Thatcher.

'Well, I've got a question,' McCartney said.

When Kinnock said he wanted to ask about the debate over passports for Hongkongers, McCartney said: 'Well, if it's such a good question, you ask it.'

Foster and another whip caught him up after the meeting and said: 'You're finished, doing that. You're on your own.' McCartney's question about a Tory MP and their activities as a private landlord led the news.

McCartney may well have followed his dad into The Office, had his first experience with whips not put him on high alert.

* * *

'You're Hugh McCartney's son, aren't you?'

A Labour whip sized up the MP for Makerfield, who had entered The Office on his first day in Parliament after the 1987 general election to see about securing a workspace.

'Yeah,' Ian McCartney confirmed.

'You'll never get an office off me then,' the whip, who had worked alongside his father in The Office, said.

McCartney frowned. 'What do you mean?'

'I'm just telling you, you're not getting an office,' the whip repeated. 'You can work in a corridor as far as I'm concerned.'

McCartney, who secured a desk after two Scottish Labour MPs intervened on his behalf, had just encountered Ray Powell, the MP for Ogmore and Labour's Pairing and Accommodation Whip. First elected in 1979, Powell, a former shop manager, elicited admiration from his fellow whips (albeit not McCartney's father, with whom he clearly did not get on) and invective from MPs outside his inner circle.

'[He] should have been the head of MI5,' says Neil Kinnock of his fellow Welshman. 'What this guy couldn't find out – God knows how he did it, but he knew everything about everybody and was encyclopaedic.' He adds: 'Very few people liked Ray because he was straight off the musical stage. He told great jokes and was very hail-fellow, but all the time, you knew he was carrying a dagger, which is a great mix as far as I was concerned.'

His cheerleaders highlight Powell's contribution to Parliament. He played a key role in the development of a building due to open at the turn of the century, which would transform the working lives of MPs and their staff, creating a slew of new offices. For eight years, he refused to take the salary he was entitled to as Pairing Whip, a position thought inappropriate to put up for election by the PLP, and therefore, for some, not a position that should be remunerated. 'Over the years, he must have been £100,000 out of pocket,' said a colleague.[1]

What's for certain is that you needed to win Powell over if you wanted an office or to secure time off. '[He] was generous and understanding, yet firm in handling often difficult situations,' said the colleague above.[2]

It was this exploitation of power that drew in Powell's enemies. Ken Livingstone, a well-known left-wing Labour politician who had served as the leader of the Greater London Council, joined the Commons in

1987. He had to wait a year before receiving an office, with Powell, seeking to put him in his place, saying curtly: 'You're not on my list.'

'You got a better room if you were a regular attendee and did what he told you,' says George Foulkes.

Alan Simpson was already good friends with left-winger Jeremy Corbyn, the MP for Islington North, when he joined Parliament in 1992. 'Why don't you just move into my office?' Corbyn proposed, as the MP he shared with, Bob Clay, had stood down. Simpson inspected the office and thought it looked great. He then designed an 'easy wheeze' to win over Powell, writing a letter along the lines of:

> Dear Ray,
>
> I'm a new member of the Parliamentary Labour Party, and I thought it would be useful to know something about me as you look to try and find appropriate accommodation. Basically, I'm a good-natured, non-smoking, vegetarian socialist from Nottingham, which, as you know, is outside London. If you can find anyone who is willing to share with such a being, then that would be great.
>
> Best wishes,
> Alan Simpson

Simpson submitted a letter and gave a copy to Corbyn, who then wrote to Powell:

> Hello Ray,
>
> I know you're juggling with accommodation. I've got a space in my room, and I'm happy to share. Can I just give you some pointers as to what would work well? Essentially, I'd like to share with a good-natured, non-smoking, vegetarian socialist from anywhere outside of London. If you come across anyone, then that would be great.

Later that day, Simpson bumped into Powell, who said: 'Why don't you go and have a quick word with Jeremy Corbyn? He's in Norman Shaw North. You might find that would be useful.'

'Oh, fantastic, Ray. That's brilliant,' Simpson said, who went back and told Corbyn: 'Jeremy, it's all worked out!'

With many of the offices already assigned, MPs who joined midway through the parliament had an even harder time getting hold of a desk. Margaret Hodge had to run in heels from her building near the Department for Education to make it to Parliament in time for votes. A colleague advised that she send flowers to Powell. Hodge did just that, and 'immediately got my room'. She smiles, telling this story, and asks rhetorically: 'Outrageous, isn't it?'

Helen Liddell, the former BBC journalist who had watched ambulances bring in sick MPs to vote during the 1974–79 parliament, wasn't given an office 'for a very long time' after joining in 1994. A former general secretary of the Scottish Labour Party, with a successful background in business, Liddell felt 'some of the whips wanted to put me in my place'.

Hers had been a poignant by-election. John Smith, who had taken over from Neil Kinnock as Labour leader in 1992, died suddenly of a heart attack in May 1994. Liddell, a good friend of Smith's, had grown up in his constituency of Monklands East. Before his death, she had been adamant that she wouldn't run for Parliament, based on what she had seen from the Press Gallery nearly two decades earlier.

At Smith's funeral, she listened to two Labour politicians who hadn't interacted for almost twenty years, after one of them ran off with the other's wife. 'Donald Dewar and Derry Irvine,' she says. 'Both talked about public service.'

As Liddell left the church, her husband said to her: 'You don't have an alternative. You have to do it.'

When Liddell first entered Parliament, with no office assigned to her, she found herself carrying out constituency casework in nooks and crannies across the estate. Top of the pile was the case of a doctor murdered by a patient in his consulting room. A whip heard her discussing this on the phone and barked: 'Get to your office!'

'I haven't got an office!' she said.

The whip then went up to Powell and demanded she be given a workspace. Liddell was duly assigned an office near Westminster Abbey. Conservative MPs would accompany her to vote in the middle of the night so that she wasn't on her own in the dark.

Powell's handling of accommodation did ruffle feathers. But many MPs' fundamental objections to his conduct stemmed from his behaviour during internal Labour elections.

* * *

Ray Powell approached a Labour MP in the Members' tearoom and asked if he could have his votes for the upcoming shadow Cabinet elections.

The MP told Powell, with whom he got on well: 'No, I'm going to make my own decisions.'

'Yes, but, you know, it will help you later on,' Powell said.

'How?'

'Well, if you need some time off or anything.'

The MP, who declined the offer, says today: 'I know for a fact that a number of MPs would hand over their vote to Ray, and Ray would, in effect, run a proxy vote for the shadow Cabinet.'

Ian McCartney had a similar experience in the Commons tearoom with Don Dixon, who took over from Norman Hogg as Deputy Chief Whip in 1987. 'The vote for the shadow Cabinet, son. As a new Member, here's the list to vote for,' Dixon said.

'I may actually vote for these people, but you can't just tell me to mark my ballot paper like this. That's just not on; I'm not prepared to do it,' McCartney said.

For decades the Parliamentary Labour Party had elected the shadow Cabinet. Though in theory empowering MPs, it also led to fierce factional lobbying by the different subsets within the PLP, all pushing for their top brass to get into the leader's team while in opposition.

Consenting to whips' advances would pay dividends. 'If you voted for the appropriate slate, then you'd be going on the delegation,' says Tony Lloyd.

For one MP, the proxy voting helped explain the 'annual miracle' of a particular person's election to the shadow Cabinet – a friend of Powell's whose success they otherwise couldn't explain. The same backbencher says that a teller for the shadow Cabinet elections had discovered that Powell would open the ballot papers the night before to check which of his 'mates' hadn't received enough support and would draw on a store of proxy votes to make up the difference. Powell, who passed away in 2001, always denied such allegations.

For the likes of Powell and Dixon, intervening in shadow Cabinet elections might have helped facilitate a more cohesive team. 'The view of Derek and Ray was that their job was to support the leader and the leader should have, in his shadow Cabinet, who he wanted,' says the MP who declined to give Powell his votes.

But others say they looked out primarily for their own. There is no suggestion that Kinnock or John Smith knew of or endorsed the whips' behaviour.

The lack of transparency extended to whips' committee appointments and overseas trips. 'There was a structure there which was neither open nor fair,' says McCartney, adding: 'Quite a lot of people with talent, if they weren't on the inside, wouldn't be chosen.'

Paddy Tipping, MP for Sherwood, was on the reserve list for an all-party trip to Russia when he received a call saying someone had dropped out. 'Would you like to go?' the person organising the trip asked, which Tipping, a Russian speaker, confirmed, 'but the whips jumped up and down and put somebody else in', he says. 'I was pretty pissed off. I had a row with [Powell] about it.'

When Tony Blair, a member of the shadow Cabinet first elected in 1983, took over from John Smith as leader of the Labour Party, his eleven years in Parliament made him certain that the whips' office needed reforming. 'Blair had a view that the office was not properly managed, wanted [Foster] gone and wanted somebody else to run the whips' office,' says an MP. 'I know Blair's view was that it was run in a way in which it shouldn't be – that it was dodgy.'

Foster quit as Chief Whip in July 1995. 'Derek's dedication to his duties, and rectitude, made him a formidable opponent for whom I retained the highest admiration,' wrote Richard Ryder, his opposite number, years later.[3] Ray Powell and Don Dixon followed soon after.

* * *

For all the allegations of corruption, the Labour whips, by the time Tony Blair took power, had overseen a tight, disciplined regime that bore considerable fruit during the Maastricht debates.

Geoff Hoon, a lawyer who had helped construct Labour's resistance on Maastricht, was one of a handful of potential ministers Tony Blair put in the whips' office on becoming leader, along with Estelle Morris and Peter Mandelson. Other whips were wary of the new arrivals, particularly Mandelson, the party's former director of communications, a familiar name to members of the press, unlike many who had worked in the whips' office.

'Those who were there before, understandably, resented the idea that we were being parachuted in without any knowledge or experience and we weren't even going to stay for long,' says Hoon.

Blair's attempts to blood would-be ministers by giving them whipping experience went out the window quickly. Impatient about the frontbench, he promoted people straight into shadow portfolios, bypassing the whips' office. One change to The Office introduced under Blair that did endure was to appoint more women. Estelle Morris was joined by Janet Anderson, Ann Coffey, Jane Kennedy, Angela Eagle and Bridget Prentice during his first parliament as leader.

Elected in 1992, Prentice turned up at the Members' entrance to Parliament with Tessa Jowell, another new joiner, and had to persuade the guarding police officer that 'yes, we really were Members of Parliament'. In the absence of formal training, Prentice instigated hourly meetings on a Wednesday morning for people to give talks to the new intake, a practice that, while welcomed by colleagues, was not well received by senior whips.

Don Dixon approached Morris and Prentice outside the tearoom. 'You'd be better off fighting the Tories than fighting the whips' office,' he said.

The 'HR' aspect of the Labour whips' office was only 'beginning to happen', Prentice says. 'Even in those days, the whips' office was seen as more dark arts than HR, really.'

With Blair's consent, Prentice worked with Labour's deputy leader John Prescott on reforming shadow Cabinet elections. Afterwards, Prentice received a call from Anji Hunter, a close Blair aide, who asked: 'Could you come and see Tony at quarter to five?'

'Oh, let me just check my diary.'

'Bridget,' Hunter intervened, 'you don't check your diary when the leader asks you to come and see them.'

Blair approached the 1997 election with veteran Donald Dewar as Chief Whip, who was gaining experience that would stand him in good stead when he came to take through the legislation that would finally deliver devolution for Scotland and Wales.

After eighteen years in the wilderness, Labour was on the brink of a landmark victory – one that would all but guarantee the government's business for years to come, but, for the whips, would present a very different kind of headache.

PART V

NEW LABOUR

CHAPTER 32

RUDE AWAKENINGS

Charlotte Atkins thought there would be twenty other Labour MPs in the room.

The MP for Staffordshire Moorlands, one of 418 Labour candidates returned six months earlier in May 1997, found herself alone sitting opposite Gordon Brown. Her whip had arranged for Atkins to meet the Chancellor to discuss plans to cut lone parent child benefit. Brown, who had committed to the Major government's spending limits for the first two years of the parliament, was determined to press ahead despite profound reservations among the party's MPs, especially newcomers like Atkins, with whom the policy didn't sit right.

For the first time since Tony Blair's landslide victory, the Parliamentary Labour Party had started to flex its collective muscle.

* * *

When it comes to whipping and government majorities, it's often said that size matters.

The tighter the majority, the greater the power in MPs' hands, and the more whips have their work cut out to barter, cajole and deliver the votes. The larger the majority, the more administrations can absorb – though not condone – dissent and concentrate on other aspects of party management, albeit they have more stakeholders to please.

But what do you do with a majority of 179? How do you make all 418 MPs feel seen and heard? How do you instil discipline, ensuring the troops get in the habit of voting, often late at night, when you're all but guaranteed to get the business with huge margins of victory? 'It's very difficult to tell individual MPs that their vote will really matter,' observes a Labour whip.

And that's only part of the story. Labour had been out of power for nearly two decades, governing for about a fifth of the twentieth century, with the Conservatives staking an audacious, provocative but increasingly evidenced claim for being the 'natural' party of government.

May 1997 presented a coveted opportunity for Labour to turn the tide and a near unprecedented capacity to deliver its business. In the lead-up to the election, Tony Blair had placed emphasis on discipline, with an urgency to put aside the ideological divides that had plagued the previous Labour government and its interim years. His rebranding of the party and accompanying policy positions had nevertheless raised eyebrows in the PLP, incurring rebellions, partially mollified by the Tories' self-implosion on the other side of the aisle.

The party's broad church, a by-product of Britain's first-past-the-post voting system, is formed of an uneasy coalition of people and views that don't always align or cohabit peacefully. Internecine rivalries and hostilities between constituency neighbours, Cabinet ministers, ideological allies and foes are also not uncommon insofar as the Labour benches are concerned, though few political parties are spared that reality.

'In many ways, it was easier to form a relationship with local Tories,' says a Labour MP. 'With your colleagues, it was almost, "Who's going to get up the totem pole quicker?"'

A Tory whip says: 'The glue that seemed to hold the Labour Party together was mutual hatred and who was up and who was down in terms of the stakes of hatedness.'

The Labour Party, however, is also a deeply tribal political force, with fierce alliances born of its collectivist nature, their mutual disdain for the Tories and its *raison d'être*. Conservatives, as demonstrated during the Maastricht debates, arguably feel more comfortable entering a division lobby with Labour MPs than the other way around; one notorious Labour dissident says they shelved a rebellion after a whip highlighted that the vote was on a Tory motion.

Labour devotees also believe they face larger hurdles than the Conservatives, including a hostile media ecosystem that predominantly leans right. For some Labour MPs, creating more barriers through dissent – and thus risking further Tory rule – is an act beyond the pale, while others view sacrificing long-held ideals to win an election – aping or conceding to aspects of the Conservatives' policy platform in the process – as similarly distasteful.

For all their pretentions otherwise, Labour MPs can save their most vehement criticism for rival factions, with whom they're often battling for influence, frequently accusing each other of betrayal or treachery.

The Labour whips needed to maintain the party's eminently penetrable united front, making dissent the preserve of a few hard-line intractable MPs for whom there was no hope, while facilitating two-way communication. That was the challenge awaiting The Office after 1 May 1997, led by Chief Whip Nick Brown and his Deputies George Mudie and Tommy McAvoy.

It was a task made only more difficult by refusing to reinstate informal pairing between MPs from rival parties. The casual approach, whereby two MPs agreed their attendance for the week ahead before running it by the whips, ceased under New Labour, save for the few who cheekily kept their back channels open. 'We ended up never going back to it because it was so essentially unfair,' explains a senior Labour whip, with pairing 'biased' towards MPs with larger majorities.

The system had collapsed six months before the election, in December 1996, after Conservative Party Pairing Whip Derek Conway offset three Tories with the same number of Labour MPs and Liberal Democrats simultaneously, helping to win a tight vote on fisheries. Donald Dewar and Nick Brown stayed in the opposition whips' office until the early hours trying to work out how they'd just fallen short. 'It was double counting,' says Brown.

Conway, for his part, stressed it was an 'innocent mistake'.[1]

Labour held a press conference the next day, with only one 'very aggressive journalist' from *The Spectator* by the name of Boris Johnson pushing back on their conclusions. 'Surely it's your responsibility to check?' he asked.

After the May election, there was also a practical reason for refusing to bring back informal pairing; there simply weren't enough opposition MPs to go around. Labour whips continued to offset some absentees, considered dispassionately by the party's hard-nosed Pairing Whip McAvoy, with Brown also watching requests 'like a hawk'. On a given night, the whips offered between fifteen and twenty pairs, allowing the opposition Chief an extra number they could let off, to be used at their discretion.

Despite this gesture, the government whips also played the odd trick, offering pairs to individual Tories ahead of big sporting events. 'You'd always catch a few like that,' Brown says.

For all the whips' best intentions, the new reality had its limitations. On the first night of voting, after seeing one large queue, some new MPs went to the smaller line and ended up in the rebel division lobby by mistake. 'The doorkeeper came in and said, "You've got to stop this!"' says Helen Liddell.

In homage to the party's Pairing Whip, The Office then curated a system of 'McAvoy days' – later moving to the 'McAvoy week' – where MPs were given time away from Parliament. A Labour MP handed a 'McAvoy week' suggests the whips had done so strategically. Brown confirms that The Office brigaded up the government's most controversial legislation and gave the most likely disrupters a week off. 'The bastards cottoned on, took the week off, but all came in to rebel on the designated day!'

At the start of the parliament, Brown and Mudie, along with Kieran Simpson, one of two special advisers in The Office, worked through the night allocating Labour MPs to select committees, ensuring those placed on 'unpopular' ones were compensated. The three men, as well as ensuring good regional and equality representation, also pushed for a committee chair to have at least one member of the left-wing Socialist Campaign Group of MPs on their team. Brown recalls George Robertson, the Secretary of State for Defence, 'flying at me' after he put a member of the Socialist Campaign Group on the defence committee. '"But he'll find out secrets! He'll bring the government down, betray us to the Russians", or whoever he thought they would betray us to,' Brown says of Robertson's misgivings.

The whips, the Chief says, gave MPs advice on how the House worked and how to make speeches. They were also told that if they had any problems, they should come and see them. 'The one thing they were not was shouted at or brutalised,' he says.

Whips like to instil good habits early, getting politicians used to the rhythms and requirements of parliamentary life, from attendance and punctuality to discipline. Though the Blair government enjoyed the party's largest ever majority, nothing lasts for ever, and within another election or two, the surplus could reduce considerably, at which point MPs would need to be well-marshalled and finely tuned. And so, the whips opted not to treat the 1997 intake any differently, despite the exceptional circumstances of the landslide election victory, delivering instructions in a straightforward and firm manner.

'There was a sense, particularly from newer whips, that they had to drill you, get you into the mode, and it wasn't a great way of dealing with people in my view,' says a Labour MP and later whip.

Whips' abrupt nature, shown across the two main parties, can be the rude awakening to politics as it really is versus how you might want it to be, leaving MPs feeling akin to lobby fodder as opposed to individuals with something to contribute. An extension of Westminster's idiosyncratic ways of working, the whips' office provides the cold shower that washes away romantic notions of what it is to be an MP with the at times bracing reality. What's more, such was Labour's success in May 1997 that some candidates hadn't expected to become MPs and thus weren't as up to speed nor as ready for brusque treatment.

The new intake, which looked different to any that had come before, was nevertheless eager to please. 'We were the keenies, but we were also the ones who were asked to do those late shifts,' says Mike Foster, MP for Worcester.

But the whips' rigidity accumulated several incidents where MPs were refused time off in hours of need, which, while no different to many other parliaments, stand out considering the government's majority. One Labour MP recalls a colleague asking to go home because their mother was very ill. The whips said no, and the MP encouraged her to go home anyway. 'She wouldn't because a sense of doing the right thing was ingrained,' they explain. 'As it happened, her mother pulled through, but she could have died.'

Margaret Hodge recalls the whips rejecting a request for a colleague to attend her child's third birthday party. 'That's shite. It just is. I've never had any patience for that.'

Huw Edwards, a Labour MP and chair of the Welsh Labour group, was told he couldn't attend the funeral of his 'dear colleague', former Cabinet minister Cledwyn Hughes, who passed away in 2001. 'You're not going, [Secretary of State for Wales] Paul Murphy is going,' his whip told him.

Stroud MP David Drew had been slipped to attend a meeting of the North Devon Labour Party at Ilfracombe Theatre – on the condition that he stuck around in Westminster until mid-afternoon before taking on the multi-hour journey. At 3.30 p.m., he received a message saying: 'The slip has been withdrawn. We've got a tight vote tonight.'

Drew rang the organiser, who barked: 'But we've booked the place! We've got people coming from all over Devon to listen to you!'

Somehow, the organiser tracked down John Prescott's number and demanded of the Deputy Prime Minister: 'What the hell is going on? Why is he not allowed to come?'

Drew says the government won the vote with a majority over 100. Prescott then had to make a trip to the south-west to make up for it.

Jacqui Smith, MP for Redditch, went to see Brown after getting pregnant in the early autumn of 1997. 'He looked at me as if he had no idea at all what [the implications were],' Smith says. Giving birth the following June in time for the summer recess, Smith was able to take three to four months of leave before returning to Parliament.

Drew says his regional whip gave Tess Kingham, the MP for Gloucester, who stood down after one term, 'a hard time'. 'She had a young child, got pregnant and had twins. It was a bit of a nightmare time for her,' Drew explains. 'For a young mother, she didn't get an awful lot of licence, even though we had this huge majority.'

Other Labour MPs had more positive experiences. Whips granted Julie Morgan time away, especially on Monday evenings, to care for her mother. 'If you had particular circumstances that they knew about, they would be generous.' Mike Gapes was shown similar treatment. One summer, after a member of Gapes's family became ill, his whip Tony McNulty told him: 'Take as long as you need. We'll see you in October.'

* * *

The 1997 election saw a record 120 women enter the House of Commons – though only nineteen represented opposition parties.

On the morning of Friday 2 May, many of the 101 female Labour MPs, sixty-five of whom were elected for the first time in 1997, gathered for a photocall on the steps of Church House in Westminster, pictured alongside the new Prime Minister.* The *Daily Mail* headlined the image 'Blair's Babes', a portent for the treatment of female MPs to come.

'I was always being told by the Tory men that it was nice to have a better class of totty around,' said Labour MP Claire Curtis-Thomas.[2] 'The Tory benches shouted things across the chamber at you, about your appearance or your size,' agreed Labour MP Beverley Hughes. Barbara Follett said Tory MPs would cup imaginary pairs of breasts. 'Even on our side, the men would stick their hands out so you'd sit on them,' she said.[3]

Labour whip Bridget Prentice collected clips of Tory MPs' remarks and headed to the opposition whips' office. 'If this isn't fixed within twenty-four hours, this is going to the media,' she said.

Newly elected female MPs were also targeted for their apparently unwavering support of the government line, likened to robots by opponents, peers and the press. Labour's Brian Sedgemore even compared his colleagues to the Stepford Wives after just one new female MP followed through on their misgivings and voted against a controversial cut to lone parent child benefit.

In July 1997, the Labour government said it was pushing ahead with plans to reform lone parent child benefit, removing the higher single-parent rate of income support and child benefit for future claimants, as part of Tony Blair's 'New Deal' for the welfare system.

Audrey Wise, a left-wing fixture during the Callaghan government twenty years earlier, put down an Early Day Motion opposing the measure, signed by fifty-five Labour backbenchers and more than eighty MPs overall. 'By that time, I was beyond the pale, and they knew that they couldn't change my mind,' says Lynne Jones, who worked with Wise on the rebellion.

The proposals, overseen by Social Security Secretary Harriet Harman,

---

* Labour introduced all-women shortlists ahead of the 1997 election in 50 per cent of the party's winnable seats.

drew the ire not only of left-wing MPs but also of newbies who felt the policy at odds with what they had come into politics to do. 'I remember thinking, this is really not right,' says Charlotte Atkins, who passed on her views to her whip.

Atkins's father Ron had served as a Labour MP, including during the 1974–79 parliament. Rather than being pinned up against a wall, he liked the whips' approach of 'Come on, Ronnie, let's go and have a coffee.' Such tactics also worked on his daughter. After meeting with Gordon Brown to discuss the changes, she says, 'Ultimately, I ended up voting with the government.'

Understanding the strength of feeling, whips sought to assure MPs that the issue would be dealt with down the line. 'Just vote for it now. I promise it will be sorted,' Deputy Chief George Mudie told waverers.

Alan Simpson says he received 'one of the best bollockings I've ever had' from Nick Brown, who, in a one-on-one meeting, explained the government line and asked if he would review his position. Simpson listened, set out his opposition and confirmed he would vote against.

'Right. I just want you to know that's a disciplinary offence,' the Chief Whip said.

'OK, that's fair enough,' Simpson said.

Simpson says that Brown paused before continuing: 'If I can add to that, and just off the record, I completely understand your position. My mum was a lone parent. I'm not sure I know how she or we would have managed without those benefits. So, at a personal level, I can completely understand the position you take up. As the Chief Whip, I'm telling you it's not the acceptable position, even if it may have been the position I find myself in too.'

Jacqui Smith also had reservations, but she didn't receive much contact from the whips, from whom she would have appreciated guidance and an explanation. 'It didn't feel as if there was much reaching out to people who weren't a problem,' she says.

Forty-seven Labour MPs voted for an amendment to the Social Security Bill against cutting child benefit for lone parents, including four members of the government, who had to resign. Fourteen MPs elected in 1997 were part of the rebellion, but only one woman, prompting Sedgemore's 'Stepford Wives' comparison. Nick Brown had predicted the vote by one. 'We were right on top of it, we knew what we were doing,' he says of the whipping operation.

As with around twenty other Labour MPs, Bill Rammell, elected in 1997, abstained. His whip warned him not to be surprised if preferment was delayed as a result. Rammell did receive preferment in 2002, briefly joining the whips' office for a two-week spell before becoming a minister. He believes his abstention might have delayed his promotion by twelve months.

MPs noticed that some of those who toed the line would soon receive a job. A future whip says: 'Some of us thought the Parliamentary Labour Party would be discussions about policy, whereas, in fact, certainly for a lot of the Blair years, it was an exercise in sycophancy as much as anything else.'

The same person says her preferment was delayed by bad relations with her regional whip, who took issue with her and another colleague for having previously blocked their candidate from running in a neighbouring parliamentary constituency. 'You don't realise at first that there are people who are basically feeding in poison about you,' the MP says.

Paddy Tipping, the representative for Sherwood from 1992 to 2010, had ongoing difficulties with his regional whip, a fellow East Midlands MP. Tipping says that during a debate on coal privatisation he wasn't chosen to speak, despite representing a constituency that 'had more collieries than anywhere else in the country'. He claims this was a result of his whip asking the Speaker not to select him. Though Tipping ended up on the committee considering the bill, his relationship with his whip was always 'a bit uncomfortable', which he believes held back his career.

A similar pattern to the lone parent vote emerged over a rebellion on plans to cut disabled benefit entitlements, with 'staunch opponents' talked round after 'heavy-handed' treatment from the whips, says Lynne Jones, who notes that one MP in particular 'completely changed'. 'She voted with the whip all the time; she never had a rebellious thought in her life after that.'

The whips warned Tess Kingham, who voted against the cuts, that resources could be withdrawn from her constituency and her political career finished if she continued to cause trouble, a *Guardian* columnist reported. After she complained to her local paper, 'the whips threatened to expose her private life in the tabloids', the columnist claimed.[4]

Though the government saw off the lone parent benefit amendment, the scale of the discontent reported to them by the whips caught the party leadership on the back foot. 'I was learning that the very discipline I thought necessary in opposition was every bit as critical, if not more so, in government; and that meant a constant interaction with the political troops,' reflected Blair.[5]

Female Labour MPs elected in 1997 argue that their conformity in the division lobbies masked the successful petitioning taking place behind the scenes. In March 1998, the Chancellor increased child benefit by £2.50 a week above inflation, with the government also producing legislation on maternity pay, childcare and part-time workers' rights. 'Perhaps, as a cohort, we should have made it clearer what we were doing policy-wise,' said one.[6]

From MPs wearing an opera hat to make a point of order through to Parliament's arcane working hours, the class of 1997 also cast fresh light on the Commons' outdated, eccentric and exclusionary ways of working, giving impetus to planned reforms that, for the whips, would have widespread consequences.

'When women started coming in, they said, "Why the fucking hell would you be voting every night at ten o'clock? Why would you have these rules, and why are you drinking so much?"' says a Labour veteran. 'The House of Commons was transformed by one thing: women.'

CHAPTER 33

A NEW DAWN

At the start of the 1997 parliament, the House nominally sat from 2.30 p.m. to 10 p.m. on Mondays to Thursdays,* but thanks to filibustering by eager Conservative MPs, the Commons could still finish well beyond midnight.

As Deputy Leader of the Commons, Paddy Tipping regularly had to oversee the adjournment debate. 'I got really pissed off with people like [Tory MPs] John Bercow and David Davis who would turn up and use it as a bit of a lark to keep us there for hours and hours,' he says.

One Labour whip woke up at 3 a.m. in the Commons Library to see the screen denoting what was taking place in the chamber had gone blank. 'I thought they'd all gone home and not told me,' the whip says. He went into the chamber to find that the lights were off, but the debate was still going, with the whip on bench duty forgetting to oppose an MP's mischievous proposal for the House to sit in private, meaning proceedings were no longer televised or public. 'The Deputy Speaker in the chair had no idea how to reassert order.'

Ian McCartney, a former filibusterer himself, could understand Tory MPs' motivations in seeking to disrupt his bill to introduce a national minimum wage, which he had nurtured since opposition. 'After a week or two, we were still on clause 1, almost line 1 [of the bill],' he says. To counter the Conservatives' delaying tactics, he asked for the whips' support in taking through the entire bill in an all-night sitting. The Office

---

* The House, as it does today, also sat on Wednesday mornings.

approved. 'It meant that the following day's proceedings were cancelled,' remembers Mike Foster, who proudly stayed up as one day entered another to vote for the landmark legislation. 'We willingly did it.'

Helen Liddell oversaw the passage of the Finance Bill on her twenty-fifth wedding anniversary. The Deputy Speaker called a break at five to midnight so that the Treasury Minister's team could buy her a glass of champagne.

While all-night sittings were the bane of many MPs' existence, they nonetheless offered the whips crucial access to and oversight of their flock. Some backbenchers who had reservations about aspects of government policy would find whips or the relevant ministers appearing beside them unannounced in the Commons Library or at a cafeteria to discuss their concerns.

But senior Labour Party figures had long been of the view that Parliament's ways of working desperately needed reforming – an opinion amplified by the 240 new MPs, many of whom had worked in modern environments unlike anything resembling the House of Commons, with one member of the 1997 intake describing filibustering and other delaying measures as 'willy-jousting'.[1]

Labour had in its manifesto pledged to create a committee to consider modernising the Commons' practices and procedures, including reforms to sitting hours. A memorandum to the aptly named Modernisation Committee from Ann Taylor, Leader of the House, indicated ministers' support for ending business on Thursdays at 7 p.m., allowing MPs to devote a full day's work to their constituency. The change was trialled for the last two years of the parliament, with Margaret Beckett now acting as Commons Leader.

The Modernisation Committee also recommended introducing programme motions for government bills, which set out the time allowed for debate at each of its stages. Before its first use in 1998, the Commons could only timetable bills through two means: the controversial guillotine motion or discussions in the Usual Channels. By the end of the parliament, most government bills were subject to programme orders, which were agreed by the Commons after a legislation's second reading. 'If John Major had the power to programme bills, Maastricht would have flown through,' comments a Tory adviser.

Tipping, as Beckett's deputy, regularly attended meetings with whips as fellow business managers. He was struck by the whips identifying some of his colleagues as 'troublemakers' when he made recommendations to fill spaces on committees, which 'would be blocked because these guys hadn't toed the line or had gone a bit too far', he explains.

In a similar incident, Home Affairs Committee chair Chris Mullin tried to recruit Labour MP Bob Marshall-Andrews – 'a bit of a serial dissident', he says – before Nick Brown intervened. 'That's not possible. He has been vetoed at the *highest* level,' the Chief Whip said, according to Mullin, who observes: 'The government is supposed to account to select committees, and yet the government was appointing them.'

Nick Brown, who, like Blair and Gordon Brown, joined the Commons in 1983, had previously been close to both figures but had migrated more towards the Chancellor. Nonetheless, he saw Blair every Monday, showing 'where we were', including a table outlining MPs' 'activity rate', such as the number of interventions they'd made in the chamber. The whips were producing a 'quality product', he says, but it was 'also true that I supported Gordon'. As the relationship between Blair and Brown soured, the Chief Whip was keen on 'discouraging' attacks against the Chancellor.

In July 1998, Nick Brown was moved to the Agriculture Department, with No. 10 believing the Chief Whip had been working primarily for the Chancellor. 'Tony realised that he was Gordon's man, not Tony's,' says a Cabinet minister, with the Prime Minister and Chancellor's relationship on a downwards trajectory. Nick Brown believes he was on the receiving end of negative briefing about his intentions or actions. 'I would say I was a victim of it more than having been an architect of my own downfall,' he stresses.

Blair appointed Ann Taylor as Brown's replacement, a veteran of the whips' office under Michael Cocks's and Walter Harrison's tutelage, and the first woman to hold the role. 'She's got terrific fortitude, and she's very honest, very direct – no bullshit zone,' says Neil Kinnock.

After joining the Cabinet as Leader of the House, Taylor said she would never have expected a 'young girl from a council estate in Bolton' to be sat around the table.[2] Viewed as being on the old Labour right, Taylor had been an MP for more than two decades, bar four years without a seat between 1983 and 1987. Opinions on Taylor vary wildly from 'the best Chief we've ever had' to 'hopeless', a charge her successors would also face in failing to push back against the No. 10 line. The first of three female Chief Whips, Taylor helped shift the dial from The Office of old, adding 'compassion' and 'inclusivity' to 'toughness' and 'discipline', says a Labour minister. 'The days of Derek Foster and Ray Powell, they're gone.'

Over the course of Labour's time in government, the whips' office began to deploy female MPs to stand in the corridors near the division lobbies ahead of difficult votes 'to reduce the tension'. 'You could have a situation where it got very heated,' says a female whip. The same whip recalls being in the upper whips' office when an MP squared up to Bob Ainsworth, a long-serving member of The Office and one of a handful of tough, old-school enforcers. 'They were really going at each other,' says the whip. The whip squeezed between the men and said: 'OK, guys, that's enough.'

Taylor would chat to MPs about their aspirations. For example, the Chief encouraged Tipping 'to do a bit more socially' to better ingratiate himself with the PLP. She was also forced to adjudicate on atypical matters.

Deputy Prime Minister John Prescott, serving as Transport Secretary, decided to overturn the Labour Party's opposition to a new road passing through the constituency of a government minister, who had campaigned locally against its mooted creation during the general election. 'You can call me a bastard, you can say whatever you want, you can vote against it. What you're saying is true; we were elected [opposing it], but I've taken a different view,' Prescott told the minister in the tearoom.

'Well, I can't support that,' the minister said.

'I don't want you to resign. You can do what you want.'

Ainsworth, the minister's whip, confronted him after he rebelled in the Commons and asked if he was going to resign. The minister told Ainsworth to speak to Prescott. Taylor then approached the minister for a quiet word. 'John's spoken to me about this. Don't do it too often because it's bad when ministers do this, but he said it's OK,' the Chief Whip said.

Taylor served as Chief Whip until the 2001 election, which saw Labour return with 412 MPs, only six fewer than the party had secured four years earlier, with the Tories upping their number by just one. Her successor was hit with the first of many generational changes to whips' powers and working lives, and a parliament that would define the government's and her party's future.

CHAPTER 34

HILARY

Hilary Armstrong and Tony Blair went way back. They had both run to be the Labour candidate in Sedgefield ahead of the 1983 election. The contest was far from hostile; Armstrong's backers had already agreed to support Blair if she dropped out. Blair did ultimately secure local party members' support, with Armstrong joining the Commons four years later as MP for North West Durham, a seat previously held by her father, Ernest Armstrong, a former whip.

Armstrong worked as PPS to John Smith, a useful exposure to the Parliamentary Labour Party and the fierce rivalries between senior figures, including heavyweights Gordon Brown and Robin Cook. 'You will find that 5 per cent of the PLP causes you 90 per cent of your work,' Armstrong wisely told Bruce Grocott, appointed Blair's PPS when he became leader.

Armstrong had never thought about serving as a whip before the Prime Minister invited her to become Chief in June 2001 – joining Donald Dewar as the second person appointed by Blair to head up The Office without prior whipping experience.

'Tony basically said to me that he knew I was political to my fingertips, and he wanted to change the view of whipping from being authoritarian, bullying, whatever, to political persuasion,' she says. 'He just thought women should be doing it to give a different view.'

Her appointment was part of a wider post-election overhaul, with several whips moved on, replaced by members of the 1997 intake, including future ministers Jim Fitzpatrick, Phil Woolas and Angela

Smith, with Jim Murphy and Charlotte Atkins soon following. The up-and-comers joined longer-serving whips such as Bob Ainsworth, Tony McNulty and Tommy McAvoy.

The whips' office overhaul extended beyond new personnel. To accommodate the scores of staff now working in No. 10, including director of communications Alastair Campbell and his media team, Blair commandeered the whips' prestigious quarters at 12 Downing Street. The move 'indicates that Downing Street is creating a Prime Minister's department in all but name', a senior political journalist said.[1]

The decision to kick the whips out of 12 Downing Street is still seen as indicative of a shift in power away from The Office to close aides, including special advisers, on whose counsel politicians had increasingly begun to rely. 'It was a humiliating state of affairs which immediately sent the message round Whitehall that the Chief Whip no longer counted,' a *Spectator* magazine columnist said of the whips' search for a new home.[2]

Successive leaders, not least Blair, have since faced accusations of drifting from the views of their backbenchers, acting presidential in a non-presidential political system, with the whips' perceived diminution – a charge that still irks veterans of The Office – seen as a potential root cause. 'If Alastair Campbell moves in and replaces the Chief Whip, it just tells you everything about what is going on,' said left-winger Tony Benn.[3] A source who later became a government special adviser in the whips' office says of the optics: 'It was the trumping of comms over Parliament.'

The whips ultimately found a home at 9 Downing Street, formerly the Privy Council building, which hadn't previously been assigned a number and which was accessed through the Cabinet Office at 70 Whitehall. 'It was hardly the Elephant and Castle,' wrote Philip Cowley, an author and expert on New Labour rebellions, in seeking to temper exaggerated analysis of the whips' apparent loss of standing.[4] Some members of The Office say that No. 9, for the whips' purposes, is more functional. Nick Brown comments: 'Hilary got the best deal she could. No one else could have done any better.'

The move, though, was undoubtedly symbolic. While the whips could still access No. 10 by heading back into 70 Whitehall and through an enclosed walkway known as Cockpit Passage – or, should they choose, by heading outside and walking along Downing Street – they were no longer joined directly, further reinforcing the narrative around different groups' standing in Blair's mind, however wide of the mark such conclusions may have been. 'If you were, say, a SpAd in No. 10, you wouldn't bump into the whips any more,' says the later special adviser. 'I think it is overblown, and I don't think it really makes a difference on a day-to-day basis, but it stops some of that more textural stuff from happening.'

The decision might just have come down to practicality. The whips certainly didn't spend all their time at No. 12 – a highly prized bit of real estate on Britain's most famous street – and No. 10 was overcrowded, bloated by the demands of a modern Prime Minister. Up against a 24-hour news cycle, No. 10 has amassed extra foot soldiers with focus on areas such as communications, strategy, polling, policy and parliamentary knowhow. Faced with the option of Campbell or Armstrong being within closer reach, Blair – perhaps understandably, given the nature of the ex-journalist's job – went with the former. Still, it was a move unthinkable to many from previous generations, for whom the whips had always played a central role. 'It would never have happened in my day,' laments former Labour whip Peter Snape.

Blair would likely see criticism of, and extrapolations about, the Downing Street rejig as greatly overstating the point, with the 1997–2001 parliament leaving him with a firm grasp of the whips' contribution. Few who dealt with Armstrong would say the Chief Whip lacked power and influence after the move.

Armstrong attended Cabinet, briefing ministers on the business and state of play. The Chief would then relay Cabinet discussions to her team, on the proviso that everything remained confidential. 'I'll tell you about that, but it can't leak, and if it does, I stop telling you,' she told her whips. Armstrong also instigated a motto: 'UGBIS' – 'Until Government Business Is Secured' – referencing all the tasks that needed completion before the whips had fulfilled their duties.

As one would expect, Blair was in regular contact with Armstrong ahead of contentious votes. She also played a key hand in reshuffles, albeit hers was one of several opinions guiding proceedings: an illustration of the pooling of influence taking place behind the scenes. The Chief was still a voice at the table – but now just one of several.

A whip stresses, however, that the Chief Whip remained enormously powerful. 'If Hilary said to Tony, "He or she's no fucking good," you were toast,' they argue. Equally, the Chief could instruct her team to bring down the Prime Minister. 'Not that we would ever have done that, but the whole narrative about the whips' office is: what power does it have over MPs? And that's so not the point; the power is over the government.'

During reshuffles, Blair would approach Armstrong with ministerial positions that he wanted filled, often based on his upcoming policy priorities. They would factor in any personality clashes and consider who the 'big beasts' – most often Gordon Brown and John Prescott – wanted to protect or promote. Armstrong would send Blair a list of who she thought had been doing well and who might need a promotion. 'That was the big problem for us,' she explains. 'We had such a big PLP, and they all thought they should be on the frontbench.'

As Blair's PPS – requiring him to be up to date with the PLP – Bruce Grocott too would be involved with reshuffles, as would the Cabinet Secretary, the most senior civil servant, who would share Whitehall's insight on how ministers were performing. Opportunistic Labour MPs would approach Grocott and the whips to convey their assessments of their own performance when jobs were in the offing; generous guidance they would largely keep to themselves. In his role, Grocott would also work alongside whips on Prime Minister's Questions, running ideas past MPs on the order paper. 'Some backbenchers will tell you to buzz off, not unreasonably … but a lot would be very happy to take suggestions,' he says.

Blair visited The Office around twice a year, occasionally attending Wednesday morning meetings, Armstrong says. One whip adds that Blair 'hardly ever' popped into The Office. 'He would invite you over for events in No. 10, but not just whips.'

The whips had the Prime Minister regularly meet backbenchers concerned over various aspects of policy. 'I don't think a leader since Tony has [done as many meetings with MPs]. It's not the [narrative], but it's true,' says Armstrong. Grocott says Blair was 'phenomenal' at handwritten notes to MPs during their hours of need. 'It was part of the whips' job and part of my job, of course, to make sure he knew if someone was having a difficult time,' he says.

But one backbencher from the Brownite wing of the PLP says Blair 'didn't mix with his MPs very much'. 'Occasionally, at the beginning, Bruce Grocott would get him into the tearoom, and it was excruciating. You began to hope that he wouldn't sit next to you because you couldn't leave until he left because it would look rude.'

The same critical MP, a potential rebel on the creation of NHS foundation trusts, went to see Blair with fellow backbenchers David Hinchliffe, Des Browne and Health Select Committee chair Frank Dobson. 'Your [local NHS] chief executive supports it,' Blair pointed out to Dobson, his former Health Secretary.

'Yes, he does, and he's a very good chief executive. But I think on this he's wrong,' Dobson replied.

Blair followed up with a phone call to the critical Brownite MP.

'Look, Tony, the problem with it is…' the MP began.

'I don't want to get into the detail,' the Prime Minister said. 'I want your vote.'

Armstrong would ask Cabinet ministers to attend a whips' meeting to explain the contents of legislation due before the House. The Chief would liaise with the Secretary of State about which MPs had an issue with a particular aspect of policy, arranging meetings with the relevant ministers. If enough people still weren't convinced, discussions would turn to any amendments that needed to be put forward by the government to address MPs' concerns.

Grateful ministers would pay tribute to the whips after a close win. 'There would be a tariff in terms of how many bottles of champagne the minister had to deliver to the whips' office,' says Charlotte Atkins, with tighter votes naturally incurring a higher tariff. 'Not that it was particularly good champagne!'

Armstrong was keen for whips to be integrated in government departments, participating in policy as well as political meetings, a task some senior ministers were better at fulfilling than others. Bill Rammell, a Foreign Office Minister, remembers his boss Jack Straw utilising intelligence gathered by the department's whip, Jim Murphy, whom he would turn to at the start of each morning and ask humorously: 'Right, Stasi, latest updates.'

* * *

Though unable to prevent their relocation, the whips resisted other mooted changes to aspects of their work.

At the turn of the millennium, senior backbench MPs suggested taking nominations for select committee membership out of whips' hands.[*] The issue came up again a year later after the whips tried to oust two Labour MPs from their parliamentary roles.

During Hilary Armstrong's first whips' meeting, she informed the team that they were opposing Gwyneth Dunwoody and Donald

---

[*] The Committee of Selection decided membership of select committees, but largely on lists supplied by whips.

Anderson remaining as chairs of the Transport and Foreign Affairs Select Committees respectively.

'Why?' asked a whip, who says the answer was, 'effectively, "Tony wants it".'

The whip told Dunwoody about the plans and said he was sorry it was happening.

'Don't worry,' she said. 'I'll win.'

The committee chairs were reinstated after more than 100 Labour MPs opposed attempts to oust them, given a free vote by Robin Cook, who took over from Margaret Beckett as Leader of the House in 2001. 'A Chief Whip's job is really to tell the Prime Minister and the Cabinet the mood of the party and to explain to the party why certain policies are being followed,' says the whip quoted above. 'Hilary was much more, "Tony says this, so we've got to do it."'

As fellow business managers, Armstrong and Cook met weekly, though their relationship was strained, with the latter's reforming zeal clashing with whips seeking to outline the potential consequences.

'I was always very conscious that he had to feel important,' says Armstrong.

In the aftermath of the Dunwoody–Anderson controversy, the Modernisation Committee proposed reforms to nominations for select committees, which Parliament narrowly rejected, amid claims the whips had faced down Cook's assurance of a free vote by whipping MPs to oppose. On this, The Office had form.

Huw Edwards, MP for Monmouth, was having dinner in central London when a whip with whom he was friendly came up to him ahead of a series of votes on House of Lords reform, including options to maintain the status quo, implement a fully appointed chamber (supported by Blair) or establish a fully or partially elected chamber (backed by Cook).

'Huw, how are you voting on these things?' the whip asked.

'Well, I'll be following Robin.'

'Tony would rather you wouldn't do that.'

'It's a free vote,' Edwards pointed out.

'Tony would rather you did not do that,' the whip repeated.

MPs failed to agree a final stage of reform for the upper chamber, but Cook did succeed in driving through further changes to MPs' hours.

In late 2002, the Modernisation Committee put forward proposals based on a memorandum from Cook for the House to sit from 11.30 a.m. and wrap up by 7 p.m. on Tuesdays and Wednesdays, with a 6 p.m. close on Thursdays. The transformational changes – which survive today bar a few tweaks in subsequent years – came into effect in early 2003, though not everyone, especially the partially neutered opposition and The Office, were happy about it.

'The whips thought this was all barking mad,' says Armstrong of some of the modernisation.

The change in hours did wonders for the London events scene, now full of Labour speakers, but nothing for MPs from constituencies outside London and the south-east still unable to return home, or for whips trying to look out for and monitor their flock, Armstrong argues.

Less than a month after the new hours came into force, a backbench Labour MP came to see Armstrong with a confession. 'I'm a bit worried; I got drunk last night and lost my wallet somewhere around Trafalgar Square and I had to be put in a taxi with some money and I'm sure somebody was snapping with a camera,' the MP told the Chief Whip. Armstrong also cites a female MP from a constituency 200 miles away who used to 'spend her time in tears in the ladies' room' as she 'wasn't with her kids but nor could she say she was working'.

The change in hours came soon after Portcullis House (PCH) opened in 2001, offering up coveted office space and new facilities to long-suffering MPs and their staff. Despite former Labour whip Ray Powell having a key role in the building's creation, Armstrong felt PCH didn't do The Office any favours either, with MPs now scattered across the estate, no longer congregating exclusively in members-only communal areas such as the tearoom or the Commons Library. Eateries and coffee spots in PCH's sunlight-lavished atrium, accessed by all passholders and visitors, including journalists mooching for intel, grew steadily more popular. 'That whole thing about how you talk to people, how you actually keep them as part of the collective, all of that was splintering, and that was a real challenge,' she says.

A senior Conservative whip agrees: 'That meant a lot of MPs would sit with their researchers rather than be in the places where it was members-only, where you could talk to people and identify not necessarily political problems but actually if somebody was lonely.'

Whips got to grips with changes to working hours, premises and their perceived standing while gearing up for one of the most significant parliamentary votes in generations and continuing to ruminate over a long-running sore: what do we do about the serial rebels?

CHAPTER 35

THE 'USUAL SUSPECTS'

OCTOBER 1983

John Prescott gathered Labour MPs to strategise ahead of the committee stage of a bill to take transport responsibility away from the Greater London Council (GLC). The legislation, introduced by Transport Secretary Nicholas Ridley, was a precursor to Margaret Thatcher's move to abolish the GLC altogether.

The year was 1983, and Prescott was serving as the shadow Transport Secretary. In his motley crew were ex-whip Peter Snape and Islington North MP Jeremy Corbyn. 'Me and Snapey will keep it going all night if that's what you want, but you'll have to stay in Parliament,' Prescott said. 'Or the alternative is we'll go and talk to Ridley, see what he's prepared to concede, come back and see if you agree with it.'

Left-winger Corbyn seemed appalled at the idea of negotiating with the Tory Cabinet minister, Snape recalls. 'Jeremy [said]: "Concede? Meet Ridley? An Old Etonian?" and all the rest of it.' Instead, Corbyn declared: 'Fight through the night! That's what we'll do.'

The group arrived at 10.30 a.m. for the first day of the committee. No Corbyn. Three weeks passed; no Corbyn. 'It turns out he was in Grenada because the Americans had just invaded,' Snape explains. Following the no-show, the group nicknamed Corbyn 'Graziani', after the Italian Field Marshal who called for an attack 'and went on leave', Snape says.

Elected in 1983, Corbyn is in prime position on the Mount Rushmore of Labour Party rebels. In the 2001–05 parliament alone, he voted against the whip on 148 occasions,[1] continuing a trend of being the most rebellious Labour MP during the party's time in power from 1997. 'No one could beat Jeremy Corbyn,' says an almost envious backbencher.

Corbyn said he rebelled over three matters: war and peace, issues of liberty and social-economic policy. When an interviewer pointed out that this set of issues encompasses vast swathes of government policy, he laughed and responded: 'I suppose it does.'[2]

The whips wouldn't spend much time trying to convince Corbyn of the arguments, nor was he one to adhere to internal Labour rules around rebellions, including writing a letter to explain the departure from the party line.

'He never did,' says Gerry Sutcliffe, who had Corbyn as part of his London flock.

Sutcliffe would confront Corbyn outside the voting lobby. 'Where's your note? Why didn't you tell me you planned to rebel?'

'Oh, I couldn't find you,' was Corbyn's usual response.

Other leading dissidents, including John McDonnell, second only to Corbyn in rebellions during the 2001–05 parliament, on 135,[3] would often abide by the party whips' expectations in informing them of his plans. 'It wasn't right, but that was fair enough,' says Sutcliffe.

McDonnell's subsequent regional whip wrote to him asking why he couldn't support a government policy. The whip says he received the note back with scribbles on it including: 'The Communist Manifesto, Das Kapital, Karl Marx'.

'It was just a list of his icons and original reading material!' the whip says. 'And just that, titles and names, no explanation.'

David Drew says McDonnell didn't speak to him for a week after he carried out more rebellions than he did. A fellow rebel MP told Drew: 'He's livid.'

Corbyn and McDonnell were leading figures in the Socialist Campaign Group of Labour MPs, which met every Wednesday evening to discuss the upcoming business. Born out of a split in the Labour left over the party's deputy leadership in the early 1980s, members of the

Campaign Group felt this one of the few times when they could properly debate issues. The group would also invite outside experts to talk through bills coming before Parliament.

Joining in 1992, Alan Simpson worked as secretary of the Campaign Group, recording the minutes of each rendezvous; the quality of his note-taking would incur 'bollockings' from veteran Dennis Skinner. Perturbed, Simpson went for tea with his mentor, Tony Benn. 'Am I out of my depth in all this?' Simpson asked. 'I just don't know what it is that I'm getting wrong.'

'You've just got to understand that this is just Dennis letting you know exactly where you stand in the order of things,' Benn explained. 'Once he feels that you know your place, you'll be fine.'

Whips would contact Simpson – the seventh most rebellious Labour MP during the 2001–05 parliament,[4] voting against the Labour whip ninety-six times – to ask how the group planned to vote. 'God knows!' he would reply.

'I wasn't being evasive or awkward when I would say, "I haven't a bloody clue!" People made their own minds up,' he explains.

Lynne Jones, the third most rebellious Labour MP in the 2001–05 parliament,[5] on 103, says of whipping the Campaign Group: 'It would be like herding cats, really.' 'We often had big disagreements,' she continues, including over the European Union. There was general agreement over domestic policy, with minor debates over issues like the potential harm of genetically modified foods. 'In the end, we'd just agree to disagree,' says Jones.

Unlike other members of The Office, the Chief Whip was aware of the splits in the Campaign Group. Armstrong says: 'I worked well with some members ... and they would tell me what was going on. They were never united, so you could always play one faction [off another].'

The Campaign Group met, in part, to understand what MPs were being asked to support. Every Thursday, the Chief Whip announced the upcoming business, accompanied by the formal issuing of the whip, a pink sheet sent out to MPs in an A4 envelope over the weekend. Even so, with MPs' hectic schedules, backbenchers regularly found themselves in the division lobbies without much immediate grasp of the policy at hand. 'Sometimes, if you said to people what is it that we're voting on exactly at this moment, people didn't know, and you could discover that you'd actually voted for something that was quite iffy,' says Simpson.

Diane Abbott, MP for Hackney North and Stoke Newington, was another Campaign Group fixture and thirteenth most rebellious Labour backbencher of the 2001–05 parliament.[6] 'You couldn't get Diane to do anything she didn't want to do,' says one of her whips. Another says: 'Diane Abbott was hard-nosed, snobby and basically very difficult to talk to.'

Efforts were made to utilise her talents. A recently appointed minister had a chat with Abbott, with whom they had served on a select committee. 'Look, you're bright. Is it your ambition to be a minister or whatever, because a lot of people are very suspicious of you?' the minister said.

'Well, yeah,' Abbott replied.

'You can come on the committee of this bill. You can do your speech and maybe vote against the government once, but if you otherwise vote with the whip, that will be fine, and no doubt people will notice that.'

Tony Blair approached the minister about his decision to include Abbott on the committee. 'Why are you doing this?'

'Well, I think she wants to be a minister.'

Blair rolled his eyes and said: 'I don't think so… On your head be it.'

The Prime Minister's cynicism was well-founded.

'She agreed this deal with me to come on the bill committee. And then she voted against the whip repeatedly and spoke against it!' the minister says.

A whip notes: 'In the early days, you're naturally full of enthusiasm and naivety, and you think you could have a conversation and appeal to people's better instincts, natures and discipline, and you finally realise that that's not going to work with certain individuals.'

The rebels' unreliability had consequences for loyal MPs forced to carry a heavier load by attending committees and other parliamentary bodies. 'People in marginal seats were actually shouldering the work because you couldn't trust certain people to vote with the party line,' says an MP and later whip. The whips were then up against it to routinely convince loyal MPs to attend committees, not least on the dreaded Finance Bill. 'The carrot was, "If you do this, I'll get you on a trip somewhere. Tell me what you want,"' says Gerry Sutcliffe.

* * *

Towards the end of the 1992–97 parliament, Tony Blair tightened up the party's rules on rebellions. The leadership also took great interest in appointments inside and outside Westminster, though they failed to prevent Ken Livingstone's bid to be Mayor of London. Livingstone ran as an independent and was expelled and banned from the Labour Party for five years.

Dennis Canavan had been an MP for a quarter of a century by 1999, when he stood in the first elections to the Scottish Parliament, created after a referendum on devolution two years earlier. The MP for Falkirk West, a proud advocate of devolution who had seen efforts to introduce a Scottish assembly thwarted during the Callaghan government, wanted to run as a Labour candidate but found opposition from within, not least from Cabinet minister and ex-Chief Donald Dewar, who had taken through the legislation that allowed Holyrood's creation.

The 'first warning shot' came from Tony Benn, who claimed Chief Whip Nick Brown had said that Canavan stood no chance of being selected as a candidate.

Canavan's independent outlook (bloody-mindedness to others) was well-known. In the 1980s, aggrieved at the Tories recruiting English

MPs to attend a committee pertaining to Scotland, and with his bid to participate rejected, Canavan staged a sit-in protest. 'I was asked to leave several times, I refused, and the committee meeting was adjourned as a result,' he says.

Arriving on the scene, Don Dixon, Labour's Deputy Chief Whip, ordered him to leave. 'Dixon, at one stage, was actually jabbing me in the back. You know, technically assaulting me like a thug, a bully,' says Canavan. 'I just told him to lay off. Eventually, I did back down because I didn't want to be suspended by the House, and I felt that I had made my point.'

Canavan, a supporter of a united Ireland, served as chair of the PLP's Northern Ireland Committee, a position he still held prior to the 1997 election. Before the committee's AGM, Canavan says he discovered that Dewar, as Chief Whip, had been urging members to oust him. 'That was just one example of where they wanted to control everything and quell what they saw as some kind of potential rebellion or a troublemaker.'

The leadership was also against his push to become a Member of the Scottish Parliament.

In the first two years of the Blair government, Canavan rebelled 'on many occasions' but insists he did so primarily on issues that 'strayed' from the party's manifesto commitments, such as the introduction of tuition fees and abolition of student grants; a template for going against the party line used by other MPs. 'The things that I voted against when I was in Westminster were not in any manifesto that I stood on,' says Labour MP Julie Morgan.

Canavan's voting record came up during his interview to run for the Scottish Parliament, with a vetting system led by fellow Scottish Labour MP Rosemary McKenna. 'Almost certainly, Donald Dewar was behind it all. He didn't want anybody in the Scottish Parliament that might be seen as a troublemaker or a rebel,' Canavan claims. He ran as an independent – resulting in his expulsion from the Labour Party

– winning in Falkirk West with more than 50 per cent of the vote. He stood down as an MP in 2000 and served in Holyrood until 2007.

* * *

As per the reforms to rebellions brought in under Tony Blair, Labour MPs were now required to consult with the Chief Whip before tabling motions or amendments. After a rebellion, the Chief could issue a written reprimand to the MP, reported to their constituency Labour Party. But the potency of this age-old punishment was starting to wane. According to a colleague, after his whip threatened to share his voting record, Harry Barnes, the ninth most rebellious Labour MP from 2001 to 2005, on eighty-one,[7] said his local Labour Party in North East Derbyshire would be disappointed he hadn't rebelled more. 'They'll think I'm a loyalist!' he said.

With rebels facing down the threats, and the government backing away from reprimanding MPs on votes such as the lone parent cuts, given the scale of the backlash, there was little whips could do beyond speaking to their flock, setting out the arguments and reporting concerns.

'Once you became a serial rebel, it wasn't really a problem,' Lynne Jones says of whipping. One whip says their job involved separating 'the Jeremy Corbyns of this world' from people who weren't regular rebels but had concerns that 'we needed to listen to'.

When a female MP indicated she would rebel, Charlotte Atkins said she knew someone in the House of Lords who might be able to persuade her not to. The peer agreed to speak with the MP but said they would keep the conversation between them. The backbencher ended up changing their mind. 'That's much more effective than a whip making threats, because it just doesn't work,' Atkins says.

Gerry Sutcliffe encouraged another female Labour MP to meet the Chief Whip and discuss her bid to allow unmarried couples to adopt, which the government incorporated into its Adoption and Children Act. 'There is a real misunderstanding about the whipping system,' says the MP. 'They're there to manage the processes and to support you.' When the MP's father passed away, Sutcliffe ensured she could be away for the week of his funeral.

Intelligent whips 'know when to pick arguments', another MP says. The Labour member, a Eurosceptic, would tell their whip 'I'm washing my hair tonight' ahead of votes pertaining to Europe, bar the times when the MP felt she 'needed to put the marker down'. On one occasion, she received a text back from the whip, saying: 'I think you'll find the shower rather crowded.'

The Office was far more preoccupied with welfare than discipline, says a whip. 'I had a couple of MPs in my flock who were really mentally fucked up, so we had to look after them.' The whip also had to manage two constituency neighbours who 'were at war with each other'.

Some are critical of The Office's lack of pastoral care for vulnerable MPs falling foul of Parliament's long hours and subsidised facilities. One longstanding backbencher says they saw a drunk MP feeling her way along the wall after coming out of a parliamentary bar. 'If someone has got a problem like that, why not try to help?' the MP asks. 'I saw a lot of people's lives ruined here and no one gave them any support.'

Fiona Jones, an MP from 1997 to 2001, passed away from alcoholism in 2007 before her fiftieth birthday, with her husband saying she would have been alive but for her period in Parliament, which first triggered her drinking. Linda McDougall, a political commentator and wife of a veteran Labour MP, wrote at the time of Jones's passing: 'The killer disease at Westminster is loneliness and isolation.'[8]

A minister says drinking was more of an issue for Labour MPs between 1992 and 1997 than after 1997. During the minister's first visit to Annie's Bar, he saw a Labour MP leaning against the bar unable to move.

Hilary Armstrong, a former social care worker, said The Office did 'a reasonable amount' on the pastoral side of things. 'There were all sorts of things going on, which was our job to be worried about.'

*   *   *

Though opting for political persuasion, The Office did dispense its fair share of threats.

Two Labour MPs said that whips would tell them on a Thursday that they had to see Hilary Armstrong the following Monday. 'You'd spend the whole weekend feeling sick,' said Helen Clark. At the meeting, it was a case of: 'Now, Helen, you've got a marginal seat… I'm sure you'd want ministers to come and support you in your election campaign…'[9]

Other MPs would settle scores by complaining about you to whips, Jane Griffiths said. Griffiths was 'shocked to be treated with so much contempt' for rebelling. 'Well, you've spoiled your record now,' a whip told her.[10]

The Labour whips say they didn't have a Black Book but did have the bench duty folder recording proceedings in the chamber. 'I rarely needed to see it,' says Armstrong.

Whips, however, would pool and share information, says Gerry Sutcliffe. 'You'd have a meeting with party staff who knew some of the things that were going on that perhaps we, as MPs, didn't know … You just build a picture of people so that you have a fair understanding of who's going to do what when.'

Derek Foster, the former Chief Whip, told one Labour MP that his predecessors had overseen a Black Book but a 'decision was made by the PLP that we could not do that, and so we haven't got one'. It is believed that Labour stopped the keeping of a Black Book in 1964.

Charlotte Atkins suggests certain intelligence was automated. 'It's one of the few things in Parliament which involves teamwork, the sharing of intelligence and the sort of computer system where they have all the intelligence on individual MPs,' she says. 'I'm not talking about scandalous stuff; I'm just talking about their history of voting and whatever. It was an impressive set-up.'

During her first stint in the whips' office, Bridget Prentice recalls a 'big chart up on the wall', colour coded to denote MPs' voting intentions. When she re-joined The Office under Armstrong, 'all of that was now computerised', with whips also starting to use email. 'We kind of lived through the evolution of technology,' she says. Whips still carried around two pagers, one assigned to members of The Office, and another given out to every MP.

Frank Field was called in to see Armstrong and told she had something that, if it were leaked to the press, 'would be very damaging', he recalled in an interview for this book before he passed away in April 2024. 'It turned out that what she was going to leak to the press was that I'd broken the rules of taking up a constituent of another MP and trying to help them,' he said. The backbencher said he had raised money from an acquaintance so that a man who had gone blind could pay privately to have his cataracts removed and keep his job. 'Far from damaging me, I thought actually, that might help me!' Field joked.

But Armstrong insists: 'I never threatened Frank in that way. I did have Frank in on a couple of occasions to ask him for help in understanding/dealing with another colleague he was close to. I do not remember anything about him dealing with someone else's constituent.'

Field, who returned to the backbenches after serving as Social Security Minister, believed the whips, from Walter Harrison and Michael Cocks onwards, 'destroyed my political career'.

Field had two brief dalliances with the Labour frontbench during his forty years as an MP. 'They made sure I didn't get anywhere,' he said of the whips. 'Then, of course, I turned into a different person by not being promoted by them. I was longing to be an insider, and all the time, I was made to be an outsider.'

Nonetheless, Field continued to believe in the need for whips, 'particularly once a government has decided what its policy is – you need a group of people who are going to see it through'.

Armstrong, a committed loyalist, had started the 2001 parliament with a high-profile run-in with an MP over prospective military action, offering a window into the era-defining disagreements to come. One government minister says: 'I would say that Hilary played the dark room of politics at times. You were never quite sure.'

CHAPTER 36

PAUL'S GOSPEL

Paul Marsden's political career got off to a stuttering start.

It began in earnest nearly a year after the 1997 election, with the 29-year-old spending his initial months as an MP caring for his wife, who was recovering from a serious car accident. Welcomed by Nick Brown in the spring of 1998, Marsden began on the back foot, conscious that he was yet to make relationships with The Office or much imprint in Parliament, bar a maiden speech in May 1997 in which he said he'd rather face the whips' wrath than his wife's.*

Marsden was a relative unknown to the party's HQ, having missed out on training sessions for candidates in key target seats. Labour had never even finished second in Shrewsbury and Atcham since the constituency's creation in 1983. Fourteen years later, the party overturned a near 11,000 Conservative majority, with Marsden unexpectedly victorious by 1,670 votes.

His first parliament passed without much interaction or confrontation with whips, bar a reprimand from Bob Ainsworth after speaking out amid the fuel crisis of 2000, with his rural constituency heavily affected.

Marsden went through a 'bruising' reselection process in his local constituency before more than doubling his majority at the 2001 election. 'I arrived in the new parliament and [still] had no real working relationship with the whips.'

---

* Marsden had asked Hansard reporters to write down his wife's name correctly after he thanked her for her support during the election campaign, fearing her 'wrath' if it was misspelled.

Labour MP Mike Foster shared an office with Marsden in Norman Shaw North, near the Red Lion pub on Whitehall, a favourite of Westminster dwellers. 'We did the first term without any problems,' he says. Britain's response to the atrocities committed by al-Qaeda on 11 September 2001 quickly altered the direction of Marsden's political career. 'He stopped being a loyal supporter of the government at that point, and that was awkward,' says Foster.

With Tony Blair pledging Britain's support as America grieved, Marsden grew concerned about Parliament having a say in military action. He spoke with a House of Commons clerk to ask how he could raise the issue. During a debate on 8 October, the day after US-led Operation Enduring Freedom began, Marsden asked Blair when UK citizens would be given a written constitution so that Parliament, 'not a Prime Minister', could authorise a declaration of war. 'I was absolutely jeered and shouted down,' he says, claiming his conversation with the clerk had been leaked to the whips' office, who 'knew all about it before I even stood up'.

Marsden followed up with an EDM calling on the government to halt bombing in Afghanistan and 'urge the United States to do likewise', amid warnings about a looming humanitarian crisis. He received a letter from Keith Hill, the Deputy Chief Whip, saying he faced disciplinary proceedings, likely for submitting an EDM without first informing The Office. Backbenchers Tam Dalyell and Jeremy Corbyn, two of the EDM's twenty-one signatories, told Marsden this set a 'dangerous precedent', although other more compliant backbenchers might have known they had to first let the whips know, as per the PLP's standing orders.

Marsden was then 'dragged in' to see Armstrong for a one-to-one. The Chief Whip, Marsden says, was clutching an inch-thick file of press cuttings pertaining to him, including articles he'd written for his local paper, speeches he had made and transcripts of radio interviews he'd given. Incensed after their lengthy and frosty exchange, Marsden went to the House of Commons Library and wrote out everything he could remember from the conversation.

A couple of days later, Marsden passed senior *Mail on Sunday* political journalist Simon Walters in Portcullis House. 'I understand you had a meeting with the Chief Whip,' Walters said. 'What happened?'

Marsden pulled out his notes. 'I'll tell you. Here it is.'

That weekend, the *Mail on Sunday* ran in full Marsden's account of his showdown with Armstrong.

'What I didn't expect was that they would publish it as a verbatim transcript and sort of hint that this was a recording,' Marsden says, insisting he hadn't taped the conversation.

The transcript included incendiary claims that Armstrong had told Marsden 'it was people like you who appeased Hitler in 1938'. Armstrong also allegedly said war is not a matter of conscience, attacked his voting and attendance record and said he had made a 'complete fool' of himself in the Commons on 8 October, didn't know the rules as he was 'too inexperienced', and 'must stop using the media' without permission, denying the party had spin doctors.[1]

'Frankly, I'd gone in there pretty damn nervous,' he says. 'After about ten minutes, I was just laughing at her because it was just a joke.'

The Office, for its part, was shocked that an MP had regurgitated a private conversation to the media in full. A handful of Conservative MPs seeking to capitalise on the backlash, including a young backbencher, George Osborne, signed an opportunistic EDM criticising Armstrong's 'heavy-handed, inept and counterproductive attempt to intimidate' Marsden. As Chief, Armstrong kept her counsel but suggests there was more to the conversation than was made public. 'There were lots of things I was talking to Paul about, and he knew he was in trouble.'

Prior to the encounter, Marsden said he'd had several weeks of 'being blanked' by Labour MPs, with otherwise friendly backbenchers 'suddenly not speaking'. He also received calls saying it had been suggested that he had been overclaiming on housing allowance. 'I'd say, "What?" They were obviously using the dark arts,' he says of the whips.

Mike Foster, meanwhile, told Ainsworth – their shared regional whip – that he could no longer work in the same office as Marsden. 'I tried to do it in a way that wasn't offensive, but that's what you use a whip for,' Foster says.

A week after the original *Mail on Sunday* story, Marsden was back in the paper once more, criticising the 'Labour smear machine', saying No. 10 officials had briefed false claims about his sexuality, mental well-being and intention to defect to the Liberal Democrats.[2]

Rumours about Marsden's imminent defection, born in part from his close friendship with neighbouring Lib Dem MPs Matthew Green and Lembit Öpik, had gathered pace. A month later, while having drinks with Öpik in Strangers' Bar after rebelling on the government's Anti-Terrorism, Crime and Security Bill, Marsden says he was approached by a handful of Labour MPs, including government whip Gerry Sutcliffe.

'Oh, you're drinking with the Lib Dems again. Are you going to leave?' Marsden claims Sutcliffe asked him.

'At first, it was a little bit jokey-jokey, and then it got to the point where … it started to get a little bit nasty,' he says. Sutcliffe, Marsden continues, put his arm across his throat, and it 'jerked my head back and smacked it against the oak panelling'.

Returning to his office, Marsden fired off a press release entitled 'Labour thugs attack MP'. In it, Marsden said Jim Dowd had prodded him in the back, while Ivan Henderson had called him a 'fucking traitor', a 'fucking disgrace' and a 'fucking arsehole'. Of Sutcliffe, he said the whip had first grabbed his arm and leg. 'He put his arm across my throat on my windpipe. My head was pinned against the wall. It hurt. His face was inches from mine,' he claimed.

The MPs denied the allegations. Sutcliffe says: 'It wasn't true, but it made good press.'

In early December, Lib Dem leader Charles Kennedy invited Marsden to his flat in Victoria, a meeting also attended by a couple of special advisers. 'He was basically trying to sell the Lib Dems to me.' Marsden joined the party on 10 December.

Later that afternoon, Marsden arrived at a parliamentary Lib Dem office ahead of a press conference confirming his defection. Kennedy joined him in a side room while photographers and reporters waited outside. 'He was just ashen-faced. He didn't say anything, and I was trying to make chit-chat,' Marsden says. Kennedy's adviser came in and 'she knew straight away that something was wrong'. Marsden thought to himself: 'Something's not right here.'

Marsden was given a round of applause during his first meeting of the Lib Dem parliamentary party. After he said he wasn't there to cause trouble, Kennedy quipped: 'Well, in that case, you can get out!'

Not long after defecting, once again in Strangers' Bar, Marsden was having drinks with a few Lib Dem MPs and a Plaid Cymru backbencher when he felt an 'almighty thump' from behind and 'landed about two metres away in the arms' of a small group, he says.

'By the time I stood up, the drink had gone everywhere,' he says of his pint. An MP told him: 'That was John Prescott. He just hit you.' Marsden went to follow Prescott out onto the terrace, but his friends pulled him back and said: 'It's not worth it, Paul.'

Marsden also encountered difficulties on the Lib Dem benches.

The MP took to heart the party's more laissez-faire attitude to rebellions. 'The Lib Dems had the view of you could speak your mind – and when you did, you were given the cold shoulder, and they still played dirty tricks.'

Fellow Lib Dem MP Sandra Gidley criticised Marsden amid a series of headlines about his private life and attempts at writing romantic poetry on his website. He admitted to having affairs and claimed at the time that Labour whips had leaked it as revenge. Andrew Stunell, the Lib Dem Chief Whip, confirmed that an intern had also asked to be moved out of his office, with a close associate telling a national newspaper that Marsden had tried to kiss her.

'Paul's got a marginal seat and I would think he would be putting his energies elsewhere – he would be advised to concentrate on keeping his constituency at the next election,' Gidley said.³ With further criticisms made in the *Daily Mail*, Marsden went to Stunell and asked if he'd authorised Gidley's remarks. 'He equivocated and I just thought, "Andrew, you know better than the Labour lot,"' Marsden says.

Lib Dems like Marsden were growing concerned about Kennedy's drinking. Invited to his parliamentary office for an event, Marsden says the party leader was 'literally draining his glass, looking around and then somebody would come out and fill it up again'. 'When then the rumours started in the parliamentary party, and it was obvious that certain people knew that he was an alcoholic, he had this disease, I just felt enormously sad and let down as well.'

Mark Oaten, a fellow Lib Dem MP, says he also felt 'huge' pressure to keep Kennedy's condition private and could have done with more support to deal with the situation. A 'core' number of figures knew about Kennedy 'for a long period of time', he says.

At this point, Oaten, who was married, says he was also drinking 'a little too much', felt depressed, had sexual doubts and was 'taking a risk with my private life'.

'What I needed was a safe, secure place to go and get support while all of the shit was going on before then,' Oaten says. 'I'm not saying that would have stopped me from doing what I did, but I was certainly unhappy, depressed, miserable and hugely stressed.'

Marsden believes he also 'probably had an alcohol problem'. 'There were times when I was in the Commons that I could barely articulate a word because I'd been drinking from late afternoon, and I saw it in other MPs, where they're literally falling asleep,' he says. 'There was a drinking culture that was just massive. Every single night. Cheap drink. Always available.'

Regarding Parliament's drinking culture, Oaten says he saw things – including fights in Strangers' Bar, drug taking and sexual misconduct – that were 'totally unacceptable'.

In July 2004, Marsden confirmed he was standing down as an MP at the next election, announcing his intention to re-join Labour in April 2005. In December of that year, Marsden wrote in the *Mail on Sunday* that Kennedy had a drink problem, a controversial intervention that the party leader's spokesperson initially denied before Kennedy resigned. Soon after, Oaten, battling headlines in the *News of the World* about his activities between 2004 and 2005 with male sex workers, quit as the party's home affairs spokesman.

Marsden's experience is a useful case study in what can go wrong if an MP isn't shown the ropes early. A rebel more by circumstance than by design – he kept his nose clean for most of the 1997–2001 parliament – Marsden plainly wasn't prepared for the cut and thrust of political life at Westminster, nor the rough edges and expectations of The Office. The reality of being a party MP didn't gel with how he saw the role, and the whips arguably mishandled him by being overly abrasive when a guiding hand may have worked better.

'Paul, we never should have lost you,' Labour's Graham Allen told him after his defection.

'It was just so badly handled from the off,' Marsden says. 'Maybe I should have obviously offered more of an olive branch, but my goodness me, my view was I'm elected, I'm supposed to stand up and say things about what I believe in.'

The trouble he encountered on the Lib Dem benches suggest Marsden was never likely to thrive as a backbencher representing a political party at Westminster. Asked what he'd do differently, Marsden admits he was inexperienced. Armstrong was 'right about that', he says.

'I probably would have attempted to speak with the regional whip,' he says, about his concerns over Parliament having a vote on military action in Afghanistan. He should have gone independent, he says, allowing both sides to cool down and potentially discuss him re-joining. But 'then you're into Iraq', he says, 'so the chances are, no, I wouldn't have'.

The confrontation with Marsden was nonetheless unfortunate for whips preparing for the most significant parliamentary showdown of the Labour government, as the Prime Minister prepared to take Britain into war in Iraq. 'That vote more than anything, both in whipping and political terms, it still reverberates through the party now,' says a Labour MP.

CHAPTER 37

IRAQ

On the morning of Tuesday 18 March 2003, Hilary Armstrong returned from 10 Downing Street to address her team. In just a few hours, from around midday onwards, MPs would begin a debate on military intervention against Saddam Hussein in Iraq. According to one of those sitting round the table, Armstrong said the Prime Minister had told her: 'I've got to win a majority of Labour MPs, and if I don't, I will resign and call a general election.'

The 'coup de grâce', the whip continues, was that Armstrong said they couldn't let MPs know, 'because we don't want to win the vote by the threat that we'll basically have a vote of no confidence'. 'We want to win the vote because we want to win the vote,' she said.

The whip thought: 'Fucking hell. This is like the Cuban Missile Crisis; this is fucking huge.'

Extraordinarily, the whip says a sixteen-year-old intern from a south London school was sitting on the floor next to him, wondering what he should say. 'Probably best you don't say anything, Oliver,' the whip says he replied.

Other members of The Office remember Armstrong's pep talk slightly differently – or not at all. One whip says: 'I remember the message coming back that he would resign, but I don't remember a general election.' A different member of The Office adds: 'I don't remember that being said, but if they said it was, then I'm sure it was.'

Armstrong, however, is adamant that it's nonsense. 'That is absolutely not my recollection, and I know it is not the truth. These myths grow up over years by people who want some drama.'

The Prime Minister's possible resignation, however, *was* a known potential outcome of the vote on Iraq, one set out to undecided Labour MPs by whips and senior ministers alike. With the Conservatives pledging support for military intervention, the government was effectively guaranteed to win the vote, but Blair knew the potential magnitude and optics of most Labour MPs voting against him, and what that would mean for his immediate future.

Few in The Office were complacent even about the government winning outright. At least two whips feared the Tories might withdraw their support, knowing it could bring the Blair government down. The whips had approached Armstrong with their concerns, who replied confidently: 'Don't worry, they won't. They've given a commitment to the White House.'

'It was the Americans who were really whipping the Tories,' Armstrong says now.

The twelve months leading up to the vote suggested that, in one way or another, Labour MPs were about to make history.

* * *

The previous autumn, Ann McKechin travelled to Rwanda as part of the first cross-party group of MPs to visit the central African country since the devastating genocide in 1994.

The Labour MP was already leaning against military intervention in Iraq, unswayed by a government dossier on the country's chemical and biological weapons capability, including an incendiary claim that Saddam Hussein's military planning allowed for some of his Weapons of Mass Destruction (WMD) to be ready within forty-five minutes of an order to use them. 'Unless a UN inspection team found [WMD], then I wasn't convinced,' she says.

Fellow Scottish MP Tom Clarke, a former minister, was also on the trip.

'Ann, I don't think I can vote for military action,' he told her in a quiet moment. McKechin, whose constituency was more left-wing and had a larger student base than that of her colleague, pondered what Clarke, a loyalist to his bones, was telling her. 'You can make a bad decision in legislation and reverse it,' she says. 'With war, there's no going back.'

The prospect of war had only grown since US President George W. Bush had cited Iraq, Iran and North Korea as part of an 'Axis of Evil' during his State of the Union address in January 2002. Two months later, Labour MP Alice Mahon put down an EDM expressing 'deep unease' at the prospect of the UK supporting military intervention, supported by 133 Labour MPs, showing the level of discontent on the government benches, and the task ahead for the whips. 'Iraq was intense, fraught. There were strongly held views on every side,' says one.

After much clamouring, MPs were recalled during the summer recess for a debate. A month later, the government produced its September Dossier.

Alan Simpson, a member of the Socialist Campaign Group, had never felt as nervous as he did around the time of the dossier's publication. 'None of us knew whether Downing Street had the smoking gun, a piece of evidence, that would justify the case for going to war and would nullify the position of those of us who were against it,' he says. On the morning of 24 September, the day the government published its claims, Simpson distributed to every Labour MP's mailbox a 'counter-dossier' of the arguments against intervention, which he had worked on with other anti-war MPs. He picked up a dozen copies of the government's dossier, ran back to his office and went through them with a team of people, dividing it into segments. After an hour, they (perhaps unsurprisingly, given they'd pre-empted the dossier with their own) concluded: 'There's nothing there that makes the case for war.' Whips, 'pretty miffed' that he'd circulated his counter-dossier, confronted Simpson as he ran back to Members' Lobby.

In November, Foreign Secretary Jack Straw committed to a debate on a substantive government motion, with MPs able to put forward amendments. Blair, unlike Prime Ministers before him, had offered a similar gesture in early 1998, after Saddam Hussein expelled UN inspectors from Iraq, putting the question of the use of force to a vote of MPs. He didn't do the same for air strikes on Iraq carried out later that year, nor for action in Sierra Leone and Kosovo, with MPs expressing their views through other parliamentary votes and means.

Straw's announcement came after United Nations Security Council Resolution 1441, which gave Hussein a final opportunity to comply with Iraq's disarmament obligations – such as allowing weapons inspectors to carry out due diligence – and thus, in the UK government's eyes, one last chance to avoid war. But many Labour MPs needed more, saying they would wait for a second UN resolution in support of intervention before voting in favour. 'They were the ones that the whips' office focused their operation on,' says an MP.

There was other context to consider, not least the pressure MPs felt at constituency level, with many undergoing reselection meetings for the next election. 'People with multi-ethnic communities were having difficulties as well,' says Gerry Sutcliffe.

Huw Edwards, a perceived loyalist, came under 'a great deal of pressure' from whips. He claims a senior member of The Office told him: 'Huw, this could affect your promotion prospects.' Edwards says dryly: 'Well a) I knew I'd be out at the next election, and b) I said to him, "What do you have in mind for me? Foreign Secretary? What is it I'm risking here?"'

Julie Morgan says she was told: 'Well, if we don't win the vote, the Prime Minister would resign.' David Drew says one MP said: 'If you knew what I knew, you'd have no worries about voting for the government and intervention into Iraq.'

Those who had confirmed their position were largely left alone. 'I've got you down in the anti-war camp,' Jeremy Corbyn's regional whip said to the backbencher.

'Well, your intelligence does you credit,' Corbyn responded.[1]

McKechin confirmed on BBC radio that she would vote against military intervention. 'Two months out before the final vote, everyone knew what my view was, and they knew it wasn't going to be changed. I didn't get any approach from the whips.'

George Foulkes also outlined his view publicly, saying he would vote in favour. His colleague Ann Clwyd had brought in Marsh Arabs and Kurds to see MPs in Parliament, outlining their treatment at Hussein's hands. 'What the fuck use is an Early Day Motion for these people who are being killed and tortured?' he says rhetorically.

Tony Lloyd, an opponent of the war, says: 'I don't remember having been heavily whipped.' A whip says: 'Although the views that were held were passionate, the conversations were rational, respectful and when you understood where people were, there was no acrimony.'

Once an MP had made up their mind, they effectively stopped talking about Iraq to people who were on the other side of the argument. 'It was a pretty horrible time in Parliament,' says one MP, who ended up voting in favour of intervention.

Sometimes disagreements spilled over in the chamber. Hilary Armstrong asked Foreign Office Minister Ben Bradshaw to make amends after he called George Galloway 'an apologist and mouthpiece' for Hussein. 'I thought I'd better do it just to keep the Chief Whip happy,' Bradshaw says.

The whips' office itself housed uncertainties over intervention. 'Five or six of them went AWOL,' says an ex-whip, who wasn't approached by The Office despite being a waverer, left to his devices as a former council leader and MP with a large majority.

As Chief, Armstrong attended a Cabinet sub-committee on Iraq which met every morning in Downing Street. She would also hand out lists of people for Cabinet ministers to approach.

'We would essentially go through the numbers and where people's arguments were. I had to be on top of every member of the PLP,' she says. The Office did what it always does, Armstrong continues, working out who MPs' friends were, who they listened to and who they respected. 'You then make sure they're talked to by the key people.'

Armstrong's two special advisers, 'who knew the PLP well', would liaise with the whips to keep updated a chart of how MPs intended to vote. 'I was able to tell the PM at every stage what I thought [the numbers were],' she says.

Edwards recalls conversations with senior Labour heavyweights Blair, Peter Mandelson and John Prescott, with the latter telling him: 'I told Tony we shouldn't have a vote. He was stupid, he didn't listen to me. Why didn't he listen to me? We don't need a vote on this.' Mandelson told him: 'Huw, this isn't about Iraq any more; it's about Tony.'

Paddy Tipping says he spoke to Foreign Secretary Jack Straw, Defence Secretary Geoff Hoon and the whips. 'One of the arguments that was put to me fairly forcefully was that Tony had made this commitment to Bush, and we couldn't let him or the Americans down,' he says. Hoon says: 'I did speak to a number of Labour MPs about what we were doing and why we were doing it … rather than telling anybody they've got to vote in a particular way.'

Jeff Ennis, the definition of a loyal MP, says he received more cajoling from Health Minister Tessa Jowell, to whom he was a PPS, than he did from members of The Office. Jim Knight, MP for South Dorset and a member of the Defence Select Committee who had met with top UN officials, including Hans Blix,* was also given a list of MPs to speak with.

Armstrong didn't call on every willing group at her disposal to try to convince Labour MPs of the arguments. 'I told the Americans they had to keep out of our way,' she says. The US embassy's political attaché

---

* Blix was first executive chairman of the UN Monitoring, Verification and Inspection Commission.

would visit Armstrong 'virtually on a weekly basis', but the Chief made clear that them talking to MPs 'would have had a negative effect', she says.

The embassy did hold two dinners for Labour MPs elected in 2001. 'They wanted to just get a sense of what our thoughts and thought processes were,' says McKechin.

In January 2003, forty-four Labour MPs used an adjournment debate to express opposition to government policy on Iraq. A month later, Labour MP Chris Smith and Douglas Hogg from the Conservatives put forward an amendment to a government motion in support of UN efforts to disarm Hussein, arguing the case for intervention was 'as yet unproven'. Some 121 Labour MPs supported the unsuccessful amendment, with twenty abstaining, the largest rebellion by government backbenchers of modern times.

Blair pledged to work on securing a second UN resolution, with senior ministerial figures including Robin Cook suggesting they would resign if one was not forthcoming. The Prime Minister also addressed the PLP during weekly gatherings on Monday evenings, where, according to Armstrong, he would say: 'Some of you are pacifists. Some of you think we should do anything rather than go to war. I respect your views, but I've got to ask you to respect that I'm doing this not to be nasty, not to be cosying up to the Americans – I'm doing it because I believe it's the right thing to do.'

Pressure ratcheted up as February transitioned to March. Cabinet ministers trawled the tearoom, with the Prime Minister even setting up at a table, meeting MPs in groups of three to five.[2] With weapons inspectors calling for more time and French President Jacques Chirac pledging to veto a UN resolution authorising the use of force in Iraq, the undecideds were firming up their choice.

On 17 March, the eve of the vote, Cook announced his resignation from the government, delivering a statement to the Commons. Commending efforts to secure a second UN resolution, Cook noted that the 'very intensity of those attempts underlines how important it was to succeed. Now that those attempts have failed, we cannot pretend that getting a second resolution was of no importance.' Without international agreement or domestic support – an estimated 1.5 million had marched in London against the war in February – Cook said he would vote against military intervention the next day. As he sat down, the House broke out in applause.

'I still think today that Robin Cook's retirement speech is the best speech I've ever heard in Parliament,' says Gerry Sutcliffe. Another whip says: 'He made a very good case, and it was extremely difficult.'

Paddy Tipping was summoned to see Tony Blair in the Prime Minister's parliamentary office on the day of the vote, with his whip also in the room.

'Oh, Paddy, I've never asked you to do anything [which wasn't strictly true, Tipping says] but I want you to vote with us tonight,' Blair said.

'I can't, Tony,' Tipping replied. The Prime Minister, according to the MP, then said: 'Well, if it makes it any easier for you, Paddy, the generals tell me it will all be over in three weeks.'

After the meeting, Tipping says his whip told him he had 'not been as helpful' as he might have been. With Tipping opting to vote against, his whip 'was really agitated about it', and it was made 'very clear to me that that was the end of my progression for ever in Parliament'.

Mike Gapes had been away from Parliament looking after his kids, with his wife very ill in hospital. The MP, a long-standing Hussein critic, wanted to vote for the war. 'If I don't, it's going to be interpreted either that I'm rebelling or people will start asking questions about why I'm not there, and I don't want to discuss my wife's illness,' he told his whip Joan Ryan.

'Ah, I'm so glad you've rung me,' Ryan, one of two government tellers on the vote, replied. 'I've been telling Tommy [McAvoy], "Leave him alone. He's got more to deal with than this."'

Blair opened the debate at 12.35 p.m. The government's lengthy and wide-ranging motion offered support to troops in the Middle East, referenced legal advice from the Attorney General backing the use of force, cited (without naming) France's blocking of a second UN resolution 'whatever the circumstances' and said the government 'should use all means necessary to ensure the disarmament' of Iraq's WMD. The Prime Minister then gave what some people felt to be his finest parliamentary performance, outlining the case for war.

An amendment by Labour MP Chris Smith argued that 'the case for war against Iraq has not yet been established, especially given the absence of specific United Nations authorisation', while also pledging 'total support for the British forces engaged in the Middle East'.

At 10 p.m., the House divided to vote on Smith's amendment first. Ann McKechin watched as Bill Tynan, an 'ultra-loyalist' Scottish Labour MP, turned and, without saying a word, went in the rebel division lobby. 'It was absolutely jaw-dropping,' she says. First-time rebels shed tears while queuing up to register their vote. 'It was an incredibly emotive experience.'

The amendment fell short by 396 to 217, with 139 Labour MPs voting against intervention, now the largest rebellion ever by government backbenchers in modern times, overtaking the vote in February. Record-breaking though this was, the majority of Labour backbenchers voted in favour of military action. Blair stayed put in 10 Downing Street.

With the amendment rejected, many MPs felt they had made their voices heard. The government motion passed by 412 to 149, with eighty-four rebels, while many more MPs abstained.*

The first Cruise missiles launched two days later.

---

* Some MPs, now that war was inevitable, didn't want to vote against a motion offering support for troops, and so abstained.

CHAPTER 38

FALLOUT

The immediate hit to the UK government from the Iraq vote came in the form of frontbench resignations. John Denham and Health Minister Lord Hunt joined Robin Cook in quitting in protest against military intervention, as did nine parliamentary private secretaries.

The longer-term damage was multi-faceted, profound and enduring.

Iraq was, for some, their first rebellion. 'Having crossed that line and voted against the whip on Iraq, since then, I've voted against the whip on a number of occasions,' says a former frontbencher. It's for this reason that whips are so eager to get hold of MPs early; rebelling against your party is a bigger deal than is often noted. Breaching the threshold becomes easier the more you do it. 'It made me more independent when it came to votes,' the MP says.

As disastrous shortfalls, consequences and blind spots in post-conflict planning revealed themselves in excruciating detail, others lost trust in the man at the wheel. 'I have enormous admiration for Tony, but it was a kind of turning point for him,' says an MP. International Development Secretary Clare Short, having hesitated prior to the March vote, resigned two months later, with a parting shot at Tony Blair's 'presidential system' of government.

Many MPs who switched their vote due to fears of the Prime Minister resigning 'deeply regretted' their choice because they could see the consequences, which were 'far bigger than for any other vote that had ever taken place', says Lynne Jones. Alan Simpson argues that not enough MPs understood that they had to exercise 'ethical judgements', which 'pulled the rug from under the case for war'. One MP says the effect of Iraq on Blair himself has been underestimated, with the PM 'feted' across the Atlantic. 'He began to think, "Look, I'm very important, and all these little people over here don't understand what I'm doing," which is when he started to use that "If you knew what I knew" argument [with MPs],' they say.

Unhappiness at local level filtered through quickly. Anti-war activists organised a protest march in Mike Gapes's Ilford South constituency after he supported intervention. 'With about 25 per cent of my constituents being Muslim, it was quite a difficult period,' he says.

Paddy Tipping, working on a by-election in Leicester South, brought mosque leaders to No. 10, realising Labour's Muslim vote 'wasn't going to come out'. 'As always, Tony thought he could fix it.' The Lib Dems took the seat on a 21.5 per cent swing.

The Office seemingly drew a metaphorical line after the vote; no letters were sent to the constituency parties of rebel MPs. One opponent of the war says his local party would have responded to such a message with: 'Stuff you!'

But Chief Whips never forget.

* * *

Pager-less Chris Mullin, who had voted against military intervention in Iraq, was about the last to find out that Tony Blair planned to appoint him once more as a minister in the Department for International Development (he had served for six months in 2001). Downing Street, unable to track him down, rang Hilary Armstrong to ask if she would find the MP.

The Chief Whip said fine, before asking if that meant she could reassure those who had lost their ministerial positions around the Iraq vote that they might now be brought back in. There was an expletive at the other end of the line. The official asked Armstrong to hold off.

Mullin, meanwhile, rang Downing Street from a telephone in Portcullis House. 'Oh, yes. He is looking for you,' an aide said, putting him on hold. When the aide returned to the phone, they asked him to call back in fifteen minutes.

Armstrong received another call from No. 10 to say that the Prime Minister was not quite ready to welcome back the frontbenchers who had resigned over Iraq. Therefore, he did not need to speak with Mullin, who, while not a frontbencher, had rebelled on intervention. 'It was not my job to tell the PM who he could appoint, but to make sure the political context around such decisions was clear,' she says.

Unaware all this was taking place, Mullin called Downing Street again. He was informed that Blair had gone home for the night and would ring him in the morning.

The Prime Minister rang the next day.

'As you realise, there's been this little difficulty. But don't worry, I've got something up your street coming in a few weeks' time,' he said.

In June 2003, Blair made Mullin a minister in the Foreign Office, with responsibility for Africa. Over the next two years, Mullin believes the whips 'did a lot of damage', regaling the Prime Minister with claims about discontent in the tearoom over his appointment. Foreign Secretary Jack Straw came back from a meeting at Downing Street and said: 'Just so you know, they're still sticking the knife in.' Mullin returned to the backbenches in 2005.

* * *

Intervention in Iraq was not the only vote that threatened to bring down the Prime Minister.

Whips were sure of defeat at the second reading of the Higher Education Bill until less than an hour before the division. Deputy Prime Minister John Prescott had even told Radio 4's *Today* programme on the morning of 27 January 2004 that the legislation might fall short.

Labour whip Charlotte Atkins was with friends in the PLP when a message came through on her pager that the government would lose the vote by five. A member of Atkins's group planned to vote against the controversial legislation, which would introduce university top-up fees, a move the party had explicitly ruled out heading into the 2001 election.[*]

'You can't vote against the government,' one MP present told the potential rebel.

'No, she has a perfect right to vote against the government,' Atkins intervened. 'Leave her alone. If she's decided she wants to vote against the government, don't bully her, she's fine.'

The MP did change her mind and voted with the party line. 'It's not about what the whips say to the individual; it's about what their friends say to the individual,' Atkins notes.

The government had produced a white paper a year before the vote proposing that universities be able to vary fees up to £3,000 a year from September 2006 onwards. Three EDMs critical of top-up fees accumulated 171 Labour signatories. Former Chief Nick Brown and his one-time Deputy George Mudie, as well as loyalists such as Angela Eagle, were key figures in the rebellion, coordinating opposition and securing concessions from Education Secretary Charles Clarke and Minister for Higher Education Alan Johnson, who took over the bill from Margaret Hodge.

'This is like finding General Eisenhower undermining Field Marshal Montgomery,' a Tory Chief said of Nick Brown's involvement.[1] For his part, Nick Brown, who, along with his sister, was raised by his mother following the death of his father, felt strongly about the implications of top-up fees for students from a working-class background.

The whips also organised for Chancellor Gordon Brown and the Prime Minister to meet rebels, with Blair's future once more in doubt

---

[*] The government insisted it wasn't going against its manifesto commitment, as top-up fees would start in 2006, during the next parliament. Ministers also argued the new variable fees would abolish the existing upfront fees and thus were not technically topping up anything.

if most of his MPs went against him. 'Of course my authority is on the line – it always is with issues like this,' he told reporters.²

One opponent of top-up fees recalls 'being shoved into a tiny room' to talk with Brown. 'Unlike Iraq, where you're on one side or not, with a bill, normally what you're trying to do is get a concession. It's more of a negotiation,' they say. A loyal MP says 'rebelling is overrated', arguing it's 'much more worthwhile' to work behind the scenes on changing a frontbench position, reserving the nuclear option for 'very narrow particular issues'.

Nick Brown and George Mudie were invited for a meeting with Blair in Downing Street. As a pair of old hands, they had to guide the officials sent to collect them on how to access No. 10 via the entrance at the Foreign Office. Blair was 'polite enough', Brown says.

'Well, if we're defeated, it will be your fault,' Blair said, according to Brown.

To which Mudie replied: 'Good.'

Among the concessions secured by the rebels were pledges to set up an independent review on the impact of top-up fees, a rise in the proposed grant level and a commitment to only changing the cap with full parliamentary consent.

Nick Brown dramatically rescinded his opposition before the debate. Some speculated that his change of heart was brought about by the Chancellor – who, it was said, had privately egged on the rebellion to destabilise Blair after he refused to set out his departure timetable from No. 10. The ex-Chief Whip bristles at the suggestion.

'What would have happened is that all the concessions … would have been withdrawn,' he says of following through on the rebellion.

With the government offering yet more assurances during the second reading debate, the bill passed by 316 to 311. Blair had met Huw Edwards on the day of the vote, who told him he would support the government. 'He was very grateful because he only won that by five votes, and I reckon I pulled two or three over with me,' Edwards says.

Labour MP Jeff Ennis, the most unnatural of rebels, was one of more than ninety Labour MPs to vote against the party line. When he saw Blair years later, he would say: 'You should have listened more to people like me, Tony. I voted against you on the Iraq War, and I voted against you on tuition fees, and I was right on both issues, wasn't I?'

With the help of whips and open-minded ministers willing to placate, assure and concede, the government avoided a damaging defeat. But one whip argues that the issue that caused Blair 'real consternation' was actually over moves to ban the hunting of wild mammals with dogs.

Insofar as the Labour government is concerned, the matter began in 1997, when the party pledged in its election manifesto to hold a free vote in Parliament on whether hunting with hounds should be banned. Later that year, Mike Foster, who had put in a bid for a Private Member's Bill, received a message on his pager to see the Chief Whip immediately. Nick Brown said: 'We don't mind what you do, so long as you don't promise to abolish the monarchy or ban hunting with dogs or something like that.'

When it became clear that Foster *did* plan to introduce a PMB against hunting with dogs, he was offered a couple of 'handout-type' bills on relatively benign matters that would carry government support, giving him the opportunity to get legislation on the statute book. 'I wasn't going to take that up,' Foster says. A whopping 411 MPs backed his PMB at second reading, before the legislation ran out of parliamentary time.

The government wanted to wriggle out of implementing an outright ban and thus avoid a painful confrontation with countryside groups and certain voters. Despite the manifesto commitment, Blair 'wasn't convinced that it was an issue we should be legislating for', says a whip. The Commons and Lords were also split on the issue, with the Tory-heavy upper chamber vigorously pushing back. But the strength of feeling in the PLP didn't dissipate; 205 MPs signed an EDM that looked forward to the 'earliest opportunity to re-affirm' the House's stance on abolition.

It's the only time one whip can remember Blair coming into the whips' office. 'So, tell me what's happening?' Blair said. 'He didn't believe what was being fed to him after all the canvassing that we did,' the whip says.

Given the strength of feeling, the whips agreed there had to be a free vote. The Hunting Act passed its third reading in September 2004.

* * *

As the rebellions piled up and anti-war MPs voiced their discontent with events in the Middle East, The Office contemplated taking action, with loyal backbenchers starting to complain that nothing was being done about the Usual Suspects.

Bridget Prentice says 'a lot of us felt' there should be a limit to how often people could break the whip without facing consequences. There was no effective penalty for Jeremy Corbyn & co., who weren't interested in overseas trips or serving on committees. 'The only way that you could punish them would have been to withdraw the whip,' Prentice says.

Keith Hill, the Deputy Chief Whip, arrived in The Office with a message from a parent. 'My mum is fed up to the back teeth of us not doing anything about Jeremy Corbyn,' he said. 'I'm going to have a look at it.'

Hill examined Corbyn's voting record across a four-month period. 'He'd voted against the Labour government more often than the Tories had voted against the government,' Hilary Armstrong claims. The Chief Whip took the evidence to Tony Blair, hoping the Prime Minister would approve removing the party whip. Blair declined.

Armstrong explains: 'Neil [Kinnock] had gone through all of that, and [Blair] now wanted a different phase in the Labour Party.' A whip says: 'There's no more loyal Blairite than me, but the boss let us down on that.'

Blair had already showcased his approach by voting, at the start of 2004, to readmit Ken Livingstone to Labour, four years after he ran as an independent against the party's candidate for Mayor of London.

With Blair refusing to budge on Corbyn, members of The Office approached a former whip with a background in the media. 'If the whips' office wanted something in the press, I did it,' the ex-whip says.

The former whip planted a story with the *Daily Telegraph* journalist Toby Helm that Labour's high command was planning 'show trials' for its most disloyal MPs, which could lead to their deselection before the next election. Helm reported that Armstrong wanted Labour's National Executive Committee to drop at least six of the most persistent rebels unless they agreed to mend their ways. The paper named Corbyn, John McDonnell, Lynne Jones, Diane Abbott, Bob Marshall-Andrews and Mike Wood as the MPs at risk.[3]

Jones, one of those singled out, says: 'They were supposed to be going heavy and interview us and tell us we had to be good girls and boys, but nothing happened.' A backbench Labour MP says: 'There was absolute uproar at the PLP. It's stupid, and it's counterproductive because it only makes people dig into their position.'

Blair was 'wise' not to expel the six MPs, Jones says. 'What they could have done is actually not done these dreadful things, and then there wouldn't have been any rebellions.'

But, for The Office, the rebels' intransigence went deeper than that. 'Jeremy and his crowd were never team players,' says the ex-whip. 'They didn't give a shit about the whip. They'd stand for Parliament as Labour, get Labour's vote, and vote against us all the time. That was our frustration. That's why we wanted Tony to chuck them out.'

CHAPTER 39

TRANSITION

With the Chief Whip still in full unadulterated flow, a female Labour MP took out a pen and scribbled a note to her neighbour. 'I don't really agree with this, do you?' she enquired, sliding the paper across a desk in a meeting room in Portcullis House. The recipient, also elected in the May 2005 election, shook his head.

Hilary Armstrong was midway through the customary post-election address to first timers. 'I don't want parliamentarians. I just want you to follow the whip. I'm not interested in what you think. I'm not interested in you caring about parliamentary democracy; just vote Labour every night, and you'll be fine,' the note-writing MP paraphrases Armstrong as saying.

Diana Johnson, the MP for Kingston upon Hull North, teasingly recalls Armstrong putting the 'fear of God in all the 2005 intake'. 'Don't sign EDMs because you could get yourself into a position where you might then have to vote against what you've signed up for,' the Chief advised.

Having enjoyed three-figure majorities in successive parliaments, Labour now had a surplus of sixty-six, with 355 MPs in total – nothing to be embarrassed about, but a good deal short of the numbers achieved nearly a decade earlier. The Conservatives had clawed their way to 198 seats, with the anti-Iraq War Liberal Democrats returning sixty-two, up eleven on the previous parliament.

As a collective, the Parliamentary Labour Party had, insofar as rebellions were concerned, broken the seal. The glue keeping the disparate elements of the party together was coming unstuck, with supporters of Gordon Brown eager for a transition, while the left pushed for post-Iraq retributions against the Prime Minister, whose Teflon armour had weakened.

In the wake of the 7/7 bombings, the deadliest terrorist atrocity committed on British soil, the government brought forward a bill to create new terrorism-related offences. At the report stage of the bill, the government proposed an amendment to increase the number of days terror suspects could be held without being charged from fourteen to ninety. Armstrong insists that Blair had said from the start: 'This isn't something we will win, but I have to demonstrate to the security services that I know what they are facing and that I'm listening to them, even if I can't persuade my MPs.' But Labour MPs including Chris Mullin argue the ninety-day policy was about 'politicians trying to look tough'.

For all that Blair was supposedly unfussed about the success of the vote, the activities of the government suggested otherwise. Emily Thornberry, MP for Islington South and Finsbury, said a whip 'threw me against a wall in the division lobby' just before the vote on ninety-day detention.[1] 'My back hit the wall and he grabbed me by the shoulders and shouted in my face,' she said. 'His face was so close to mine I got spit in my face.' Tom Watson, a government whip, also shouted 'traitor' at her as she went into the rebel division lobby.* Gordon Brown and Foreign Secretary Jack Straw returned from overseas trips to vote in the division, with the government suffering its first defeat since coming to power, losing 322 to 291.† Blair left the chamber shaking his head. Armstrong faced briefing about her future following the loss. 'I just ignored it,' she says. 'I was not in trouble at all for that vote.'

Armstrong did, however, find herself in hot water as the government lost two votes on its bill to combat racial and religious hatred,

---

* Thornberry said Watson wasn't the whip who pushed her against the wall.
† MPs opted to increase the detention period to twenty-eight days.

with Blair contributing by missing the second division, which was lost by just one. 'Tony was furious because he didn't know [defeat was coming],' she says.

By May 2006, Armstrong had become the longest-serving Labour Chief Whip in government. Unapologetic for her confrontational style, she had navigated The Office through its stormiest seas, keeping, until the 2005 parliament, a near-perfect record. 'I loved it. I had a great time. I learned a lot about politics; about how things get done,' she says.

Some Labour MPs still cling to the Chief's acts of kindness. Iain Wright took a couple of days off after his grandmother died in 2006, returning to Parliament before the end of his permitted absence from the Commons.

'What the hell are you doing back? I don't want to see you here,' Armstrong told him.

'But, Hilary, I want to be. It helps me,' Wright replied.

Armstrong added: 'Any time you need to be away, get away.'

Given her approach to the role, not everyone was a fan. 'She wasn't a very skilful whip. She was too crude and tubthumping,' says an MP elected in 2005. Some people you can bully, others you can bribe, but there's a good deal more 'who have to be caressed, stroked and listened to and whose considerations must be taken into account', the MP adds.

Another says: 'She really divided the PLP into sheep and goats. She was a really bad Chief Whip because she believed that her job was simply to pass on the dictates from on high without listening to anyone.'

A year after the election, Armstrong was moved to the Cabinet Office, while Blair lined up a new Chief Whip for what would turn out to be his final year in 10 Downing Street.

* * *

The moment he heard the rumour on Sky News, Mike Foster picked up his phone and searched for Jacqui Smith's number. The two West

Midlands MPs were old friends; Foster's wife had done teacher training with Smith, while Foster had acted as her election agent in Redditch at the 1992 election. Knowing Smith was on a train to London, he rang her mobile.

'The speculation is you're going to be the Chief Whip,' he told Smith, who, he says, 'swore at me, as she does. She didn't believe it until she got off the train.'

Though incredulous, for the rest of the train journey, Smith pondered the idea. 'Oh, I quite fancy that,' she thought. Smith had never served in the whips' office but had views on how it might be run, based largely on her brief experience on the backbenches. As Schools Minister, she had also just helped take through the Education Act, which required 'hard graft' to secure MPs' backing. After receiving the offer from Tony Blair, Smith returned the favour to Foster.

'Sit by your phone,' she said. 'You're going to get a call from the Prime Minister.'

The Downing Street switchboard rang that evening to ask if Foster could hold. 'I want you to join the whips' office,' Blair told him. Foster received his first invitation to a whips' meeting the next day, greeted by Roy Stone,* the principal private secretary to the Government Chief Whip, who said: 'Welcome, Minister.'

Given her unfamiliarity with The Office, Smith was understandably nervous of how she'd be received by a group with a 'certain amount of mystique around it'. Her Deputy would be Bob Ainsworth, a veteran of eleven years who she believes had wanted to become Chief. 'There were a couple of days that were, to say the least, a little bit tricky.' She adds: 'I have to say that Bob then turned into an absolutely brilliant Deputy and really, really supportive.'

Smith sought to change how whips engaged with MPs, instigating a policy of ringing round their flock 'on a regular basis', says Foster.

---

* Roy Stone took over from Murdo Maclean in 2000.

'Jacqui's approach to it was probably more proactive.' Smith also carried out a survey on what subject areas MPs were interested in, their outside connections and how their expertise could be utilised.

Every Wednesday, Smith would walk through the Cabinet Office to No. 10 and spend half an hour with the Prime Minister. The Chief would fill him in on 'colour': the upcoming business, how people were feeling, who was being a pain, who was being good. A lot of Smith's time was spent meeting MPs, summoned or appearing unannounced because they 'weren't behaving as we would hope', they had personal issues or they wanted a job.

Unusually for a Chief, Smith spoke to the press, including doing the media round the morning after local elections. 'I never subscribed to the view that everything had to be kept secret,' she says. Smith had 'made a deal' when she took on the job 'that I didn't want to be completely silenced, and I still needed, on occasions, to talk publicly'.

Smith had inherited from her predecessor a PLP discontented with aspects of government policy, not least on Iraq, and split over its future leadership – a live discussion in Westminster ever since tensions between Labour's two biggest beasts had become known.

Alan Simpson was on his way to a PLP meeting when prying journalists waiting outside the committee room asked his thoughts on the Prime Minister and the Chancellor.

'Which side are you, Blair or Brown?' a journalist asked.

'No,' he replied.

'No to whom,' the journalist followed up.

'Just no.'

'You've got to be on one side or the other.'

'No. I'm being offered a choice between Saddam and Uday [Hussein], and my answer is neither. I'm not on either side,' he said.

Smith hauled Simpson in after his remark went public.

'If you're going into a war of choice on a completely fabricated set of arguments, don't expect me to pretend that you're any different,' he said. Simpson also revealed that he'd written to UN Secretary General Kofi Annan for a ruling on the legality of the Iraq invasion.

Smith responded by persuading the PLP to change its standing orders to allow a Chief to suspend MPs who make insulting remarks about colleagues and refuse to apologise. 'He made several public statements that were enormously insulting to the Prime Minister and … more than disrespectful to the Parliamentary Labour Party,' Smith says.

Though arguably more approachable than her predecessor, Smith was also a stickler for loyalty; the new Chief Whip had never rebelled as an MP. 'Sometimes, of course, I asked MPs to come and see me, and they chose to resign the whip rather than come – and that's Clare Short,' she says of the disgruntled former Cabinet minister who now sat as an independent MP. Smith also had a clash with Diane Abbott over her voting record, telling the backbencher at the end of an intemperate clash to 'fuck off out of my office'.[2]

* * *

On 31 August 2006, Defence Minister Tom Watson and a handful of Labour MPs dined at the Bilash restaurant in Wolverhampton. Over chicken vindaloo, saag paneer and a pint of beer, Watson discussed 'concerns' about Blair's leadership.[3] The frontbencher had held similar talks with Siôn Simon and others from his 2001 intake for several months. The MPs signed the restaurant's visitors book, their glowing reviews picked up by the *Mail on Sunday*.

'The whips' office had their own intelligence of where they thought rebellions might come from,' says Ann McKechin, a fellow MP elected in 2001. What whips had failed to grasp was the 'dynamic that exists' among people elected in the same intake, she continues.

Watson travelled to Scotland the next day for a weekend at a golf hotel in St Andrews, briefly visiting the Chancellor Gordon Brown during his stay. Watson insisted the two men didn't discuss a private letter he had been formulating calling on the Prime Minister to go.

After the dinner in Wolverhampton, the West Bromwich East MP and other conspirers rang up colleagues in pursuit of signatures. 'It was all done by phone calls,' says McKechin, a signatory after factoring in local views on Blair in the wake of Iraq.

The first Jacqui Smith heard of the plot was when somebody rang her up trying to recruit her to the cause. 'That didn't work!' she laughs. Some whips, however, were sympathetic. 'I tried to make sure that people understood their wider responsibility as whips for getting the business through, and I tried to rebuild the team and the cohesiveness of the team.'

The plotters sent the private letter, signed by seventeen MPs, to Downing Street. Smith instructed her whips to ring those who had put their names to it. Tommy McAvoy, the Pairing Whip and Comptroller, asked McKechin if she planned to say anything to the media. She said no, and McAvoy replied: 'That's fine, thank you very much.'

Iain Wright had joined the Commons as MP for Hartlepool at a by-election in 2004 but says the 2001 intake 'took me as their own'. Early on, he had tea in the Pugin Room with his whip after he accidentally voted in the wrong division lobby. His whip encouraged him to fess up to his local paper and explain: 'I was stupid, I was new. You don't get a floorplan for security reasons; I turned the wrong way.'

After Wright, a PPS, signed the letter calling for Blair's resignation, Smith spoke with him in her office.

'I'm going to work with you on the assumption, Iain, that nothing's changed, that we can trust you, that you've got the best interests of the Labour government at heart, and to that extent, I'm more than happy, if you want to be on committees, we will consider that,' she said.

Wright joined a select committee early the next year.

McKechin explains: 'They couldn't punish any of the backbenchers because we'd signed a private letter and we'd not spoken to the media.'

For all the plotters' silence, the letter *did* find its way to the media, with McKechin pointing the finger at No. 10. 'As a way of handling it, [they leaked it], yes.' Watson resigned as Defence Minister, with others, including Wright, following suit.

Though considered a fairly ineffectual coup, the Curry House Plot *was* successful in forcing Blair to announce his departure date, set for June 2007. Before his last goodbyes, the Prime Minister pushed through pending policies, including a tight vote to renew the Trident nuclear deterrent, which corresponded with Foster's birthday; in jest, he brought in a cake with a Campaign For Nuclear Disarmament badge stuck on in icing.

Smith managed to avoid defeat during her year as Chief Whip. 'I lost no votes, but I did lose a Prime Minister.' Wanting to preserve party unity, she helped oversee a smooth transition to the new leadership, with Gordon Brown elected unopposed after left-winger John McDonnell failed to get the required forty-five nominations from MPs to force a contest.

In between tight votes and coups, the whips squeezed in social occasions, with the team attending the premiere of *Whipping It Up*, a play by Steve Thompson, with actor Richard Wilson, who had a drink with The Office after the performance, portraying a Tory Chief.

The evening before Brown took over, the whips dined together, an occasion they dubbed 'The Last Supper'. The next day would bring in a new regime, one that would implement changes to The Office. There were, however, some who survived the transition, including one particular mainstay who would last the entirety of the New Labour government.

'If you're looking at the heavies,' an MP says, 'the trail leads on the Labour side to Tommy McAvoy.'

CHAPTER 40

TOMMY

The new-look Labour whips' team gathered in 9 Downing Street for their first weekly meeting since Gordon Brown became Prime Minister. Trays of bacon and sausage sandwiches lined tables pressed up against the wall, with tea and instant coffee also on offer; this being a gathering of Labour, not Tory whips, there were no goblets of champagne to be seen.

Diana Johnson, a newly appointed whip, grimaced as she surveyed the breakfast offerings. 'What about yoghurt and some fruit?' she asked, prompting Scotsman Tommy McAvoy, with his austere glare and thin, pursed lips, to remark: 'You cannae put brown sauce on yoghurt.'

Beyond pitching healthier breakfast alternatives, when dealing with McAvoy, a legend of The Office not just for his remarkable longevity, the most egregious error one could make was to refer to him as Glaswegian. When an MP who had been refused a pair described him as a 'Glaswegian thug', McAvoy pointed out that he was from Rutherglen.[1] Elected MP for his native Glasgow Rutherglen in 1987, he successfully pushed to take the burgh out of Glasgow and back into Lanarkshire. His seat became Rutherglen and Hamilton West in 2005.

McAvoy's passion for Rutherglen was matched only by his commitment to his party, religion and family, including his wife of more than fifty years and their four sons. 'Central to his character was he's Catholic,' says a colleague. Nick Brown says: 'He was Catholic not by faith or conviction but tribally. Born into it, that was the side he was on, and my God, he was.'

Some MPs knew the way to McAvoy's heart. A Labour Member who had missed a vote while overseas came to The Office armed with an offering from Lourdes in south-western France, known for its Catholic pilgrimage site.

During his life, McAvoy had to adjust to the changing approach of younger generations to the sectarian divide in Glasgow. When a youngster turned up at his house wearing a Rangers shirt – the football team traditionally supported by the city's Protestants – saying he was there to see his son, McAvoy was certain he was at the wrong house.

'No, it's all right, I'm coming down shortly!' his son shouted down.

McAvoy's whipping story began in 1990, joining the opposition whips' office under Neil Kinnock, where he remained for three years, returning in 1996. From 1997, McAvoy was in charge of the floor of the House as Comptroller, also acting as Pairing and Accommodation Whip, through whom MPs would have to travel in pursuit of time off or better workspaces.

'Tommy was absolutely old-school scary,' says a whip.

Midway through the 1997 parliament, with a handful of Tories and Northern Ireland MPs filibustering in the Commons, Chris Mullin went to see McAvoy at 3.40 a.m. The government had enjoyed a majority of 220 in the last vote, and Mullin wanted to go home.

Finding McAvoy slumped in an armchair watching a television programme about Stalin, his red braces 'stretched across his large belly', Mullin sought to reason with the senior whip. 'Tommy, do we really need to win every division by a majority of 200 plus?'

'Can you guarantee for me, Chris, that the Tories won't suddenly turn up and vote?'

'They will if we keep this nonsense going until they return refreshed from a night's sleep.'

'This is class war, Chris,' McAvoy said.

'In case you haven't noticed, Tommy, the other class is at home in bed.'

Mullin's efforts 'cut no ice'.[2]

In the first parliament of the Labour government, Ben Bradshaw made a similar attempt for MPs to go home during a late-night sitting.

'What do you want?' McAvoy asked.

'I haven't had sex for ages. I just want to go home!' Bradshaw replied, according to an MP. Bradshaw remembers the exchange slightly differently; after business wrapped up in the chamber,* he said: 'At last, I can go and have sex with my husband!'

'Well, off you go then,' McAvoy said with an open mouth.

One evening during Blair's first parliament as Prime Minister, the Conservatives had seemingly left the estate, with the government believing they had gone home for the night. Tory MPs had, in fact, gathered nearby and returned to Parliament in time for votes. The government wasn't defeated, but the act 'kept them on their toes much more and made sure that more of them had to stay around every evening', says a Conservative MP.

McAvoy would explain to whips: 'It's all very well people coming to me and saying, "My cat's sick and I need to go home," but actually, what they don't understand is that all these other people are absent, we're concerned that there might be an ambush being made against us, that's why I need to keep a really tight hold on who gets to be slipped and who doesn't.'

Some MPs question McAvoy's methodology in approving pairs. 'He, obviously being a Scot, would always say to [Scottish MPs], "Oh yeah, off you go,"' says a fellow whip, highlighting that it often took other MPs – who didn't have the option of flying – longer to return to their constituencies. 'I didn't feel that he was particularly fair.'

An MP who sought time off for an Armed Forces Parliamentary Scheme event was told by her whip that McAvoy wasn't keen and had said she was 'always off the whip'. 'I looked at my record, and I hadn't

---

* McAvoy would tell MPs 'away with ye' when they could finally go home.

missed a vote – not one,' says the MP. Her whip investigated and found that was the case. The same MP says McAvoy demanded she come back after attending an event, requiring her, on a Thursday, to travel to Yorkshire, return to London, then head north again to her constituency. 'I didn't because it was stupid,' the MP says.

Some McAvoy rejections proved short-sighted. Alan Simpson submitted a slip asking to be paired so that he could attend a meeting in Tyneside. After thinking it over, McAvoy rejected his request late on. Simpson then received a call from a BBC *Newsnight* producer asking if he could do an interview. The following morning, Simpson went into the whips' office.

'Oh, Tommy, I'm not sure whether I owe you an apology or a vote of thanks,' Simpson said.

'What do you mean by that?'

'Well, I was a bit miffed that I couldn't do the Tyneside meeting last night, but as it turned out, I got this request from *Newsnight*, so I was able to go and put my arguments in front of a much bigger audience on television... So, I owe you one!'

McAvoy paused, before saying: 'I think you should just fuck off now before you're in any more trouble than you are already. Just fuck off.'

On rare occasions, McAvoy could overlook unapproved absences – when provided with an adequate explanation. He rang up Huw Edwards after the backbencher missed a series of votes the previous evening.

'Where were you? What were you doing?' he demanded.

'Tommy, I was playing cricket. We had a parliamentary cricket game,' Edwards responded.

'You were playing *cricket*?' McAvoy said in disgust. 'You can't be playing cricket when we've got votes here!'

Edwards took out his team sheet and read out the list of people who played, featuring four Labour MPs and seven Conservatives, meaning the Tories had lost a net of three votes.

'Ah, Huwie, you're a great man! You're a great man!' McAvoy said.

McAvoy was less impressed with Edwards the first day back after the 2001 election, finding him at the Members' entrance wearing a stripey blazer.

'Where are you going?'

'Sorry, Tommy, we're going to Australia on a [parliamentary] rugby tour.'

'You can't go on a tour!' the whip fumed.

'Tommy, I was going on this tour, win or lose. I've won, you've got a majority of [more than 100], and we're on the plane to Australia.'

Jim Knight was at a dinner in 1 Parliament Street also attended by ex-Labour frontbencher Martin O'Neill when the division bell went midway through proceedings. 'Don't worry about it... Stay here; it will be fine,' O'Neill told him. McAvoy later 'tore me off a strip', Knight says. 'That was part of my learning that I shouldn't listen to the old lags.'

For all he could aggravate MPs, McAvoy received a rare outpouring of love when, in July 2006, he became the longest-serving Comptroller and government whip since records began. No fewer than 137 MPs signed an EDM recognising McAvoy's 'outstanding achievement' and 'the difficult task he has of securing government business whilst accommodating the ... requirements of 352 Labour colleagues'. Signed by five Conservatives, including members of the opposition whips' office, the EDM acknowledged 'the respect he has earned from all sides' and wished him well 'in a role that with his unique qualities, he has made all his own'.

* * *

If people came into the whips' office with an impression of Tommy McAvoy, they often left with an entirely different one.

'We absolutely loved him. We would die for him. We were in awe of him. Secondly, he was the most frustrating fucker I've ever worked for,' a whip says. McAvoy, they add, was 'boring, brilliant, scrupulously fair and ruthless'. The whip remembers being in a car with McAvoy after visiting John Prescott at the Deputy Prime Minister's Dorneywood residence. For ninety minutes, McAvoy looked ahead without saying a word.

McAvoy, who had a plaque saying 'Feminism spoken here' and a dead piranha on his desk,[3] was known for his acerbic wit. Braver members of The Office would even give McAvoy a bit of grief. Mike Foster still has photos of fellow whip Alan Campbell sitting in McAvoy's chair with his feet on the desk. 'Tommy would have killed us had he seen it.'

Not everyone in The Office got on with McAvoy. 'I found him a bit of a bully,' says the whip who complained about McAvoy prioritising Scottish MPs, who worked alongside him in the upper whips' office. In late 2003, MPs were given a free vote on enforced fluoridation of water supplies. When someone asked how you spell fluoride, McAvoy responded: 'P-o-i-s-o-n.' The whip, who was pro-fluoride, says: 'I remember thinking, "I'm going to have a real problem with Tommy here."' Chief Whip Hilary Armstrong defused the tension by saying before voting: 'Healthy teeth this way.'

McAvoy had little truck with ministers he felt failed to meet their parliamentary obligations. When Jacqui Smith was Home Secretary, for the first time in her decade in politics, she went home ill at lunchtime. At five o'clock, she received a call saying she had to come back to vote. 'I could not even have half a day off ill when I wasn't a notorious skiver.'

Early on in Diana Johnson's time as a whip, a member of her flock – a senior Cabinet minister no less – asked to be slipped as they were having a 'very important' dinner party. 'I obviously was a little bit naive, and I put this down on a form,' Johnson says. McAvoy came running down the stairs to the lower whips' office clutching the form, on which he'd put a big red cross. 'A London dinner party wasn't going to get someone off the whip,' she notes.

Most unnerving for the whips, McAvoy was well across events on Committee Corridor. When a whip lost a vote unexpectedly at committee stage, word had reached the upper whips' office before they had even made it back to their desk. 'What happened there? You better get it sorted,' McAvoy said.

As Schools Minister, Jim Knight took through the Education and Inspections Act. The departmental whip, 'who shall remain nameless', had miscalculated in allowing people to take holiday in the run-up to Easter, which coincided with a Labour member of the committee going on compassionate leave. Taken together, the respective absences meant the government would lose its majority on the committee the following week.

Knight approached McAvoy, who was 'pissed off' with all involved, for advice. 'You're going to have to finish the bill tonight, however late that goes, but you're not allowed to tell anyone until it's very late in the evening,' he said.

The session, which was due to finish at 6 p.m. that Thursday, finished at midday Friday. 'It was all a bit outrageous,' says Knight, with opposition parties and the committee chair blindsided. 'But it's the way whipping works if you realise you haven't got the votes.'

With Gordon Brown in No. 10, McAvoy adjusted to life under his fifth Chief Whip since the start of the Labour government, entering his eleventh year as Comptroller of the Household. Little did he or The Office know of the seismic economic and political tests to come.*

---

* In March 2024, McAvoy, by now a Labour peer and a whip in the upper chamber, passed away at the age of eighty. Nick Brown and George Mudie, two of his close friends from The Office and fellow senior whips, visited him in hospital in Glasgow before cancer took his life. 'All three of us were stuck for something to say to each other,' says Brown. '"Are you all right?" is a slightly hapless thing to say to someone who you know isn't. In adversity, he was as brave and as firm of purpose as he was in life.'

CHAPTER 41

CRISES

Geoff Hoon was an unusual choice for Gordon Brown's first Chief Whip; even the former Defence Secretary knew that. It's not that he lacked experience. On the contrary, unlike the previous two Chiefs, he'd already served in the whips' office, with a year as Leader of the House on his résumé to boot. But as a 'card-carrying Blairite', he wasn't a natural fit for the role under Brown, who worked with a close-knit and largely impregnable group of politicians and advisers, not least 'the two Eds' – Balls and Miliband – now senior frontbenchers.

But then, that's why the Prime Minister appointed him.

'Gordon wanted to reach across the divide in the Labour Party,' Hoon says. The Prime Minister was 'very flattering' in their meeting, offering assurances and carrots that 'were never really delivered'. Hoon accepted the position – only to regret it. 'You can't have a Chief Whip who is neither trusted nor part of the Prime Minister's circle.'

There was a third man in Hoon and Brown's relationship.

'I was Chief Whip in name, and I had the office and the trappings, and I did the job as best I could, but I always knew that the real Chief Whip was Nick Brown.'

Nick Brown, a close confidant of the new Prime Minister and veteran whip, was back in The Office as the number two. Hoon remembers going into Nick Brown's office, where his Deputy 'very quickly' shut down a telephone call that he guessed was with the Prime Minister. Nick Brown says these claims of him being the de facto Chief Whip are 'not unfair'. 'He just left me to run it, and I did. He sort of thought strategic thoughts,' Nick Brown says of Hoon.

A Labour MP says that, on 'certain things', Nick Brown and George Mudie, the former Deputy Chief Whip, were running an 'unofficial' whips' office. 'I was unofficially working with them,' the MP says. Nick Brown confirms: 'We had auxiliaries, people who were runners who might come into the whips' office later under a different regime.'

Gordon Brown is a man known for his fierce loyalty, underpinned by a pronounced and limiting insecurity, as well as for his celebrated intellectual heft and political talent. Such loyalty is a rare commodity in politics; Brown regularly pushed for his acolytes at government reshuffles. On the other hand, when times got difficult, he 'surrounded himself with those people and didn't really go beyond that', Hoon says. 'That was a terrible mistake.'

The whips' office was 'a little bit more disjointed' during the transition to a new administration, Mike Foster says, with incumbent Blairites joined by the likes of Tom Watson, the point man of the Curry House Plot, who was back as an assistant whip. 'There was more of an edge to our meetings, shall we say.' At the weekly gatherings, whips were encouraged to speak out. 'That's when you might get the odd frosty exchange.'

Though outside the inner circle, Hoon would go over to No. 10 at 7 a.m. mid-week to help with prep for Prime Minister's Questions. Often he had the feeling that Brown 'had been pounding his word processor for several hours already'. Hoon says he was involved in the first of Brown's reshuffles, discussing individuals with the Prime Minister, but doesn't think he reviewed any Cabinet-level appointments. His relative marginalisation 'freed' him to concentrate on the 'HR' side and running of The Office, tasks often associated with the Deputy, Nick Brown and Hoon almost reversing roles. He put Foster in charge of moving The Office from pagers to texts, requiring negotiations with service providers.

Though 'quite a laidback individual', as one of his whips describes him, Hoon gave his fair share of dressing downs. A Eurosceptic pushing for a referendum on the EU's Treaty of Lisbon says Hoon 'just screamed at me for five minutes'. Jim Knight, a government minister, had committed to speak at a GMB Union conference in Plymouth, but Hoon wanted him back in the Commons. 'He told me that if I didn't get back for the vote, he would recommend my dismissal to the Prime Minister,' he says. Knight duly took a flight to London.

The change in leadership briefly neutralised dissent, with Labour MPs wanting to give Brown, as Hoon says, 'the benefit of quite a lot of doubt'.

Soon, the sands would shift.

* * *

In his last budget before taking over as Prime Minister, Gordon Brown announced plans to abolish the 10p rate of income tax, taking the lowest earners into the 20 per cent tax bracket. With his successor, Alistair Darling, reaffirming the proposals in April 2008, he faced a sizeable nascent backlash.

Unease could also be found inside the whips' office. Mike Foster and Sarah McCarthy-Fry, both accountants and the latter Geoff Hoon's PPS, made the case against abolishing the 10p rate, which they believed to be regressive. 'We had sat down and crunched the numbers between the two of us, and we were going, "This is just not good,"' Foster says. The pair asked Hoon to raise their concerns up the food chain.

The threat to the government came from Labour MP Frank Field, who tabled an amendment to Darling's Finance Bill, backed by forty-six Labour MPs, to prevent the abolition of the 10p rate until measures had been put in place to protect those affected. Field headed to the Commons to find out when his amendment would be called and was told by the whips that there would first be a vote before his debate would begin. Walking slowly back to his office in Portcullis House, Field thought the whips 'could rat on me'. He ran back to the chamber.

As he pushed his way in, his amendment was being called. 'The whips had decided not to have a debate on the amendment before mine and hoped mine would fall because I wouldn't be in the chamber to move it.'

Speaker Michael Martin allowed Field to find his place and move the amendment, to which Darling responded, announcing a compensation package. 'The government didn't restore the 10p [rate], but I think spent more money on concessions than they made from the 10p's withdrawal,' says Field, who withdrew his amendment after Darling's announcement.

Later in the year, the government was forced to shelve plans to extend terror detention from twenty-eight to forty-two days after a resounding defeat in the Lords. The Office had narrowly secured a victory in the Commons by 315 to 306 thanks to some smart whipping and an agreement with the Democratic Unionist Party (DUP).

Inviting two MPs intending to abstain to his personal office near the Commons chamber, Nick Brown asked an official to bring up a canvass return outlining how the whips thought the result would turn out. 'The youngster brought up a previous iteration, so it was worse than it would have been by five o'clock, with the vote at seven – much worse,' Brown says.

Surveying the projection, the MPs said: 'We had no idea! All right, then...' and voted with the government.

In the chamber, Ian Paisley, the former DUP leader, 'crossed the chamber very dramatically' and shook Nick Brown's hand, saying: 'We've had our losses', in reference to violence in Northern Ireland. A colleague in the whips' office, noticing Tory discontent at the DUP's support, told the Deputy Chief Whip: 'Nick, you better just get the vote moved.'

With the bill later withdrawn, The Office got stuck into Sadiq Khan, the whip overseeing the measure. Foster gifted him a copy of *The Hitchhiker's Guide to the Galaxy* at Secret Santa that Christmas, in which forty-two is the number from which all meaning can be derived.

Throughout the year, the world had teetered on the edge of a global financial crisis, the first signs of which had appeared, as far as the UK was concerned, in September 2007. Darling was forced to guarantee all deposits at Northern Rock after the first run on a bank in 150 years. In the subsequent period, the Treasury's most senior civil servant, Nick Macpherson, called a former colleague, Helen Goodman, who was serving as Deputy Leader of the House.

'We might need to take emergency legislation on the banks this week. How quickly can you get it through?' he asked.

'As quickly as you like,' Goodman responded.

'In twenty-four hours?'

'Yep, sure. We can do that.'

Goodman briefed Hoon on the conversation. 'He was very pissed off with me… He said, "Helen, I've got to get everyone to stay all night, and you've landed me with that."'

The pretence of Nick Brown acting as Deputy ended in October 2008, when he formally reclaimed the mantle of Chief Whip. Hoon's indifferent and frustrating year in The Office ended with a move to the Department for Transport as Secretary of State. Nick Brown implemented a moniker for the whips to follow: 'We don't do policy, we do process.'[1]

After eleven years as Comptroller, Tommy McAvoy served once more as Nick Brown's Deputy Chief Whip, this time in the position of Treasurer of Her Majesty's Household. The Office, with additions from the 2005 intake and a few Brownites to boot, was arguably more cohesive. 'Which was a good thing, because we spent most of our time trying to keep the government from disaster,' says a new joiner.

The reshuffle came at the height of the maelstrom in financial markets, with the Prime Minister playing a pivotal role in shaping the international response. For the whips, the largest burden from the crisis fell on the shoulders of the Lord Commissioners, who were called in abruptly to countersign enormous (and exceptionally urgent) cheques. One whip, after signing sensitive documents, 'was then locked in a room until the markets opened', recalled Labour whip Helen Jones.[2] Another Lord Commissioner burst into The Office and declared: 'I've just bought a bank!'

The global financial crisis and its subsequent handling made little difference to the whips' day-to-day lives, with the peril, if not the consequences, largely outside the parliamentary estate. The same could not be said for an imminent era-defining Westminster scandal.

* * *

While issuing a three-line whip, the government put forward a motion to exempt MPs' expenses from disclosure under a Freedom of Information request, following a long-running dispute with transparency campaigners seeking to pull back the curtain. Under widespread opposition, the proposal was dropped, and disclosure of MPs' expenses was set for July 2009. The *Daily Telegraph*, however, got hold of the details a few months in advance.

Incrementally, day by day, the newspaper revealed claims made by MPs and ministers that shocked, appalled and angered the public in equal measure. In time, six MPs would be convicted of criminal offences, with hundreds called on to repay their expenses.

The issue arguably has its roots back in 1971, when MPs' salaries and expenses were separated. Ministers, wary of sending out the wrong signals to the public at a time of economic hardship, preferred to raise allowances as a means of upping MPs' pay,* which has not kept pace with the growth in average earnings since 1911, the first year they

---

* From 1971, MPs drew primarily on four main allowances: a car allowance, a secretarial allowance, an additional costs allowance and a London supplement (for those unable to claim the additional costs).

received money.* Concurrently, the role of an MP, particularly with regards to constituency casework, was becoming more burdensome; the number of letters sent to the Commons rose from 10,000 a week in 1964 to 40,000 a week in 1997. A 2011 parliamentary inquiry said that 'several MPs and former MPs' suggested that the whips had encouraged them to make up for 'deficiencies' in salary by claiming 'as much as possible as allowances'. The Committee on Members' Expenses cited one backbencher who said that in 1976, following a meeting about pay with then Leader of the House Michael Foot, word came back from the whips that it was 'untimely' to increase salaries significantly 'but a new range of allowances would be put in place and nobody would ask too many questions about claims for them'.

'None of this meant that the allowances could be claimed regardless of whether the costs were incurred,' the committee wrote in its report. 'Rules and principles existed, even though the requirement for evidence and the checking of claims were lax.'

In time, the additional costs allowance granted to MPs covered 'some expenditure which would otherwise have been paid out of salaries, such as white goods, home furnishings and home improvements', the committee wrote. 'Thus the separation of salary and expenses envisaged in 1971 was muddied, eventually with disastrous results in 2009.'[3]

The fallout from the expenses scandal would last for years and, for the whips, be of high consequence. Gordon Brown oversaw the introduction of the Independent Parliamentary Standards Authority, taking responsibility for MPs' expenses and salary away from the Commons. He also initiated the Reform of the House of Commons Committee, known as the Wright Committee, whose suggestions for restoring faith in Westminster included wholesale changes to select committees and other aspects of parliamentary life in the whips' gift.

---

* MPs took home £400 in 1911.

The Office, too, was caught up in the initial scandal, on what became known as 'Whips' Day' in the *Telegraph*'s tranche of reports. On the morning in question, Nick Brown walked into The Office and asked: 'How many of you have had emails from the *Daily Telegraph*?' Those who had received a request for comment raised their hands; those who hadn't took on their duties, so that the whips could respond to the newspaper.

While answering for their own expenses, the whips also had to pick up the pieces for their MPs, many of whom faced remonstrations and vitriol, with an irate public seeking answers. A whip had people shouting outside their house at night. 'I had letters that were quite threatening... calling me a thief, all this sort of stuff.' The same whip says MPs' spouses were spat at in supermarkets. Some MPs had panic attacks. A Tory MP's police officer son was spat at while on duty. 'That's for your dad,' said the culprit.

'We were in a place where we genuinely feared that someone might take their life,' says a SpAd. 'We had whips who had young children or teenagers at school who were getting bullied as a result.'

When two of the MPs caught up in the *Telegraph*'s reporting died four months apart, Labour's David Taylor and Ashok Kumar – the former from a heart attack and the latter of undisclosed natural causes – a whip said: 'That's manslaughter by the *Daily Telegraph*.' Another wonders: 'Who knows if those people would have still been alive without the extra worry they had?'

A separate whip, after an MP claimed expenses for pet food, was walking in the park with her dog when someone shouted: 'We're paying for your dog's dinner!' Helen Goodman, who joined The Office in October 2008, says: 'Criticism was extremely strong, and rightly so. People were very shocked by it, so there was a lot of unhappiness among parliamentarians.'

Conservative MP Charles Walker says he got 'frightfully upset at being positioned as a crook' and handed in a letter to the party's Chief

CRISES

Whip, Patrick McLoughlin, saying he was resigning from the 1922 Committee of backbench Tory MPs. He took the same letter to Sir Michael Spicer, the chair of the 1922 Committee, of which Walker was an executive member.

'Oh my God, Charles, you've just resigned the whip,' Spicer told him.

'No, I haven't. I've resigned from the 1922 Committee.'

'But we're all on the 1922 Committee. What you meant to write was that you wanted to resign from the *executive* of the 1922 Committee!'

Spicer rang up McLoughlin. 'He hasn't resigned the whip, Patrick. I've got him here. No, no.' Walker heard a 'chuckle down the phone'.

Margaret Hodge was away throughout the period, on compassionate leave taking care of her husband, with her job as a Culture Minister kept open until her return. While she was called in once or twice to vote, the whips didn't put any pressure on Hodge, but nor did they ask after her circumstances. 'They're not good at that supporting of individuals,' she argues. Hodge's husband passed away in June 2009. She resumed her ministerial role in the autumn.

Speaking about the whips' purpose, one member of The Office says: 'You may be able to help people on certain things, but your primary duty is to deliver the votes. A lot of nonsense is talked about whips' offices as personnel departments, to be honest.'

The whips navigated the fallout from the expenses scandal and the uncertainty of the financial crisis with tight votes in the Commons. An adviser nicknamed 'Grid Boy' would put together the lists ahead of divisions. While the government started with a majority, in reality, given the rebellious fever spreading through the PLP, it often didn't.

In April 2009, twenty-seven Labour MP supported a non-binding Liberal Democrat motion, put forward on an opposition half-day, offering all Gurkhas equal right of residence, ushering in Brown's first significant defeat as Prime Minister. Nick Brown thought he had negotiated a deal with the Labour MP leading the rebellion, who he says failed to pass on the news to his fellow backbenchers.

On Committee Corridor, inexperienced members of The Office dropped the ball. One whip lost a vote because 'he had forgotten what Labour policy was', shouting 'aye' to a vote on an amendment he should have opposed, with other Labour committee members following his lead.[4] Another whip, Dawn Butler, failed to ensure MPs arrived on time for a committee session at 9 a.m. Tory shadow minister John Hayes, teaming up with Lib Dem members, managed to 'defeat a whole clause before the skills minister, Siôn Simon, and chums' turned up, *The Guardian* reported.[5] McAvoy demanded the committee sit until it finished business, going until 4.30 the next morning, adjourning for four hours before resuming.

In between crises, the whips held an annual photo with the Prime Minister, who was a rare visitor to The Office, except after closely fought votes. He invited the team to a reception at Downing Street also attended by regional journalists, with parched and hungry whips descending like a plague of locusts on the wine and the snacks.

Brown saw his Chief Whip regularly. 'I had a tremendous amount of access to him,' says Nick Brown. The Prime Minister instructed an official to draw up plans to turn the meeting room in 12 Downing Street, the whips' former home, into a hub of people whom he often wanted to summon immediately. Nick Brown met the person putting together the proposal. 'In the corner, outside the door of the old Chief Whip's office, there was one desk unallocated,' he recalls. After explaining where the different functionaries would be, the official wavered over who would have the unallocated desk.

'Don't you dare. Don't you even try it,' Brown pre-empted.

'Right,' the official said. 'I thought that's what you might say.'

The expenses scandal ran concurrently with ill-feeling towards Brown's leadership flourishing on the backbenches, graced with grandees and discontented former ministers, many of whom were from the Blairite wing of the party.

Diana Johnson had John Prescott, the former Deputy Prime

Minister, in her flock. When she rang to say she was his whip, he replied: 'Don't bother ringing me, I will speak to Gordon.'

Angst over Brown could also be found in the Cabinet. Nick Brown instructed Helen Jones, the departmental whip in the Department of Culture, Media and Sport, to 'find out what [Secretary of State James Purnell] is doing and stop it'.[6] Purnell resigned in June 2009 and called on the Prime Minister to follow suit.

In her book on how to be a whip, Jones recalled how, via an insider, the whips uncovered where a group of ministers plotting against the Prime Minister would meet, with their dinners recorded indiscreetly in their diaries.[7] Nick Brown says of handling potential coups: 'You have to know what you're doing, keep to the point, front them down, sometimes argue them down and focus on the key job, which is to get the parliamentary business through.'

In January 2010, former ministers Geoff Hoon and Patricia Hewitt wrote to Labour MPs calling for a secret ballot on the party leadership. The ex-Chief Whip explains: 'I knew lots of MPs who were profoundly unhappy but knew there was an election coming, who didn't feel it was the right time to change leaders. The Tories would have done it in a heartbeat.'

An election loomed, with the Labour government having navigated two transcendent crises that would affect the UK economy and political system for years to come. But were the Tories ready to capitalise?

CHAPTER 42

P. M.

Labour frontbencher Gerry Sutcliffe, sporting a tie with the parliamentary crest and a faint outline of a whip, arrived at a committee on science without knowing anything about the subject at hand. With Lord Sainsbury, the Science Minister, unable to attend, Sutcliffe was called upon to take one for the team by delivering a speech and fielding questions.

As an ex-whip, he did his duty.

'I used to wear the whips' tie when it was a dodgy day of business,' he explains. 'Whips or anybody who had been a whip on the opposition side wouldn't put you under pressure.'

Perhaps spying signs of a vulnerable, unbriefed minister, Conservative MP Cheryl Gillan asked detailed questions about space policy, despite having also passed through The Office. Sutcliffe tried to bat her off with delaying answers, and Labour MPs put forward 'daft' questions about *Star Wars* to buy him more time.

Conservative whip Michael Fabricant handed Sutcliffe a note.

> Gerry, the reason she knows so much is because her husband was the director general of the British National Space Centre.

Gillan, who, in her political career, also served as secretary of the all-party group on space policy, hadn't declared her husband's background.

'When I found that out, I went to town, and she apologised,' Sutcliffe says.

He said to Fabricant afterwards: 'Why did you do that?'

'Us whips have got to stick together,' Fabricant replied.

Aided by a jaded cynicism about their colleagues, of whom they have seen all sides – good, bad, exceptionally ugly – whips from rival parties can share a close relationship. 'Some of the Labour whips that I dealt with both in opposition and in government are people that I get on extremely well with still,' says a senior Conservative Party whip.

The Conservative and Labour whips who served during Tony Blair and Gordon Brown's premierships were no different to any other generations. While the minister and their opposite number were going at it hammer and tongs, whips would negotiate when to finish.

A government whip acting as a teller stood at the top of the division lobby next to their opposition counterpart, ready to count MPs registering their vote with Commons staff. The whip, who had been to a whisky tasting, 'was completely pissed, absolutely pissed out of my head', he confesses. His Tory opposite number, Geoffrey Clinton-Brown, 'propped me up and counted the vote for me'. 'I put the vote down at 286 and he said, "No… it's 386." You depend on that relationship to make it work,' the Labour whip says of the Usual Channels.

The Labour whips had a particular respect for an enduring member of the opposition whips' office, Patrick McLoughlin, a former miner who first joined The Office in 1995. Three years later, McLoughlin had been promoted to Deputy.

The whisky-tasting whip, no longer in The Office, recalls McLoughlin coming to his aid midway through the 2001 parliament. A copy of the Queen's Speech was sent to Buckingham Palace the evening before the monarch was due to read it out in the Lords as part of the state opening of Parliament. The ex-whip says when they received the speech back, it had been cut in half. 'We completely shat ourselves.' The minister rang Buckingham Palace asking – tentatively – for an explanation. 'The Queen's private secretary said, "Yes, she's going to Ascot. She needs to get away early."'

The minister continues: 'The problem was we'd already press-released it, so I had to phone Patrick.'

He told McLoughlin: 'Patrick, the Queen is not going to read out the whole speech. Don't you fucking dare play politics with this, because if the press notice, they're going to blame us, and you better not blame us because we can't blame the Queen.'

'I assure you,' McLoughlin said. 'I won't do that.'

* * *

After the bloodbath of the 1997 election, the Tories had to be strategic in their whipping.

Left with a rump of 165 MPs, the party couldn't land many blows against the Labour juggernaut. The Office, with James Arbuthnot as Chief and Patrick McLoughlin as Deputy, prioritised Committee Corridor, Commons-related mischief and tactical skirmishes, negotiating with MPs to ensure their attendance. The whips also pushed hard to make sure the party had representation in the chamber, rather than an 'endless stream of government speakers', as one whip puts it. But a new joiner, appointed to the frontbench within a year, recalls a debate where the Tory attendance was just him, the whip on bench duty and an MP.

With several of the Tory old guard surviving the cull, the whips had to convince grandiose colleagues – who could no longer be tantalised with ministerial roles – to put in the hard yards, opting for a mixture of charm, placation and bartering. One whip asked a former minister, 'who was quite important in his mind', why he had missed a vote. After the MP 'went off on me', the whip wrote a grovelling letter, making reference to all the important roles they'd held during their career. 'Junior Minister in Charge of Widgets? Wow, that really must have been very, very important.' The MP eased up after the flattery.

Another whip would invite a grandee for a glass of whisky, asking him about Parliament when he was first elected nearly thirty years earlier. At the end of the trip down memory lane, the MP would often say: 'Well, dear boy. I've thoroughly enjoyed this. I was going to vote against the Conservatives on this, but I will abstain. How's that?'

The whip explains: 'The job of the whips' office, of course, is to prove that if you cooperate, there will be rewards. It's like the Society of Jesus in the eighteenth century; you show them the bible but also the instruments of torture.'[1]

Induction for the 1997 intake was minimal. 'Can I get some instructions as to how to do this?' an MP asked.

A whip responded: 'Well, Churchill didn't have to ask that.'

Arbuthnot worked hard on cultivating a team atmosphere, meeting with backbenchers to set out what the party wanted to do in the week ahead. The whips distributed questions for PMQs and made use of the Parliamentary Research Unit, relying on willing filibusterers to keep Labour ministers at the despatch box, before the controversial change to Commons sitting hours, which diluted this prized piece of opposition power.

Nick Brown says the Tories under William Hague focused on trying to disrupt the Labour government however they could, blanketly opposing measures and looking at conventions, such as refusing to allow questions to be taken together as a block, even if they related to each other. Arbuthnot, the Tory Chief Whip, was a 'nice person, totally rational'. But the Tories 'tried every single thing they could think of within the rules – just', Brown contends.

Ahead of one PMQs, McLoughlin approached Ann Widdecombe with a tip that, prior to the government introducing the national minimum wage, a Labour donor was paying his workers less than the proposed baseline hourly rate. 'I wouldn't have had that hit but for the whips' office and Patrick,' says Widdecombe.

In March 2001, McLoughlin and Widdecombe took part in a sit-in protest at the amount of time given to discuss the committee stage of a bill on law and order, with the government hoping to drive the legislation through before that year's general election.

The Office also indulged in wry mischief. McLoughlin would later recall to aides the time whips made up a rumour that a Labour minister was due to make a statement, forcing a Secretary of State to deliver one to the Commons, succumbing to an expectant media.

McLoughlin, as Deputy Chief Whip, didn't let the Conservatives' reduced standing alter discipline in The Office, not least on timekeeping. A new whip, known among his friends and family for tardiness, arrived one morning on the fifth bong of Big Ben for his first whips' meeting, with everyone else present before the top of the hour. The Chief looked at his watch and said: 'Good afternoon.'

The whips were expected to give reports on their flock and know what they were covering. 'We were permanently out there, hunting MPs down in the Smoking Room or wherever to have conversations,' says a whip. The whips also maintained the system of notes, with the safe's password still the leader's birthdate.

'We were keeping track of people's foibles, but more to do with behaviours,' says a whip. 'If somebody was drinking too much, perhaps, and we could see that they may need a little bit of help getting home in the evenings if we were asking them to stay for late votes.' The notes were kept for two weeks only.

Given the diminished number of MPs, The Office adapted the system for allocating whips' flocks. David Maclean, who succeeded Arbuthnot in 2001, asked whip Stephen O'Brien to produce a report on how best to do it. With the Maastricht rebel Iain Duncan Smith taking over from Hague as leader, the party ruminated on how to get the right-winger better press. As part of this, in his report, O'Brien suggested organising whips 'into regions which match the television stations', with a view to 'making sure that we could then, within our flocks, find ways of getting stories [into the press]'. Stories could relate to issues such as local truancy figures, literacy levels or hospital waiting lists. 'That gave us the coverage for the political programmes, particularly on Fridays and the weekends,' the whip explains.

The whips' office as a collective didn't dabble with leaking stories to the press – though some individuals would take on the task. 'People who were very comfortable and skilled at the dark arts would … appoint themselves,' O'Brien says. 'People knew it was happening and then would channel either real or false information through them.'

A future member of The Office says: 'They were absolutely, expressly – and still are – not supposed to do this.'

Throughout Duncan Smith's time as leader, the whips picked up on unrest among MPs, the majority of whom hadn't supported his bid for the top job, with the Eurosceptic winning via the newly introduced party membership vote against Ken Clarke. On his return to Parliament in 2001,* Alistair Burt, a centrist One Nation Conservative, worked, at the whips' request, as Duncan Smith's PPS. 'Look, Iain's in trouble. He's only got one PPS, Owen Paterson, and they both speak the same language, and we don't think he's listening. We need another voice in there,' a senior whip told Burt.

After a member of The Office asked Graham Brady, a Tory MP since 1997, if he would lend his support to Duncan Smith at PMQs and a meeting of the 1922 Committee, the whip paused and said of the party leader: 'The trouble is, he is shit, isn't he?'[2]

Some members of the parliamentary party felt the whips' team, led by Maclean, was unnecessarily abrasive. 'They were trying to be hectoring and old-style military, and it just didn't work,' says a frontbencher. John Hayes, Pairing Whip from 2001 to 2002, carried a clipboard 'which would ostentatiously appear at PMQs', jotting down who was there, who wasn't and the quality of questions asked. 'It was just all so obvious and ridiculous.'

Douglas Hogg, a barrister, would humour Hayes by putting in

---

* Burt had lost his seat at the 1997 election.

writing the days he would be in the Commons or in court. The Pairing Whip would duly write back: 'I give you permission to be away.'

'Honour was satisfied on both sides,' the frontbencher says.

Maclean, referred to as a 'rusty nail cocktail, the fiery blend of malt whisky, tempered by Drambuie',[3] had served in Margaret Thatcher's whips' office from 1987 to 1989. In his tenure as Chief, he navigated the tempestuous seas between an increasingly disgruntled parliamentary party and the leader's office while also adjusting to life with multiple sclerosis.

When more than thirty Conservative MPs abstained on the issue of gay adoption – with Duncan Smith controversially ordering his troops to oppose – Maclean wrote a letter insisting that they had done nothing wrong.[4] The night before Duncan Smith's notorious 'quiet man' speech at the 2003 Tory Party conference, Maclean caught wind that up to fifteen rebels had signed letters of no confidence in the party leader, just ten short of the number needed to force a ballot. Maclean approached the tight-lipped Sir Michael Spicer, chair of the 1922 Committee to whom Tory MPs privately send no-confidence letters, who said: 'Don't even ask.'[5] After the event, with Duncan Smith facing negative briefing to the BBC at the hands of disgruntled Conservative MPs, Maclean put together plans to interview those suspected of being responsible.[6] Around ten days later, after taking soundings, Maclean told Duncan Smith that he 'had one last chance to bow out gracefully or face a vote of no confidence', *The Independent* reported.[7] Duncan Smith fought the contest, losing by 75 to 90.

Shortly after Duncan Smith's departure, Maclean stood down, writing to MPs that, having defended the leader, it is now 'vital' The Office is seen to be 'neutral and impartial'.[8] But, on taking over, Michael Howard reappointed his ex-Home Office colleague. 'We had a very easy relationship in which we spoke to each other whenever we needed to,' Howard says.

Under Howard's leadership, the party sought to impose greater discipline. He removed the party whip from Ann Winterton after she refused to apologise for a widely condemned racist joke about the death of twenty Chinese cockle pickers in Morecambe Bay. He also sacked as party chairman and removed from the candidates list Howard Flight after he criticised Tory spending plans.

'I was the fourth leader in six years,' Howard notes of the need for a change in approach.

The Tories won 198 seats at the 2005 election. Howard and Maclean stood down from their roles, with young up-and-comer David Cameron elected party leader.

His Chief Whip? One Patrick McLoughlin.

'Patrick is the nicest man in the world, and he would protect you if you had problems. Nevertheless, he would also kill you if you caused him problems,' says a Tory frontbencher. 'That's the ideal combination for a Chief Whip; charm with menace behind it.'

* * *

In his four years outside Westminster, Alistair Burt worked as a headhunter at a firm that also focused on personal development and coaching. 'I wanted to bring some of this into the party,' Burt says. While politics is far from a meritocracy, Burt formed the view that no one should leave Parliament 'without feeling they'd had a chance to be as good as they could be'.

He cites as evidence the experience of Archie Norman, a successful British businessman – the first person to serve as chair of a FTSE 100 company and MP simultaneously – who 'got nowhere because everybody thought, "Well, we'll teach him a lesson. He may be a smart arse who's run Asda, but what does he know about being a Member of Parliament?"'

Burt approached his party leader, David Cameron, and said: 'I think we should do more.'

Cameron appointed Burt as the whip responsible for personal development, putting together 'much better induction' for new members and a plan to help MPs work towards their goals, be they ministerial, constituency-based or otherwise (some in the whips' office thought this the wrong approach, believing it would give MPs a sense of entitlement).

Efforts had been made to improve the onboarding process for MPs. In 2001, at the invitation of Tory whip Mark Prisk, John Bercow and Julian Lewis, friends and experts in public speaking, held a 'fairly intensive seminar' on parliamentary techniques, titled 'Tricks of the Trade'. Extending the offer to the 2005 intake, Lewis wrote in an email that the induction was to prevent MPs having to learn 'the hard way' things 'which could be imparted at the outset'.

The whips also gave their customary talk. Adam Holloway, elected in 2005, recalls one whip saying that, even if you receive a fifty-page letter from a constituent in green ink, 'somebody in your office must read every word of it, in case a constituent says, "That's why I'm going to kill myself on Thursday" or whatever'. He says: 'So, that was quite impressive.'

Not everyone was taken with the induction. 'It was a largely sink-or-swim kind of approach,' says Philip Davies, the MP for Shipley. Another new joiner received a reprimand from her whip for attending a reception at Lambeth Palace and missing votes. 'I had no idea what a "three-line running whip" meant at all. I just thought I'd be voting at seven,' the MP explains.

The whips were keen to get new MPs onto select committees, handing out forms to rank their preferences by subject area. Davies, a free-spirited backbencher with no political ambitions beyond being a constituency MP, had put a line through his sheet.

'Philip, you're not on a select committee, are you?' Andrew Robathan, the Deputy Chief Whip, asked Davies in the division lobby. 'Would you like to go on one?'

'No, not really,' Davies replied.

'Well, humour me. If you had to go on one, which one would it be?'

'I don't know, Andrew. Probably Culture, Media and Sport.'

'We've got a vacancy,' Robathan said. 'You're on!'

Later in the parliament, Davies visited the whips' office for a catch-up.

'Before you leave, Philip, what's your view of modernisation?' Robathan asked.

'Andrew, the very thought of the word fills me with horror,' Davies, a traditionalist, replied.

'Excellent,' Robathan said. 'I'm putting you on the Modernisation Committee.'

The whips sent the long-serving Nicholas Winterton along with Davies. 'Our job was to stop any modernisation from happening at all,' Davies says.

Though better inducted, the 2005 intake still showed similar patterns to those who had come before. One MP, Holloway says, would sit in the tearoom, absorbing information before visiting the whips. 'I just thought I'd tell you; I was with so-and-so in the tearoom, and I must say, they were being very disloyal,' the MP would say.

Burt worked on his project up to the 2010 election, but found himself moved to the Foreign Office as the Conservatives adjusted to an uncertain life in tandem with a rival party.

A new era for the whips was about to begin.

PART VI

UNNATURAL COALITIONS

CHAPTER 43

POSTURE TO POWER

The Liberal Democrats' new Chief Whip Alistair Carmichael boarded the 159 bus to take him on the short journey from Kennington in south London to Westminster. The Orkney and Shetland MP navigated through the passengers, coming across, by sheer coincidence, another Kennington local, Patrick McLoughlin. The first meeting of the two most senior whips in the coalition government therefore took place at the back of the 159 bus.

As the 159 moved along Kennington Lane, past the Imperial War Museum on its way to the perennially crowded Westminster Bridge, the only certainty was that this parliament would be different. Two rival parties had formed a coalition government, the first since the Second World War. For the whips, the unknown of the new administration coincided with wholesale changes to their powers of patronage.

The coalition had agreed to bring forward in full recommendations made by the Wright Committee to improve the procedures and relevance of Parliament in the wake of the expenses scandal. While not all measures would come to pass, many did, including the introduction of e-petitions. Crucially, MPs would now elect chairs and members of select committees, stripping the whips of a key prize in their arsenal of goodies. No longer could The Office veto nominees or appoint potentially malleable chairs. 'That was an enormous bit of patronage the whips gave away,' says a Tory minister. 'It's always useful for the whips to have carrots to hand out, and there were now far fewer carrots than there used to be.'

Despite McLoughlin's pleas, Cameron also did not waver in keeping the Tories' manifesto commitment of introducing Backbench Business Days, with debates on non-binding motions chosen by a cross-party committee, as per the Wright reforms, to better empower non-ministerial MPs.

Attuned Eurosceptics spied an opportunity.

'He was the most likeable and trustworthy colleague you could wish for,' Cameron said of McLoughlin. 'But we didn't see eye to eye on everything.'[1]

The events around an early debate produced by the Backbench Business Committee were informative. The issue at hand – contaminated blood transfusions – touched people across the House; Lib Dem MP Lynne Featherstone's nephew had died after being infected with hepatitis C. But the coalition took issue with the motion's wording, which ministers felt would 'just compensate without limit', says Carmichael. 'In government, you can't really do that.'

Ministers worked on an amendment with Treasury and cross-party support, but John Bercow, the Speaker of the Commons since 2009, didn't select it. 'He said it was the government trying to wreck a Backbench Business Committee Motion,' Carmichael says.

The government whipped to oppose, with a precedent set for amendments to Backbench Business Motions after Bercow's ruling. 'The Speaker undermined for his own personal vainglory the standing of the Backbench Business Committee,' argues Carmichael. Though the coalition, for now, continued to whip backbench motions – entangling themselves in trouble – future governments would ignore such votes, unbound by the outcome.

'That was a learning day for a lot of people,' Carmichael says, not least on the combative approach of the controversial Speaker and the ongoing friction it would incur with senior members of The Office.

McLoughlin, especially, had a difficult relationship with Bercow, who viewed the whips with suspicion and, in many ways, as anathema to his reforming zeal, which centred around empowering MPs. 'He always regarded us as the enemy,' said a whip.[2]

Later in the year, McLoughlin heckled by the Speaker's chair after Bercow repeated his question to help a Labour MP who had intervened prematurely state their objection correctly. In a fiery exchange typical of the irascible Speaker, Bercow barked 'Order!' eight times and demanded McLoughlin return to the chamber. 'We all saw you!' the Chief said.

McLoughlin slammed the door after arriving back in the whips' office. John Randall, the Tories' Deputy Chief Whip, looked at McLoughlin's adviser and said, 'Leave it,' before heading to speak with him. 'It was one of those examples of Bercow publicly humiliating Tories,' said the adviser. A whip said: 'It sounds silly with a small man and a big guy, but that was the dynamic of a bully.'[3]

The Speaker was fond of comparing the whips to sewers, an analogy first used by his one-time political hero Enoch Powell. 'I had a relationship with my whips characterised by trust and understanding. I didn't trust them, and they didn't understand me,' Bercow would tell audiences.

McLoughlin and Carmichael would have to navigate The Office's new reality – many of the modernising reforms of the previous ten years had worked against the whips' stranglehold on aspects of parliamentary life – while also keeping backbenchers onside about the merits of coalition government, sacrifices, compromises and all.

* * *

The first inkling Alistair Carmichael got that his Chief Whip prayers would be answered came midway through the 2010 election.

Lib Dem leader Nick Clegg, riding a wave after strong performances at televised debates, travelled to Scotland on a campaign visit along with his deputy chief of staff, Alison Suttie. Over a drink, Suttie told

Carmichael: 'In the event that we're in government, we're going to need to run a different sort of whipping operation than the one that we've traditionally had.'

She cited the Scotsman as probably the right man for the task.

On 6 May 2010, the British public returned at a general election the first hung parliament since February 1974. David Cameron's Conservatives won 306 seats, twenty short of an overall majority, with Labour on 258 and the Lib Dems fifty-seven, a disappointing and unexpected loss of five on their 2005 showing.

The result triggered negotiations between the Tories and the Lib Dems – and separate talks between Clegg's team and Gordon Brown's Labour Party – on forming a potential coalition government.

The Lib Dems held a meeting on the Saturday after the election for backbenchers to pitch in their thoughts on the negotiations. Carmichael was getting 'quite jumpy' that the party hadn't yet spoken to Labour representatives, and McLoughlin warned senior colleagues that a Lib–Lab arrangement would be legitimate. But by mid-week, Lib Dem MPs and peers were voting on the initial coalition agreement with the Conservatives, covering eleven areas, including deficit reduction, immigration and education. 'Repairing the public finances was the glue that held the whole thing together,' says Carmichael. Two Lib Dem MPs voted against, including former leader Charles Kennedy. The party also held a special conference in Birmingham, offering members a vote.

'That was very important for me as Chief Whip,' Carmichael says. If MPs were unhappy with a policy choice, the party's whips could say: 'Well, look, this is what you voted for.'

The Tories had no such votes or endorsements. 'I was particularly incensed with the coalition,' says arch-Thatcherite Christopher Chope. 'Why should we go along with it? It wasn't in our manifesto.' In time, Carmichael says, McLoughlin confessed to him: 'I know how you got to your decision, and I sometimes wish I had the same thing I could point to.'

The lack of buy-in also diluted the impact of a letter from the Chief Whip to an MP's constituency party chairman. 'That all went with the coalition, because so many of our associations saw the Tory dog being wagged by the Lib Dem tail,' says a senior whip. With reduced powers, a later member of The Office *did* threaten to pass on an MP's poor attendance record to their constituency chairman – but was met with incredulity.

'[The MP] was apoplectic; that was like, crossing the line,' the whip says. 'I just thought, "Well, what levers have I got?"' The whip didn't follow up on the threat.

Cameron did at least update his assembled backbenchers on how talks were progressing. By the Tuesday evening, expectant Conservative MPs gathered again. Walking to the centre of Committee Room 14, McLoughlin formally introduced Cameron, who was joined by his wife Samantha, to his new role.

'Colleagues, the Prime Minister,' he said.

'It was a good piece of theatre because some of us had done thirteen years in opposition,' says a government minister. 'That was Patrick enjoying his moment in the sun.'

In the preceding days, the Tory whips had smartly kept MPs in Parliament. They attended an induction, including one of three sessions with Julian Lewis and Charles Walker, who had filled in for John Bercow. While helpful – a reflection in part of Alistair Burt's efforts to improve the onboarding process – some suspected the whips also encouraged attendance as it prevented MPs from speaking to the media about the proposed coalition.

Many MPs gathered in Parliament now had more sophisticated mobile phones. Between 2005 and 2010, iPhones arrived in the UK, while BlackBerry had around a 20 per cent share of the smartphone market. Charles Walker recalls the whips distributing BlackBerrys to Tory MPs.

'I don't understand any of that crap, so I gave it back. I thought it was utter shit,' he says. Generally, Walker liked to make himself as uncontactable as possible. 'And they knew that.'

The whips, however, were 'quite good' at tracking Walker down. With MPs called in for a vote, Walker went 'off the radar', deliberately ignoring his phone while driving to a fishing trip with his friend and fellow Tory MP George Hollingbery. Knowing about Walker's hobbies and friendships, a whip rang Hollingbery.

'Hi, George. We have a suspicion that Charles is sitting next to you. Can you put the phone onto him now, please?' the whip said.

Another time, Walker was fishing with Hollingbery on the banks of the River Spey in Scotland when another whip rang his mobile. 'Look, Charles, we're going to have to call you back in because we've got this vote on the badger cull, and numbers are looking tight,' the whip said, with the government pushing in favour of a cull.

Walker, the MP for Broxbourne, replied: 'OK... I just want to explain something. "Broxbourne" – "Brox" is old English for badger. Broxbourne means "badger stream". My election literature has me standing next to a full-sized badger... If you expect me to come back, I can assure you I will be disappointing you as regards to which lobby I'm in.'

The whip said: 'Understood. Enjoy your week's fishing.'

* * *

On 12 May 2010, Carmichael was made Lib Dem Chief and Government Deputy Chief Whip. On offering the position, Clegg had told him: 'You've got the right skillset for the job, you have the ear of your colleagues, you have a degree of emotional intelligence that you'll need and, frankly, sometimes you can look like a bit of a thug.'

Carmichael was 'given licence' – McLoughlin an 'instruction' – 'to build a machinery in coalition that worked', he says. They each took responsibility for discipline and internal management in their parties. 'We then came together to manage the business of government.'

The two whips' teams would meet separately before the business started in the Commons, the Lib Dems gathering in the whips' office assigned to the third largest party, also just off Members' Lobby. All the whips would then meet together. A senior Tory whip says: 'They did their own HR, they did their own pairing, although that was involved with our Pairing Whip. We had joint meetings … We included them in our rotas.'

The Conservative whips had previously selected their own. But this became 'increasingly disrupted' by Cameron and George Osborne, says Brooks Newmark, who joined The Office in 2007. '[They wanted] to have control as to who went into the whips' office.'

A senior Tory whip comments: 'You suddenly had people put in there who you're a bit doubtful of.'

The whips, however, did still have their rituals. Fabricant, a close associate of businessman Andy Street, through whose ties he could track down some good wines, was made the Social (or 'Entertainment') Whip. The whips also maintained a system of notes, two members of The Office say, although how or whether they were collected, stored or gathered remains unclear. 'Very much so. There wasn't a Black Book. There was a folder. Whips' notes,' says Fabricant, potentially alluding to the bench duty notebook rather than the Black Book. But another whip says: 'I've never seen it, but I do believe there is a record, yes.'

A member of The Office who joined later in the parliament created their own spreadsheets of data and feedback from their flock. 'Every time I had a conversation, I'd log it,' they say.

Perhaps some MPs wouldn't be pleased to learn of another of The Office's rituals, which involved the whip returning from bench duty, who would read out a summary of events in the chamber as documented in the notebook to the rest of The Office. 'There were obviously in-jokes and nicknames for various MPs. That was quite funny,' says a whip.

The Tory whips, according to Fabricant at least, initially continued nominating a Shit of the Year. Early in the coalition, Fabricant was the last of the whips to put forward a suggestion.

'Come on, who are you nominating?' McLoughlin urged.

'We've covered all the obvious ones,' Fabricant replied.

'Well, name somebody.'

Fabricant says he named somebody 'perfectly reasonable' and was challenged for it.

'Patrick… this is like we're denouncing somebody. I'm not going to name a name for the sake of naming a name.'

The Shit List then 'rather died down'. 'We didn't do it after that,' Fabricant says.

As other whips 'felt very uncomfortable' dealing with certain personal issues, Fabricant stepped up to take on pastoral support. Fabricant, who is bisexual, used to joke that he was the 'sexual deviants' whip', he says. 'I did deal with difficult situations, particularly one person who was married with kids, and he then left his wife for a bloke, and it was causing problems in the association, and he was… anyway. Humanity.'

Increasingly, Fabricant felt the whips should monitor MPs' staff turnover as potential signals of workplace mistreatment. 'There were certain people whose staff would leave after two or three months,' he says. One MP, who left the Commons in 2015, 'would be throwing things at people and goodness knows what else'.

Issues related to policy and strategy in the coalition were centralised in 'the Quad', with Nick Clegg and Chief Secretary to the Treasury Danny Alexander from the Lib Dems and David Cameron and Chancellor George Osborne, a key Tory strategist, directing proceedings.

When an issue arose that wasn't codified in the coalition agreement, the parties came up with workarounds. Clegg and Cameron made separate statements in response to the Leveson Inquiry into the culture, practices and ethics of the press, triggered by the phone-hacking scandal. 'We had the two-state solution,' says Alistair Carmichael light-heartedly.

Carmichael didn't tap up MPs who had served during Jim Callaghan and David Steel's Lib–Lab pact for advice, believing that to be a different parliamentary scenario, but Clegg's team did bring over Liberals who had been in coalition in continental Europe. One speaker said the most difficult job in any Liberal party within a coalition is that of the business manager.

'Your job is like wheelbarrowing frogs,' he said.

Should he write one, Carmichael says he will call his book *Keeper of the Frogs*.

McLoughlin and Carmichael had grand offices at 9 Downing Street, with chandeliers, sofas, large desks, giant TVs and large portraits on the wall plucked from the Government Art Collection. Carmichael spent most of his time in Parliament, bar occasions like the whole whips' team meeting, which now took place in 9 Downing Street on Monday mornings.

'The whole point of being in Downing Street was that you'd be close to what was happening in No. 10, but actually, not being in No. 10, it didn't work quite the same,' Carmichael says. 'You don't get the same access to decision-making upstream that they traditionally had.'

Both Chief Whips sat in on Cabinet, with Carmichael, as Deputy, seated around the perimeter of the room while McLoughlin was at the table. They also attended various Cabinet committees on policy, joined weekly business managers' meetings and liaised with their respective counterparts in the Lords. McLoughlin, as Chief Whip, attended the 8.30 a.m. and 4 p.m. internal senior Tory meetings in 10 Downing Street, joined by aides, Cameron and the likes of Osborne or Foreign Secretary William Hague. Carmichael met once a week with Clegg and attended weekly gatherings of the Lib Dem parliamentary party.

In the face of the received wisdom that the coalition was doomed to fail – in part because of doubts over the Lib Dems' discipline and ability to do the difficult things in government – the parties were extra motivated to prove the doubters wrong.

At the coalition's first Queen's Speech, McLoughlin and Carmichael, standing in the middle of the chamber directing events, devised a seating plan for the frontbench so that those who needed to would be seen. As Cabinet ministers came in, they instructed: 'Right, you sit there' or 'No, Chris, for fuck's sake, get back to the other end!', Carmichael jokes.

The two Chiefs also agreed to occupy the benches on the government side that mirrored those the parties had taken in opposition, with the Tories on the right and the Lib Dems on the left. 'It was things like that sent signals to the outside world that this was an operation that was being done properly, professionally and collaboratively.'

After years of critiquing from the backbenches, it was important for the Lib Dems to 'show that we were capable of doing our own share of the heavy lifting', Carmichael concedes.

Things, insofar as whipping was concerned, would have to be different.

* * *

The Lib Dem whips' office was initially made up of Alistair Carmichael, Mark Hunter as his number two and Norman Lamb, with a dedicated SpAd in Ben Williams, plus other officials.

The team worked harmoniously with the Conservatives whips' office, both sides speaking glowingly of their working relationships. 'We all loved the coalition government,' says a Tory whip. In collaboration, Tory and Lib Dem MPs conjured a significant majority, meaning routine votes were guaranteed and difficult ones could, for the most part, be navigated – although the academic and whips expert Professor Philip Cowley has calculated that the coalition government was the most rebellious of the post-war era, defeating the previous record set between 2005 and 2010.

Michael Fabricant, appointed government Pairing Whip, got on 'extremely well' with his Lib Dem equivalent, who confided about the challenge of transitioning to government. A senior Tory whip says: 'The Lib Dems hadn't really had any whipping before.'

Mark Oaten, MP for Winchester from 1997 to 2010, puts this down to two reasons. First, Lib Dem MPs often feel that they have secured their typically marginal seats largely off their own bat and are therefore individualistic or idiosyncratic. Secondly, in normal times, the Lib Dem whips haven't got much by way of patronage or sticks at their disposal to marshal MPs. 'You arrived at party discipline through debate, persuasion, small meetings, discussion and the leader occasionally saying: "Come on, guys, we should stick together on this,"' he says.

Jim Wallace, Lib Dem Chief Whip from 1987 to 1992, says the party's 'philosophical approach to whipping was that every vote was a free vote, except you were expected to vote with the party line'. The process for a rebellion was first to tell the Chief Whip, then to speak to the party spokesman privately and listen to their speech in the chamber, and if after that you still wanted to vote differently, 'there were no recriminations', Wallace explains.

As a minority party, Liberal whips would use personal relationships and parliamentary tools to try to curry influence. David Alton, Chief Whip from 1985 to 1987, met every week with Jack Weatherill in Speaker's House, eating cake made by Weatherill's wife, to discuss the next week's business. 'I found Jack incredibly fair,' says Alton, who would push for Liberals to be called at Prime Minister's Questions. 'He would go out of his way even to suggest opportunities that might arise.'

Alton, in turn, could convince Weatherill to select Liberal amendments. 'We haven't had an innings on any of these things recently. Isn't it our turn?' he would ask.

As Deputy Chief Whip from 2006 to 2010, Adrian Sanders would attend the mysterious 'Administrative Committee', which met every Wednesday in Committee Room 13.

'I'm probably not allowed to say that because it's a secret committee of the whips that meet,' he reveals. At the twenty-minute meetings, attendees from the Tories, Labour and the largest minority party discuss who they want on a particular committee and 'give their approval' to suggestions, which sounds a lot like the work of the Committee of Selection, a known body.

'It's pretty much a rubber-stamping exercise, but it's an exercise that has to be gone through,' he says. The Lib Dem spokesperson also had to ask other minority parties who they wanted represented. 'My job was to reveal that name at that meeting.'

While operating differently from their counterparts, Liberal whips would still offer support. 'There were moments where you had to sort out intensely personal things,' Alton says. In one instance, he spoke to a Liberal MP, who had serious financial issues, about the huge debts he'd run up in the House of Commons. 'It was only when we sat down and talked about it that we were able to find a way around that to help him through it and sort it.'

Sanders recalls approaching an MP who was always late into the voting lobby. 'Well, I'm slightly deaf, and I can't hear anything when there's loads of people heading to vote,' the MP told Sanders, who passed on the explanation to the Chief Whip and asked if there was anything they could do to help or accommodate his hearing difficulties.

The first test of Lib Dem cohesiveness amid the new demands of life in government came with George Osborne's first budget in the summer of 2010. Lib Dem MP Andrew George faced down party procedure by tabling an amendment to limit a planned rise in VAT. But it was an issue that the party had explicitly ruled out in the election campaign that would truly challenge the resolve of Liberal Democrats in the coalition government.

*　*　*

Alistair Carmichael's wife could see the effect the job was having on her husband and the father of their boys. 'Even when you're here, you're not actually here,' she told him. The Chief was physically present but spending his time putting out fires over his party's calamitous position on tuition fees.

In the party's manifesto, the Lib Dems had committed to phasing out tuition fees, while MPs had signed pledges vowing not to vote for any increase following a report commissioned by the outgoing Labour government. But within the party hierarchy there were varying levels of support for free tuition, which some felt would be ruinously expensive. In the coalition agreement, the Lib Dems had agreed to wait for the findings of Lord Browne's review of higher education funding and could abstain on any subsequent proposed fee rise. 'If we'd done that, then actually we could have held reasonable discipline,' says Carmichael. 'But we didn't. We started to flake.'

To boost university funding, the Browne Report recommended ending a cap on fees altogether, but the government responded by increasing the limit to £9,000 a year. Business Secretary Vince Cable, having previously said all Lib Dems would abstain, now said he would vote for the proposals he was overseeing, including increasing the salary level at which fees are repaid by £6,000, and other mitigations. After a period of equivocation and uncertainty, Clegg told his MPs that all Lib Dem ministers would vote for the changes.

'Well, for me, that was the end. I had no time for Clegg after that,' says Adrian Sanders.

A friend in the House of Lords was brought in to speak with Sanders. 'You've got lots of friends in the upper house, no doubt you're going to end up there one day, but it probably won't happen if you [rebel],' the peer said.

Sanders was now 'even more determined' to vote against the proposals. He has never joined the House of Lords.

The fallout from the party's U-turn went well beyond the confines of the parliamentary estate. Irate students, many of whom had been lured into supporting the party by the manifesto commitment on tuition fees, marched on London for the day of the vote.

The Commons backed the proposals by 323 to 302, with twenty-one Lib Dems rebelling, twenty-seven voting in favour and eight abstaining. Former leaders Menzies Campbell and Charles Kennedy were among those in the rebel lobby, while two PPSs quit. In central London, the student march descended into chaos, with windows smashed, graffiti sprayed and statues defaced.

Patrick McLoughlin and Carmichael would often have a dram of whisky to reflect on the day or the week just gone. The first time the Tories took an 'absolute shellacking from their own backbenchers on Europe' – an issue that would return time and again for Cameron's party – McLoughlin said to him: 'I guess this is my tuition fees day.'

Carmichael replied: 'Really? Go to the window, look out and tell me how many riot police you see on Whitehall.'

McLoughlin had the 'good grace' to laugh and concede: 'Yeah, it wasn't quite the same.'

The Lib Dems would feel the ripple effect of the tuition fee vote for years to come.

CHAPTER 44

PLEBISCITES

Andrew Mitchell, the International Development Secretary, frowned as he saw an incoming call from the Prime Minister's chief of staff. 'Don't worry, it's good news,' Ed Llewellyn reassured him.[1]

The summer recess of 2012 was nearing its end, and the Prime Minister was formulating a reshuffle. Patrick McLoughlin, after seventeen years in The Office, seven of those spent as Chief Whip of the Conservative Party, had been angling for a move. Mitchell, a whip during John Major's time in government, had absorbed from previous conversations with senior Cabinet ministers like George Osborne that he could be in the running as a successor.

With Eurosceptics flexing their muscles, a Chief with a Maastricht grounding made sense.

The recess came shortly after a tumultuous summer for the coalition, suffering its largest rebellion to date as ninety-one Tory MPs opposed plans for a mainly elected House of Lords, a Liberal Democrat hobby horse. The government, fearing defeat, had pulled a vote on the programme motion and later withdrew the bill, despite winning at second reading. Chris Pincher, MP for Tamworth, had faced down a warning from his whip about his promotion prospects if he rebelled on the issue. 'If you go down this route and choose to vote against the government, then you remove yourself from the gene pool,' his whip said. As with other rebels, Pincher didn't receive preferment until after the 2015 election.

The Lib Dems had already had their hopes of an alternative voting system for electing MPs dashed at a referendum, with the Tories opposing the move during the campaign. Furious after the Lords reform vote, Clegg pulled his party's support for changes to constituency boundaries. 'That was probably the first time the coalition had been put under some strain. It needed to settle down,' says a Tory whip.

For Mitchell, the position of Chief had been a long-held dream. 'He absolutely loves the whipping side of things,' says a ministerial colleague. 'He enjoyed the power over people that that brings.'

Neither had he left his whipping instincts behind. Charlotte Atkins, the former Labour whip, recalls being 'very irritated' by Mitchell, then a shadow minister, seeking to negotiate with her during the committee stage of a bill. His experience, shrewdness and nature had others convinced of his credentials.

Cameron invited Mitchell for a chat in his study at No. 10 and outlined his pitch. But Mitchell, who had enjoyed his two and a half years at DfID, was hesitant. 'I'm not sure I can return to the serpentine world of whipping, which brings out the darker side of my character,' he said.[2] Mitchell also feared that, after spending time abroad in his current role, he was unfamiliar with the parliamentary party.

The Prime Minister pushed back: 'They'll all want to get to know you as Chief.'[3]

Cameron asked him to mull it over, hinting that William Hague wouldn't stay in the Foreign Office for ever, and would one day leave a vacancy to be filled. After taking calls from Llewellyn, Osborne and Hague, and running the idea by close acquaintances, Mitchell accepted the offer, with various provisos. He argued that whips can't work effectively if MPs go around them directly to the Prime Minister's staff and vice versa. He asked for whipping to be left to him, including on appointments, and not interfered with by Downing Street. He would handle the parliamentary party and participate in promotions at reshuffles, especially at junior level, an aspect of the role that had faded in opposition. 'I had made clear that if they wanted me, this reversion was non-negotiable, and the Prime Minister had agreed,' he later wrote.[4]

The new Chief also put his stamp on The Office, bringing in promising talents such as Nicky Morgan and Anne Milton while reinstating former whips, including Greg Knight as his number three. John Randall, with his 'institutional memory', was kept as Deputy, though Mitchell had plans for Knight to, in time, serve as his number two.[5]

There were several casualties in The Office revamp. Brooks Newmark, a five-year whipping veteran, found himself jobless despite various assurances of preferment that never quite came to fruition. In opposition, he had worked as the shadow Treasury whip, sitting in on meetings with Osborne, who didn't always take to Newmark's contributions and insight from his time as a senior partner at a private equity firm, among other roles in financial services.

Newmark says that Philip Hammond, the number two in the shadow Treasury team, pulled him aside after a meeting and said: 'Brooks, your role there is to keep quiet, to listen and not give your opinion.'

The whip had found himself in hot water twice already during the coalition. While driving from his Braintree constituency, he heard on the radio that Sir Mervyn King, the Governor of the Bank of England, was planning to implement further quantitative easing to help boost the UK's stagnant economy. Newmark, an opponent of the policy, pulled to side of the road on the A120 and wrote a tweet, which partly read: 'QE is the crack cocaine of monetarism.'

Half an hour later, driving on the M11, Newmark received a call from Osborne. Fuck, he thought as he answered the phone.

'Did you fucking tweet something about quantitative easing?' Osborne asked.

When the whip said that the Bank of England is separate from government policy, Osborne replied, 'You're a member of the government. I'm there to support the Governor of the Bank of England when he does things, you're not supposed to do that' and then 'sort of slammed the phone down', Newmark says. He rang Chief Whip Patrick McLoughlin to let him know and said he would resign if expected. Defence Secretary Liam Fox, facing his own scandal, beat him to the punch, preventing Newmark's early exit from the whips' office.

Newmark had already upset the party leadership after attending a private meeting in Damascus with Syrian President Bashar al-Assad, with whom he had engaged over a five-year period, amid the outbreak of the country's civil war. Newmark, an expert on Syria, had received permission from the Foreign Office to attend the requested meeting and discussed a five-point plan for how he intended to approach the rendezvous with Hague.

While on the plane back to the UK, an international news agency, in reporting the encounter, issued a photo of Assad and Newmark having tea, taken during a previous meeting.

'Literally, from the time I take off to the time I land, I'm then front-page news of four national newspapers,' says Newmark. Though the Foreign Office knew of the trip, the Prime Minister did not.

McLoughlin had stuck with Newmark. Mitchell opted to go in a different direction.

* * *

The new Chief had a penchant for the whips' traditions, reinstating the silver goblets with champagne for the weekly meetings. 'It actually taints the taste,' says a disappointed quaffer. Mitchell also took the team on a weekend retreat and for dinner at the Gran Paradiso in Belgravia.

The Chief's abrupt style quickly put noses out of joint in No. 10, however, with one official complaining that Mitchell was 'throwing [his] weight around'.[6]

Though too late to make suggestions, Mitchell assisted Cameron with his first major reshuffle by informing colleagues their ministerial services were no longer required. On the evening of Wednesday 19 September, Mitchell was running late for an event where he was due to speak.

'I raced out of No. 9, grabbed my bike and rushed down towards the gates of Downing Street...' he said. 'I had no inkling of the havoc the next forty-five seconds would unleash.'[7]

A whip says: 'It was only about two days after my appointment that "Plebgate" happened, and the Chief Whip found himself in the news in a way that Chief Whips should not.'

No. 10 officials heard about the incident at the Downing Street gates that very night, but Mitchell only caught wind that the matter had escalated after receiving a phone call from Ed Llewellyn the following afternoon.

The Chief Whip stood accused of swearing at police officers as he tried to exit through the main vehicle gates at Downing Street, allegedly referring to them as 'fucking plebs'. Mitchell apologised for swearing but vehemently denied referring to the police as plebs, later saying he told officers: 'I thought you guys were supposed to fucking help us.'

In his memoir, Mitchell said: 'Although words were exchanged over ... how I could get my bicycle out ... and what I perceived to be an unhelpful attitude by the officers, the problem was resolved and I left ... through the pedestrian gate.'[8]

The next day, Deputy Chief Whip John Randall received an email claiming to be from a constituent, giving a detailed eyewitness account of the altercation, seemingly corroborating allegations made in a police log and, soon, the *Sun* newspaper. Randall passed the message onto Downing Street, believing, after a follow-up query, that it was credible. At midnight, *The Sun* released its front page, which screamed: 'Cabinet Minister: Police are plebs'.

The political pressure grew with each passing day. The Labour Party publicly and disgruntled Conservatives privately were calling for Mitchell to resign. All except two in the whips' office were loyal. Cameron stood by the Chief despite initially believing he should go on receipt of the email from Randall's alleged constituent. 'David, how will you feel in six weeks' time if this email is exposed as bogus?' Mitchell asked the Prime Minister, who backed down.[9]

In the corridors, MPs approached some whips with the verdict: 'He's got to go. All my policemen are up in arms.' Nicky Morgan says: 'It was a difficult story for everybody because nobody entirely knew what had happened. It put The Office under strain.'

Mitchell agreed to meet with three local representatives from the Police Federation in his constituency of Sutton Coldfield. After a 45-minute meeting, recorded by a Tory press officer, the three representatives told the press that Mitchell had refused to disclose what he'd said on Downing Street. The audio recording, contradicting these claims, was later leaked to the media.

On 19 October, a month after the incident, Mitchell travelled to Chequers to work through his resignation as Chief Whip. 'It was a very unpleasant business,' says a whip. 'It finally unwound.' In his resignation letter, Mitchell once more denied the allegations, conceding he had sworn but insisting he had not used the word pleb, and said his 'damaging publicity' meant he could no longer carry on as Chief.

For Mitchell, the story was far from over.

Two months later, Channel 4 broadcast CCTV footage which cast doubt on the police officers' accounts of the exchange. The following November, PC Keith Wallis was charged with misconduct in public office, accused of sending the email to John Randall, the Deputy Chief Whip, in which he posed as a member of the public who had witnessed the incident. He pled guilty and was sentenced to twelve months in prison. Another officer, PC James Glanville, was sacked for gross misconduct after being identified as the police source of the *Sun* story. PC Gillian Weatherley and PC Susan Johnson were also sacked for leaks to the press, while the three Police Federation officers who had attended the Sutton Coldfield meeting were investigated and hauled before MPs on the Home Affairs Select Committee.

Mitchell launched a civil libel case against *The Sun*, while PC Toby Rowland, the police officer on duty at Downing Street, in turn sued Mitchell for libel after he said any officer who maintained he used the word pleb was not telling the truth. The joint libel trial ended with the judge ruling against Mitchell on the grounds that he deemed Rowland lacked 'the wit or imagination' to have invented the story.

The ex-Chief's reputation in future whips' offices was not overly positive. 'People like Andrew Mitchell were a pain in the arse,' says a later senior whip. A party staffer says The Office effectively stopped assigning Mitchell a dedicated whip, given how difficult he was to handle.

One whip says Randall, who had worked closely with Patrick McLoughlin but never gelled with Mitchell, was 'instrumental' in 'keeping the rest of the office on track' during Plebgate. Seeking a period of stability after the failed experiment, Cameron turned to a politician with a steeped history in The Office to serve as Chief: The 'Bicycling Baronet', two-time serving whip under Margaret Thatcher – in opposition and in government – Sir George Young.

'He had the right approach, he had gravitas,' says one backbencher. 'A Chief Whip who everybody respected, who, yes, was on the Wet side of the party but was just an extraordinarily strong person,' says one of his whips.

In his previous iterations as a whip, rival offices had spent time locked in arguments over timetabling, which, following the advent of programme motions and amid cordial discussions with Labour, were no longer as prevalent. Young met weekly with Rosie Winterton, his opposition counterpart, to 'talk things through'. 'Quite a lot of it would be about mutual problems – expenses, how you manage that, people behaving badly in select committees,' he says.

Young, who removed the whip from Conservative backbencher Nadine Dorries for controversially entering *I'm a Celebrity... Get Me Out of Here*, instigated annual appraisals with MPs and his whips. 'I tried not to take them for granted,' he says of his team.

One of his first hurdles came through the introduction of gay marriage, which split members of The Office. Desmond Swayne, who whipped the bill, says it was the most difficult challenge he encountered while in post. 'Although it was a free vote, the fact is we desperately wanted that legislation through. Cameron was very committed to it,' he says.

Swayne had to navigate the restrictions of a free vote while also outlining the bill's merits. Parliament passed the legislation soon before the summer recess in July 2013, which, in due course, would come to a premature end.

* * *

In the early hours of Wednesday 21 August, a suspected chemical weapons attack took place on the outskirts of Damascus in Syria, killing more than 1,400 people. US President Barack Obama led calls for deterrent military action against Syrian President Bashar al-Assad.

Alistair Carmichael, the Lib Dem Chief, was volunteering for a legal aid organisation in Cameroon when the word came through that the government wanted to recall Parliament. The decision to formally bring back MPs came the Monday after the attack. Carmichael quickly accrued a £250 mobile phone bill.

George Young, on holiday in Europe when the news broke, had advised David Cameron against recalling MPs. 'We were going to come back in a few days anyway,' he says. Scarred by events in Iraq and Afghanistan, with further doubts over the success of the UK's involvement in Libya two years earlier, many were hesitant to endorse military action.

'MPs had been away from Westminster, so they had all been wound up by their constituencies,' says Carmichael.

Unable to tell backbenchers the exact wording of the motion to come, Tory whips struggled to grasp the extent of a rebellion over potential air strikes 'because we couldn't do the ring-round', says Young. His advice was to get the Labour Party onside. 'Firstly, because of the numbers. But secondly, if we're going to war, we don't want to split Parliament.' The Prime Minister began negotiations with Labour leader Ed Miliband to secure his party's backing.

By the day of the vote, held on Thursday 29 August, Cameron had agreed for MPs to have a second vote on taking part in US-led air strikes after UN weapons inspectors had completed their investigations. He also released an assessment from the Joint Intelligence Committee which said it was 'highly likely' the Assad regime was behind the chemical weapons attack.

Despite the efforts and concessions, Miliband instructed his party to oppose intervention, believing the case was as yet unproven.

Carmichael flew back from Cameroon to Heathrow Airport, arriving at The Office for a call at 8 a.m. It was 'pretty obvious', he says, it was heading for 'trainwreck territory'.

The whips had partaken in an 'intensive lobbying' exercise, encouraging and lining up 'grandees' to speak at meetings to try to influence the 1922 Committee, says Desmond Swayne. Another says: 'You were trying to get people back from different parts of the world. You haven't had a chance to look at them, have ministers talk to them and everything else.'

Philip Davies, known to have reservations about air strikes, was asked to see the Prime Minister at four o'clock that afternoon. 'Of course,' he replied. You know the government is in a mess, Davies jokes, 'when they're contacting me'.

It had happened before. Matt Hancock, a government minister, had rung Davies on a Sunday while he was watching his son play football ahead of a tight vote. 'I knew instantly the government was stuffed at that point,' he laughs. Hancock lobbied Davies, to no avail. The Shipley MP is what you might call unmalleable. He is without ministerial ambitions and needs no second invitation to speak his mind. Despite this, he reveals that the Prime Minister once asked him to join the whips' office in government – an offer Davies also declined.

After mulling his position on Syria, Davies decided the conversation with the Prime Minister wasn't going to end well. He rang his whip and asked them to pass on to No. 10 that he was pulling out of the meeting.

Waiting that evening to vote against a Labour amendment requiring 'compelling' evidence that the Assad regime was responsible for the chemical weapons attack, Cameron approached Davies and another Tory MP, Martin Vickers, about the government motion.

'Look, the next vote, I need you,' he told them.

'Prime Minister, I'm sorry, I just can't do it,' Davies said, with Vickers agreeing.

'Well, Martin, thank you for at least seeing me this afternoon,' Cameron said.

The Labour amendment was comfortably defeated, but the government nonetheless lost its vote to pave the way for intervention by 272 to 285, with thirty Tories and nine Lib Dems voting against. Ten ministers didn't vote, including two whips, with some on approved absences while others inexplicably missed the division.

Cameron confirmed that, following the defeat, the UK would not take part in air strikes.

A constituent subsequently sent Adam Holloway, a former soldier and Tory rebel on Syria, an 'unpleasant' email, saying 'how she hoped that I would be haunted by the screams of Syrian children'. After pondering for a few days whether to click send, the Tory MP replied: 'Fuck off and bomb someone else with your ignorance.'

When word reached Young, he asked Holloway to see him and write a letter of apology to the constituent. 'Since when are Conservative MPs who have served in the Armed Forces supposed to apologise to people who call them a coward?' Holloway asked. Young 'did get that, to be fair,' Holloway says.

The morning after the vote, Carmichael awoke to more news from

Syria. 'I watched a report about Assad having bombed a school with napalm, and I felt utterly desolate,' he says. The Lib Dem Chief was 'more emotionally invested in that vote than any other. It was a failure of leadership, a failure of party management, it was a failure of media – it was the long tail of the intervention in Iraq and the lack of trust that there was by that time in government.'

The coalition government lost the vote without immediate recriminations for the whips' office. Carmichael's period as Chief was coming to a natural end regardless, and Young, who had already called time on his ministerial career before replacing Andrew Mitchell, would have almost a year before Cameron shuffled the decks, despite copping his fair share of criticism for the operation's shortfalls.

But, for whips of all hues, a dormant volcano was about to erupt.

CHAPTER 45

WESTMINSTER'S SECRET SERVICE

Michael Cockerell, the renowned broadcaster with an assertive and rhythmic voice, was back in Parliament making his latest documentary, *Inside the Commons*. Almost twenty years had passed since the BBC first ran his revealing, colourful and explosive hour-long film on the whips, *Westminster's Secret Service*, in May 1995.

Naturally, not everyone had been pleased with Cockerell's attempts to lift the lid on the whips' office. 'Some whips like Andrew Mitchell saw me as an enemy,' the journalist recalls.

'I know none of us spoke to him,' says a member of John Major's whips' office (which is not *quite* true – David Lightbown gave a response when doorstepped at a Tory Party conference). Several former whips had spoken out, however, 'which went down like a lead balloon'.

Richard Ryder had gathered his predecessors for a meeting, setting out why The Office didn't want anyone to take part, forgetting to invite Willie Whitelaw, who had served as Chief in opposition.[1] Whitelaw, with whom Cockerell had good relations from a previous project, was 'wonderfully indiscreet' about matters such as the 'Dirt Book'. 'We got a lot of coverage about that,' says Cockerell.

Working with two colleagues, Cockerell approached around eighty people who had passed through the whips' office. 'Almost all refused to talk to us,' he wrote in his book, *Unmasking Our Leaders*. 'But a handful agreed to speak off the record and another half-dozen agreed to take part.' The documentary included some form of contribution from Tristan Garel-Jones, Stephen Dorrell and Lightbown.

Cockerell had an easier time securing footage with the Labour whips' office, who allowed him to film their operations off Members' Lobby and interview members of the team. He put on a reunion event for whips from the 1974–79 parliament, only for Michael Cocks to lament his lack of invitation, despite having turned down an interview request. A Labour whip who doesn't appear is Geoff Hoon, who 'consciously avoided being involved'. 'I just didn't see it at the time as being helpful to a prospective Labour government,' Hoon explains.

In 2014, Cockerell aspired to infiltrate the whips' office once more for his latest documentary. Rosie Winterton, the Labour Chief Whip, agreed to speak, and Desmond Swayne, one of the more colourful members of the government office, also signed up. But in George Young, the Government Chief Whip, he encountered a similar sentiment to twenty years earlier. When they passed each other in Portcullis House, Young would just say, 'Omertà', and walk off.

Westminster's Secret Service had confirmed long-held rumours about aspects of the whips' routines, from the Black Book through to Shit Lists. It also contained hitherto unseen correspondence from Martin Redmayne, the ex-Tory Chief, to the then Prime Minister, Alec Douglas-Home. But the most explosive aspect of the documentary related to claims from a Tory whip under Ted Heath, which, nearly two decades after the film first aired, would resurface and, scrutinised in a new context, cause consternation across Westminster.

During his 1995 interview, Tim Fortescue, a Tory whip in the early 1970s, said an MP in trouble 'with any sense' would come to the whips and ask for help.

'It might be debt, it might be… a scandal involving small boys, or any kind of scandal in which a member seemed likely to be mixed up in,' Fortescue said. If the whips could help, they would, he continued. 'And we would do everything we can because we would store up brownie points … if we could get a chap out of trouble then, he will do as we ask for ever more…'

The comments re-emerged at the height of calls to investigate alleged child sexual abuse in Westminster; the Tory peer Norman Tebbit had told the *Andrew Marr Show* the previous weekend that 'there may well have been' a 'big political cover-up' in the 1980s. Cockerell's phone blew up with calls from journalists, but he decided not to talk as he was courting Tory whips for his new documentary. 'To have this dragged out again did not help my chances.'

In July 2014, Home Secretary Theresa May announced an independent inquiry into child sexual abuse, which, as part of its fifteen investigations, considered issues pertaining to Westminster, and what whips, party leaders and senior figures did or didn't know about the activities of their MPs.

With the words from Tim Fortescue and Norman Tebbit as a basis, the Independent Inquiry into Child Sexual Abuse took evidence from members of The Office across the decades. Contributors were asked to comment on how whips obtained details of confidential matters and whether this information was used to apply pressure; if they knew of allegations of criminal conduct relating to MPs; and whether a whip did nothing or took active steps to suppress such allegations.

As part of its investigation, the inquiry considered the keeping of a Black Book. Evidence sessions established that Labour ceased the practice in 1964. As for what it included, Ken Clarke, a Tory whip under Ted Heath, explained that 'you reported things which you thought might have been of interest'. The bulk of notes, whips insisted, related to matters of parliamentary business, legislation and policy.

The inquiry examined whips' notes provided by Michael Jopling, Chief Whip from 1979 to 1983, which contained reference to MPs' personal lives (the notes also included information on members from other political parties and prospective parliamentary candidates). Some scribes mentioned scandals likely to break, including an affair involving a Scottish Tory MP. 'The purpose of this note was so that the Chief Whip was aware of situations … with regards to the members,' Jopling explained.

Jopling arguably had overseen greater retention of papers than many of his associates. A coalition-era whip remembers the ex-Chief producing rebel Nicholas Winterton's voting record from his wallet during a dinner for an outgoing senior member of The Office.

The inquiry reported that it had seen notes about the state of an MP's marriage and a forthcoming issue of *Private Eye* containing 'a little snippet in it, suggesting that there is a "Sex Scandal in a Sauna Bath", which involves a Cabinet Minister'. The inquiry also saw a note about a Conservative MP being seen 'in the lower office with his secretary and two others. All rather pretty young men.'

The 'most significant' note for the inquiry related to a telephone call from the Attorney General. The note, which has been redacted and isn't easy to decipher, said: 'Telephone call from Michael Havers to tell Chief Whip that it would be likely to break within 48 hours that [redacted] present woman a Call Girl also a letter of homosexual nature in existence from [redacted] to a boy.'

Jopling said the note was the 'most serious' one he received from the whips while Chief. 'Shock and horror went through the entire office at the time, having read that.' Given Havers, the Attorney General, was aware of the issue, Jopling understood that the matter was being properly handled by the investigating authorities.

Due to the passage of time and 'patchy retention' of notes, 'it is not possible for us to conclude one way or the other whether allegations of child sexual abuse or exploitation featured in other whips' notes', the inquiry said.

In written evidence, George Young, who kept personal notes on his iPad for his eyes only while Chief Whip, said if anything of a criminal nature came to the whips' attention, the advice would be to report the matter to the police. Like others, he said he had no recollection of any allegation of child sexual abuse against any MP and stressed he wasn't aware of instances where whips used their knowledge of confidential matters to pressure backbenchers. 'I want to be absolutely clear such behaviour was not part of the culture of the office I led; nor would I tolerate any member of my office using such tactics,' he said.

In its summary on matters related to the whips, the inquiry said 'it would be speculation to conclude that personal information was used to pressure MPs'. Its final report stated: 'Based on the evidence we have seen, we cannot conclude that the whips and whips' offices concealed or suppressed allegations of child sexual abuse by persons of public prominence, or used it as a form of leverage.'

The inquiry was more assertive on another aspect of its investigation into Westminster.

In his September 2010 obituary of Cyril Smith, Michael Meadowcroft, the Liberal Party's ex-Deputy Chief Whip, acknowledged allegations surrounding the Rochdale MP. 'Efforts by *Private Eye* to implicate Smith in scandalous activities with boys never stuck and appeared to have no effect on his electability,' he wrote.[2] Three years later, Channel 4 contacted Meadowcroft and asked if he would take part in a *Dispatches* programme on Smith.

'Well, why me?' he asked.

'Because you were the only person who mentioned this in your obituary,' came the reply.

Meadowcroft was surprised by the number of people who arrived at his house in Leeds to film. 'There were two cameras, a bloke outside in the garden filming established shots, producer, the lot,' he says. Meadowcroft was interviewed for an hour and ten minutes.

'Question after question, you could see the elephant trap opening up in front of you: why didn't we do something about it?'

In September 2013, Channel 4 aired *The Paedophile MP: How Cyril Smith Got Away With It*. After the documentary came out, Meadowcroft received an email from Jill Pratt, the widow of Garth Pratt, who had been deselected as the party's candidate in Rochdale in 1970, with Smith, a former Labour councillor, his replacement. Jill told Meadowcroft that when the party's chief agent Ted Wheeler visited Rochdale, they informed him there was a Baptist minister who had reported allegations about Smith. Wheeler, Meadowcroft said, visited the Baptist minister, who handed on the names of boys who alleged they had been abused.

'Who could have sent him?' asks Meadowcroft of Wheeler's visit to Rochdale. 'It could only have been the leader or the Chief Whip: Jeremy Thorpe or David Steel. The chief agent doesn't come off his own back for something like that. So, all the protestations about not knowing were certainly not circumstantially the case.'

What senior Liberal figures did or didn't know about Smith when he became a prospective parliamentary candidate (PPC) in 1970, and when he was reselected as the Liberal candidate for Rochdale ahead of a by-election in 1972, remains hotly contested. The inquiry felt similarly to Meadowcroft, concluding it was 'highly unlikely' the Liberal Party in Westminster knew nothing about the allegations concerning Smith at the time he was selected as a PPC.

But David Steel stresses: 'I said that's absolute rubbish, because we didn't know about it.'

David Alton, who joined Parliament in 1979 and served as Chief Whip from 1985, says: 'I wish now that someone had brought that kind of information to us, because if they had, then something would have been done about it. But it wasn't.'

Smith was elected in 1972, serving as Liberal Chief Whip from 1976 to 1977. In 1979, the *Rochdale Alternative Press* alleged that Smith had spanked and sexually abused boys aged between fifteen and eighteen at a hostel set up by an association of which Smith was a secretary. The police had investigated similar claims in 1969, but no prosecution was brought. *Private Eye* followed up the story, which Steel asked Smith about during 'a casual conversation at the lunch table'. Smith said the story was correct, insofar as he'd been interviewed by the police and they'd taken no further action, Steel says now. 'That was the end of what was a very brief conversation.'

Giving evidence, Steel said he came away from the interaction assuming Smith had committed the offences. Asked if that provided more reason to hold an inquiry, he said: 'No, because it was ... before he was even a member of my party. It had nothing to do with me.'

When his remarks went public, the Liberal Democrats suspended Steel pending an investigation. His supporters, of whom there are still many in the House of Lords, insist that Steel had difficulties hearing the questions asked of him while giving evidence. 'They rather mishandled David because actually he couldn't hear what they were saying,' says Alan Beith. 'His hearing is not very good.' His suspension was later lifted by the Lib Dems.

'When I was giving evidence, I should never have gone beyond what I'd given them in written evidence, which was that he had probably abused his position as a Labour councillor,' says Steel. 'But I didn't know any more than that. The idea that I should conduct an inquiry when ... three [Directors of Public Prosecutions] had looked at the police investigation and each had decided that nothing could be done about it. That was not mentioned in the report.'

In its conclusions, the inquiry highlighted a 'significant problem' of deference towards people of prominence, saying political parties and police had turned a 'blind eye'. The report cited how senior Conservative figures including Margaret Thatcher and Norman Tebbit were aware of rumours regarding Peter Morrison – the Prime Minister's last PPS in office and a former deputy party chairman – having, as one witness attested, a 'penchant for small boys'. (Expanding on his remark to the *Andrew Marr Show* about a political cover-up in the 1980s, Tebbit, while giving evidence, referred to suggestions that Morrison had an interest in 'young men' of about 'sixth form age', as well as alluding to allegations concerning Smith, Jimmy Savile and senior members of the Church of England and the Catholic Church.)

The inquiry also said the Conservative whips' office had tried to protect their party's image by 'playing down rumours and protecting politicians from gossip or scandal at all costs'. The report was especially critical of Steel, accusing him of a 'failure to accept the seriousness of what he had been told by Smith'.

Steel says he wrote to the chairman of the inquiry highlighting what he claimed were eleven mistakes in the report. 'All I got was a reply from one of the well-paid lawyers supporting the inquiry saying that nothing could be done but my letter had been noted,' he says.

The former Liberal leader and Chief Whip stood down from the Lords a month later, in March 2020, on the fifty-fifth anniversary of the by-election that first brought him into Parliament. 'It still rankles with me, but I decided that it wasn't worth bothering about,' he says of the inquiry. 'I could have taken them to judicial review if I had enough money, but I didn't, so I decided to leave it.'

The inquiry's launch in July 2014 coincided with a significant change to the Conservative whips' office, as David Cameron replaced George Young, due to stand down at the next election, with an unlikely character.

CHAPTER 46

CULTURE CLASH

'Out, all of you!' Don Foster, the Liberal Democrat Chief Whip, demanded. Shocked Cabinet ministers and frontbenchers meeting with Michael Gove scarpered through one of the few exits from the Government Chief Whip's office.

The two Chiefs had agreed that their parties would issue at the same time separate press releases setting out their respective positions on a policy area that they couldn't reach a consensus on in coalition. But, while attending a meeting of the Lib Dem parliamentary party, Foster caught wind that the Conservatives had sent out their press release an hour earlier than planned. Gove, Foster believed, had tried to steal a march on the Lib Dems.

He made a beeline for Gove's office to confront his coalition colleague.

'I'm seeing Michael now,' Foster had said to Gove's staff.

'You can't,' one replied. 'He's in a meeting.'

'I don't care,' Foster said.

He flung open the door to end Gove's ministerial get-together.

'My behaviour, incidentally – I'm prepared to admit – was absolutely appalling and unacceptable,' Foster says.

The 'screaming match' with Gove lasted for five minutes before calming down. 'It never occurred to me that the people outside were all standing there with their ears up against the door,' Foster says of the ministers he had booted out earlier. The row officially ended after a knock on the door, with Ed Vaizey, the Arts Minister, entering before being summoned.

'Don,' he said. 'Is it all right if I get my jacket now?'

The encounter, in fact, served to ease tensions between Gove and Foster, the former having to put his political cunning on ice to maintain good inter-coalition relations. 'From that moment on, Michael realised that he had to behave differently – at least with me.'

* * *

Unlike his predecessor, Don Foster, the MP for Bath, had no interest in becoming Liberal Democrat Chief Whip.

Content in the Department for Communities and Local Government, Foster had already tried to point Nick Clegg in another direction, suggesting a colleague to take over from Alistair Carmichael, who was due to become Scottish Secretary. When Clegg informed him over the phone that his candidate had already fallen through, Foster teased: 'Oh, I'm the second choice, am I?'

Lib Dem buy-in for the coalition had been under considerable strain. The party felt aggrieved at the handling of and commitment to its core constitutional asks on Lords reform and the AV referendum. Senior leadership, with one eye on the election, wanted to set more space between themselves and the Conservatives, particularly in response to backlash over policy areas such as the controversial 'bedroom tax', which reduced benefits for claimants deemed to have a spare bedroom, part of a slew of austerity measures implemented by the coalition to cut back public finances.

'Having learned that that was really screwing us, we began the process of being much more open,' Foster says. By the end of the parliament, the Lib Dems took the unprecedented step of unveiling an 'alternative' budget to the one set out by the Chancellor George Osborne.

Foster navigated difficult votes and increasingly restless MPs while enforcing new rules for Lib Dem frontbenchers. A minister who failed to vote in a division without permission or a good reason was fined a bottle of Famous Grouse whisky for the whips' stockpile, ready for MPs seeking to pass time in The Office during evenings in Parliament.

A studious Chief, Foster investigated after a minister claimed he had missed a vote because the lift in his department wasn't working. 'Little did he know that I'm the sort of guy who checks every detail,' Foster says. He spoke with the relevant engineers, 'only to discover this was a complete falsehood'. The minister was promptly fined a bottle of Famous Grouse.

When a Secretary of State said they hadn't heard the division bell, Foster ascertained that he had booked a meeting in the one room in the building where he knew that it wasn't working. Foster confirms: 'He was fined a bottle of Famous Grouse whisky as well.'

The Lib Dem Chief found in his Conservative Party colleague George Young an 'incredibly effective operator' who grasped coalition politics. 'He very much understood that, whether you like it or not, you've got to work with the bloody Lib Dems,' Foster explains.

Years on from their notorious press conference in the Downing Street garden, in which Cameron and Clegg unveiled their plans for a coalition, the two leaders had a firmer handle on the role of The Office, Foster says. But Foster's confidence in Cameron's understanding changed exponentially in July 2014, when he appointed Michael Gove as Tory Chief Whip.

Gove, a true political operator, had spent four controversial years in the Department for Education (DfE), unapologetically taking on the educational establishment he collectively termed the 'blob'. But Cameron, frustrated at Gove's political fingers reaching into pies outside the DfE, and seeking to change the narrative about his party ahead of an election, wanted to find Gove a new home. He recalled a conversation in 2013 in which he said Gove had told him: 'If you were ever to give me another job, I'd love to be Chief Whip.'[1]

The Prime Minister invited Gove to his flat in No. 10 and ran the idea by him. According to Cameron, Gove confirmed the next day he would take the job, before emailing to change his mind. 'You must realise that I divide the world into team players and wankers. You've always been a team player. Don't become a wanker,' Cameron texted.[2]

Gove relented, but neither man fully realised the implications of the appointment; Gove took a £30,000+ pay cut as an attendee of Cabinet rather than a full member. The move was seen as a demotion. 'A shabby day's work which Cameron will live to regret,' Sarah Vine, Gove's wife, tweeted of the reshuffle.

Gove had an inauspicious start to life in The Office – his first whipping job – after getting stuck in a toilet and nearly missing a vote.

'I used to love it when Michael Gove was Chief. He was the biggest gossip,' Michael Fabricant says.

Fabricant recalls showing someone around Parliament, pointing out a window in the whips' office that overlooks 'a tiny bit of courtyard'. 'That's where the whips are based along there, and the Chief Whip's office is there,' he told his guest. Suddenly, the window flew open, and out leaned Gove, who said, 'Cooey, Michael. I'm the Chief Whip!' before closing it again.

A Tory MP observes: 'Michael Gove was like a smiling assassin when he was Chief Whip. He would absolutely put his arm around you and twist the knife in your back at the same time as he was giving you a hug.'

Foster was closer with Rosie Winterton, the Labour Chief Whip, than he was with Gove. With an election looming and pollsters forecasting another hung parliament, 'the conversations with Labour increasingly were at a point of recognising that things were going to change in the not-too-distant future,' he says. 'So, a relationship with Labour had to be thought of in terms of the future as well as the present.' All told, Foster spent as much time, if not more, 'talking, planning and plotting to some extent' with Winterton as with Gove.

Gove's tenure as Chief Whip is arguably best remembered for a plot that went wrong.

A select group, including Gove and William Hague, the Leader of the House, had been working on the plan for around a month. 'Cabinet members didn't know,' said an oblivious member of the top team.³ Cameron and Osborne, while keeping their distance and holding contrasting views on the endeavour's merits, were also aware; the former was more eager than the latter to see the back of John Bercow. On Thursday 26 March 2015, the final day of the parliament, the government planned to vote on a motion calling for the Speaker's re-election – usually a foregone conclusion – to be decided by secret ballot.

The motion wouldn't guarantee Bercow's removal – but it could, theoretically, help bring it about once MPs returned to cast their vote on the chair after the May general election.

Without fear of retribution, such as rarely being called by an unforgiving Speaker, MPs could decide as they wished on Bercow's future, knowing he wouldn't find out how they had voted. Given the extent of the Speaker's unpopularity in certain corners of the Tory Party, it was possible that, subject to the general election result, Bercow *could* lose.

Despite the plan's execution, which gave the opposite impression, the plotters had thought things through carefully. The Tories were kept in Westminster on a three-line whip, *officially* for a pre-election meeting with Australian political strategist Lynton Crosby. Labour MPs, eager to begin campaigning ahead of the general election – not least the considerable and under-pressure Scottish contingent – were expected to leave en masse for their constituencies on the afternoon of Wednesday 25 March, the day before the vote.

A senior whip said the idea of the secret ballot was put forward by a Labour MP. 'It was suggested by Natascha Engel,' they said.⁴ Engel denied involvement and said she had no recollection of tipping off the plotters. In fairness, the Procedure Committee under two chairs had called for MPs to vote on such a move, but ministers, until the very end of the parliament, had failed to allocate time to discuss its latest report on the floor of the House.

For some, the endeavour fell short when Hague went to visit Bercow at 5.30 p.m., an hour earlier than planned, about the soon-to-be-laid government motion. Grasping the implications, Bercow quickly contacted Rosie Winterton, the Labour Chief Whip, and Angela Eagle, Hague's opposite number. 'Honestly, if they had told him half an hour later, we wouldn't have been able to stop them,' admitted Eagle.[5]

Eagle burst into Hague's parliamentary office and entered his study, instructing one of his advisers: 'Get out!' A member of the leader's office joked about the Labour MP leaving behind an 'Angela Eagle-shaped hole' in the entrance door.[6]

Winterton, meanwhile, dealt with Gove. Her whips put out a message for MPs to attend Westminster the next day, preventing some from returning to their constituencies.

For Eagle, Hague's body language suggested he had been forced into the move. A senior whip said Hague, who was retiring from politics, was keen on the idea, though his aides wanted more insight on the operation. 'Have the whips got the numbers?' one aide kept asking. The same aide requested to see The Office's spreadsheets with the names of the MPs signed up. 'I was quite annoyed at the time that they didn't show me,' they said.[7]

For fear of the plot leaking, the whips involved with the plan had not told some of the more vociferous anti-Bercow backbenchers about their intentions. The rest of The Office were briefed after the motion was tabled.

While Bercow had plenty of Tory detractors, he also had several admirers who liked the way he championed the House and backbenchers in the face of perceived executive overreach. Among them were Julian Lewis, a close friend; Charles Walker, chair of the Procedure Committee, who learned in astonishment of the government's intention to use his report for its own advantage without consulting him; and David

Davis, an ex-whip, who, on hearing about the plot, delayed his flight to a family skiing holiday to attend Parliament the following day.

With the Commons on Thursdays sitting from 9.30 a.m., Bercow granted three Urgent Questions, which allowed for more Labour MPs to return to Westminster before the debate on the government motion. By the time Hague stood to lead the discussions, he had taken a beating, with members from across the House lining up to condemn the government – and him personally. An aide to Hague argued that the whips had fallen short by failing to secure enough people to speak in favour of the motion.

A key plotter said the Leader of the House turned to Gove during the debate and urged: 'I think we should pull this.' Gove apparently replied: 'No, we're going to hold firm here, William … We're going to have the vote, win or lose.'[8]

With the House applauding a barn-storming speech from Walker, the writing was on the wall. MPs voted by 202 to 228 against the government motion. Tom Brake, Deputy Leader of the House and Lib Dem whip, while supportive of moving to a secret ballot, said the issue became conflated with Tory angst against the Speaker, rather than being seen as merely a procedural rejig. 'The House chose otherwise because they did see it as being a direct attack on John Bercow.'[9]

A senior whip went to see Cameron in No. 10. 'Sorry, David, we didn't quite pull it off.' The move was 'worth trying', the Prime Minister replied.[10]

The plotters split between those close to Hague and Gove as to who was to blame. 'I thought the reason was that Hague tipped off Bercow … too early,' said the senior whip. But the aide to Hague said: 'The whips promised No. 10, DC and William that they could deliver the votes.' An aide to Cameron said: 'People were pretty fucked off about it because the optics looked really, really bad … It was classic Gove playing parliamentary games and messing up.' A Cabinet minister said: 'If you're going to shoot somebody, make sure you kill them.'[11]

Bercow's death stare at Hague after reading out the result spoke volumes. Never had the Speaker felt more motivated to assert the will of the House against the executive.

It was not as if the Speaker needed extra motivation. He had already shown how far he was willing to go in making the government's life as uncomfortable as possible, not least on a subject area that had plagued the Conservatives for decades, and for which he was about to become a household name.

CHAPTER 47

THE R GROUP

EARLY 2011

Eight Conservative MPs gathered for their weekly Tuesday meeting at 8.30 a.m. in Room R of Portcullis House. The aptly named R Group, comprising Peter Bone, Steve Baker, Philip Hollobone, Douglas Carswell, Christopher Chope, David Nuttall, Mark Reckless and John Baron, formed, according to one of their own, the 'essential awkward squad'.[1] All bar one had been elected after the turn of the millennium, taking their cue from their forerunners, the Eurosceptics who led the charge against Maastricht – and learning from their mistakes.

At the start of the parliament, the incumbent members of the R Group spotted the tremendous opportunity presented by the newly established Backbench Business Committee. If they could secure spots on the committee itself, they could shape what the group put forward. 'The government whips didn't pay any significant attention to the committee's creation and … didn't attempt to influence who was elected,' argued Peter Bone, who, along with Philip Hollobone, got onto the committee.[2] In Natascha Engel, they found a sympathetic chair.

Sitting in the tearoom next to David Cameron, who had faced down Chief Whip Patrick McLoughlin's pleas against implementing a Backbench Business Committee, Bone asked: 'Isn't it great that we can have debates and votes on issues we want?' Cameron 'spluttered his cup of tea', Bone claimed. 'He hadn't realised the significance.'[3]

With UKIP leader Nigel Farage gaining notoriety for abrasive speeches in the European Parliament, and a petition carrying more than 100,000 signatures calling for an EU referendum finding its way to Downing Street, Cameron was under pressure on Europe. After the Lisbon Treaty in 2007, the latest iteration of European Union development, his party had entered the 2010 election vowing a 'referendum lock' on any new transfer of powers.

The party had been keen to clamp down on anti-Europe dissent in opposition. When, a month or two after his election in 2005, Philip Davies said in the Commons that he supported a referendum on EU membership – and confirmed that he would vote against remaining – he received a message on his pager to see the outgoing Chief Whip David Maclean immediately.

Maclean 'tore a strip off me and told me that what I said was not party policy', Davies recalls.

'I never said it was party policy. It's my policy!' he replied.

Maclean printed out a statement for Davies to sign saying that he supported the Conservative Party line on the EU, which, the MP says, was pretty much 'being in Europe but not run by Europe'.

'Can I take it away and think about it?' Davies asked.

'Yes, you can,' Maclean replied.

Davies went to his office and chucked the statement in the bin. He returned to see Maclean a few hours later.

'Well, this won't do,' the Chief Whip said.

Davies said: 'Look. I'll do you a deal. If you can get [arch-Europhile] Ken Clarke to sign a statement to say that he agrees with Conservative Party policy on Europe, I'll sign one.'

That, Davies says, was the end of the matter.

Carswell, a member of the R Group who, like Davies, was elected in 2005, got a taste for what was to come before even entering Parliament. The whips summoned Carswell in after he was confirmed as a candidate for Clacton and quizzed him on whether he lived in the constituency. After his election, Carswell says he was summoned to see a whip who told him that he was too closely politically affiliated with

Daniel Hannan, a Conservative MEP and anti-EU campaigner, and if he wanted a career in Westminster, he should rethink his ties.

'If the moron I was talking to had any idea as to who I was and what animated me, and what caused me to go into politics...' Carswell says. 'Of course, I smiled sweetly and ignored him.'

The Maastricht wounds still ran deep on both sides of the Europe debate.

Charles Walker went for training with other prospective MPs in 2005 – including those who had previously lost seats – hosted by people who had served in the whips' office under John Major. One candidate, a former MP, turned to Walker and said: 'They're all jokes and smiles now, but they were absolute bastards.'

The R Group opted not speak to the whips or those who 'colluded' with them, says Carswell, operating instead in 'complete purdah'. 'The "Men of Maastricht", I suspect, were in difficulty probably because they did play the game with the whips,' he argues. Gradually, the R Group started a counter-whipping operation, carrying out around a dozen phone calls each over the weekend. 'I had a spreadsheet, and we started really, really small,' Carswell says.

Unlike their predecessors on Maastricht, the Eurosceptics opted – for now – not to brief the press, keeping instead their plans a tight secret, away from the whips.

The MPs had been conjuring up a motion on an EU referendum, seeking consent from other like-minded souls to coalesce around one position. A space came up in the list for backbench debates and the R Group went into overdrive. They chose Nuttall to propose the motion, rather than a more prominent Leave figure, who could put other senior MPs' noses out of joint. Nuttall presented the motion and Bone and Hollobone lobbied.[4]

The committee selected Nuttall's motion for debate on Thursday 27 October 2011.

Under Cameron, the coalition government had chosen to whip

Backbench Business Motions, elevating their importance, despite such votes' non-binding status. The government also opted to move the debate to the previous Monday to allow Cameron and William Hague, both away on overseas trips, to attend, giving it primetime focus.

The Conservative Party leader issued a three-line whip to reject the motion, and The Office went to work – despite having members on both sides of the debate. 'I had no problem doing that,' says Michael Fabricant, a whip and supporter of leaving the EU.

'The government went in very, very hard,' said a Eurosceptic. Hollobone claimed: 'People were told their careers wouldn't even get off the ground; there would be eternal retributions.'[5]

Carswell appointed Baker as Chief Whip of the Eurosceptics – an astute signing that would pay dividends – leading to the website Guido Fawkes coining him 'the Rebel Commander'. 'Successive Chief Whips have got a lot to thank Douglas Carswell for!' Baker joked.[6]

Downing Street hoped that Speaker John Bercow would select one of three amendments to the rebels' motion, believing that would split the vote and dilute the impact of a one-off rebellion. He did not.

On the day of the vote, Stuart Andrew, MP for Pudsey, met McLoughlin. He presented the Chief Whip with a leaflet he'd been asked by the party to distribute ahead of the 2010 election, featuring a picture of the previous Labour MP with his fingers in his ears and a caption accusing him of ignoring the public's views on Europe. Andrew was escalated up to see the Prime Minister but followed through on his conviction of voting for a referendum.

In the division lobby, Cameron gave Baker, who had earlier said he would vote for a referendum even if McLoughlin were standing with a machine gun at the lobby's exit, a 'look of absolute thunder and fury'.[7] The government defeated the motion by a resounding 483 to 111, but eighty-one Tory MPs rebelled on a three-line whip, including two PPSs and forty-nine from the 2010 intake of MPs.

Two months later, Cameron sought to block a new EU-wide treaty, triggering the coalition's most serious row to date, having failed to consult Nick Clegg. 'It was one of the few points when I thought, "Jesus, this whole thing could collapse,"' says Alistair Carmichael. When, a year hence, Cameron said he would use the UK's veto on any increase to the EU budget above inflation, Tory MPs, with Labour support, put forward an amendment calling for a real-terms cut, which Bercow selected. The non-binding amendment won by 307 to 294.

Reflecting on the 81-MP rebellion, Cameron defended opposing the motion but said his tactics 'may have been cack-handed'. The rebellion 'showed the extent to which the ground was moving beneath us', he said.[8] In January 2013, Cameron announced his party would hold a referendum on EU membership if it secured a majority at the next general election.

Bercow made another significant intervention soon after, breaking with convention by accepting an amendment to the Queen's Speech from a backbench Tory MP lamenting the government's lack of legislative commitment to a referendum. The amendment lost 130 to 277, but Bercow's intentions were clear in seeking to give voice to backbenchers. 'Bercow was regarded in the whips' office as being somebody who was rarely helpful, virtually always unhelpful and often actively conspiring against the government,' said a whip.[9]

In August 2014, in the wake of Nigel Farage's UKIP winning the European elections, Carswell defected from the Tories. Fellow R Group member Mark Reckless followed suit a month later. Both men won their by-elections, called after leaving the Conservatives, with Carswell given a windowless office on his return by the whips. 'It's folly at just so many levels. If that really is your revenge, why brief it? It just makes you look like a jerk,' he says.

The 2015 election saw Cameron's party win an unlikely majority, teeing up the countdown to an EU referendum, while Ed Miliband stood down as leader, winning just 232 seats. The Labour Party spent the summer debating a successor, with a left-field candidate, who only just received the required thirty-five nominations from MPs to make the ballot,* the clear frontrunner. On 12 September 2015, the Labour Party membership overwhelmingly elected Jeremy Corbyn, the long-term scourge of successive whips' offices, as the Leader of the Opposition.

'It was quite interesting for me years later when he became leader and he's demanding loyalty,' says one of Corbyn's whips. Another, who had urged Tony Blair to take the whip away from Corbyn, the most rebellious MP on the Labour benches, reflects: 'When Corbyn won, the boss might have regretted it, but during his period as Prime Minister, he didn't.'

The fallout from Corbyn's leadership and, most significantly, the EU referendum, pencilled in for 23 June 2016, would have untold consequences for party unity across the House and leave the whips – already stripped bare – largely powerless to stop the rot.

---

* Sadiq Khan, a former whip, was one of the last to nominate Corbyn for the leadership.

CHAPTER 48

DOING A WALTER

On the morning of 9 June 2017, Gavin Williamson turned to his principal private secretary and asked: 'Do you think we could do a Walter Harrison?' Roy Stone mulled the implications, nodded and told the Chief Whip: 'I suppose we can. In fact, we're going to have to.'[1]

Theresa May had gambled away the Tories' small majority at a snap election. Ironically, the Prime Minister, now described by an ex-Cabinet colleague as a 'dead woman walking', had called the election to strengthen her hand in negotiations with the European Union.

In fairness, May had done so amid highly favourable polling, with her party nearly twenty points ahead of the struggling and increasingly fractious Labour opposition. But the Tories now had 317 seats, nine short of a majority, with Labour, confounding all expectations under beleaguered party leader Jeremy Corbyn, who had already survived an attempt to unseat him, on 262.

For the whips, the electorate had brought about another hung parliament at the worst possible time.

* * *

Just shy of twelve months earlier, the UK, in a result that reverberated across Europe and beyond, voted to leave the EU by 51.9 per cent to 48.1. David Cameron, who undertook a leading role in the Remain campaign, had emerged on the winning side in two prior referendums: the first on the Alternative Vote in 2011 and the second on Scottish independence in 2014. On Friday 24 June 2016, his good fortune having run out, Cameron announced his intention to resign.

By comparison with what followed, the run-up to the EU referendum had, from the whips' perspective, been fairly smooth. Mark Harper – a minister but a whipping novice – took over from Michael Gove as Chief Whip, working alongside Anne Milton, who was now Deputy.

The Commons still saw its share of drama. In December 2015, MPs voted in favour of air strikes against Islamic State targets in Syria by 397 to 223 – with Corbyn giving his troops a free vote while opposing intervention, while his shadow Foreign Secretary Hilary Benn passionately argued the case *for* action from the despatch box – more than two years after Cameron's defeat over Bashar al-Assad's regime.

'A lot of ministerial time was taken up with talking to colleagues who had a problem,' says a Tory whip involved in the operation.

Not every vote was successful. MPs rejected by 317 to 286 plans to overhaul Sunday trading laws, with Chancellor George Osborne – who had already been forced to climb down on cuts to tax credits following a defeat in the House of Lords – pressing ahead with the vote despite warnings from the whips about a potential loss. 'We were absolutely clear about the numbers,' a whip says, but Osborne stressed: 'No, I still want you to have the vote.'

Most significantly from a constitutional perspective, the whips marshalled the historic bill enacting the referendum. In February 2016, Cameron, having renegotiated the terms of Britain's EU membership, returned with his new deal for the UK inside the bloc, which Brexiteers lined up to attack in the Commons. Cabinet ministers were allowed to declare for either side of the debate, with Michael Gove and the newly installed MP for Uxbridge Boris Johnson joining the Leave campaign. Steve Barclay was about the only whip to follow suit.

Gavin Williamson, the MP for South Staffordshire since 2010, had spent nearly three effective years as Cameron's PPS by the time of the

Prime Minister's resignation. 'There wasn't a backbencher he didn't know, didn't chat to, there were no wallflowers,' an MP says.

Soon to be a free agent, he offered to run the numbers for the parliamentary side of Home Secretary Theresa May's leadership campaign. 'He was very good at knowing how people were going to vote,' says a Cabinet minister. A former whip says Williamson sidled up to him at breakfast in Parliament and asked: 'Look, I'm going to ask if you'll vote for Theresa?'

The ex-member of The Office recalled May's whip in opposition, who shadowed her departmental team, tearing his hair out, saying: 'She doesn't talk to anybody. There's no corporate spirit there!' At whips' meetings, McLoughlin, the Deputy, would defend May, arguing: 'It doesn't matter. She gets things done, and she can be trusted with her brief.'

Despite these reservations, the former whip told Williamson: 'I know her warts and all. I know all the negative side, but I will vote for her.'

Boris Johnson, the face of the Leave campaign, was widely regarded as the frontrunner for the leadership but opted not to stand after Michael Gove spectacularly put his own name forward with a hefty swipe at his Brexit ally. With MPs narrowing the choices to Brexiteer Andrea Leadsom and Remain-voting May, who kept her nose clean in the referendum and led among backbenchers, the contest went to the membership. But when Leadsom pulled out, May was elected unopposed on 11 July 2016.

'Brexit', May told all-comers, 'means Brexit.'

In her reshuffle, May appointed Williamson as Chief Whip. 'He's very good at convincing people that he knows a lot,' says a one-time colleague. One of his appointees, Mark Spencer, says: 'He's somebody that I respected. He was very clear about what he wanted and wanted to achieve.' But another MP says simply: 'He's a prat of the first order.'

Williamson retained Milton as Deputy, but relations between the number one and number two in The Office were strained from the outset. 'Any group of ministers is a coalition of sorts, but I think it would be fair to suggest they didn't necessarily gel,' a colleague says.

A former nurse who was garnering a reputation for the pastoral elements of the role, Milton had wanted to replace Harper as Chief and suspected Williamson wanted her gone. Williamson's team, who, with no handover between Chiefs, were already having to gather intelligence from the ground up, found it took time to build trust with Milton, who was wary about sharing information – particularly personal information – with the Chief Whip. Milton, a whip says, viewed herself as a 'dam' between MPs and Williamson.

Milton acted as the liaison with the in-house Parliamentary Health and Wellbeing Service, securing from the Speaker additional funds for supporting MPs in need. In her time, she helped arrange for a psychiatrist to visit the home of an MP on the verge of suicide. MPs, whips and staff would report issues to Milton, such as accounts of people drinking to excess, misbehaving on the parliamentary estate or abusing their position. 'The whips would report to her: "I saw X in a club, really drunk,"' says a colleague. Milton also confronted Tory MP Bob Stewart after he made a sexist remark to *Spectator* journalist Isabel Hardman.

Much of the information she was privy to – some of which was intensely personal or potentially serious – Milton wanted to keep away from Williamson. 'Anne had to tell Gavin about some things, but she told him as little as possible because she didn't trust him,' says a colleague. One whip is grateful that Williamson didn't inherit a 'Black Book' from his predecessors. 'That would have been his ticket to a lot of things.'

Milton's reservations, people who worked with Williamson attest, were well-founded. 'I felt he embraced the caricature of what a Chief should be, that slightly Francis Urquhart, *House of Cards* mentality and being menacing,' says a colleague, who got on well with Williamson. 'He was always keen to have information on people who needed help, all that kind of stuff.'

In an interview with *Channel 4 News*, Milton later claimed that Williamson 'loved salacious gossip'.[2] The Chief would come into The Office and say guess who enjoys some form of sex or another, Milton said. She also remembered Williamson handing her a cheque to pass on to an MP in financial difficulty. 'He waved it under my nose and said: "Make sure when you give him this cheque, he knows that I now own him,"' she said.[3]

A Tory MP and future minister, meanwhile, accused Williamson of raising details of her private life in an apparent attempt to silence her. Allies of the Chief Whip said he had done so in a 'pastoral capacity'.[4]

Craig Whittaker, a whip who 'quite liked' Williamson, remarks: 'Parliament is about power, pure power. Gavin grasped that to the nth degree and used it and milked it for every ounce he could squeeze out of it.'

Williamson, he says, is the only one in his experience who 'used the dark arts', though he also concedes: 'That's not entirely true; you clearly come up with plans occasionally with how you're going to deal with somebody and that may not be in a good way. Gavin was much more, "Just fucking get it done!" He was more in your face, threatening.'

Within a few months, news trickled out that Williamson kept a pet tarantula called Cronus on his desk, named after a Greek god who came to power by castrating his father before eating his own children to ensure they couldn't get rid of him. 'Cronus is a perfect example of an incredibly clean, ruthless killer – absolutely fascinating to rear,' he said theatrically.[5] Visiting the Chief, Michael Fabricant asked if he could stroke Cronus. 'Personally, I think the thing was dead. It didn't even move. But no, I'm sure it wasn't,' he says.

His advocates insist that Williamson had an astute political snout worthy of the office he held. 'Gavin Williamson was a brilliant Chief Whip,' says Philip Davies. 'He was interested in people; he took the time to find out what made people tick.'

A colleague recalls the Chief's reaction when Labour MP Carolyn

Harris, who, in the late 1980s, required a loan to pay for her eight-year-old son's funeral, led efforts for a fund to cover children's burial and cremation costs. No. 10, while naturally sympathetic, felt a blanket fund, as opposed to a targeted one to help those most in need, was not the right way to go as some people didn't require a grant to pay for a funeral. 'Gavin saw the politics straight away of: "Well, it doesn't matter, does it? These are kids who have died,"' says the colleague. Williamson talked No. 10 around to avoid putting MPs in a position of having to oppose the measure.

On his approach to whipping, Williamson told the Tory Party conference: 'Personally, I don't much like the stick, but it is amazing what can be achieved with a sharpened carrot.'

Regarding the carrots at his disposal, Whittaker says Williamson looked towards an exclusive sovereign body. 'Gavin used the Privy Council as an incentive to people to get things done and put through unprecedented numbers of privy counsellors during his time as Chief Whip.'

In building up intelligence, Williamson's special advisers put together spreadsheets of the parliamentary party and instructed, as per the Chief's wishes, the whips to do regular ring-rounds and interviews with their flock, working out MPs' career aspirations, feedback from their patch and long-term plans. 'Getting that tapestry is so important,' an aide in The Office says.

New members of The Office received a pack, around six A4 pages long, on how to be a whip. Increasingly communicating with their flock by text or WhatsApp – with the weekly issuing of the 'Whip' now done by email – the dynamics in The Office, if not the job, were changing.

Whittaker says he would type up all his conversations before going to bed. As to whether there was still physical note-taking, one whip who joined in the coalition says: 'I think we had notes at the beginning, and then somebody forgot the code for the safe. It had all but gone.'

Another whip says Williamson expected 'detailed' feedback. 'Just writing, "This person isn't going to vote with us" was meaningless information,' they say. 'What he wanted to know was the specifics of why.'

The Tories had talked about bringing the party back together after the fractious referendum. But the cracks remained, with a growing number of Remain-voting MPs disgruntled at how the new Prime Minister approached Parliament on issues regarding the EU. The government, however, had yet to lose a vote on Brexit. Its Article 50 Bill to trigger the two-year negotiating process – required following a Supreme Court ruling – sailed through the Commons.

Chris Pincher, the whip on the bill, had spent time considering how MPs act when they're in a group, devising a 'herding mechanism' to first get them into the chamber before votes, so that they couldn't just hide, dip into the lobbies and then run away. During divisions, two people would also be assigned to shepherd MPs – one of whom would be 'a bit more impressive' – watching out for specific targets they wanted to get into the 'right' lobby.

He also sought to break up the group of Remain MPs who sat in the top right corner of the Tory benches by instructing other backbenchers to submit prayer cards at the start of the day to reserve their seats. 'When they're sat together, you can't get to them,' Pincher says.

For Theresa May, things were looking rosy. After June 2017, everything changed.

* * *

Stuart Andrew, one of many MPs whose majorities had dropped substantially after the 2017 election, arrived at 9 Downing Street to see the Chief Whip about a role in The Office. 'I'm really keen to join, but given I've got a marginal seat, my one anxiety is that I won't be able to speak in the chamber,' he said.

Gavin Williamson, with a smile on his face, joked: 'I've heard you speak. I don't think you'll be much of a loss to your constituents.'

With Milton moved to the Department for Education, Julian Smith took over as Deputy Chief Whip. As Chief, Williamson helped broker a confidence and supply agreement with the Democratic Unionist Party. In The Office, thoughts turned to other measures that could help shore up the Tories' position in Parliament.

In his conversation with Roy Stone, the principal private secretary to the Chief Whip, Williamson had presciently evoked the memory of Walter Harrison. In 1976, Labour's Deputy Chief proposed a surprise motion on a sitting Friday to grant the government, which had lost its majority in the House, a majority on standing committees. Stone, in seeking to work out how the minority government could operate, proposed evoking this precedent.[6]

Andrea Leadsom, the Leader of the House, put forward plans for bill committees where there was an odd number of MPs to have a government majority of one. With the support of the DUP, the measure passed. 'It was based on that understanding that the government of the day has the right to get its business through,' argues a member of The Office. Others deemed it a constitutional outrage.

To further steady the ship, the whips sought agreement from the opposition to provide pairs. They achieved this through good relations with Labour whips Alan Campbell and Mark Tami in particular, both of whom had served in government. 'Thereby, we got ourselves a little bit of wriggle room,' says Chris Pincher.

The Office also instigated a system of 'sweepers' and 'bogwatchers', with whips touring the usual haunts across the Palace of Westminster to ensure MPs voted. The Lords terrace was one such spot, which became popular with Tory MPs for its smoking area. It was also difficult to hear the Commons bell from this vantage point, though there was an annunciator. Other key areas included the Lords dining room and the basement (where there is no bell or phone signal). 'You would send people off to make sure that they hauled out anybody in there to come back to vote because we needed everyone,' Pincher says. Whips would also take up the 'usual exits' to stop people leaving between divisions.

The May government opted to instruct its MPs to abstain on

Opposition Day Motions, rather than whip and incur rebellions. The government lost votes on the rollout of universal credit, social care funding and NHS pay. The Labour Party also attacked the Tories for eating into parliamentary time with ministerial statements, criticisms amplified by Speaker John Bercow.

In response, the Labour Party deployed an antiquated procedure known as a humble address to compel ministers to acknowledge the will of the House. Though the Tories pointed the finger at Bercow as the source of the suggestion, Nick Brown, who returned as Labour Chief Whip in 2016, counters: 'The clerks cleared the humble address idea when the Labour whips' office under me … came up with the idea.'

Tory MPs had their suspicions about the relationship between Labour whips and Bercow, with Brown referred to as the Speaker's 'line manager', which the Chief rejects. He does recall the Speaker asking for Thangam Debbonaire and Bambos Charalambous to be the party's tellers at an upcoming vote, likely so that Bercow could enjoy announcing their names in his usual over-the-top style.

Armed with greater power than before the 2017 election, Tory MPs sceptical of Brexit flexed their muscles. 'Gavin Williamson was a nightmare to deal with,' says a Remain-voting MP. 'Slippery, couldn't be trusted, all the rest of it.' Williamson would agree on an amendment only for MPs to discover the 'wording had shifted'. 'He can flip from being relatively charming to trying to be threatening very quickly. He's slightly a snake oil salesman type.'

Cabinet minister Michael Fallon, facing accusations of inappropriate behaviour, resigned as Defence Secretary at the end of October, the first casualty of the brewing Westminster harassment and bullying scandal. Williamson succeeded Fallon in the Ministry of Defence despite never having served in either the department or the Armed Forces. In November, Julian Smith, his Deputy and close ally, took over as Chief.

'Julian Smith was a lot more straightforward but ultimately found it difficult to deliver,' says the Remain-voting MP. Chris Pincher, who would go on to serve as Smith's Deputy, says: 'Nobody worked as hard as Julian. He put himself through hell to try and help Mrs May.'

With all eyes on Parliament and its key players, Smith was a more ubiquitous figure than other Tory Chief Whips. As the Brexit chaos unfolded, he looked increasingly haggard, working all hours in 9 Downing Street. When, after midnight, Craig Whittaker would email summaries of his conversations during the day, 'two seconds later my phone would ring, and it would be Julian Smith'.

'The guy never slept,' Whittaker says. 'He was questioning you about stuff all the time.'

Despite praise for his undoubted efforts in the face of much resistance, some who worked with Smith believe his fraught demeanour was a symptom of erratic ways of working, not being across the detail, and struggles with delegating. 'I found Julian really hard to work for,' says a colleague. 'He doesn't trust very easily.'

The critical co-worker compares Smith's approach to candy floss. 'It looks voluminous, there's a lot there, but it's not going to fill you up,' they say. 'It's actually air; it's empty. That's how I would describe a lot of his activity as Chief Whip.'

Left with an emerging harassment scandal, Smith, in December 2017, also had to tackle a nascent rebellion from Remain-voting Tory rebels, who had begun meeting regularly and were led, in this instance, by former Cabinet minister Dominic Grieve.

The ex-Attorney General met whips with around ten demands for the government's European Union Withdrawal Bill. The government consented to the majority – but not an amendment seeking to legally guarantee Parliament a so-called meaningful vote on May's Brexit deal.

The Prime Minister had already committed to put her deal to Parliament, but Grieve pushed to prevent the government from implementing a Withdrawal Agreement before MPs had voted on it. In May's first Commons defeat over Brexit, eleven Tory MPs, including vice-chair Stephen Hammond, backed Grieve's amendment. For the rebels, everything changed.

'That's why it was important to do it, because the whips suddenly thought, "Hmm, there's another game in town here. We need to worry about this lot as well,"' says a rebel.

Remain-voting Tory MPs say they were 'pretty rigorous' in informing the whips of their intentions – but those in The Office argue they were harder to deal with than Brexiteers, regularly shifting goalposts and changing demands. 'At least with [Brexiteers], their word was almost their honour,' says Whittaker. Another person says: 'They were less angry. If you did a deal with Jacob Rees-Mogg, for example, he tended to stick to it. You couldn't do a deal with Anna Soubry or Dominic Grieve.'

The next summer, as the European Union Withdrawal Bill entered its ping-pong stage with the House of Lords, officials contemplated how a so-called meaningful vote on the Brexit deal should work. Grieve, who had worked with like-minded peers in the Lords seeking to prevent Britain crashing out of the EU empty-handed, pushed an amendment to give MPs the power to amend and vote on any government motion if there was no deal by a certain date.

But advisers in No. 10 and the whips' office felt you couldn't have a meaningful vote without potential consequences, learning from the experience of John Major during Maastricht, when he made the matter a confidence issue and finally secured the legislation. No. 10 aides Nikki da Costa and Stephen Parkinson worked up an amendment[*] to say that, if MPs voted no twice, they would trigger a general election. They showed it to the Prime Minister, who liked it. But Smith did not.

The Chief feared being bounced without stress-testing the idea, believing MPs – who, in a minority government, wield significant power – would be apoplectic if blindsided by such an audacious move. A

---

[*] Insiders say that the amendment would have navigated the restrictions imposed by the Fixed-term Parliament Act, introduced by the coalition government under David Cameron.

general election could also usher in a Jeremy Corbyn-led government. A colleague in The Office says Smith secured May's consent to run the proposed amendment by Oliver Letwin, a former senior minister, noted as an intellectual and, for at least one whip, a 'pain in the arse'.

Letwin visited the Chief's office in No. 9.

'This is what they want to do,' Smith said, handing over the details (the person who witnessed this conversation laments the Chief's use of 'they', rather than 'we').

Letwin read through the proposal before concluding, 'No, no, no, you can't do that.'

'This vote with consequences was dismissed,' says the witness regretfully.

But, approached to comment, Smith counters: 'I thought the idea was crackers, as did the parliamentary party. It has nothing to do with Oliver Letwin. It was fundamentally a daft idea that could have gifted an election to Corbyn. Barking mad!'

Chris Pincher, by then Smith's Deputy, argues: 'I think if there had been a confidence vote, it would have been lost. There was just too much distrust of her and her team's motives, if I'm honest, to make it possible.'

After the negotiations with Remainers, the government agreed on wording that committed to putting a Brexit deal to the Commons and passing a bill in both Houses of Parliament. In the event of MPs rejecting the deal, the government had to produce a next-steps statement within twenty-one days. 'Letwin', a government aide says, 'designed this alternative.'

With pairing abandoned for the vote on the Grieve amendment, heavily pregnant MPs Jo Swinson and Laura Pidcock were brought in, as were sick Labour backbenchers Paul Flynn and Naz Shah, the latter wheeled through the division lobbies holding a disposable sick bag. After government compromises and assurances, the amendment fell short by 319 to 303.

With the European Union Withdrawal Act wrapped up, attention turned to the Trade Bill, to which Smith had diverted eager rebels seeking to amend other pieces of government legislation. When the Trade Bill finally came up for debate, it had so many attachments that 'it was like a bloody Christmas tree', Craig Whittaker, the whip for the legislation, jokes.

MPs prepared to vote on an amendment calling for the UK to remain in a customs union with the EU if the two sides couldn't negotiate a trade deal. In a sign of Smith 'not being across the numbers' and thinking 'just do it', says a colleague, he asked three Tory MPs to breach pairing arrangements, including party chairman Brandon Lewis, who was paired with Jo Swinson, a Lib Dem MP away on maternity leave. The government won the customs union vote by six.

Smith, who hadn't realised that Lewis was paired with a pregnant MP, tweeted that Lewis had been 'asked to vote in error'. Though No. 10 didn't deny that MPs had been asked to break pairs, the Chief survived calls for his head.

Other ministers, in due course, opted to leave. Foreign Secretary Boris Johnson, a perpetual headache-inducer for successive Prime Ministers, resigned from the Cabinet over May's so-called Chequers plan for Brexit, which included a common rulebook between the UK and the EU for food and goods, to avoid a hard border on the island of Ireland. Brexit Secretary David Davis and Steve Baker also walked.

Smith worked on another reshaping of the top team; he had already spent one Christmas carefully formulating a frontbench that would include more women and more black and minority ethnic MPs. (Wendy Morton, Rebecca Harris, Nusrat Ghani, Amanda Milling, Kelly Tolhurst and Mims Davies all joined the whips' office in January 2018.) Further reshuffles, amid resignations and sackings, would come.

In just a few months, the Prime Minister would return to London with her draft Withdrawal Agreement and a political declaration on the future UK–EU relationship. For everyone concerned with Parliament, not least the whips, all hell was about to break loose.

CHAPTER 49

THE MEANING OF STRIFE

When, in January 2017, Theresa May delivered a speech at Lancaster House setting out her Brexit vision, Leave MPs could hardly believe their ears. The Prime Minister confirmed that, as part of exiting the EU, the UK would opt out of the single market, and she left the door open to waving goodbye to the bloc's customs union. No deal, she said, is better than a bad deal.

Even the perennially oppositional Nigel Farage cracked a half-smile. 'Real progress,' he tweeted.

By the summer of 2018, Leavers' enthusiasm had waned, tainted by signs of a change in approach after the snap general election. With the vexed issue of preventing a hard border between Ireland and Northern Ireland steering May down a particular Brexit path, MPs switched gear. 'We were in shock for a few days, frankly, that the Downing Street machine seemed to turn against the Eurosceptics,' said Bernard Jenkin of May's Chequers proposal.[1]

The European Research Group (ERG), first formed in the aftermath of Maastricht, had re-formed under Steve Baker's guidance following the EU referendum. Baker set about professionalising the outfit, establishing a steering committee of leading Leave MPs, who met on Mondays in former leader (and Maastricht rebel) Iain Duncan Smith's office.

Over two years, the government had appointed three of its chairs – Baker, Chris Heaton-Harris and Suella Braverman – to ministerial roles in the Department for Exiting the EU, in attempts to bring them onside. Jacob Rees-Mogg, a fierce Eurosceptic, was now at the top of the ERG tree, transitioning from an eccentric backbencher to a household name.

'We ended up in this spiral where both sides of the argument were being driven further apart by their desire to maintain their own media profile,' says a whip of Remainers and Brexiteers.

With former whip Mark Francois joining Baker in leading efforts to marshal MPs, the ERG ran an effective whipping unit, with members of the counter-operation known as 'buddies' to avoid outside detection.[2] An ERG member confirms: 'We knew how everybody was going to vote ... We had a database. It was absolutely a parallel whips' office, and it was remarkably effective.'

Forgetful MPs left copies of the ERG 'whip' on the Commons benches, claims an ex-Cabinet minister. 'In previous times, people would have been thrown out of the party for that.'

In November 2018, May returned to London with her draft Brexit deal. UK and EU negotiators had agreed to a so-called backstop arrangement – seeing Britain enter a single customs territory with the bloc if both sides failed to agree a trade deal before the end of a transition period – to avoid a hard border on the island of Ireland.

The DUP, the government's confidence and supply partners, vehemently opposed the plan, as did Brexiteers and certain members of the government who wanted a time limit on the backstop – views Julian Smith increasingly had to reflect to the Prime Minister. Brexit Secretary Dominic Raab and his minister Braverman, the former ERG chair, resigned.

With the draft agreement pleasing very few – some Remainers had hoped for a softer landing, while others now wanted nothing short of a second referendum, known as a People's Vote – the whips had an impossible task. The Chief, after a ring-round in The Office a month before the draft deal came back, had already reported to No. 10 that 130 Tory MPs might rebel.[3] Smith later said the news went down poorly with Downing Street officials, who argued that it was his job to deliver the votes.[4] No whip could make up that deficit.

Before the meaningful vote, planned for 10 December, Smith, in a stark departure from his predecessors' approach, invited ITV to report from inside his office, including a meeting of his team and an awkward confrontation with Philip Davies over the issue of the backstop.

Cabinet ministers, meanwhile, got to work on the various Brexit groupings. 'I would be asked to speak to the people who were hardline Remain,' says David Lidington, the de facto Deputy Prime Minister, with whom Smith would attend the 8.30 a.m. meetings in No. 10. 'Michael [Gove], the Chief and Theresa would focus on the Leavers.'

Despite Smith's insistence to ITV that the meaningful vote, due in December, was going ahead, the government pushed it back, days after MPs found May's administration in contempt of Parliament for refusing to disclose in full the Attorney General's advice on the deal.

The Conservatives, led by key members of the ERG, held an internal no-confidence vote in their party leader, with the required forty-eight MPs submitting a letter to Sir Graham Brady, the chair of the 1922 Committee. May survived by 200 to 117.

Francois, who had called for May to go, delivered a small case of 'fairly decent' Margaux to the whips' office, placing it on the Deputy's desk with a note:

To the Office, with the compliments of Dad's Army.'[5]

* * *

On 8 January 2019, Dominic Grieve visited John Bercow in the Speaker's apartment. He had just tabled an amendment to the government's business motion detailing the timetable for the new meaningful vote. MPs had already agreed the business motion for the postponed vote, with paragraph 9 stating: 'The question on any such motion shall be put forthwith.'

As such, the second business motion, which varied the first, appeared unamendable. Bercow disagreed.

'You do realise it's controversial?' Grieve pointed out to Bercow, after the Speaker said he'd asked for it to be put on the order paper so he could think about it overnight.

'Of course I know it's controversial. I will make up my own mind,' he said.[6]

To the consternation of the government – and in apparent disagreement with advice offered by House of Commons officials – Bercow selected Grieve's amendment calling for May to announce within three days details of her Plan B for Brexit if MPs rejected her deal.

In the Commons, as Tory MPs lined up to attack the Speaker, Julian Smith was overheard telling Bercow his ruling was 'totally out of order'. A No. 10 aide says Smith would often enter the Prime Minister's parliamentary office with his 'eyes glazed' after another 'difficult evening' with a 'recalcitrant' Speaker.[7] MPs backed the Grieve amendment 308 to 297.

The run-up to the meaningful vote coincided with some Brexit-backing MPs receiving knighthoods, including ex-Cabinet minister John Redwood and former whip John Hayes, while Edward Leigh found himself on the Privy Council. The timing prompted cynicism from opposition parties about the government's motivations and the long arm of The Office.

'I suppose if you go back to why people have queries about the whips' office, it is a key part of the Prime Minister and government's patronage,' concedes a senior whip.

On 15 January, the House rejected May's Brexit deal by an eyewatering 230 votes, the heaviest defeat by a Prime Minister in the democratic era. Among the many Tory rebels was Gareth Johnson, who quit the whips' office to vote against the Prime Minister's proposals.

'[Smith] had a very, very difficult hand to play,' says a pro-EU MP who voted for the deal. 'He was dealing with people convinced by their own position who would not move.'

Labour Chief Nick Brown, sitting on the opposition frontbench, took out a KitKat from his pocket as a pre-agreed signal for colleagues to table a motion of no confidence in the Prime Minister. The idea, taken from a recent book about a KGB agent turned defector, fell short when an MP walked between the Chief and the watching TV cameras at the crucial moment.

Luckily, the team had a back-up plan. Text.[8]

May survived the Commons no-confidence vote by 325 to 306, with Tory and DUP MPs voting in favour of the Prime Minister.

* * *

After MPs resigned en masse and attempted to unseat him as leader, Jeremy Corbyn appointed veteran Nick Brown as Chief in late 2016, replacing Rosie Winterton, who had served for six years.

'Nick was a pretty straightforward and professional person,' says an aide in Corbyn's office. James Matthewson, an adviser to Labour chairman Ian Lavery, says the Chief was 'central to holding so much stuff together'.

Brown hadn't expected to receive the offer. 'Well, it's got to be vacant,' he said of the Chief Whip role.

'It is,' Corbyn assured him.

Brown had left The Office in autumn 2010, after Ed Miliband replaced him as Chief with Winterton. Two of his former colleagues suspected Brown accepted Corbyn's offer partly as a 'tit for tat' with Winterton but also to get back a paid job. Wrong on both counts, Brown insists.

Early on in his tenure, Brown, in reference to his previous stint in The Office, joked to the PLP that 'there's nobody in this room who's had more dealings with Jeremy and has got to know him better'. A senior Tory whip remembers doing a joint session on The Office for overseas visitors with Alan Campbell, Labour's Deputy Chief. After talking about people not getting promoted for rebelling, Campbell joked: 'The only job they get is leader of the Labour Party.'

Given Brown had served as Chief in the New Labour government, some frontbenchers were sceptical of his motives. 'Nick Brown isn't bought into your project ideologically. You need to be very careful,' Ian Lavery warned Corbyn.

The Labour leader's rebellious record made it nigh-on impossible for the whips to impose discipline. Though admiring of Brown's efforts, aides felt the whips in general failed to crack down on MPs for sending 'abusive' messages to Corbyn, shouting at him in corridors or flagrantly leaking PLP meetings to journalists. 'In terms of trying to push the party's lines on issues in general terms, I don't think the whips' office did any of that,' says a Corbyn aide.

Brown, as Chief Whip, would also get the 'brunt' of MPs' wrath at PLP meetings on Mondays at 6 p.m. while outlining the upcoming business. 'The hatred ran every bit as deep at the end as it did at the beginning,' he says of discontent with Corbyn's leadership.

Mike Gapes still has framed on his office wall a written reprimand from Brown, time-limited for six months, after voting against triggering Article 50 in breach of a three-line whip. 'You are required to comply with the whip in the future,' Brown wrote. 'If you wish to contest this letter on the grounds of accuracy of your voting record, please contact me.'

Seeking to overturn the massive deficit from the first meaningful vote, the government held talks with Labour MPs from Leave-voting constituencies who, outwardly at least, wanted to see Brexit delivered. But Labour, gradually working its way to supporting a confirmatory referendum under shadow Brexit Secretary Keir Starmer, put the squeeze on. David Lidington says he knows of Labour backbenchers who were in tears after being warned about voting for the Prime Minister's Brexit deal. Brown, meanwhile, says around twenty Labour MPs who represented Leave seats would 'gang up and come and see me en masse, demanding that I did what they wanted'.

Brown, though, was a supporter of inserting a referendum as a clause in the legislation and cutting a deal with the Tories not to take it out. A Corbyn aide remarks: 'By the end, the whips' office was in effect the whips' office for the People's Vote campaign, not for the leadership.'

But not everyone in the Labour whips' office felt the same. Stephanie Peacock resigned to vote against moves to hold a second national vote.

Privately, Brown says that Corbyn was 'toying with the Wilsonian idea' of 'letting them each go their own way', allowing his MPs to campaign while he as leader remained neutral. 'As soon as he tried that, his office … told him no.'

Gapes, an MP since 1992, had always got on well with Brown but recalls the Chief Whip trying to block him from rebelling during Corbyn's leadership.

'No, we're in that lobby, not this one,' Brown said.

'Excuse me,' Gapes said. 'I'm doing a Jeremy.'

On 18 February 2019, in protest at Corbyn's leadership and amid damaging claims of antisemitism within the party, Gapes and six other MPs quit and set up The Independent Group. Fellow Labour MP Joan Ryan joined a day later, quickly followed by three pro-EU Tory MPs, Anna Soubry, Heidi Allen and Sarah Wollaston. 'There were far more than the seven of us who went initially,' says Gapes.*

Parliament was riven with counter-whipping operations, with MPs on opposing sides linked by their respective positions on Brexit. One cross-party group formed in late 2018 called itself 'Trains and Buses' – named after founding members who had served as Transport

---

* Gapes, speaking in early 2024, continues: 'We were in discussions with twenty-five, thirty at the time, some of whom are now in senior roles within the Starmer shadow Cabinet.'

Ministers – with pro-EU MPs from across the House joining its eponymous WhatsApp group.[9]

Another grouping, referred to by some as 'the grandees', who sought a cross-party compromise and were vehemently opposed to a no-deal Brexit, featured the likes of Oliver Letwin, Nick Boles, Hilary Benn, Margaret Beckett and Yvette Cooper.[10] The Common Market 2.0 group, who advocated a Norway-style exit, also gathered interest.

Labour MPs who voted against triggering the Brexit process had already set up a WhatsApp group known as 'Beyond Article 50'.[11] Labour MP Ben Bradshaw says his colleague Stephen Doughty was 'kind of the unofficial whip of the backbench PLP faction' that 'wanted to shift Corbyn into a more progressive' position on a second referendum.

Brexit-supporting Labour MPs such as Frank Field and Kate Hoey also went their own way, liaising with like-minded souls across the Commons. 'We would do our organising of our vote on the floor of the House. They would see us doing it,' said Field of the Labour whips. The ERG and the DUP paid close attention to each other's moves, united by their opposition to May's deal and their revulsion at the backstop, with Julian Smith pushing for a solution, knowing the impasse wouldn't be broken without it.

On 12 March, MPs once more rejected Theresa May's Brexit deal, this time by 149 votes, after the Prime Minister returned from Brussels having sought further changes. The House then rejected leaving the EU without an agreement, with five Cabinet ministers abstaining, huddled in a room just off the Commons chamber, rather than voting against as instructed.

'We did it on the basis that the Prime Minister couldn't possibly fire all of us,' says one Cabinet rebel. 'I do look back on that and think, "What the hell did that achieve?" I should have just supported the government; I was a minister.'

The divides on the backbenches were mirrored in the Cabinet. Those on the Remain-voting wing concerned about the influence of the ERG, including the Chancellor Philip Hammond, David Gauke and Greg Clark, met weekly. The so-called 'Pizza Club' of Brexit-backing ministers, including Andrea Leadsom, Chris Grayling and Michael Gove, also linked up.

Parliament requested an extension to Article 50, though eight Cabinet ministers voted against May's motion calling for a delay to Brexit. Smith and other whips abstained. 'The problem with the backbenchers was made worse by the fact that discipline at Cabinet was clearly breaking down,' says David Lidington. 'The frequency of leaks was deeply shocking.'

* * *

After Labour asked for a clarification, John Bercow, citing a precedent from 1604, warned that a motion or an amendment already ruled upon during a parliamentary session could not be brought forward again. A third meaningful vote would have to be on a sufficiently different motion.

Seeking to break the impasse, Theresa May invited opposition leaders to a meeting in her parliamentary office, but Jeremy Corbyn, believing the terms of the rendezvous had been breached, refused to take part after Change UK* representative Chuka Umunna turned up. Ian Blackford, the SNP's group leader in Westminster, took his place as the main point man.

The Prime Minister offered opposition parties negotiations with David Lidington to find a way forward. Blackford told May that, for this to work, 'nothing must be off the table', including the prospect of the UK remaining in the EU's single market and customs union. 'But, Ian,' May replied. 'Brexit means Brexit.'

With cross-party talks attended by Smith and other Chiefs now

---

* The new name for the Independent Group.

under way, the whips worked seven-day weeks seeking a breakthrough. Smith would often ring his team late at night, asking things like: 'Can you get this information before dawn?'

Despite the enormous pressure, there was still time for more light-hearted moments. Mark Spencer, a farmer, was racking up record numbers of parliamentary defeats as the Comptroller, who deals with the business on the floor of the House. He was also copping flak from his colleague Alister Jack, who owned a thousand-acre estate in Scotland.

'You've got a market garden, old boy,' Jack would tease of Spencer's East Midlands farm.

With The Office – and Parliament more broadly – suffering an infestation of mice, Spencer set Jack a challenge. 'I tell you what. If you think you're so bloody good at land management, let's have a competition to see who can catch the most mice,' he said.

Both men brought in mouse traps marked with their names. Spencer sailed ahead, but then his tally dried up. Perplexed, Spencer tried different types of cheese and bait for the mice. One day, he accidentally dropped his pen onto one of the traps by his desk, but it didn't go off.

Jack, it transpired, had sabotaged the traps with superglue. 'He is a rat of the highest order, that Alister Jack!' jokes Spencer.

By this stage, Craig Whittaker had reluctantly taken on the role of Vice-Chamberlain, writing each day to the Queen with a report on the extraordinary impasse in Parliament. After Smith met him three times trying to persuade him to succeed Andrew Stephenson in the post, he finally caved. 'I just didn't feel as though I was up to writing to our Queen on a daily basis,' he confides.

Buckingham Palace issued the usual instruction to share gossip from Parliament – with a caveat. 'But perhaps not as much gossip as the previous Vice-Chamberlain gave her,' he was told. Whittaker explains: 'Andrew can be quite flamboyant with his language sometimes.'

Eight weeks after he took on the position, Whittaker had an audience with Her Majesty at Buckingham Palace but didn't think to look over his previous daily messages in advance, believing 'there is no way the Queen is going to remember what I wrote to her'.

For twenty minutes, and without notes, the Queen grilled Whittaker on matters in his daily reports. Sweating, Whittaker thought: 'Shit, did I really say that?' He held two more audiences with Her Majesty after that meeting. 'I wasn't caught out again,' he says.

* * *

On 29 March, MPs voted for a third time on May's Withdrawal Agreement.

The Speaker had been satisfied that the motion, this time just on the exit deal and not on the future relationship, was sufficiently different to the previous two votes. Despite whispered assurances emanating from The Office that May wouldn't cling to No. 10 following a victory, the House rejected the deal by 344 to 286, with thirty-four Tories voting against. Brexiteers who held the line referred to themselves as 'The Spartans'.

One so-called Spartan, Adam Holloway, says he was called up to have tea with an ex-Chancellor – a friend of his parents – and a former MI6 officer whom he knew well. 'I knew these were the tentacles [of the whips' office],' he says. Another friend sidled up to him on the day of the vote and urged: 'Just abstain tonight.'

With the Commons at deadlock, Oliver Letwin put forward an amendment calling for a series of indicative votes on a way forward with Brexit, including for outcomes such as another referendum, a so-called Norway-style exit or remaining in the customs union.

This, for Remainers, was their opportunity.

Labour MP and former whip Helen Goodman, who says she had come up with the idea of holding indicative votes, did the whipping operation on the customs union Brexit option, spearheaded, on her suggestion, by Tory grandee Ken Clarke. She negotiated with MPs across the House, while Tory MPs Rory Stewart and Alex Chalk took care of their benches.

Those in favour of the UK remaining in a customs union with the EU joined a WhatsApp Group, predictably titled 'Customs Union'. Members included Stewart, Chalk, government minister Alistair Burt, Caroline Spelman, Damian Green, Richard Benyon and Sarah Newton.

The customs union option came closest to passing the House, falling short by three votes, with advocates of different options, including a People's Vote, refusing to compromise. This 'perfectly encapsulated where we were: everyone knew what they were against, but they couldn't agree with what they were for', says a member of the whips' office.

A supporter of the customs union option alleges that Tory whips told ministers to sit the vote out. 'I know the whips' office told ministers at the time, "Do not engage with this, do not indulge, do not vote" and all the rest of it,' they say. Goodman argues: 'It's terrible that people were putting their personal agenda [first]. There was a lot of ambition.'

Bercow's rulings from the chair failed to surprise anyone in The Office. 'There was always a degree of certainty in that relationship because we knew he hated the government,' says a member. Nonetheless, when the Speaker allowed Oliver Letwin and Labour's Yvette Cooper, via standing order 24 of the House, to take control of the order paper and bring forward a bill, even they were taken aback. The bill – designed to prevent a no-deal exit without MPs' approval – went through its Commons stages in one day. The only surprise, insofar as the whips were concerned, came when Bercow voted *with* the government on a tied amendment.

The paralysis ultimately did for May, who stood down as leader. The summer leadership contest saw Jeremy Hunt and Boris Johnson emerge as frontrunners. Gavin Williamson, the former Chief Whip and deft sniffer of political wind, who had been sacked as Defence

Secretary following a leak inquiry, helped marshal Johnson's campaign behind the scenes, eventually securing, in the process, a return to the Cabinet table.

In July 2019, Johnson, the leading Brexit campaigner, entered 10 Downing Street, vowing to leave the EU by 31 October, the newly agreed exit date. The Prime Minister and his new Chief Whip were willing to tread where their predecessors had stopped short.

PART VII

THE FINAL THROES

CHAPTER 50

BIG FARMER

EARLY SUMMER 2019

Roy Stone, the principal private secretary to the Government Chief Whip, called in a special adviser for a quiet word. 'We have a problem,' he said. 'We need to identify who the next Chief Whip is going to be.'

Both men agreed that, given the extent of the parliamentary challenge before them, Julian Smith's successor must, as a prerequisite, have prior experience of The Office. (The Chief's ties to Theresa May's administration, and thus to its many defeats, errors and shortcomings, meant no one expected him to remain in post once the new leader came in.)

'Who is it, then?' Stone asked.

The SpAd considered the question. 'I think the only person in that office is Mark Spencer,' he said of the Comptroller, who had been a whip since June 2016.

Stone replied: 'Well, you need to go and have a word with him then.'

The SpAd grabbed Spencer – an affable personality with a background in agriculture, known by Boris Johnson as 'Big Farmer' – and advised him to speak with the expectant Prime Minister about the idea of him becoming Chief Whip. 'Why don't you make a pitch for it?'

Armed with several pages of notes, put together with the help of the SpAd, Spencer told Johnson: 'When you win, these are the things you need to know about whipping, here's the parliamentary party, here's the detail, these are what I think our challenges are going to be, this will be my strategy.'

Three weeks before the result of the leadership election, Spencer took a phone call asking if he would meet Johnson and his soon-to-be chief of staff, Eddie Lister. At the end of the discussion, Lister turned to him and said: 'Would you consider being our Chief Whip?'

Johnson, a furiously ambitious politician whose eyes had long been set lustfully on the keys to No. 10, had, in fact, already tapped up another MP as a possible head of his whips' office.

'I'm minded to make you Chief Whip,' he told Paul Beresford, the imposing antipodean and former leader of Wandsworth Council.

Beresford says Johnson won't remember this exchange 'because Boris just says these things'. In any case, the MP turned it down as his style of whipping is 'a bit heavy' for today's world.

Johnson, an aspiring people pleaser by word if not by deed, had also offered assurances to Craig Whittaker that he would become Deputy Chief Whip, only for Amanda Milling to receive the appointment. Whittaker quit in anger. 'That was me chucking my toys out of the pram,' he says.

On 1 September, the whips arrived at Chequers. Drinking Balfour English sparkling wine on the terrace before a social lunch,[1] talk turned to rumours that Oliver Letwin was planning on taking control of the order paper again, seeking to prevent a no-deal Brexit. Spencer and his team wanted to send an email to Tory MPs welcoming them back from the summer break and reminding them subtly – or, rather, informing them – that votes on Europe are a matter of confidence. But Johnson's advisers preferred a more confrontational approach, briefing that rebels would lose the whip.

'It was clear from the Johnson operation and Dominic Cummings that they were very determined not to repeat what they considered to be the mistakes of Theresa May's government,' says Alistair Burt.

The May administration hadn't always pulled back from taking action over Brexit. Michael Heseltine, the former Deputy Prime Minister and passionate Europhile, had the Lords whip removed after saying he would vote Liberal Democrat in the European elections. Midway through dinner with his wife in central London, Heseltine received a phone call from John Taylor, the Chief Whip in the Lords, asking him to meet.

Taylor, Heseltine says, was 'acutely embarrassed'. 'It was quite obvious he'd been ordered to take the whip away from me.' Heseltine, who retained his membership of the party, was still allowed to sit on the bench in the upper chamber reserved for ex-Tory Cabinet ministers. He had the whip restored in July 2024.

MPs were already wound up by Johnson's decision to ask the Queen to prorogue Parliament after the conference recess – a move the Supreme Court later ruled unlawful – in an apparent bid to heighten pressure on backbenchers to reach a verdict, with the clock ticking down to 31 October, the EU exit date.

Spencer invited Letwin into his office for a conversation about his bill.

'Chief, I know what you're going to ask me to do. You're going to ask me to pull this,' a witness recalls Letwin saying.

'Well, yeah,' Spencer replied.

'Let me tell you, I've been working on this for a very long time,' Letwin said.

The witness comments: 'That was the moment that all the bits of the jigsaw went together for me. I can remember sitting there thinking: "You clever little fucker."'

To the surprise of no one, John Bercow allowed Letwin to introduce a motion under standing order 24 to take control of the order paper and bring forward his and Labour MP Hilary Benn's bill. The government removed the whip from twenty-one rebels, including a slew of ex-Cabinet ministers, former whips and grandees, as Parliament voted 328 to 301 in favour.

Burt, one of the twenty-one, received a letter from the Chief Whip informing him of the news. 'It reminded me that being a member of the parliamentary party was a privilege, not a right. I couldn't write back and tell him to fuck off because I don't do that,' he says.

Burt, instead, 'gently took him to task' over his thirty-two years of loyalty, which contrasted with that shown by some members of the Cabinet. He sent the letter but never received a reply.

'They weren't Conservatives, they aren't Conservatives, and they're not going to be Conservatives in the future,' he says of Johnson's inner circle. 'They wanted to promote the harshest Brexit they could, use Parliament to do so and in the meantime cause a few casualties.'

Taking the whip from the rebels 'shocked a lot of people' but sent a 'really strong' message to the electorate that the government was serious about seeing through Brexit, Spencer says. 'The mistake was giving [the whip] back to some of them, but that was Boris. He's the most forgiving man in the world.'

Compelled to ask the EU for a delay until 31 January 2020, Johnson called an election for 12 December, promising to 'Get Brexit Done' and urging Britain to back his 'oven-ready' deal.

The UK honoured his request, with the Tories winning 365 seats to Labour's 202.

Parliament approved Johnson's Brexit deal, with Roy Stone instrumental in helping to usher the EU Withdrawal Agreement Bill through both Houses against a hard deadline on 30 December. Britain technically left the EU on 31 January, entering a one-year transition phase.

All seemed well for the Johnson administration and its whips, handed a healthy government majority and momentum, until an emerging international crisis reached Britain's shores.

* * *

When Stuart Andrew, who had been appointed Deputy Chief Whip in February 2020, would board a train to London from Leeds, he'd often be battling for a seat. But commuting in early April, he wandered through a series of empty carriages. Arriving in the capital, he walked to the Underground and hopped on a vacant Tube, while Mark Spencer was driven to Westminster from King's Cross Station in his ministerial car, passing few, if any, vehicles en route.

Many agree that the Covid-19 pandemic was a whip's worst nightmare. Conservative MPs were spread across the country, unable to congregate in Parliament. The pandemic was especially disruptive for the large and varied 2019 intake, on whom the whips had yet to get a handle, with the UK entering lockdown three months after the election. 'That basically is the root of the problems of the Boris administration, in that we weren't able to assimilate those people into Parliament,' says Spencer.

Rather than whips putting an arm around their shoulder in the division lobbies or in Parliament's myriad corridors, The Office primarily had to communicate over the phone. The Chief Whip still hadn't met some newcomers in person before the UK went into lockdown in late March 2020. From home, MPs messaged their whips to inform them of a rebellion.

'It's much more difficult to walk by the Chief Whip or the Prime Minister and say, "I'm sorry, I'm going in the wrong lobby" than it is to send a text to your whip,' Spencer argues.

The new intake, some of whom had won unexpectedly in constituencies across Labour's so-called Red Wall, had already shown signs of independence, a potential lack of biddability, and resistance to the notion of whipping. After a misreport of their true number, the 107 new Conservative MPs formed a WhatsApp group ironically named 'The 109 Group', with a description reading: 'Our intake, no whips!'[2] They were also, perhaps less enthusiastically, members of a group formed by the whips named 'The New Intake', which distributed instructions. 'We are different. We are definitely younger, more northern, even more gay,' said an MP.[3]

'For the whips, controlling this intake is going to be tricky,' a *Times* columnist noted.[4]

From providing support to imbuing a sense of teamwork, every aspect of the whips' job was harder. When two unacquainted neighbouring MPs facing boundary changes competed over a new constituency, one tried to get the other deselected, a symptom, a whips' office insider says, of the lack of comradeship. 'MPs not getting to know each other created problems.'

As the pandemic crept its way ominously towards Britain, and other countries took the painful decision to lock down, the whips' office considered how to operate in a world of Covid-19.

'When the official Boris Johnson government narrative was "Haha, look at Italy and Spain, they're a bunch of namby-pambies", we were discussing how you would legislate for a situation where there were rotting bodies in the streets,' says the whips' insider.

With Britain locked down, staff in the whips' office fielded calls from their gardens about setting up TV screens in the chamber and how electronic voting would operate, with Parliament due to return after the Easter recess. They faced frustrations with the Speaker Lindsay Hoyle – John Bercow's successor – whom they felt was 'all over the place'. Nonetheless, Hoyle helped oversee the installation of a virtual Parliament, which lasted until Jacob Rees-Mogg, the Leader of the House, effectively put paid to it in May, amid rumours he had done so on behalf of the whips. 'We wanted it to end, but we didn't want a superspreading Parliament in the process,' says the insider. MPs took part in the bizarre endeavour of voting amid social distancing, queues snaking around the estate (though curiously, as the Palace of Westminster has royal status, its inhabitants only had to be one metre apart, rather than two).

As per Covid restrictions, no more than two people at a time were allowed in the Chief Whip's office. The rest of the whips had to operate within a bubble, rotating over who would be allowed to work from

Parliament. Andrew, a popular Deputy Chief Whip, took it upon himself to act as a proxy for Conservative MPs. 'I had 347 votes to cast,' he says.

In January 2019, the House had begun a year-long trial for proxy voting, which had been expanded during the pandemic.* Before a division, Tory MPs would message Andrew outlining how they wished to vote. One evening, as the Commons considered five Lords amendments to a bill, he had to keep across how the 347 MPs planned to vote for each division. As the whip on duty, he would vote in the Aye lobby and say 'plus' however many MPs. He'd then go to the No lobby and cast the votes for the rest, saying, 'Not me.' Finally, he would send an email to the Public Bill Office with the list of how people had voted.

Andrew decided to have some fun with his new role. At one vote, he went to the No lobby first, where Labour MPs, confused at seeing the Tories' Deputy Chief Whip, decided they must be in the wrong place and headed for the other division lobby. While more conniving deputies would consider casting their proxies as they pleased, Andrew did not, nor did he use the opportunity for one final plea when MPs submitted their requests.

In May 2020, *The Guardian* and the *Daily Mirror* released a joint investigation into a trip taken by Dominic Cummings from London to Durham two months earlier while his wife experienced symptoms of Covid-19. A separate trip to Barnard Castle while based in Durham and recovering from the virus faced further scrutiny, amid claims that he had broken the government's own lockdown rules. Under intense pressure, Cummings defended his actions during a press conference in the No. 10 garden. The furore amplified Tory MPs' unease with Johnson's administration, which, one aide argues, had underestimated the level of discontent. Subsequently, the whips facilitated Zoom calls with ministers, so backbenchers had more opportunities to ask questions about

---

* In September 2020, MPs agreed to make permanent arrangements for proxy voting where MPs are away because of childbirth, care of an infant or a newly adopted child, or complications related to childbirth.

the government's response to the pandemic, realising they couldn't just expect them to toe the line for tough, draconian measures.

With Keir Starmer appointed Labour leader, the whips also faced a different challenge from the new opposition. Though Nick Brown was still Chief Whip, at least for the time being, there were suddenly far fewer pairs available, an insider says.* Labour submitted motions for an upcoming Opposition Day later in the afternoon, to which the government had to prepare a response, only to put forward a 'completely different set of motions' just before the House rose on Tuesday evenings, forcing officials to work late into the night.

Aides had to sit Spencer down and say: 'Nick Brown has crossed the road to have a fight with you this evening.'

* * *

Insofar as it could, the business of government continued amid the restrictions of a pandemic that ebbed and flowed.

Tory MPs who rebelled received a six-month 'cooling off' period before they could secure a meeting with the whips' office. 'You don't get any points for voting with the government; you just lose points for voting against the government,' says a whips' office expert.

Mark Spencer had on his desk a burdizzo, a clamp used for castrating cows, in faux-homage to Cronus the tarantula. 'Mark's thinking was that the burdizzo, as well as being farming-themed, was so utterly ridiculous that it was funny,' explains a colleague. In non-serious meetings where The Office might need a favour from someone, Mark would hold the burdizzo, look sternly at the person, and clip the castrator

---

* Brown left The Office in May 2021, with Alan Campbell, his Deputy, taking over. Brown, facing an investigation into accusations of wrongdoing, lost the Labour whip eighteen months later. He subsequently quit the party, saying he could no longer engage with the 'fundamentally, and inexcusably, flawed' internal disciplinary process, and announced he would stand down at the next election. Brown denies the allegations against him, which date back to 1998 and were made, he said, by a political rival within the Labour Party.

together. 'Nobody thought it was a genuine attempt to intimidate,' the colleague stresses. 'It was hilarious.'

A mice infestation continued to plague The Office. Following the passage of a contentious piece of legislation, Spencer hosted 'smoothing-over' drinks, during which a mouse made an appearance. 'Pandemonium erupted as several men tried to catch this mouse,' says the colleague. 'Mark almost had it, but it slipped through his grasp.'

In a continuation of the administration's tough approach to dissent, the whips warned Theresa Villiers about her place on the joint Intelligence and Security Committee (ISC) after she rebelled on the sale of chlorinated chicken and hormone-treated beef in the UK. (Johnson rang her amid reports that she'd lost her place to say her membership would go ahead.)

A statutory body rather than a parliamentary select committee, the ISC oversees the work of the UK's intelligence and security services. With Dominic Grieve, one of those who lost the Tory whip, standing down at the 2019 election, the ISC needed a new chair.

Conservative MP Julian Lewis, starting his twenty-third year in Parliament, had taken the decision not to run again for chair of the Defence Select Committee, with a large part of his weekends taken up with going over materials ahead of upcoming evidence sessions. After making that decision, the thought occurred that he could return to the ISC, of which he had previously been a member, as he wouldn't be able to take the confidential papers home with him.

Lewis visited a senior member of The Office to let him know that he would like to sit again on the committee, preferably as chairman.

'Oh, well, it will rather depend on the Prime Minister,' the whip said.

While the Prime Minister has a say on who serves on the ISC, given its nature and exposure to important matters of state, in 2013, Parliament ruled that its members should decide on the chairmanship – a fact Lewis now pointed out.

'Well, that may be the theory, Julian,' the senior whip said, 'but in reality, the Prime Minister tends to make it known who they want.'

Lewis made a mental note to watch out for this as events unfolded.

Later, he spoke to Spencer in his office. 'I'm afraid the Prime Minister wants it to be Chris Grayling,' the Chief said of the ISC chairmanship.

Johnson had told Grayling, a former whip who had faced ridicule in the media for his tenures in various Cabinet posts, that he couldn't offer him a top job. When the Prime Minister asked him to think about what role he would like to do instead, Grayling said he'd like to be ISC chair.

Knowing the scale of work involved and the importance of the role, Lewis was outraged at this planned appointment, especially given No. 10's interference and the fact Grayling hadn't, to him, shown much interest in defence or security matters. He took soundings from other ISC members and found the majority were of the same opinion. Lewis ran for the chairmanship – and won.*

Spencer was furious. In their conversation, he felt he'd received a commitment from Lewis to support Grayling as chair if he joined the ISC. But Lewis says if that were true, it would not have been necessary for the Chief to text him an hour before the vote to confirm that he would back Grayling. 'Almost certainly, Mark thought that the mere fact that he had *told* me about the PM's preference was enough to secure my compliance,' he says.

'Julian, what the fuck is this about?' Spencer said after the vote.

According to the Chief, Lewis replied: 'Look, I said to you I would support him as chair, but at no point did I say I'd vote for him. If he became chair, of course I would support him.'

The government removed the whip from Lewis, who had served as a Tory MP since 1997.

Lewis saw a missed call from the Prime Minister and rang him back. The two men spoke for about an hour, with Johnson saying Lewis could have the whip reinstated and stay on the committee, so long as he stood

---

* Grayling left the ISC a month later.

down as chair. To which Lewis responded: 'Well, if I had wanted to do that, I wouldn't have run for the chairmanship in the first place.'

The fault, Lewis felt, was not in the whips' office but in No. 10 for seeking to influence the outcome of the ISC chairmanship.

Lewis carried on as though nothing had happened, sitting on the government benches and voting with the Conservatives as often as he would otherwise have done.

After a few months, Lewis had tea with the Chief Whip, who, in light of his 'obvious' loyalty to the party, said: 'We're minded to offer you the whip back.' Lewis had the Conservative whip reinstated at the end of December 2020, a decision pushed by the Prime Minister, rather than Spencer. 'I wouldn't have done it,' he says.

Regardless, Lewis says this was a case of 'sensible restraint on both sides' to end an unnecessary quarrel brought about by 'inappropriate behaviour in No. 10'. He adds: 'Not for the last time – as it turned out!'

CHAPTER 51

FEELING THE PINCH

Julian Smith took over as Chief Whip on 2 November 2017, slap bang in the middle of Westminster's harassment scandal, as a list of sexual misconduct, peccadilloes and affairs pertaining to forty MPs was circulating across Parliament, the veracity of which was in question. A whip says the spreadsheet seemed 'partially made up', though there were some 'real cases'.

Michael Fallon had already stepped down, with Damian Green, the Deputy Prime Minister, soon to follow. Other MPs would, in due course, get caught in the firing line, not least John Bercow, as focus pivoted towards allegations of bullying and staff mistreatment. Smith, who had made significant interventions during his time as a whip to offer pastoral support to those in need, spent weekends dealing with the aftermath of the scandal.

The Office had, for some time, seen staff come forward to make complaints about MPs, especially as more women joined the team. A coalition-era whip says: 'I had a couple of staff members approach me about issues they had with their MPs, which we would try to deal with and all the rest of it. Even ten years ago, it was a very different cultural attitude.'

Within three days of Smith's appointment, attention turned to inside the whips' office.

Chris Pincher, the MP for Tamworth since 2010, had joined The Office in July 2016. 'If you think Gavin Williamson was Machiavellian, this guy was an amateur compared to Pincher,' says a colleague. 'Pincher went to great lengths to destroy people.'

Pincher says he didn't believe in threatening people and says it's unfair to say he did things in a 'Machiavellian way'. 'I liked being very precise, knowing what was going on, and getting The Office to act as a team to try to deliver whatever it was that we were trying to deliver.'

The critical colleague in The Office suspects that Pincher was behind the leaking of the controversial list of allegations and rumours about Tory MPs, potentially as a way of deflecting from his own troubles, which would soon surface. But Pincher insists he had nothing to do with the list, either in its drawing up or in its leaking. 'My understanding is it was produced by two researchers who essentially cobbled things together they'd heard or made up.' The researchers then put it into a forum that could be picked up by the media, he says. 'I certainly had no knowledge of it or involvement in it, either prior to or subsequent to.'

On 5 November, Pincher referred himself to the police and the party structures after Alex Story, a party activist and former Olympic rower, accused him of making an unwanted pass while dressed in a bathrobe in 2001, describing him as a 'pound shop Harvey Weinstein'.[1] He was also accused of 'touching up' ex-Labour MP Tom Blenkinsop. Pincher was cleared following a party investigation, rejoining The Office in January 2018 as Deputy Chief Whip.

Pincher could be quite 'officious', former whip Wendy Morton says. 'It often felt like it was his way or no way.'

That November, Smith announced to The Office Pincher's appointment to the Privy Council. Soon after, Pincher had Elizabeth II's coronation playing out on his laptop, reciting the words said by the bishops, commentator and the Queen, claims a witness. 'His whole life was built around that kind of stuff, and woe betide anybody that wasn't of the same ilk.'

In April 2019, Smith issued an apology to Johnny Mercer after Pincher stood accused of seeking damaging information on the Tory MP from a former colleague in the army. Pincher says the story, first reported by the *Daily Mail*, has 'all been ridiculously overplayed'. 'Put it like this, if anybody was going to the press to talk about it, it was Johnny himself,' he says.

It would be Pincher's extracurricular activities, and the Prime Minister's reaction to them, that would seal the Johnson administration's fate.

* * *

In the wake of the harassment and bullying scandal, with two investigations into Westminster producing damning reports, Theresa May announced a new procedure for staff to deal with allegations of misconduct. In 2018, Parliament's Independent Complaints and Grievance Scheme (ICGS) came into force.

In 2019, the ICGS remit expanded to consider historical cases. The following summer, more than twenty new Conservatives voted to deny MPs the right to debate the most serious sanctions determined by an independent expert panel. With the ICGS in place, whips, now able to avoid accusations of sitting on or trying to contain serious allegations, directed people filing complaints to the relevant authorities.

'That was quite a big shift and the right shift as well to make,' says a senior whip of the ICGS. Another insider says: 'The whips' office does not have the power, is not skilled up to investigate these complaints and actively does not want to do it.' A Tory MP notes: 'The room for whips to be real fixers is diminished, and rightly so, I would suspect.'

A senior whip even accompanied a staff member to the police to discuss a serious allegation. 'It wasn't for her to report it, but just so she could talk through with the police what the process would be, so she could make that decision with an informed mind,' they explain.

Though able to pass on complaints, The Office faced criticism for not suspending the whip from MPs accused of serious wrongdoing, including one backbencher who faced a police investigation into an allegation of rape. 'Once [the police have] come to that conclusion, then we can assess where we're at and the position that the MP finds themselves in,' Spencer, the Chief Whip, explained in a statement.[2] The MP later had the charges against them dropped.

The approach differed from that of the May government, which had suspended two MPs facing allegations of sexual misconduct before, months later, reverse-ferreting. In December 2018, the Conservatives restored the whip for Charlie Elphicke and Andrew Griffiths so that they could take part in a vote of no confidence. Griffiths had resigned as a minister and been suspended in July of that year for sending hundreds of sexually explicit messages to two women in his constituency. In separate allegations, he was later found by a family court to have raped and domestically abused his wife. In July 2020, Elphicke was found guilty of three counts of sexual assault; he was sentenced to two years in prison.

* * *

Amid probes over the Prime Minister's holidays, No. 10 refurbishments and the activities of his aides and Health Secretary Matt Hancock, who resigned after footage emerged of him breaching Covid-19 restrictions by kissing a colleague with whom he was having an affair, Boris Johnson's government, like John Major's before it, found itself increasingly mired in scandal.

Its MPs were also growing impatient with voting through Covid restrictions. Mark Harper, a former Chief Whip, led along with Steve Baker the Covid Recovery Group to challenge the use of lockdown measures. 'We were saved by the bell, and the bell was the vaccine,' says a member of the whips' office. 'It was unsustainable, and it was going to break.'

The government had taken to defending those at the centre of media storms, not least Cabinet minister Priti Patel, whom Johnson had urged MPs to 'form a square around' after a damning report into allegations of bullying civil servants, which she denied. Johnson's approach was no different when Kathryn Stone, the independent Parliamentary Commissioner for Standards, found Owen Paterson to have committed an 'egregious' breach of lobbying rules. The former minister said the investigation did 'not comply with natural justice' and had contributed to his wife's suicide. MPs on the Standards Committee recommended Paterson be suspended from the House of Commons for thirty sitting days.

With MPs due to vote on the suspension, the whips under Mark Spencer as Chief urged backbenchers to support an amendment to establish a new Tory-led committee to reconsider the case. The government won by 250 to 232, but opposition parties vowed to boycott the new body. Amid fierce media uproar, the government U-turned and Johnson apologised. 'It was a massive, massive misstep,' says a member of The Office.

Spencer had told aides that he'd received calls from around forty MPs who wanted to support Paterson. 'What about the others?' asks the person above. Paterson stood down as an MP in November 2021.

The saga, which preceded reports in the *Daily Mirror* and on ITV about festivities in No. 10 during the pandemic – known as 'Partygate' – led to ruminations over Spencer's future, with the Chief also facing explosive accusations from a Tory MP.

* * *

After losing her job in the Department for Transport at the February 2020 reshuffle, Nusrat Ghani, a former whip and the first female Muslim minister to speak from the Commons despatch box, sought an explanation from the Chief Whip.

Mark Spencer would usually have one of his three advisers with him for meetings of this nature, but not on this occasion. Part of the issue was that his SpAds were based in an office about five minutes away. The former post room, tucked in a forgotten corner of the Palace of Westminster, didn't even have an entrance door with a handle. 'My single mistake was meeting her on my own,' Spencer says.

The two parties couldn't have more different accounts of what was said in the Chief's office on 4 March. This is Ghani's version, as relayed to the *Sunday Times* nearly two years later.

When Ghani sought clarity over her sacking, a whip,[*] she claimed, said her 'Muslimness' had been raised as an 'issue' at a reshuffle meeting in No. 10, and that her 'Muslim woman minister' status was making colleagues uncomfortable. The whip also reported concerns that she hadn't done enough to defend the party against allegations of Islamophobia.[†]

At a second meeting with the whip, Ghani says she was told there was no Islamophobia in the party and that she was actually fired for saying that Boris Johnson had a 'women problem'.

The following is Spencer's account of what took place.

The story, insofar as the Chief Whip is concerned, began prior to the 2019 election, when he was with his wife on their way to campaign. Ghani called and said she had done her time in the Department for Transport and wanted to be moved to the Foreign Office. Given the election, Spencer said now wasn't the moment to talk about that. Ghani said she was fed up with her role and if she couldn't go to the Foreign Office, she'd rather go to the backbenches.

Spencer's wife, who overheard the conversation, said: 'Well, we know where she's going then.'

After the February reshuffle, Ghani rang Spencer to complain. On

---

[*] Ghani didn't identify Spencer in her statement to the *Sunday Times* in January 2022.
[†] An independent inquiry into allegations of Islamophobia in the Conservative Party was taking place at the time.

4 March, Spencer relayed what she had said to him about going to the backbenches if she couldn't join the Foreign Office. Ghani said she was just sounding off. 'Well, I can only take you at face value. But look, leave it with me. Let me think about this for a week and see what we can do to help,' Spencer replied.

According to Spencer, Ghani rang again asking for another meeting. On 23 March, Spencer, joined by one of his SpAds, says he offered Ghani a position on the UK delegation to the NATO Parliamentary Assembly. He had also spoken to the Speaker and got her a post on the Panel of Chairs, which oversees Commons committees.* 'There were lots of little sweeteners that we could do to help,' he says. 'I thought it went reasonably well and off she went.'

His SpAd gives the same account of the meeting. 'My notes [which the SpAd submitted to a subsequent inquiry but no longer has] were literally "NATO Parliamentary Assembly", a list of names, including Nus's, and a tick and some vague niceties. It was a cordial meeting.'

Word reached Spencer via 1922 Committee chair Sir Graham Brady that Ghani was telling people he'd cited her faith as a reason for her sacking. If that were correct, Spencer argues, Ghani would surely have attended the second meeting 'all guns blazing'. Spencer claims that he was not surprised that 'she didn't raise that at the second meeting because it wasn't raised at the first meeting', making the point that 'at the first meeting, I didn't have a witness'.

In a rendezvous brokered by Brady, Ghani saw the Prime Minister in No. 10 on 1 July. But in briefing Johnson beforehand, Spencer had only mentioned the second meeting on 23 March, a fact he was criticised for when Ghani's allegations were reviewed in an inquiry, which was unable to conclude with 'sufficient confidence' what 'was or was not said at these two meetings'. Spencer said the omission was an oversight and admitted he should have taken more care in providing

---

* Ghani took up both these roles in 2020.

information to the Prime Minister. 'I said to Boris, "Look, there's nothing here for me to say or to do. If you want to meet her, you can,"' Spencer says of a previous conversation.

Johnson encouraged Ghani to lodge a formal complaint and take part in the Islamophobia inquiry into the Conservative Party. The MP responded by saying she didn't believe either process to be the correct forum for this complaint.

The row surfaced in January 2022 when the *Sunday Times* caught wind of the claims. In a statement to the paper, Ghani also said she had been warned by the whips that persisting in raising this allegation would see her ostracised by colleagues and her career and reputation destroyed. When the story went live, Spencer identified himself on Twitter as the whip at the centre of Ghani's allegations, which he described as defamatory and asserted that they had been cleared by the Islamophobia inquiry. He then deleted and reposted his statements.

Ghani's allegations devastated Spencer. 'He was and remains partly tortured and traumatised by the idea that people think he had the capacity to behave in that way,' says a colleague.

What can we conclude?

Given much of this is one person's word against another, there's not much we can. There is a dispute over what happened in the second meeting, with the SpAd echoing Spencer's version of events. 'It was literally a meeting about the NATO Parliamentary Assembly members, and I don't remember any chitchat about anything that she's alleged,' the SpAd reiterates, though stressing that the issue rests primarily on the first meeting. The inquiry by Sir Laurie Magnus, the Prime Minister's independent adviser on ministers' interests, said that while he found no evidence to suggest the comments about Ghani's faith were made, it was not possible to conclude 'absolutely that such comments were not made'.

If the allegations aren't true, as Spencer claims, then where did they come from? He speculates that Ghani might have sought to 'weaponise' the Prime Minister's reputation around Islamophobia.* 'I can lie in bed at night and not worry about it. I don't know how she feels about that, really. I'd love to one day know how she must feel.'

Ghani declined an interview for this book and didn't respond to a request for comment.

* * *

In the wake of the Paterson scandal, and with the Nusrat Ghani story about to break, the last thing Mark Spencer needed was a threat to the running of The Office.

In late 2021, with Partygate in full swing, former whips Chris Pincher, Chris Heaton-Harris and Nigel Adams approached the Prime Minister pitching to run a shadow whipping operation. 'We thought that he needed essentially a political campaign team to get people refocused on the real enemy, the Labour Party, rather than the internal fighting,' Pincher says.

With concerns for the PM's future, the trio, whom some say enjoyed the dark arts of whipping, speculated as to how many letters of no confidence MPs had submitted to Sir Graham Brady. At a meeting with the Chief and his aides, the three men insisted they sought to support the work of The Office. But those around Spencer had deep reservations.

'What's going on?' Craig Whittaker, who had rejoined The Office in September 2021, asked Spencer in a quiet moment.

'What do you mean?'

'How much support have you got from No. 10?'

'Where are you going with this?'

'Well, there's an alternative whipping operation. What the frigging hell is that all about?'

Spencer told Whittaker that Johnson wanted it for different reasons.

---

* In a 2018 article, Johnson had said women wearing the burka looked like 'letterboxes'.

'OK, Chief, it's not for me to overstep the mark, but it's my view, you watch your back,' Whittaker warned.

He was far from alone in being concerned. Another colleague remembers Spencer being called to No. 10 for a meeting, only to return and say: 'We didn't really talk about anything.' The colleague believes that Johnson had been supposed to let the Chief Whip go at the meeting but stopped short because Spencer was 'his guy'.

At the start of February 2022, Whittaker asked when Spencer had last received No. 10's full backing. 'I'll give you until the end of the week unless you do something drastic.'

Spencer replied: 'You're pessimistic, Whittaker, it's fine. Leave it alone. It will work out.'

Coming out of a restaurant mid-week, Whittaker saw he had forty missed calls. 'I knew straight away what had happened.'

That morning, a journalist had rung a member of Spencer's team regarding rumours about the Chief's future. The aide passed on the message that Johnson had lined up a replacement. Spencer returned at lunchtime, confirming: 'You're fucking right.'

In the end, it was Heaton-Harris whom Johnson appointed Chief, with Pincher his Deputy, after rumours the latter was in line for the top job. Spencer moved to become Leader of the House. Whittaker, no fan of Pincher, quit.

A check by the Cabinet Office propriety and ethics team, which gave the all clear, delayed Pincher's announcement. Spencer says he was told that the new Deputy walked into The Office on his first day and said words to the effect of: 'Don't worry, guys. I'm here to save the reputation of the whips' office.' A former Conservative Party staff member remembers travelling in a car with Pincher after a social event that year, asking what he most liked about being Deputy Chief Whip. Pincher, who had been drinking, allegedly replied: 'The power.'

After Johnson took on the leadership in July 2019, Pincher had served in the Foreign Office. But several sources in The Office say he was moved to become Housing Minister following complaints from Foreign Office officials. 'It was about staff being kept on late and a culture of drinking with the minister,' a government source told *The Times*. 'The advice was that he should be moved before the situation escalated.'[3]

The events surrounding Pincher came to a head at the end of June 2022, after he was accused of drunkenly groping two guests at the Carlton Club, acts seen by, among others, government whip Sarah Dines. One of the victims approached Dines soon after, asking if she would raise the incident with the Chief Whip. Dines agreed and empathised, but then asked if the man was gay, arguing that it didn't make it 'straightforward' if he was. A source told the *Sunday Times*, which reported this encounter, that Dines was attempting to establish the full circumstances of what happened and later followed up the issue with the Chief Whip.[4]

The next day, 1 July, Pincher resigned as Deputy Chief and had the whip suspended after one of his accusers made a formal complaint. 'I'm not sure I do want to say very much about it. It was just very, very unpleasant,' says Pincher of the scandal that followed. He jokes that he now has 'more pill boxes than a beach in Normandy'.

'I'm still getting over it, is the short answer.'

That weekend, the Sunday papers reported new allegations about Pincher's conduct, including making unwanted passes at MPs. Downing Street denied that Johnson had been aware of any 'specific' allegations against Pincher at the time of his appointment, only to confirm that the PM did know about some of the claims, saying they were either resolved or did not proceed to a formal complaint. Johnson also didn't deny that he had once referred to the whip as 'Pincher by name, pincher by nature'.[5]

When it emerged Johnson knew more than he had let on about Pincher – and as more people came forward with claims surrounding the former Deputy Chief Whip – minister after minister, fatigued at the never-ending scandals emanating from No. 10, not least from Partygate, resigned from government.

Johnson, begrudgingly, announced he would step down from the job he had long coveted.

CHAPTER 52

TRUSS ISSUES

Of all the reforms, economic or otherwise, that Liz Truss floated on the campaign trail to become the next Conservative Party leader, one, from a whips' perspective, stood out.

'I would… move the whips' office back into No. 12 Downing Street,' she said.[1]

In the wake of the successive scandals that ultimately secured Boris Johnson's demise, Truss wanted to emphasise MPs' importance and that of parliamentary democracy. 'We need that restoration of standards, discipline, but also support.' Unfortunately for Truss, she wouldn't be around long enough in Downing Street to fully see the restitution through.

A long-serving Cabinet minister, devoted proponent of British foods and reformed Remain-voter, Truss led the pack in the race to succeed Johnson, pledging to boost the UK's stagnant economy with a host of tax cuts and other rejuvenating measures. Despite a transparent desire to become Prime Minister, evidenced particularly during her most recent time as Foreign Secretary, those close to Truss say she wasn't well-prepared to run for the leadership. 'The first campaign meeting I went to was a blank page,' says Craig Whittaker.

Whittaker had known Truss for many years: not only was he once her campaign manager at a general election, he was also the godfather to one of her children. Having returned to The Office to help plug the holes left by the mass government exodus over the summer, he stepped back from helping her leadership bid formally.

With polls of the wider membership indicating a victory over Rishi Sunak, MPs' top choice to replace Johnson, thoughts turned to her senior team. An aide to Truss rang Whittaker around a week before the vote of the party membership. 'Liz thinks you'd like to do some international travel,' she said. 'How would you feel about going into the Foreign Office?'

Whittaker stressed that he wanted to remain a whip.

The aide asked which role within The Office he'd like. 'I want to be Chief Whip,' Whittaker said (he says jokingly). Truss, however, had already offered that role to someone else.

Where the Labour Party trailed the Tories on electing female leaders – the Conservatives would shortly choose their third – the roles reversed when it came to the whips' office. Ann Taylor, Hilary Armstrong, Jacqui Smith and Rosie Winterton had all served as Labour Chief Whips. The Tories had never appointed a woman to head up The Office.

Wendy Morton, the MP for Aldridge-Brownhills, had served as an assistant whip from January 2018 to July 2019. She had overlapped briefly with Truss at the Foreign Office in late 2021. On 6 September 2022, she became the Tory Party's first ever female Chief Whip, with Whittaker as her Deputy.

Morton, who had never coveted the position, nonetheless thought: why not? 'It was a hellish role at a very difficult time in politics. But it was a great honour and a privilege.'

The new Chief implemented some quick changes. She removed from the mantelpiece in 9 Downing Street two old whips which had been donated, keeping the ones preserved in a frame. Morton also sought to provide 'a bit more coffee' and 'a little less alcohol' for visitors. As for the move to 12 Downing Street, Morton insists that it was in process.

'I had an office [there],' she says. Morton even has an England football shirt with her name and a No. 12 on the back. The whips, who couldn't all fit into their old haunt, remained in No. 9.

Truss's indiscriminate sacking of ministers such as Michael Gove, Nadine Dorries and Grant Shapps, replaced with allies who had backed her campaign, stacked the Tory backbenches with effective, peeved and motivated operators. Like Iain Duncan Smith before her, while Truss had won among party members, she didn't have the majority support of her MPs.

In The Office, there were plenty of fresh faces.

'For me to be successfully whipped, the whip has to be credible,' says an independent-minded Tory MP. 'When Liz Truss stacked the whips' office with people who were elected in 2019, that was always going to be difficult.'

Soon after their appointment, the two most senior whips met for breakfast at Morton's flat in Marylebone to discuss how they planned to run The Office, agreeing a pact that 'if one goes, we both go'. 'We stand and die together,' explains Whittaker of their ethos.

* * *

On 8 September, Morton was pulled into a meeting of Operation London Bridge, the meticulous and long-established plan to deal with the death of the sitting monarch. It was two days after Queen Elizabeth II, the UK's longest-serving monarch, had invited Truss to form a government.

Morton walked to Downing Street, entering through the back door, and awaited updates. Earlier, in the chamber, word had reached Truss that the Queen might soon pass. Her Majesty died later that day, aged ninety-six.

For the three members of the royal household in the whips' office – Whittaker, Rebecca Harris and Jo Churchill – this had significant implications, with each playing a ceremonial role at the funeral to come, including walking in front of the procession leading the Queen's coffin. Whittaker also had an organisational function to carry out, deciding which privy counsellors would attend certain events related to the funeral.

'OK, this is your job for the next twenty-four hours. I need you to sort that,' Morton told him. She says: 'Craig and I worked on it, and he was a great help.'

They had to consider two aspects: who attended the gatherings of the Accession Council, and the Queen's coffin's arrival into Westminster Hall. 'There was also an element where a selection of privy counsellors went to the physical funeral as well,' Whittaker says.

Typically – though it had been seventy years since an event of this nature – all privy counsellors would attend the Accession Council, but with Chief Whips including Gavin Williamson stacking the sovereign body with politicians, that could no longer be the case. The powers that be had changed the rules a year earlier so that attendance would be sorted by ballot. 'Nobody on the Privy Council had realised this had happened,' Whittaker says.

Whittaker decided that privy counsellors who won at the ballot wouldn't be considered for the arrival of the Queen's coffin into Westminster Hall. He emailed all the privy counsellors in Parliament with words to the effect of: 'Sorry, we're limited on numbers, this is my method of working it out. I think this is fair, please feel free to ring me if you don't.'

Everyone thought it was a fair process bar three people, one of whom was so incensed that they went to Speaker Lindsay Hoyle and got a ticket directly.

For the funeral, given the limited space and sky-high demand, they took the 'pragmatic decision' that they could offer the Cabinet and two Deputy Speakers a place, Morton says. One of those unhappy with his lot was Williamson. (Morton suggests Julian Smith was also displeased.)

'I don't know whether they were not happy with it or it was just used as another way of having a dig and stirring up trouble,' Morton says.

'Let's just say, there was an element of incoming flak coming from all sorts of quarters at that time.'

On the afternoon of 13 September, in messages seen by the *Sunday Times*, Williamson messaged Morton to say it was 'very poor' that privy counsellors 'who aren't favoured' were excluded from attending the funeral. Morton insisted this wasn't the case, but he pushed back: 'Well certainly looks it which [I] think is very shit and perception becomes reality. Also don't forget I know how this works so don't puss me about.' Williamson accused Morton of rigging the system and said it was 'disgusting' that she was using the Queen's death to 'punish people who are just supportive'. When Morton insisted again that this wasn't the case, Williamson said: 'Well lets [sic] see how many more times you fuck us all over. There is a price for everything.'[2]

Morton went on to file a bullying complaint against Williamson, which an independent expert panel upheld, ordering that he apologise to the House of Commons and undergo training. 'I will do my utmost to ensure this does not happen again,' Williamson told MPs.

* * *

By 20 October, six weeks after she entered No. 10, Liz Truss's premiership was teetering on the edge.

Forced to sack Chancellor Kwasi Kwarteng for the maelstrom caused by his mini-budget, whose swingeing tax cuts the markets profoundly mistrusted, Truss, who was inextricably linked to the policy platform outlined from the Treasury, struggled to steady the ship.

The Prime Minister plucked Jeremy Hunt from the wilderness to serve as Chancellor, unpicking the mess left behind by his predecessor. Home Secretary Suella Braverman – a previous leadership rival – was a law unto herself. Truss was in office, but not in power.

The whips were just focused on the evening ahead.

Labour had pushed for a motion that would allow it to seize control of the order paper and schedule a vote to prevent the government's planned reversal of a ban on fracking, a move symptomatic, one backbencher says, of the improved output of the opposition whips' office.

Alan Campbell, after more than a decade as Labour Deputy Chief Whip, was now running The Office, though he had to liaise primarily with Craig Whittaker, after the two Chiefs clashed early on in Morton's tenure.

For The Office, the Labour motion was a clear-cut confidence issue. 'What government in their right mind would hand over power to the opposition for the day?' asks Whittaker.

The Deputy wrote to MPs: 'I know this is difficult for some colleagues, but we simply cannot allow this. We are voting no and I reiterate, this is a hard three line whip with all slips withdrawn.'[3]

The whips had done as they usually do, triaging meetings with all the relevant senior ministers, including Business Secretary Jacob Rees-Mogg, the man overseeing the changes, posted up at his parliamentary office. 'It was probably the most technically perfect whipping operation day that you could have,' Whittaker says.

The whips thought there would be eight Tory MPs voting against the government, of whom two might abstain. 'We had the numbers. We'd been so focused on it. It *was* a confidence vote,' Morton says.

Increasingly, Morton and Whittaker felt that key players in Truss's team – both ministers and aides – 'were putting their oar in', Thérèse Coffey among them. 'Never have I had a call from the Deputy Prime Minister to say, "The optics of the chamber look pretty poor today,"' Whittaker says. 'She was interfering on such a minute level.'

That afternoon, Braverman was sacked for allegedly leaking sensitive information.

Fracking, part of Truss's solution for combating sky-high energy bills, was far from universally popular on the Tory benches. Despite the whips' instructions, MPs such as Chris Skidmore, a leading advocate for net zero, said he would vote against the government line.

In his memoir, Sir Graham Brady revealed that he spoke to No. 10 about changing the whipping on the vote, believing around twenty MPs might rebel. Whether this is the conversation that changed No. 10's mind is for debate. Either way, an aide passed on a message to the PPS on the frontbench, who told the minister, Graham Stuart, to change the whipping while addressing the House of Commons. Around 6.50 p.m., in a direct contradiction of the message issued from the whips' office, Stuart said, 'Clearly this is not a confidence vote.'

Morton asked Whittaker, who was on the floor of the House, to join her in The Office.

'They want us to change the whipping,' she said.

'Absolutely not,' he replied.

Morton said Coffey was adamant the whipping should change. Around ten minutes before the vote, Whittaker asked the Chief to invite Coffey to join them. 'We had a blazing row in the whips' office with her,' Whittaker says.

The Deputy Prime Minister said they couldn't guarantee a win, to which Whittaker says he replied: 'How the fecking hell would you know whether we're going to win a vote or not?'

Failing to reach agreement, the Deputy Chief Whip departed for the voting lobby. There, he found a 'horde of people' who were 'absolutely screaming at each other', the bedlam caused by Stuart's message from the despatch box. 'It was an absolute bun fight,' Whittaker says.

According to her number two, Morton, who was also supposed to act as a teller with Whittaker during the vote, said: 'Right, that's it. I'm done! I'm going!' and walked away. Whittaker saw Truss in the division lobbies and informed her that she'd just lost her Chief Whip and, given their pact, would lose her number two in The Office as well.

'You need to come and sort this mess out because it's your team's fault this has happened.'

Truss urged him to come to her parliamentary office, which he said he would do once the vote was over. After clearing the lobbies,

Whittaker caught Stuart's eye and asked if he would issue a retraction. The minister said no, and Whittaker stormed off around the back of the Speaker's chair towards the Prime Minister's parliamentary office, telling a colleague who asked if he was OK: 'No, I'm fucking furious, and I don't give a fuck any more.'

Finally in a room alone with Truss, the Prime Minister told him: 'You can't resign.'

'Wendy's already gone; she's telling people that she's resigned. You better get her down here too,' he said.

Meanwhile, the rest of the whips gathered in The Office. They pivoted from 'what the fuck is going on?' to 'let's have some wine and we'll find out in due course', says Adam Holloway.

Morton joined Whittaker in Truss's parliamentary office. A 'real shouting match' ensued. The Prime Minister asked her two top whips to stay, but Whittaker said he would only do so if No. 10 issued a press release saying the night's events were due to a mistake by Downing Street. Truss rang her team and asked them to come over, though this never materialised.

'Look, I'm going to have to speak to the guys at No. 10, but I don't think we can do what you're asking,' she said.

'Well, fine, but that's it, we'll be down in the whips' office; come and get us when you want us,' Whittaker said, leaving with Morton.

After the pair updated the team, other whips said they would also walk.

Truss invited the Chief and the Deputy back to her office and said she would have to accept their resignation. Morton 'stormed out' again, according to Whittaker, who warned Truss as he was leaving that the rest of her whips were preparing to pack their bags. 'You may want to try and convince them to stay.'

With Morton and Whittaker at the back of the room, Truss visited The Office.

'Craig, if you don't mind me divulging our conversation, I've already asked you to stay, I want you to stay, what do you guys think?' she asked her whips.

'Well, Prime Minister, I hope you don't mind me further divulging that conversation, but as you know, Wendy and I will both stay. However, we want a public statement saying it was a cock-up and I want you to restore power to this lady,' Whittaker said.

Truss looked at the whips and asked again: 'Well, what do you think?'

No. 10 did issue a statement in the early hours, but 'the damage was done'. The Conservative powers that be let Truss know that she could no longer continue as Prime Minister. After forty-four tumultuous and consequential days in Downing Street, she announced her resignation.

CHAPTER 53

THE LAST WORD

In July 2024, Keir Starmer's Labour Party won a landslide general election victory, securing just seven seats short of Tony Blair's tally in 1997, with 411 MPs. Rishi Sunak's Conservatives fell to a party record low of 121 seats, decimated after fourteen years in power.

Labour Chief Whip Alan Campbell joined the Commons in 1997 and the whips' office in 2005. He reflected deeply on the first few years of the New Labour government when taking on the role of Chief. He sat down with two of his predecessors, Ann Taylor and Hilary Armstrong, and discussed the lessons that could be drawn from the period and how to handle such a large majority. Both ex-Chiefs talked about the system of 'McAvoy weeks', but Campbell and his aides decided against reinstating this policy of allowing backbenchers one week a month in their constituency, instead focusing on kickstarting interest in Parliament.

'With every new intake, you notice the cultural resistance to actually being in Westminster,' says a whips' office insider. For the first six months of the parliament, The Office was keen to impress upon MPs, some of whom harbour concerns about re-election in marginal seats, that the Commons can be used to campaign for issues that matter to their constituents.

Armstrong and Taylor stressed the importance of having regular conversations with MPs. The whips do the Sunday ring-round twice a month but prioritise meeting their flock face to face. The ex-Chiefs also discussed spotting the early signs of backbenchers feeling alienated

– from the party and in their personal lives – as the realities of being an MP sink in. The Office has focused on supporting MPs, some of whom never expected to be elected, struggling to adapt to life in Parliament away from their families and under the spotlight.

The Office also spends time outlining the nuance of policies to some would-be rebel MPs; on a vote to uprate benefits, for example, whips had to explain that it was a take it or leave it scenario rather than a discussion about the size of the increase. In other words, if you rebel because you don't think it's enough, you're voting against benefits being uprated full stop.

These are not the only areas where the whips' office has drawn lessons from the past.

* * *

Back like a re-formed, middling '90s pop group is the Modernisation Committee, looking into ways of adapting Parliament's practices, including the working hours. With 231 new Labour MPs taking their seats, therein lies the opportunity for a fresh perspective on how Westminster operates. 'In this parliament, you've probably got the potential for the biggest change in culture in the way the place works,' says a former Labour whips' office SpAd. This is likely to the chagrin of peers in the Lords, who believe the quality of legislation from the Commons has diminished in recent years because of MPs spending less time in Parliament.

What other similarities are there? Like Mike Foster's awkward Private Member's Bill on hunting with dogs, an MP brought forward (admittedly this time with the Prime Minister's apparent backing) a controversial proposal to introduce assisted dying in the UK. Most starkly, there was an early rebellion over welfare policy.

In July 2024, the SNP put forward an amendment to Labour's first King's Speech for fourteen years, calling for an end to the two-child benefit cap. Keir Starmer issued a three-line whip to vote against the amendment, but seven Labour MPs, including Zarah Sultana and John McDonnell, voted in favour. The MPs lost the whip for a minimum of six months.

'During this period, you are not suspended from the obligations of the whip,' the Chief wrote to the seven rebels (The Office continued to email the MPs the whip on Thursday afternoons). With the six-month suspensions drawing to a close, it emerged the whips would review each on a case-by-case basis, factoring in MPs' commitment to follow the party line. Four – Richard Burgon, Ian Byrne, Imran Hussain and Rebecca Long-Bailey – were handed back the whip at the end of the period.

In the wake of the vote, a couple of the rebels came to the whips' office and asked why they had taken this decision despite McDonnell and Corbyn voting against the New Labour government on hundreds of occasions. 'We were actually able to say: "Jeremy and John, they might have been rebels, but they never tried to amend a Labour Queen's Speech,"' says a member of The Office. The same person says things might have been different if they had sought to amend a bill at report stage, but on The Office's hierarchy of rebellions, the King's Speech (and a budget) are at the very top.

Still, those who had lobbied for Tony Blair to kick out Corbyn & co. were pleased. 'Good for him,' says a former Labour whip of Starmer's decision. (Analysis by Professor Philip Cowley, the doyen of parliamentary rebellions, revealed how Labour MPs had grown more rebellious while in government, outstripping previous records with each parliament under New Labour.)

A government aide says: 'The idea that you could have a Jeremy-type character who's racking up easily into triple-figure rebellions over the course of a government these days is for the birds.'

Others argue that the decision sent out a clear signal of The Office's expectations. Of Gordon Brown's first parliamentary defeat in 2009 on allowing all retired Gurkhas to settle in the UK, a SpAd remembered MPs hurrying to the whips' office after the vote. 'If I'd known we were going to lose the vote, I wouldn't have rebelled!' one said.

The ex-adviser says: 'On some of this stuff, you just have to find a way of drawing the line.'

Starmer had already shown his intentions after stripping (and refusing to reinstate) the whip from Corbyn while in opposition, following his statement in response to a report into antisemitism in the Labour Party. A person who worked with Starmer says: 'It's Keir's view that having the whip is a privilege, not a right. You have to behave yourself accordingly.' In July 2025, Sultana announced she was leaving Labour to co-lead a new party with Corbyn. 'The writing was on the wall for her,' says the government aide of Sultana's future in the Labour Party. 'She jumped before she was pushed.'

In Campbell, Starmer has a Chief Whip of longevity with institutional memory of life in government and a man with the humour and disposition worthy of the role.

Stuart Andrew served as interim Conservative Chief Whip while the party elected a new leader after the 2024 election. He remembers first coming across Campbell in the corridor years earlier. 'He looks stern and severe,' he thought. But when they both served as deputies for their parties, he realised the extent of Campbell's dry wit. 'Alan is a man I've got a huge amount of respect for. I just think he is brilliant,' Andrew says.

Rebecca Harris, a veteran Tory whip, took over as Conservative Party Chief in November 2024. A Labour whips' office insider says she is well thought of and gets on with Campbell. However, with the Tories stripped of so many MPs and Kemi Badenoch bedding in as leader, one observer believes the new Chief has faced difficulties working out exactly what her party plans to do and communicating that to her Labour counterparts through the Usual Channels.

Starmer's tough clampdown on rebellions was further evident in September 2024, during a vote to remove winter fuel payment from most pensioners. Ultimately, the rebellion was restricted to fifty-two Labour MPs who abstained and one, Jon Trickett, who voted against the plans, though he retained the party whip.

But then, as so often is the case, MPs found their voice. Emboldened after disappointing local election results in May 2025, backbenchers helped bring about a government U-turn on the cuts to winter fuel payments. Labour whip Vicky Foxcroft then quit over plans to slash disability benefits, with Starmer forced to climb down to get the remnants of his proposals through the Commons at second reading.

Any suggestion that the government's iron grip had softened was dashed after four 'persistent' Labour rebels – Neil Duncan-Jordan, Brian Leishman, Chris Hinchliff and Rachael Maskell – lost the party whip before the summer recess; three other MPs were stripped of their trade envoy roles.

Insofar as the whips are concerned, The Office is fulfilling its job of communicating in both directions; the speed at which No. 10 is acting on their advice is for debate. A person in The Office notes a 'slight disconnect' with 'those who live over the road' about the whips' purpose. 'As well as an intelligence-gathering service, the whips' office acts as a reality check for the centre,' they say. 'It isn't the Bullying and Arm-Twisting Department, as depicted in the caricature.'

Regardless of the government's majority, its stranglehold on backbenchers can only last so long, which explains the leadership's initial clampdown. The signs of Starmer's 'Stalinist' approach – as one New Labour rebel puts it – were there long before the summer of 2024.

* * *

The experience of the Conservatives and even the SNP, whose heavily fortified wall splintered dramatically after years of a dominant showing in Scotland, show that cohesiveness cannot be taken for granted, and nor is it, realistically, enduring.

'I'm a great supporter of Keir Starmer, but Tony was characterised as a control freak. If anything, I've observed from the outside, it's even greater under Keir,' said a former New Labour-era minister, speaking several months before the 2024 general election. This, the person said, 'will store up problems, not initially, but the longer we're in government'.

The first warning sign for many was the way Starmer handled a November 2023 vote on an SNP amendment calling for a ceasefire in Gaza, in which he had instructed his MPs to abstain. His backbenchers were already riled up after he appeared to back Israel's right to withhold power and water from Gaza after the atrocities committed by Hamas on 7 October.

A former whip said: 'He made a terrible error at the beginning, which led to a bigger rebellion than he needed to have because it annoyed people so much.'

Fifty-six Labour MPs defied the party line, including eight frontbenchers, who resigned. In an interview for this book in the aftermath of the vote, former Chief Whip Jacqui Smith said: 'Keir needs to give some thought to how he wants the PLP to be handled in government, and I'm not sure he's quite got it right at the moment.'

Smith, now a Labour peer and minister, said that when she was Chief Whip, she spent time 'getting upstream of where people might have concerns' by building relationships and ensuring MPs could speak to the relevant stakeholders. 'I'm not sure – well, my view is – that didn't happen,' she said of the Gaza vote.

Learning the lessons from Blair, MPs, speaking before the party took power, warned Starmer not to lose touch with the PLP. 'That trips you up eventually,' says a former minister. An ex-whip and MP says: 'We know there's going to be some hard decisions taken and you need to really have a good relationship with the PLP. That relies on a good whips' office and a good whipping operation.'

When compared with the Conservatives, some interviewees for this book, historically at least, expressed signs of an inferiority complex with regards to Labour's whipping operation. 'In my time, the Tories were always better organised, their whipping arrangements more sophisticated and their whole practice of dealing with the whips' office was better,' says former Labour Chief Whip Geoff Hoon.

In recent years, MPs have reported progress. When, in 2012, Mike Gapes tragically lost his daughter, the whips visited him in his constituency and organised for other MPs to do likewise. When he was forced to come back to Parliament for a three-line whip,* the whips took Gapes through the lobbies, 'put me out on the terrace, and just tried to look after me', he says.

After the bruising 2014 Scottish independence referendum, the whips kept a close eye on the party's contingent representing seats north of the border. 'The whipping arrangements changed to more or less a care and welfare basis,' says a Scottish Labour MP.

Harriet Harman, whose Labour MP husband Jack Dromey died in January 2022, says the whips wound up his parliamentary affairs. 'I didn't even ask them to, but I was hugely appreciative and grateful. That wouldn't have happened in the old days,' she says.

Not everyone felt the whips' helping hand. In 2017, Margaret Hodge's daughter-in-law was killed in a car accident. The MP rushed to help look after her son's three children while Harman informed The Office that Hodge wouldn't be in for an extended period. 'That was fine, but they never rang to say, "Are you OK? Is there anything we can do to help?"' Hodge says.

Despite the shortcomings, Hodge says that, compared to her early days in politics, 'the whole culture in Parliament is better than it was'.

In June 2021, Victoria Warren replaced Roy Stone as the principal private secretary to the Government Chief Whip, becoming the fifth person – and first woman – to hold the role. 'I always found Vic easy to get on with and very competent,' says Wendy Morton.

---

* Labour had just pushed for a no-confidence vote in then Culture Secretary Jeremy Hunt.

Stone left Parliament as an 'institution in his own right', according to a former colleague.

'Roy was as tough as old boots. Absolutely straight. Completely discreet,' says Nick Brown, the former Labour Chief Whip.

Stone was pivotal at various crucial moments in recent political history, helping to marshal the government's Brexit bill through Parliament before the end of 2020 and playing a key role in the running of the coalition government. 'Roy Stone is the oil that made the government engine function,' says ex-Liberal Democrat Chief Whip Alistair Carmichael.

While praised for his rigged neutrality, Stone, described by an acquaintance as something of an 'Essex boy', had his own views, but never did these impact his work. He would offer up some of his unparalleled insight to newcomers – if they asked the right questions. 'He was very willing in private – obviously – to share his thoughts about how things were going or how things had gone in a previous administration and so on,' says Don Foster, another former Lib Dem Chief Whip. 'A great guy.'

Stone passed away suddenly on 12 May 2025, aged sixty-three.

* * *

That this book includes contributions from over sixty people who have passed through the whips' office, and more who have worked within it, shows how much has changed. 'The theory was that you never talked about what went on in the whips' office until your dying day, as though you worked at Bletchley Park,' says a former Tory whip.

A journalist writing a book of this nature thirty years ago would arguably have far fewer pages to show for it. Indeed, Gyles Brandreth, the author, broadcaster and former whip, received in the post a blank piece of paper with a black spot, a mark of shame, after the publication of his acclaimed diaries. Various trailblazers – Brandreth very much included – set the path for others to follow. People like Andrew Mitchell, a devotee of The Office's rituals and norms, would never have discussed The Office in an autobiography but for those who had broken the seal.

Many interviewees felt confident they hadn't spilled the beans to such an extent that all the whips' secrets would be on display in bookshops. Some were certain they had been of no use whatsoever. Each, however much they thought otherwise, offered a snippet that helped put these pages together, shaping the recent journey of whips and whipping in Westminster.

At the end of this journey, what can we conclude?

The clearest point is that many of the modernising reforms – be they elections for select committees, the changed working hours or otherwise – have reduced the whips' influence over Parliament. People involved in these decisions argue that they were more about empowering backbenchers and creating other career paths than about undermining The Office. Still, the diminution in whips' powers of patronage coincided with a breakdown in party discipline, seen most acutely in the aftermath of the EU referendum, which placed a huge strain on the UK's parliamentary democracy. Without as many goodies and unable to apply old-school solutions, the whips struggled to contain the fallout. 'The fundamental mistake is the conditions and the ineptitude of leaders who must have deluded themselves – and it is a delusion – into thinking that, in and of itself, a Chief Whip and a whips' office can make the difference in those circumstances,' argues Neil Kinnock.

Technology has also altered things. With a few angry slaps of a QWERTY keyboard, a disgruntled MP can share on social media details of a rough encounter with a whip. MPs with a significant social media presence may also feel more accountable to their followers than they do the whips. 'They've almost found their own conception of what being an MP is, and it's not necessarily our conception,' says a government aide of some Labour backbenchers.

The way The Office operates has equally moved on: whips create WhatsApp groups for their flock, distribute the Whip by email and can, if they wish, monitor MPs' Twitter feeds. Formerly shared members-only spaces, meanwhile, have fragmented. 'You can't build personal relationships by WhatsApp,' says Philip Davies, who lost his seat in 2024.

Life for those in The Office has also changed. The bell that used to connect to the Commons no longer works; the Chief Whip's table in the Members' Dining Room isn't the fixture it once was. 'Whips' Trips', where members of The Office were sent to different countries on ministerial visits, are basically no more. With tighter budgets, away days at Chequers or Dorneywood also rarely take place. 'It's definitely a more Westminster-based office these days,' says a member of the whips' office. Gone from the weekly Whip is the much-maligned 'two-line' whip – seen as a halfway house that posed more questions than answers – with Labour assigning a three-line whip for government business and a one-line whip to issues like Private Member's Bills or Backbench Business Debates.

Conservative whips today submit feedback via email. 'Every Chief Whip insists on all feedback going in, but it's like everything, it's the quality of the feedback,' says Craig Whittaker, who put every conversation he had with an MP in a folder, which has been burnt. 'If I was on the email system now, you'd get one [whip] saying, "no issues, no issues, no issues" next to somebody's name, whereas I had quite a portfolio.' The former Deputy Chief would hold back certain private information. 'You might put in, "He's having some personal issues" or something, but I wouldn't do thread to needle on some of the stuff.'

Information accrued by one Chief Whip is often not passed on to their successor. 'There's a misconception that the Black Book gets handed over to the next Chief Whip,' Whittaker says. However, in his diaries, Simon Hart, Chief Whip under Rishi Sunak, revealed that his predecessors shared 'troubling' cases when they took office in

November 2022. This included allegations of rape and coercive control against an MP and another in which the Crown Prosecution Service was considering charging a former MP with child sex offences.

Adam Holloway, a whip from July to October 2022, would write, as required, a report for the Chief after doing a ring-round of his flock. Sometimes he would call an MP back and make sure they were happy for him to report their candid remarks about a particular issue. 'That way, you build up trust,' he explains.

Where once The Office had charts, aides now prepare spreadsheets with MPs' voting intentions and any additional colour for Chief Whips. (Aides stopped providing these spreadsheets for one particular Tory Chief after they started sharing them with No. 10. 'If this ever gets back to the parliamentary party, they stop telling you stuff,' says an ex-SpAd.)

The former insider says of intelligence gathering: 'It wasn't what you would characterise as a Black Book-type note at all, it was just the day-to-day business.' The information would be crucial in keeping abreast of upcoming votes, with The Office updating the relevant departmental minister on what to expect – and what needed to be done.

New intakes, illustrated by their increasingly disbelieving responses to the whips' induction briefings, simply wouldn't put up with The Office's output of old. Many whips also look down on tactics that their predecessors used freely. An ex-senior Tory whip reprimanded a junior colleague who 'had gone way out on a limb' and phoned an MP's local party. 'Look, you might win the vote tonight, but you have made an enemy,' the whip said.

In January 2022, Conservative backbencher William Wragg met with police to discuss his claims that government whips were threatening to withdraw investments from constituencies. The accusations centred around the distribution of the government's Levelling Up fund. The truth, one person who worked in The Office at the time claims, is more nuanced than the headlines.

Rather than whips suggesting that already allocated money would be withdrawn, it instead related to projects that had not yet been signed off, for which MPs were competing. Why, the person says, would the Chief Whip recommend a rebel receive the unallocated funding over someone who has toed the line?

The injection of fresh perspectives on Westminster's idiosyncratic ways of working has brought about much of the change we've seen in Parliament. The Office has – many people would say fairly – fallen foul of this trend. Whips are no longer the sole judges of MPs' misdeeds. Given their standing, some, like Conservative peer Eric Pickles, feel whips should become more of an HR department than a disciplinary organisation.

Efforts have been made to this end, with one MP facing mental health difficulties assigned a whip while he was in the House of Commons, Pickles says. 'When I first came in, they really wouldn't have done that.' Pickles also mentions that David Waddington, Margaret Thatcher's penultimate Chief, spoke about his mental breakdown only after he stopped being an MP.

'Michael Dobbs wrote that whips were throwing people off the top of buildings,' says a former senior Tory whip. 'These days, whips talk people down from the top of buildings.'

But while Pickles believes whips should focus more on providing support, others believe they're not the right port of call for such matters. 'Unless somebody has a particularly good HR background, they're not the people to deal with pastoral issues,' says an ex-Tory whip. One ex-Deputy Chief Whip believes serious HR issues should be dealt with by an independent body. 'The whips' office should not be the recipient of all those complaints.'

There is an obvious friction between whips being privy to personal information and convincing MPs of the party line. It relies on a belief in the 'good chap' principle that the person before you is of the requisite moral value. Recent years have shown that some characters can slip through the net and seek to take advantage of their largely unscrutinised powers; whips don't face a 'whips' office select committee' or MPs on the floor of the House.

The grievance scheme has freed whips of the responsibility for looking into allegations of serious wrongdoing, creating a formal system for staff to lodge complaints, complementing a complex web of committees monitoring MPs' adherence to standards and values. However, some MPs feel that The Office has gone from self-regulating to another extreme. 'As soon as you're accused of anything remotely credible, they withdraw the whip,' says an ex-Tory minister. 'As a result, the feeling gets out in the backbenches that "they haven't got my back".'

Conservative Neil Parish, who resigned as an MP in 2022 after admitting to watching porn in Parliament, says whips need to offer support to those forced to leave politics. 'I did not commit murder, but I don't think I would have been treated any worse had I done that,' he says. With one notable exception, Parish said he didn't hear from any whips after he left Parliament. 'There needs to be more care taken and more aftercare.'

Craig Whittaker, who checked in with Chris Pincher amid his scandal, agrees: 'Even if they haven't got the Conservative whip at this particular moment in time, you need to make sure they're not going to hang themselves off Tower Bridge or do something really, really stupid.'

Pincher says of being in the firing line: 'When the sharks smell blood, all sense of proportion and sanity goes out of the window and it is a very, very unpleasant thing to be a part of and probably also unpleasant to watch.'

Brooks Newmark, who resigned as a minister in 2014 after a newspaper sting, says the whips are good at HR only on the small things. 'In the modern era, we need to have better mechanisms to [provide] support.' A former Labour minister argues there should be more post-Parliament care for MPs in general. 'There was never once any advice or counselling on how you might manage or what you might do after you lost your seat,' they say.

With one or two exceptions, not many people believe that the British political system could simply do away with whips. 'I can see the necessity for them, but I didn't always want to do what they wanted to be done,' said Frank Field.

Labour's Ben Bradshaw, who stood down at the 2024 election, notes that party discipline in countries like Germany, thanks in part to a different voting system, 'is far stricter than it is here'. 'It's become much laxer here in recent years, contrary to the whips' fearsome reputation,' he says. 'Part of that is because of issues like Brexit that have torn the parties apart.'

An aide to Jeremy Corbyn believes the UK could look to the likes of South Africa, where the Chief Whip and the Leader of the House are effectively the same role, with the business manager speaking publicly. 'That could be done in a more open, less shadowy kind of way,' they argue. In this regard, the Chief would be held to account by MPs in the chamber.

After a period of flux, some long for the return of core whipping principles, such as a combination of long-serving and newer whips in the Tories' office. 'What it did was it brought a collective memory,' says Liam Fox. Since Patrick McLoughlin stood down in 2012, the Tories have had twelve Chief Whips. Labour, over the same period, has had three.

Much has been written and will continue to be written about the activities of whips. In many ways, The Office could help itself by disavowing a ban of silence and speaking openly, if not overly candidly, about how it operates. There's plenty to suggest that the tropes about whips are precisely that – tropes – and that the bad eggs are far fewer in number than the good.

But without direct scrutiny and oversight of their endeavours, there will likely still be examples of whips who misuse the powers at their disposal – of which there remain several, despite all the protestations otherwise – undermining the efforts of the compliant majority.

For as long as the system exists in its current form, this will probably be ever thus. A former senior whip concludes: 'We all like power of some description. Just being a parliamentarian gives you a level of power. But it's how you use that power, isn't it?'

ACKNOWLEDGEMENTS

For this book I am indebted to many people, none more so than Ioana, without whose love, support and warmth I would still be, in more ways than I can say, stuck on page one.

I would like to thank Mum, Dad, Sally, Granny, Adie, Jane, Lucy, Chloe, Will, Harry, Louisa and Matilda, and members of my extended family, Petruța, Cătălin, Coco, Geo, Omar, Alex, Florin and Ștefan, the bedrock of our lives. Also to Peter and Anthea for your generosity.

To those resting in another place, thank you for everything. Bill and Judy, I'll never forget what you did for us. Chris, I miss your infectious laugh; we talk about you all the time.

A special shoutout goes to Jon, Ralph and James M, the first people to read extracts of this book, whose advice was, and always will be, hugely appreciated. I also owe much to David, whose invaluable knowledge and open mind I plundered many times during this project. I look forward to a few long lunches over the coming years to showcase my gratitude.

To the likes of Andy, Marina and Bosco, Basti, Chloe and Eliza, Pete and Francesca, George and Hattie, Ada and Yaroslav, Andreea, Rad and Aaron, Gabi, Layla and Greg, Ștefi, Luke, Jeremy (close friend and illustrator extraordinaire, who designed the cover for this book), Peter (Nash and West), Emilio and Graham. You may not realise it, but you all spurred me on when I needed it, be it through your excitement, advice or just sitting there while I rambled on. And how could I forget the #notagoodlook crew?... I love you all. Even you, James.

Kate and Jack, whose guidance during my two years at *POLITICO* made me grow as a journalist. Dan Bond, whose backing led me to first write a book. Olivia, James, and the entire Biteback team for working with me again, editing my words with such care. Finally, I'd like to thank the 157 people who contributed to this project, including more than sixty of you who passed through the whips' office, sharing a glimpse into this fascinating world.

NOTES

HISTORY IN BRIEF
1. Tim Renton, *Chief Whip: People, Power and Patronage in Westminster*, Politico's, 2004
2. P. D. G. Thomas, *The House of Commons in the Eighteenth Century*, Clarendon Press, 1971
3. Tim Renton, *Chief Whip*, op. cit.
4. Viscount Gladstone, 'The Chief Whip in the British Parliament', *American Political Science Review*, Vol. 21, No. 3, August 1927
5. Ibid.
6. Tim Renton, *Chief Whip*, op. cit.
7. Sir John Gorst's office, 'London Letter', *Western Daily Press*, 12 December 1990
8. Michael Rush and Claire Ettinghausen, 'Opening Up The Usual Channels', Hansard Society, 2002
9. 'Lord Hugh Cecil's charges', *Daily Mirror*, 5 April 1911
10. Michael Rush and Claire Ettinghausen, 'Opening Up The Usual Channels', op. cit.
11. J.C., 'When rowdyism was rampant', *Meath Herald and Cavan Advertiser*, 23 October 1926
12. Tim Renton, *Chief Whip*, op. cit.

CHAPTER 1
1. Chris Moncrieff, 'Whipping boys…', *Hull Daily Mail*, 5 December 1995

CHAPTER 2
1. Jennifer Walpole and Richard Kelly, 'The Whips' Office', House of Commons Library, 10 October 2008
2. Michael Rush and Claire Ettinghausen, 'Opening Up The Usual Channels', op. cit.
3. Helen Jones, *How to Be a Government Whip*, Biteback Publishing, 2016
4. Sebastian Whale, 'The unusual channels: how to whip MPs in the age of coronavirus', *The House*, 30 June 2020

CHAPTER 3
1. Eliot Wilson, 'I'm just the chief whip. I put a bit of stick about', Substack, 21 November 2022
2. Michael Cockerell, *Westminster's Secret Service*, BBC 2, 21 May 1995
3. Michael Rush and Claire Ettinghausen, 'Opening Up The Usual Channels', op. cit.

CHAPTER 4
1. Janet Anderson, 'I was the Queen's official gossip', *Daily Mail*, 21 April 2012
2. Wally Thomas, 'Why someone, somewhere down the Mall writes a letter to Her Majesty every day (except Fridays), *Neath Guardian*, 13 July 1978
3. Tim Renton, *Chief Whip*, op. cit.
4. Janet Anderson, 'I was the Queen's official gossip', op. cit.
5. 'MPs back TV in house', *Derby Daily Telegraph*, 10 February 1988

CHAPTER 5
1. John Lewis, 'The whip cracks', *Birmingham Daily Post*, 19 December 1974
2. 'Always the bridesmaid and never the bride,' he quipped to reporters after meeting with the Prime Minister in 10 Downing Street.
3. David Bradford, 'Party almost cracked the Whip', *The Scotsman*, 19 December 1974
4. John Beavan, 'A Life in Focus', *The Independent*, 27 April 2019

5   Michael Cockerell, *Westminster's Secret Service*, op. cit.
6   Tam Dalyell, 'Obituary: Lord Mellish', *The Independent*, 11 May 1998
7   Bob Mellish, 'The Job That Gave Him a Heart Attack', *Sunday Post*, 16 February 1975
8   Tam Dalyell, 'Obituary: Lord Mellish', op. cit.
9   Ibid.
10 Ibid.
11 Bob Mellish, 'The Job That Gave Him a Heart Attack', op. cit.
12 Ibid.
13 Tam Dalyell, 'Obituary: Lord Mellish', op. cit.
14 'Mellish may quit Whip's job', *Birmingham Daily Post*, 26 July 1974
15 Bob Mellish, 'The Job That Gave Him A Heart Attack', op. cit.
16 Patrick Cosgrave, 'Obituaries: Lord Colnbrook', *The Independent*, 7 October 1996
17 Emmeline Ledgerwood, 'When every vote counted', The History of Parliament, 13 September 2017
18 'Cabinet seat for Chief Whip', *Aberdeen Press and Journal*, 15 June 1974
19 Gordon Jackson and Bill Doult, 'It looks like autumn now', *Newcastle Evening Chronicle*, 21 June 1974
20 'Mellish may quit Whip's job', op. cit.
21 Charles Reiss, 'Wilson unveils his Grand Strategy', *Birmingham Daily Post*, 30 October 1974

CHAPTER 6

1   'Division won by fraction – of an MP', *Birmingham Daily Post*, 30 May 1968
2   'Filibuster, charges Macleod', *Liverpool Daily Post*, 30 May 1968
3   'Whip is accused of calling members out of committee', *The Scotsman*, 30 May 1968
4   Tam Dalyell, 'Walter Harrison: Labour whip whose efforts did much to keep the party in power in the 1970s', *The Independent*, 24 October 2012
5   'Obituaries: Walter Harrison', *Yorkshire Post*, 27 October 2012
6   Ibid.
7   'Wigan MP is among eight new government whips', *Liverpool Echo*, 15 April 1966
8   Tam Dalyell, 'Walter Harrison: Labour whip whose efforts did much to keep the party in power in the 1970s', op. cit.
9   'Guillotine: Labour MPs declare all-out war', *Daily Mirror*, 22 January 1971
10 'A House divided against itself', *Nottingham Guardian*, 25 January 1971
11 'Walter Harrison', *Daily Telegraph*, 22 October 2012
12 'Froth on the party whips' beer', *Cambridge Daily News*, 6 February 1971
13 'Row flares after strikes bill vote', *Hull Daily Mail*, 5 August 1971
14 'Walter Harrison', *Daily Telegraph*, op. cit.
15 Jack Straw, *Last Man Standing: Memoirs of a Political Survivor*, Pan Books, 2012
16 Ian Hernon, 'Stepping in as Foot's legman', *Bristol Evening Post*, 15 January 1981
17 Peter Snape, 'Forceful types with the job of whipping MPs into a frenzy', *Birmingham Daily Post*, 27 December 1996
18 Alan Goddard, 'Johnson is stuck for a stick', *Hull Daily Mail*, 5 November 1982
19 'Walter Harrison', *Daily Telegraph*, op. cit.
20 Andrew Roth, 'Walter Harrison obituary', *The Guardian*, 23 October 2012
21 'Double for Morris brothers', *Manchester Evening News*, 7 March 1974

CHAPTER 7

1   David Bradford, 'Party almost cracked the Whip', op. cit.
2   Sebastian Whale, 'Betty Boothroyd: "I am a bit timid. But I'm dealing with the giants"', *The House*, 26 April 2018
3   Ibid.
4   James Naughtie, 'John Stonehouse: Bizarre tale of the MP who faked his own death', BBC News, 27 July 2001
5   Sebastian Whale, 'Betty Boothroyd: "I am a bit timid. But I'm dealing with the giants"', op. cit.
6   'Stonehouse held in Australia', *Coventry Evening Telegraph*, 24 December 1974
7   'Mellish quits over Labour rebellion', *Cambridge Daily News*, 18 December 1974
8   David Rose, 'Mellish stays to avoid crisis', *Liverpool Daily Post*, 19 December 1974
9   David Bradford, 'Mellish to stay as Chief Whip', *The Scotsman*, 19 December 1974
10 'Whip resigns', *Birmingham Daily Post*, 24 January 1975
11 Bob Mellish, 'The Job That Gave Him a Heart Attack', op. cit.
12 Desmond McCartan, 'Fitt holds whip hand at Westminster', *Belfast Telegraph*, 28 October 1975

NOTES

13   Bob Mellish, 'The Job That Gave Him a Heart Attack', op. cit.
14   Ibid.
15   Emmeline Ledgerwood, 'When every vote counted', op. cit.
16   'The lonely wives of Westminster', *Birmingham Daily Post*, 28 January 1975
17   'Promise of relief for sex-starved members', *The Scotsman*, 26 March 1975
18   Preston Witts, 'Will Bob do it again?', *Liverpool Echo*, 19 December 1974
19   Bill Doult, 'Labour MP rebels over vote', *Aberdeen Evening Express*, 22 August 1975
20   'Walter Harrison', *Daily Telegraph*, op. cit.
21   'Mr Callaghan and Labour whip clash over Market', *Hull Daily Mail*, 8 April 1975
22   'Tory fury over left-wing "deal"', *Belfast News Letter*, 13 June 1975
23   Ernest Prince, 'Harold survives, but rift deepens', *Wolverhampton Express and Star*, 12 March 1976

CHAPTER 8

1   'Obituary: Jack Weatherill', *Daily Telegraph*, 8 May 2007
2   Bernard Weatherill, 'Election of Speaker', Hansard, 15 June 1983
3   George Young, 'Tributes (Speaker Weatherill)', Hansard, 10 May 2007
4   Bernard Weatherill, 'Election of Speaker', op. cit.
5   Patrick Cosgrave, 'Obituary: Lord Colnbrook', *The Independent*, 7 October 1996
6   Emmeline Ledgerwood, 'When every vote counted', op. cit.
7   Ibid.
8   'Sir Carol Mather', *Daily Telegraph*, 5 July 2006
9   Tim Renton, *Chief Whip*, op. cit.
10   Ibid.
11   James Graham, *This House*, National Theatre, October 2012

CHAPTER 9

1   'Double vote "joke" move', *Nottingham Evening Post*, 28 July 1975
2   Ibid.
3   George Jones, 'Fortnight of trouble ahead for Wilson', *The Scotsman*, 28 July 1975
4   David Perry, 'MP hits minister', *Newcastle Journal*, 5 March 1975
5   John Lewis and Charles Reiss, 'Government survives on jobs crisis', *Birmingham Daily Post*, 30 January 1976
6   *The Night the Government Fell: A Parliamentary Coup*, BBC Parliament, 28 March 2009
7   Robert B. Semple Jr, 'Wilson, stunning Britain, quits as prime minister; Laborite leader 13 years', *New York Times*, 17 March 1976
8   Tam Dalyell, 'Obituary: Lord Mellish', op. cit.
9   John Deans and Ken Smith, 'Dramatic appeal to Ryman', *Newcastle Journal*, 17 January 1976
10   Ernest Prince, 'A hollow victory', *Wolverhampton Express and Star*, 20 January 1976
11   Charles Reiss, 'Election comes into picture as Stonehouse quits Labour', *Birmingham Daily Post*, 8 April 1976
12   Peter Simmonds, 'Govt. given a thrashing', *Aberdeen Press and Journal*, 11 March 1976
13   James Callaghan, *Time and Chance*, William Collins Sons & Co., 1987
14   Ibid.
15   Tom James, 'Bill scrapes through', *The Scotsman*, 28 May 1976
16   Ian Aitken and Peter Cole, 'Red Flag is waved at the Tory bull', *The Guardian*, 27 May 1976
17   Ibid.
18   Ibid.
19   Gordon Jackson, 'We shall not be moved, says big Jim', *Aberdeen Evening Express*, 28 May 1976
20   Ian Aitken and Peter Cole, 'Red Flag is waved at the Tory bull', op. cit.
21   Tom Pendry, *Taking It on the Chin*, Biteback Publishing, 2016
22   Ibid.
23   Gordon Jackson, 'We shall not be moved, says big Jim', op. cit.
24   Ibid.
25   Ibid.
26   Ibid.
27   'Resignation for MP would be "silly"', *Stamford Mercury*, 4 June 1976
28   Preston Witts, 'More hazards ahead over "pairing"?', *Liverpool Echo*, 4 June 1976
29   'Tories believe they have the upper hand', *Belfast News Letter*, 11 June 1976
30   'Kruger round-up', *Birmingham Daily Post*, 9 June 1976

31 'Commons uproar: MP claims "flaw" in bill leaked to Tories', *Leicester Daily Mercury*, 28 May 1976
32 Charles Reiss, 'Callaghan and Tories call a truce', *Birmingham Daily Post*, 23 June 1976
33 'Sir Harold refused "pair"', *The Scotsman*, 18 November 1976
34 Paul Callan, 'Maggie maroons Heath', *Daily Mirror*, 30 July 1976
35 Tom James, 'Ships bill likely to be "sunk" by Lords', *The Scotsman*, 22 November 1976
36 Robin Hodgson, 'Diary of a new man about the House', *Birmingham Daily Post*, 15 November 1976

CHAPTER 10

1 Editorial, 'Stop this scandal', *Aberdeen Press and Journal*, 26 July 1976
2 *The Night the Government Fell*, op. cit.
3 John Deans, 'Hospital man hits at "silly woman"', *Aberdeen Press and Journal*, 30 July 1976
4 Editorial, 'Stop this scandal', op. cit.
5 Michael Cockerell, *Westminster's Secret Service*, op. cit.
6 Peter Snape, 'Forceful types with the job of whipping MPs into a frenzy', op. cit.
7 Ibid.
8 Joe Ashton, 'Who's for a whip-round?', *Retford, Gainsborough & Worksop Times*, 31 December 1976
9 Peter Snape, 'Forceful types with the job of whipping MPs into a frenzy', op. cit.
10 'Sick MP runs away with a wife', *The People*, 24 April 1977
11 Francis Wheen, 'Buddy, can you spare a tank?', *The Guardian*, 28 February 2001
12 'MP's wife admits arson', *Belfast News Letter*, 14 May 1978
13 John Lewis, 'Callaghan's big gamble comes off', *Birmingham Daily Post*, 15 June 1978

CHAPTER 11

1 Andrew Roth, 'Obituary: Lord Cocks of Hartcliffe', *The Guardian*, 27 March 2001
2 *The Night the Government Fell*, op. cit.
3 Eric Price, 'Week Ending', *Western Daily Press*, 30 July 1977
4 Michael Cockerell, *Westminster's Secret Service*, op. cit.
5 Peter Snape, 'Forceful types with the job of whipping MPs into a frenzy', op. cit.
6 Ibid.
7 Eric Price, 'Week Ending', op. cit.

CHAPTER 12

1 'Jim parries Maggie's killer blow', *Western Daily Press*, 24 March 1977
2 Gordon Jackson, 'It's a deal!', *Newcastle Evening Chronicle*, 23 March 1977
3 'Now the leaders face the grassroots', *Belfast Telegraph*, 24 March 1977
4 Chris Moncrieff, 'Bad day for Britain – Thatcher', *Belfast Telegraph*, 24 March 1977
5 Peter Gavan, 'Toe the line or we go, Jim says', *Western Daily Press*, 22 June 1977
6 Julia Langdon, 'Obituary: Audrey Wise', *The Guardian*, 5 September 2000
7 Derrick Hill, 'President's warning on future of Lib–Lab pact', *Liverpool Echo*, 27 September 1977

CHAPTER 13

1 *The Night the Government Fell*, op. cit.
2 James Callaghan, *Time and Chance*, op. cit.
3 Ibid.
4 John Lewis and Peter Gavan, 'Callaghan to gamble all on 1979 election', *Birmingham Daily Post*, 8 September 1978
5 Ibid.
6 *The Night the Government Fell*, op. cit.
7 'Crisis? What crisis?', BBC News, 12 September 2000

CHAPTER 14

1 *The Night the Government Fell*, op. cit.
2 Ibid.
3 Roy Hattersley, 'The party's over', *The Observer*, 22 May 2009
4 *The Night the Government Fell*, op. cit.
5 Ibid.
6 Ibid.
7 Ibid.

8   Ibid.
9   Ibid.
10 Ferdinand Mount, 'The boycott and the bomb', *The Spectator*, 7 April 1979
11 Ibid.
12 *The Night the Government Fell*, op. cit.
13 Ibid.
14 Ibid.
15 Emmeline Ledgerwood, 'When every vote counted', op. cit.
16 Roy Hattersley, 'The party's over', op. cit.
17 *The Night the Government Fell*, op. cit.
18 'Parliament to tighten security', *Belfast Telegraph*, 1 November 1975
19 *The Night the Government Fell*, op. cit.
20 Ibid.
21 Ferdinand Mount, 'The boycott and the bomb', op. cit.
22 Terence Lancaster, 'Battle starts after defeat by one vote', *Daily Mirror*, 29 March 1979

CHAPTER 15

1   Peter Snape, 'Forceful types with the job of whipping MPs into a frenzy', op. cit.
2   'Tories scrape through – and spring elections on way', *Belfast Telegraph*, 29 March 1979
3   George Jones, 'New Palace Yard horror stuns MPs', *The Scotsman*, 31 March 1979
4   'House stunned as whip tells of blast', *Belfast News Letter*, 31 March 1979
5   Emmeline Ledgerwood, 'When every vote counted', op. cit.
6   Andrew Roth, 'Walter Harrison obituary', op. cit.
7   James Callaghan, *Time and Chance*, op. cit.

CHAPTER 16

1   Alan Travis, 'Margaret Thatcher papers reveal how close Tories came to a split in 1981', *The Guardian*, 17 March 2012
2   Ibid.
3   Andrew Grice, 'I watched the last time MPs worked on a Saturday, in 1982. Unlike today, it was a political high point', *The Independent*, 19 October 2019

CHAPTER 17

1   John Major, *John Major: The Autobiography*, Harper Collins, 1999
2   Ibid.
3   'A tall story', *Daily Mirror*, 10 April 1974
4   'Westminster weight-watchers whip up will-power wager', *Liverpool Daily Post*, 22 January 1980
5   Michael Brown, 'They take risks – and how! – which is why we need our gay MPs and their scandals', *Daily Telegraph*, 29 January 2006
6   Michael Brown, 'Were we all alcoholics in Parliament back then?', *The Independent*, 30 August 2006
7   Geoffrey Wheatcroft, *The Strange Death of Tory England*, Penguin, 2005
8   Simon Hoggart, 'Another Pint of Claret', *New Humanist*, 31 May 2007
9   'Father of the House fights to deny Thatcher', *The Herald*, 8 July 1996
10 Patrick Kidd, 'The Times Diary', *The Times*, 15 July 2014
11 Matthew Parris, *Chance Witness: An Outsider's Life in Politics*, Viking, 2002
12 Robert Boscawen, *Armoured Guardsmen: A War Diary*, Pen & Sword, 2010
13 Anne Keleny, 'Robert Boscawen: Tank commander who survived terrible injuries to become a respected and admired Conservative MP', *The Independent*, 14 January 2014
14 John Major, *John Major*, op. cit.
15 'Leon Brittan: Tory Home Secretary whose rise was halted by Westland affair', *The Independent*, 23 January 2015
16 Amy Davidson Sorkin, 'How the I.R.A. almost blew up the British Government', *New Yorker*, 3 April 2023
17 'IRA Brighton Bomb: Doctor who treated victims recalls blast', BBC News, 21 June 2022
18 Liz Lightfoot, 'He'll never walk again, they said', *Western Daily Press*, 14 December 1984

CHAPTER 18

1   David Rose, 'Maggie's not dried up on the wets', *Liverpool Echo*, 6 January 1981

CHAPTER 19

1. 'Complaints against the "lists" system', *The Scotsman*, 21 February 1911
2. Rodney Brayton, 'Margesson', *Manchester Evening News*, 15 February 1941
3. Gyles Brandreth, *Breaking the Code: Westminster Diaries*, Biteback Publishing, second edition, 2014
4. Ibid.
5. Ibid.
6. Michael Cockerell, *Westminster's Secret Service*, op. cit.
7. Ibid.
8. Emmeline Ledgerwood, 'When every vote counted', op. cit.

CHAPTER 20

1. John Major, *John Major*, op. cit.
2. Andrew Mitchell, *Beyond a Fringe: Tales from a reformed Establishment lackey*, Biteback Publishing, second edition, 2022
3. Tim Renton, *Chief Whip*, op. cit.
4. Tim Sainsbury, *Among the Supporting Cast: Reminiscences and Reflections on Three Careers*, Adelphi, 2020
5. John Major, *John Major*, op. cit.

CHAPTER 21

1. John Major, *John Major*, op. cit.
2. Ibid.

CHAPTER 22

1. 'Dobbs deals House cards', *Northampton Chronicle and Echo*, 6 May 1989
2. 'Tristan Garel-Jones, Tory "wet" and able deputy chief whip under Margaret Thatcher', *Daily Telegraph*, 24 March 2020
3. 'Lord Garel-Jones obituary', *The Times*, 28 March 2020
4. Chris Moncrieff, 'Wet and Dry tallyman of Tory traits', *Derby Daily Telegraph*, 4 December 1987
5. Gordon Jackson and David Perry, 'Mrs. T faces party crisis', *Belfast Telegraph*, 7 October 1981
6. 'Thatcher defeats "no confidence" move', *Belfast Telegraph*, 29 October 1981
7. 'Lord Garel-Jones obituary', *The Times*, op. cit.
8. Ibid.
9. Mike Steele, 'Janner bids to give roughneck an object lesson', *Leicester Daily Mercury*, 27 April 1984
10. David Bradshaw, 'Ministers rally to defence of accused whip', *Western Daily Press*, 24 February 1986
11. Tim Renton, *Chief Whip*, op. cit.
12. 'Lord Garel-Jones obituary', *The Times*, op. cit.
13. Chris Moncrieff, 'Wet and Dry tallyman of Tory traits', op. cit.
14. Ibid.

CHAPTER 23

1. Tim Renton, *Chief Whip*, op. cit.
2. Ibid.
3. Ibid.
4. Ibid.
5. Ibid.
6. Ibid.
7. Ibid.
8. Tom Condon, 'Life after Maggie', *Scotland on Sunday*, 25 November 1990
9. Tim Renton, *Chief Whip*, op. cit.
10. Margaret Thatcher, *The Downing Street Years*, Harper Press, 1993
11. Tim Renton, *Chief Whip*, op. cit.
12. Ibid.
13. Margaret Thatcher, *The Downing Street Years*, op. cit.
14. Tim Renton, *Chief Whip*, op. cit.
15. Ibid.
16. Margaret Thatcher, *The Downing Street Years*, op. cit.
17. Ibid.

NOTES

CHAPTER 24
1. Gyles Brandreth, *Breaking the Code*, op. cit.
2. John Major, *John Major*, op. cit.

CHAPTER 25
1. Jerry Hayes, *An Unexpected MP: Confessions of a Political Gossip*, Biteback Publishing, 2014
2. 'MPs in tears after a good whipping', *Illustrated London News*, 1 December 1988
3. Nigel Nelson and Kim Bartlett, 'Hanky-spanky as top Tories keep quiet over shares in pervert Proctor's business', *The People*, 30 October 1994
4. Patrick O'Flynn and Mark Langford, 'A legendary enforcer of the party line', *Birmingham Daily Post*, 13 December 1995
5. Sue Fisher, 'I didn't thump anyone!', *Tamworth Herald*, 12 November 1993
6. Ibid.
7. Sue Fisher, 'I'm sharpening my axe – "bloody furious" MP', *Tamworth Herald*, 26 July 1991
8. Patrick O'Flynn, 'Loyal Tories who must try to stop the rot', *Birmingham Daily Post*, 10 February 1994
9. Michael Cockerell, *Westminster's Secret Service*, op. cit.
10. 'MP explains decision on gay sex poll – the "most difficult vote" of his career', *Lichfield Mercury*, 24 February 1994
11. David Lightbown, 'A new boy in Westminster', *Lichfield Mercury*, 15 July 1983
12. Kurt Calder, 'I'll name that MP in…', *Lichfield Mercury*, 8 June 1984
13. 'MP escapes from an Ulster mob', *Coleshill Chronicle*, 22 August 1986
14. Dan Collins, 'DHSS cash "conspiracy" say Labour', *Atherstone News and Herald*, 19 September 1986
15. Sue Robinson, 'Benefits claim that shocked MP', *Tamworth Herald*, 26 September 1986
16. Andrew Mitchell, *Beyond a Fringe*, op. cit.
17. Timothy Kirkhope, 'Obituary: Sir David Lightbown', *The Independent*, 14 December 1995
18. 'MP recovering after collapsing in House', *Staffordshire Newsletter*, 25 January 1991
19. Timothy Kirkhope, 'Obituary: Sir David Lightbown', op. cit.
20. Nigel Morris, 'Bruiser with a heart of gold', *Birmingham Daily Post*, 23 July 1993
21. John Rentoul, 'MP's death cuts government majority to five', *The Independent*, 13 December 1995

CHAPTER 26
1. 'Whips crack down to save day', *The Scotsman*, 5 November 1992
2. Teresa Gorman, *The Bastards: Dirty Tricks and the Challenge to Europe*, Pan Books, 1993
3. John Major, *John Major*, op. cit.
4. Ibid.
5. Ibid.
6. Teresa Gorman, *The Bastards*, op. cit.
7. John Major, *John Major*, op. cit.
8. Ibid.
9. Teresa Gorman, *The Bastards*, op. cit.
10. John Major, *John Major*, op. cit.
11. Gyles Brandreth, *Breaking the Code*, op. cit.
12. John Major, *John Major*, op. cit.
13. Ibid.
14. 'Bully-boy tactics on Tory rebels denied by whips', *Newcastle Journal*, 6 November 1992
15. Tom Condon, 'The whipping boys', *Scotland on Sunday*, 8 November 1992
16. Peter Collins, 'Whips' tactics lashed', *South Wales Echo*, 5 November 1992
17. 'Bully-boy tactics on Tory rebels denied by whips', op. cit.
18. Ibid.
19. Peter Collins, 'Whips' tactics lashed', op. cit.
20. Tom Condon, 'The whipping boys', op. cit.
21. Joy Copley, 'Maastricht battle victory wrung out with blood, sweat and tears', *The Scotsman*, 6 November 1992
22. Tom Condon, 'The whipping boys', op. cit.
23. John Major, *John Major*, op. cit.
24. Tom Condon, 'The whipping boys', op. cit.
25. Andrew Mitchell, *Beyond a Fringe*, op. cit.
26. Tom Condon, 'The whipping boys', op. cit.
27. Teresa Gorman, *The Bastards*, op. cit.

28 John Major, *John Major*, op. cit.
29 Janet Leet, 'Revealed: MP's note to the PM!', *Lichfield Mercury*, 12 November 1992
30 John Major, *John Major*, op. cit.
31 Teresa Gorman, *The Bastards*, op. cit.
32 John Major, *John Major*, op. cit.
33 Teresa Gorman, *The Bastards*, op. cit.
34 Peter Collins, 'Whips' tactics lashed', op. cit.
35 Janet Leet, 'Revealed: MP's note to the PM!', op. cit.
36 Peter Collins, 'Whips' tactics lashed', op. cit.
37 Nigel Morris, 'Whipping up the right support', *Birmingham Daily Post*, 6 November 1992
38 David Bradshaw and Alastair Campbell, 'Blackmailed by Major's sex thugs', *Daily Mirror*, 6 November 1992
39 Nigel Morris, 'Whipping up the right support', op. cit.
40 David Bradshaw and Alastair Campbell, 'Blackmailed by Major's sex thugs', op. cit.
41 Tom Condon, 'The whipping boys', *Scotland on Sunday*, 8 November 1992

CHAPTER 27
1 John Major, *John Major*, op. cit.
2 David Bradshaw and Alastair Campbell, 'Blackmailed by Major's sex thugs', op. cit.
3 Andrew Mitchell, *Beyond a Fringe*, op. cit.
4 Ibid.
5 Ibid.
6 John Major, *John Major*, op. cit.

CHAPTER 28
1 John Major, *John Major*, op. cit.
2 Ibid.
3 Andrew Mitchell, *Beyond a Fringe*, op. cit.
4 Colin Brown, 'The Maastricht Debate: Waverers met with more subtle methods', *The Independent*, 22 July 1993
5 Ibid.
6 Ibid.
7 John Major, *John Major*, op. cit.
8 Ibid.
9 Ibid.
10 Andrew Mitchell, *Beyond a Fringe*, op. cit.

CHAPTER 29
1 Patrick Wintour and Stephen Bates, 'Major goes back to the old values', *The Guardian*, 9 October 1993
2 Patrick Wintour, Duncan Campbell and Louise Jury, 'MP's lurid death shocks Tories', *The Guardian*, 8 February 1994
3 'Tory MP drank himself to death alone in his flat', *The Independent*, 27 February 1997
4 Ibid.
5 Andrew Mitchell, *Beyond a Fringe*, op. cit.
6 Phil Murphy, 'Ex-whip to face probe into sleaze row note', *Aberdeen Press and Journal*, 16 October 1996
7 Colin Brown and Christian Wolmar, 'Sensation! Tory minister does the decent thing', *The Independent*, 12 December 1996
8 Gyles Brandreth, *Breaking the Code*, op. cit.
9 Ibid.
10 Ibid.

CHAPTER 30
1 'Sir Anthony Grant, Conservative MP and influential trade minister – obituary', *Daily Telegraph*, 17 October 2016

CHAPTER 31
1 Tam Dalyell, 'Sir Ray Powell', *The Independent*, 10 December 2001
2 Ibid.
3 Richard Ryder, 'Letter: Derek Foster obituary', *The Guardian*, 24 January 2019

NOTES

CHAPTER 32
1   Jon Craig, 'History shows House of Commons "pairing" row is nothing new', Sky News, 24 July 2018
2   Rachel Cooke, 'Oh babe, just look at us now', *The Observer*, 22 April 2007
3   Ibid.
4   George Monbiot, 'Break the whip', *The Guardian*, 12 June 2001
5   Tony Blair, *A Journey*, Hutchinson, 2010
6   Sebastian Whale, 'Whatever happened to the class of 1997?', *The House*, 29 September 2021

CHAPTER 33
1   Tess Kingham, 'Cheesed off by willy-jousters in a pointless parliament', *The Guardian*, 20 June 2001
2   Ray Dunne, 'Ann Taylor: Chief Whip', BBC News, 5 March 2001

CHAPTER 34
1   Nicholas Watt, 'Whip shown the door of 12 Downing Street to make way for Blair's staff', *The Guardian*, 25 June 2001
2   Peter Oborne, 'Blair downgraded the Labour whips – and now he is paying the price', *The Spectator*, 17 January 2004
3   Sarah Womack, 'Campbell ousts the Chief Whip', *Daily Telegraph*, 7 September 2001
4   Philip Cowley, *The Rebels: How Blair mislaid his majority*, Politico's, 2005

CHAPTER 35
1   Philip Cowley, *The Rebels*, op. cit.
2   Ibid.
3   Ibid.
4   Ibid.
5   Ibid.
6   Ibid.
7   Ibid.
8   Linda McDougall, 'The Babe who fell from grace', *Daily Telegraph*, 9 February 2007
9   Rachel Cooke, 'Oh babe, just look at us now', op. cit.
10 Ibid.

CHAPTER 36
1   'Those that are not with us are against us', *The Guardian*, 22 October 2001
2   Simon Walters, 'How Number 10 tried to smear me, by Labour MP', *Mail on Sunday*, 28 October 2001
3   Kevin Maguire, 'MP warned after intern asks to leave', *The Guardian*, 29 November 2003

CHAPTER 37
1   Philip Cowley, *The Rebels*, op. cit.
2   Ibid.

CHAPTER 38
1   Tim Renton, *Chief Whip*, op. cit.
2   'Blair: No retreat on top-up fees', BBC News, 2 December 2003
3   Toby Helm, '"Show trials" to axe MPs disloyal to Blair', *Daily Telegraph*, 2 March 2004

CHAPTER 39
1   Simon Hattenstone, 'Emily Thornberry: "A whip threw me against a wall. He was so close I got spit in my face"', *The Guardian*, 20 February 2023
2   Alex Macpherson, 'Political Counterfactual: How Jacqui Smith Became…', iaindale.com, 2 April 2021
3   Jonathan Oliver and Christine Challand, 'Baltgate: How Brown supporters had secret meeting to curry on plotting', *Mail on Sunday*, 17 September 2006

CHAPTER 40
1   George Foulkes, 'Tribute to Lord McAvoy', *The House*, 12 March 2024
2   Chris Mullin, *A View from the Foothills: The Diaries of Chris Mullin*, Profile Books, 2010
3   Helen Jones, *How to Be a Government Whip*, op. cit.

CHAPTER 41

1   Helen Jones, *How to Be a Government Whip*, op. cit.
2   Ibid.
3   Committee on Members' Expenses, First Report, 'The Operation of the Parliamentary Standards Act 2009', 6 December 2011
4   Ibid.
5   'Good morning, anyone?', *The Guardian*, 7 April 2009
6   Helen Jones, *How to Be a Government Whip*, op. cit.
7   Ibid.

CHAPTER 42

1   Sebastian Whale, 'The unusual channels: how to whip MPs in the age of coronavirus', op. cit.
2   Graham Brady, *Kingmaker: Secrets, Lies and the Truth about Five Prime Ministers*, Ithaka Press, 2024
3   Karen Barden, 'The fighting spirit of David Maclean', *Westmorland Gazette*, 7 August 2003
4   Andrew Grice, 'Tory Chief Whip sends letter of apology to adoption "rebels"', *The Independent*, 9 November 2002
5   Colin Brown and Francis Elliott, 'Was this the week the Quiet Man lost the plot?', *Daily Telegraph*, 12 October 2003
6   'Tory MPs face written warnings', BBC News, 11 October 2003
7   Paul Waugh and Andrew Grice, 'Tory chief whip to Duncan Smith: Go now or face leadership battle', *The Guardian*, 23 October 2003
8   'Tory chief whip quits post', *Evening Standard*, 13 April 2012

CHAPTER 43

1   David Cameron, *For the Record*, William Collins, 2019
2   Sebastian Whale, *Call to Order*, Biteback Publishing, 2020
3   Ibid.

CHAPTER 44

1   Andrew Mitchell, *Beyond a Fringe*, op. cit.
2   Ibid.
3   Ibid.
4   Ibid.
5   Ibid.
6   Ibid.
7   Ibid.
8   Ibid.
9   Ibid.

CHAPTER 45

1   Michael Cockerell, *Unmasking Our Leaders: Confessions of a Political Documentary-Maker*, Biteback Publishing, second edition, 2022
2   Michael Meadowcroft, 'Sir Cyril Smith obituary', *The Guardian*, 3 September 2010

CHAPTER 46

1   David Cameron, *For the Record*, op. cit.
2   Ibid.
3   Sebastian Whale, *Call to Order*, op. cit.
4   Ibid.
5   Ibid.
6   Ibid.
7   Ibid.
8   Ibid.
9   Ibid.
10 Ibid.
11 Ibid.

CHAPTER 47

1   Sebastian Whale, 'Whatever happened to the 2011 Eurosceptic Rebels?', *The House*, 24 October 2021

NOTES

2 Ibid.
3 Ibid.
4 Ibid.
5 Ibid.
6 Ibid.
7 Ibid.
8 David Cameron, *For the Record*, op. cit.
9 Sebastian Whale, *Call to Order*, op. cit.

CHAPTER 48

1 Mark D'Arcy, 'Whitehall's whispering mandarin', *The Critic*, May 2022
2 Cathy Newman, 'Exclusive: Gavin Williamson's former deputy alleges "wholly inappropriate" threat made to MP in financial trouble', Channel 4 News, 8 November 2022
3 Ibid.
4 Steven Swinford and Gabriel Pogrund, 'Gavin Williamson's "tacit threat to MP over private life"', *The Times*, 7 November 2022
5 Rowena Mason, 'The tarantula stays: Tory chief whip won't remove pet spider from office', *The Guardian*, 23 November 2016
6 Mark D'Arcy, 'Whitehall's whispering mandarin', op. cit.

CHAPTER 49

1 Sebastian Whale, 'The ERG: a party within a party?', *The House*, 27 September 2018
2 Mark Francois, *Spartan Victory: The inside story of the Battle for Brexit*, independently published, 2021
3 Gavin Barwell, *Chief of Staff: Notes from Downing Street*, Atlantic Books, 2021
4 Anthony Seldon with Raymond Newell, *May at 10: The Verdict*, Biteback Publishing, 2020
5 Andrew Gimson, 'Interview: Francois insists that the ERG wants the backstop ditched altogether – not tweaked', ConservativeHome, 23 January 2019
6 Sebastian Whale, *Call to Order*, op. cit.
7 Ibid.
8 Jon Craig, 'Labour's KitKat plot to topple Theresa May inspired by spy thriller', Sky News, 22 January 2019
9 Meg Russell and Lisa James, *The Parliamentary Battle Over Brexit*, Oxford University Press, 2023
10 Ibid.
11 Ibid.

CHAPTER 50

1 Boris Johnson, *Unleashed*, William Collins, 2024
2 Matt Chorley, 'Inside the minds (and WhatsApp groups) of the new Tory MPs', *The Times*, 15 January 2020
3 Ibid.
4 Ibid.

CHAPTER 51

1 Alex Story, '"You will go far in the Tories... let me slip into something more comfortable": Olympic rower and Conservative activist ALEX STORY tells of "awkward Carry On moment with party whip"', *Mail on Sunday*, 4 November 2017
2 Peter Walker and Rajeev Syal, 'Chief whip defends lack of action against Tory MP accused of rape', *The Guardian*, 3 August 2020
3 Oliver Wright, 'PM was warned five times about Pincher's conduct', *The Times*, 6 July 2022
4 Caroline Wheeler and Harry Yorke, 'Chris Pincher accuser: I was furious and shell-shocked', *Sunday Times*, 3 July 2022
5 Rowena Mason, 'Chris Pincher: a timeline of allegations and investigations', *The Guardian*, 4 July 2022

CHAPTER 52

1 Video, 'Liz Truss would move whips' office back to No. 12 Downing Street', Mail Online, 28 July 2022
2 Gabriel Pogrund, 'No 10 refuses to endorse Gavin Williamson as threatening texts revealed', *The Times*, 5 November 2022
3 Camilla Turner, 'Chief Whip Wendy Morton quits – then returns – amid reports MPs "manhandled"', *Daily Telegraph*, 20 October 2022

INDEX

1922 Committee 196, 225, 361, 370, 441
92 Group 185–6, 198

Abbott, Diane 302, 336, 342
abstention 9, 68, 79, 84, 113, 125, 137, 138, 368, 432–3, 446, 493
Accommodation Whip 11, 52, 262
Adams, Nigel 475
'Administrative Committee' 388
Ainsworth, Bob 286, 287, 290, 314, 340
Ainsworth, Peter 11–12
air strikes, votes on 398–400, 426
Aitken, Jonathan 44–6, 171, 186, 200, 221–2
Al Fayed, Mohamed 247, 251
al-Assad, Bashar 394, 398–401
alcoholism 145, 247–8, 306, 316
Alexander, Danny 384
Allason, Rupert 242
Allen, Graham 317
Allen, Heidi 445
Alton, David 125–6, 233, 387, 408
Anderson, Donald 294–5
Anderson, Janet 32, 268
Andrew, Stuart 28, 30, 422, 431, 458–9, 461, 492
Anne, Princess 28
Arbuthnot, James 367, 368, 369
Archer, Jeffrey xii–xiv, 42, 167
Armstrong, Ernest 58, 289
Armstrong, Hilary 289–97, 323–5, 489–90
    2005 intake 337
    on Blair 338
    Campaign Group and 301
    character 339, 350
    on Corbyn 335
    Iraq and 319–20, 330–31
    Marsden and 313, 317
    on pastoral care 306–7
Ashdown, Paddy 231
Ashley, Jack 42
Ashton, Joe 82, 93, 94–5, 96, 128, 130
Assistant Government Whip 11
Atkins, Charlotte 271, 279, 290, 294, 305, 307–8, 332
Atkins, Humphrey 44–6, 74–5, 77, 84, 88–91, 117, 127, 139–41
Atkins, Robert 137, 139
Atkins, Ron 279
Aye lobby 9, 81, 229, 461

Backbench Business Committee 378, 419, 422, 498
Badenoch, Kemi 492
Baker, Kenneth 189
Baker, Steve 419, 422, 437, 439
Balls, Ed 353

Bank of England 393–4
Barclay, Steve 426
Barnes, Harry 305
Baron, John 419
Bassam, Steve 13
Beckett, Margaret 284, 446
Beith, Alan 84, 92, 105–7, 109, 120, 126, 233, 409
bell, division 74, 95, 172, 349
bench duty 151–2, 234, 307, 367, 383–4
Benn, Hilary 426, 446, 457
Benn, Tony 100, 290, 301, 303
Bennett, Nicholas 170, 171, 172, 196, 199
Benyon, Richard 450
Bercow, John 415–18
    Grieve and 441–2
    Letwin and 457
    as speaker 378–9, 422, 423, 433, 447, 450, 467
    Tipping on 283
    'Tricks of the Trade' 373
Beresford, Paul 177, 213, 456
Berry, Sir Anthony 148
bill committees *see* standing committees
Black Book 157–64, 234, 247, 251–2, 307, 403, 405–6
Black Wednesday (1992) 224
Blackford, Ian 17–18, 447
Blair, Tony
    Abbott and 302
    Armstrong and 289–93
    Campbell and 290–91
    control freak 494
    Corbyn and 335–6, 424, 491
    Edwards and 333
    elected PM 272
    Ennis and 334
    Gordon Brown and 285
    and Iraq 319–27
    Jacqui Smith and 341
    as Labour leader 267
    Mudie and 333
    reshuffles 292
    security services and 338
    whips' office visits 293, 335
Blenkinsop, Tom 468
Blix, Hans 324
Blue Chip Dining Group 137, 170
Boateng, Paul 260
Body, Richard 244
Boles, Nick 446
Bone, Peter 22, 419
Booth, Hartley 223, 247
Boothroyd, Betty 59–61, 206, 209, 228, 241
Boscawen, Robert 'Bob' 146, 176
Boswell, Tim 207

Bottomley, Peter 66, 117
Bowis, John 212, 236, 245–6
Bradshaw, Ben 323, 347, 446, 502
Brady, Sir Graham 370, 441, 473, 475, 485
Brake, Tom 417
Brandreth, Gyles 252–3, 496–7
Braverman, Suella 439, 440, 483, 484
Brexit 426, 427, 431, 434–7, 439–42, 444–7, 448–51
Brighton Grand Hotel bombing (1984) 148
Brittan, Leon 138, 147
Brocklebank-Fowler, Christopher 138
Bromley-Davenport, Walter 9
Brooker, Peter 206
Broughton, Alfred 'Doc' 92, 116–17, 119, 121–2, 125, 129
Brown, Gordon
  becomes PM 345
  as Chancellor 292, 332–3, 338
  Charlotte Atkins and 271
  Cook and 289
  first significant defeat 361, 491–2
  Nick Brown and 362
  oversees IPSA 359
  as PM 353–4
  reshuffle 357
  Watson and 342–3
Brown, Michael 144
Brown, Nick 273–5, 279–80, 332–4, 443–5
  accusations of wrongdoing 462
  on Armstrong 291
  Canavan and 303
  de facto Chief Whip 353–4, 357
  expenses scandal and 360
  Gordon Brown and 361, 362–3
  on Hague 368
  Ian Paisley and 356
  Jacqui Smith and 277
  Marshall-Andrews and 285
  McAvoy and 345, 351
  returns as Chief Whip 433
  on Stone 496
Browne, Des 293
Browning, Angela 206–7, 209, 256
Bruinvels, Peter 172
Brunson, Michael 243
Buchanan-Smith, Alick 78–9
Buckley, Sheila 60–61
Budgen, Nicholas 244
Burgon, Richard 491
Burt, Alistair 242–3, 252–3, 370, 372, 381, 450, 456, 457–8
Bush, George W. 321, 324
Butler, Dawn 362
Byrne, Ian 491

Cable, Vince 389
Callaghan, James 'Jim' 84–5, 111–14, 117–19
  cartoon of 92
  Cocks and 85, 103, 108, 119
  Harrison and 68, 129
  Healey and 96–7
  Lib-Lab pact 107–10
  Snape and 99
  Thatcher and 88, 90–91, 123
Cameron, David 372–3
  and Backbench Business Committee 419
  Bercow plot and 415, 417
  Con-Lib Dem coalition 381
  Gove and 413–14
  McLoughlin and 378
  Mitchell and 392, 396
  as PM 383, 384, 385
  referendums and 425–6
  resigns 426
  Syria and 400
  three-line whip and 10
  under pressure on Europe 419–23
  whips and 410
Campbell, Alan 350, 432, 462, 484, 489, 492
Campbell, Alastair 290
Campbell, Menzies 390
Canavan, Dennis 67, 69–70, 87, 303–5
Carlisle, John 231, 241
Carlton Club 175, 176, 221, 477
Carmichael, Alistair 377, 378–80, 382, 385–6, 389–90, 398–401, 412, 423, 496
Carrington, Peter 139
Carson, John 117–18
Carswell, Douglas 22–3, 419, 420–21, 422, 423
Carttiss, Michael 229, 230, 244
Cash, Bill 221, 223, 240
Castle, Barbara 91, 92, 94
Chalk, Alex 450
Chapman, Sydney 13, 250
Charalambous, Bambos 433
Charles III, King 26–7, 29, 212
Chief Whip 15–23
  briefings by 21–2
  bullying by 3, 4
  day-to-day 21–2, 168
  history 7, 502
  House of Lords xv, 136
  longest-serving 15
  office breakdown 19–21, 40
  PrPS to 17–19
  'the other view' 22–3
  Usual Channels 16–19
  women as 286, 289–97, 480
Chirac, Jacques 325, 327
Chope, Christopher 200–201, 380, 419
Churchill, Jo 481
Clark, Alan 152
Clark, David 56, 100
Clark, Greg 447
Clark, Helen 307
Clarke, Charles 332
Clarke, Ken 236, 370, 405, 420, 450
Clarke, Tom 321
Clay, Bob 263
Clegg, Nick 379, 380, 382, 384, 385, 389, 392, 412, 423
Clinton-Brown, Geoffrey 366
Clinton-Davis, Stanley 82
Clywd, Ann 323
Cockerell, Michael 403–4, 405
Cocks, Michael 99–103, 115–16, 127–8, 308–9
  Beith and 106, 107, 120
  Callaghan and 85, 103, 108, 119
  Cockerell and 404
  dealing with tight votes 95
  deploys whips 122
  Hayman and 90, 92
  Kinnock and 102–3, 129, 259
  marginal seats 111, 112
  Neave's death 126
  Snape and 83, 97
Coe, Sebastian 209, 255
Coffey, Ann 268
Coffey, Thérèse 484, 485
Coleman, Donald 30
Committee Corridor 3, 14
Committee of Selection 84, 294, 388
Comptroller 11, 25, 27, 351, 448
Con-Lib Dem coalition (2010–15) 380
Concannon, Don 144
Conservative Research Department (CRD) 73
Conway, Derek 247–8, 273–4
Cook, Robin 45, 289, 295–6, 325–6
Cooper, Yvette 446, 450

520

INDEX

Corbyn, Jeremy 263-4, 299-300, 443-5
    Armstrong on 335
    Blair and 335-6, 424, 491
    Iraq and 312, 323
    as Labour leader 425, 436
    May and 447
da Costa, Nikki 435
counter-whipping operations 445-7
Covid-19 pandemic 459-62, 470, 471
Cowley, Prof. Philip 290, 386-7, 491
Cran, James 221
Crosby, Lynton 415
Crouch, David 161
Cummings, Dominic 456, 461
Cunningham, George 112
Cunningham, Jack 87-8
Currie, Edwina 153-4, 155-6, 214, 216, 217
Curry House Plot (2006) 342-4
Curtis-Thomas, Claire 278
'Customs Union' 450

Dakin, Nic 29
Dalyell, Tam 42, 312
D'Arcy, Mark 57-8, 122, 129
Darling, Alistair 355, 356, 357
Davidson, Arthur 99
Davies, Bryan 115, 119, 122-3
Davies, Mims 437
Davies, Philip 373-4, 399-400, 420, 429, 498
Davies, Quentin 252
Davis, David 170, 208-9, 283, 416-17, 437
    Maastricht Bill and 220, 222-4, 229, 230, 235, 237, 239, 242
Debbonaire, Thangam 433
Democratic Unionist Party (DUP) 356, 432, 440, 443, 446
Denham, John 329
Denham, Lord (Bertram 'Bertie' Bowyer) 136
Deputy Chief Whip xv, 3, 22, 25, 27, 55, 71-8
devolution 69-70, 108, 112, 114, 268, 303
Dewar, Donald 264, 268, 273, 289, 303, 304
Dines, Sarah 477
'Dirt Book' *see* Black Book
Dixon, Don 265, 266, 267, 268, 304
Dixon, Samantha 29
Dobbs, Michael, *House of Cards* xiii, xvi, 73-4, 78, 123, 181-7, 200, 500
Dobson, Frank 293
Dormand, Jack 85, 100, 101, 117, 141
Dorrell, Stephen 138, 403
Dorries, Nadine 397, 481
Doughty, Stephen 446
Douglas-Home, Sir Alec 77, 404
Dowd, Jim 314
Drayson, Burnaby 163
Drew, David 276-7, 300, 322
Dromey, Jack 495
Dubs, Alf 128
Duncan, Alan 200
Duncan-Jordan, Neil 493
Duncan Smith, Iain 10, 369-70, 371, 439
Dunwoody, Gwyneth 250, 294-5
Durant, Tony 154

Eagle, Angela 268, 332, 416
Early Day Motion (EDM) 222, 224, 278, 312, 313, 321, 323, 332, 334-5, 337, 349
Edelman, Maurice 83
Edge, Geoff 67
Edwards, Huw 276, 295-6, 322, 324, 333, 348-9
Elis-Thomas, Dafydd 61-2
Elizabeth II, Queen 26, 28, 29-32, 448-9, 468-9, 481-2
Elphicke, Charlie 470
Engel, Natascha 415, 419
Ennis, Jeff 324, 334

EU referendum 420-22, 425, 426
European Economic Community (EEC) 43, 67-8
European exchange rate mechanism (ERM) 189, 224
European Research Group (ERG) 439-41, 446-7
Evans, David 223
Evans, Gwynfor 61
expenses scandal (2009) 358-61

Fabricant, Michael 208-9, 365-6
    EDMs and 222
    EU referendum and 422
    framed cheque 34
    on Gove 414
    on Lightbown 212
    Major and 228-9, 231, 243
    Pairing Whip 387
    Social Whip 383-4
    on Williamson 429
Fairbairn, Nicholas 230, 247
Falklands War (1982) 138-40, 161
Fallon, Michael 170, 433, 467
Farage, Nigel 419-20, 423, 439
Featherstone, Lynne 378
Field, Frank 54, 308-9, 355-6, 446, 502
Fields, Terry 260-61
Finance Bill (2008) 355-6
fines, whisky 413
Fitt, Gerry 63, 113, 118, 119, 120-21, 125
Fitzpatrick, Jim 30, 31-2, 34, 289
'Fix It Four' 100
'fixer' 21
Fletcher, Diane 183
Flight, Howard 372
'Flusher' duty 95
Flynn, Paul 436
Follett, Barbara 278
Fookes, Janet 122
Foot, Michael 84, 100, 103, 112, 122, 125, 128, 129, 359
Ford strike (1978) 113-14
Fortescue, Tim 160-61, 404, 405
Forth, Eric 239
Foster, Derek 259-60, 261, 266, 267, 307
Foster, Don 411-14
Foster, Mike 276, 284, 312, 314, 334, 339-40, 350, 354, 355, 490
Foulkes, George 127, 263, 323
Fowler, Gerry 101
Fowler, Norman 227
Fox, Liam 22, 222, 249-50, 394, 502
Foxcroft, Vicky 493
Francois, Mark 440, 441
free vote 8, 68, 78, 223, 295, 398, 426
Fresh Start Group 223
Fry, Peter 88-9
'Fuck-Up Squad' 71-9

Galley, Roy 172-3, 178
Galloway, George 323
Galpern, Myer 87
Gapes, Mike 277, 326, 330, 444, 445, 495
Gardiner, George 185-6, 198
Garel-Jones, Tristan 137-8, 166-7, 170-71, 184-7, 191-2, 219-20, 237-8
    argument with Leigh 243
    night games 177
    Skinner and 32
    teetotaller 152
    Thatcher and 197, 199
    TV interview 403
Gauke, David 447
George, Andrew 388
Germany 502
Ghani, Nusrat 437, 471-5
Gidley, Sandra 315-16

Gill, Christopher 219, 221, 231, 244
Gillan, Cheryl 256, 365
Glanville, PC James 396
Goldstone, Basil 109
Goodlad, Alastair 192, 250, 252–3, 255
Goodman, Helen 357, 360, 449–50, 450
Gordon-Lennox, RAdm Alexander 87
Gorman, Teresa 221, 229, 243, 244
Gove, Michael 411–17, 426, 427, 441, 447, 481
Government Chief Whip's Office (GCWO) 19–21
government whips 10–11
Government Whips' Admin Unit (GWAU) 21, 22, 29
Gow, Ian 138
Graham, James, *This House* xiii–xiv, 130–31
Graham, Ted 116
Grant, Anthony 255–6
Grant, George 88
Grayling, Chris 447, 464
Green, Bert 85
Green, Damian 450, 467
Green, Matthew 314
Greenway, Harry 226, 237
Grieve, Dominic 434–5, 441–2, 463
Griffiths, Andrew 470
Griffiths, Jane 307
Grimond, Jo 105–6
Grocott, Bruce 67, 94, 111, 117, 289, 292–3
Guido Fawkes 20, 422
Gummer, John 237

Hague, William 255, 368, 385, 392, 394, 415, 416, 417, 422
Hamilton, Archie 135, 137, 151, 155, 162–3, 165, 169
Hamilton, Jimmy 70
Hamilton, Neil 196, 247, 251
Hamilton, William 87, 123
Hamling, William 66
Hammond, Philip 393, 447
Hammond, Stephen 435
Hancock, Matt 399, 470
Hannan, Daniel 421
Hardman, Isabel 428
Harman, Harriet 8, 127–8, 129, 278, 495
Harper, Joe 94, 95, 106
Harper, Mark 426, 470
Harris, Carolyn 429–30
Harris, Charles 18
Harris, Rebecca 437, 481, 492
Harrison, Walter 49–58, 63–4
    Ashton's play 128
    Beith and 106, 107
    Broughton and 117, 119
    Callaghan and 129
    EEC and 68
    Field and 308–9
    Graham's play 130
    on Hayman 92
    Kinnock and 129
    looking for Litterick 97–8
    Maguire and 125
    Neave's death 126
    non-voters and 81
    pastoral care 61
    Stradling Thomas and 127
    Weatherill and 121–2
    whips' duty roster 95
    Williamson and 432
Hart, Simon xv, 498–9
Hattersley, Roy 117–18, 123
Hatton, Frank 95
Havers, Michael 406
Hayes, Jerry 211–12
Hayes, John 362, 370–71, 442
Hayman, Helene 55, 89–90, 91–2, 111

Hayward, Robert 128, 148, 186, 197, 199, 205–6
Healey, Denis 68, 69, 84, 97
Heath, Ted 9–10, 39, 45, 53, 77, 91, 145, 192, 194, 228
Heathcoat-Amory, David 229, 239
Heaton-Harris, Chris 439, 475, 476
Heddle, John 217
Heffer, Eric 68, 148
Helm, Toby 336
Henderson, Douglas 88
Henderson, Ivan 314
Heseltine, Michael 168–9
    Europhile 457
    illness 240
    leadership bid 193–4, 195, 200
    Maastricht and 219, 229, 230
    mace incident 86–7, 88
    Pendry sues 91
    Proctor and 167
    Westland crisis 147
Hewitt, Patricia 363
Hicks, Maureen 212
Higher Education Bill (2004) 331–4
Hill, Keith 312, 335
Hinchliff, Chris 493
Hinchliffe, David 293
Hodge, Margaret 245, 264, 276, 361, 495
Hodgson, Robin 91
Hogg, Douglas 325, 370–71
Hogg, Norman 259
Hollingbery, George 382
Hollobone, Philip 419
Holloway, Adam 373, 400, 449, 486, 499
Hoon, Geoff 236, 267, 324, 353–5, 357, 363, 404, 495
Hooson, Emlyn 109
Horam, John 42
House of Cards (book/TV series) xiii, xvi, 15, 181–7, 200, 428
House of Lords xv, 13, 391
Howard, Michael 371–2
Howarth, Alan 245–6
Howarth, Gerald 223, 229
Howe, Geoffrey 136, 138, 189, 190–91, 193
Hoye, Kate 446
Hoyle, Lindsay 460
Hughes, Beverley 278
Hughes, Cledwyn 112, 276
Hughes, Robert 13, 65, 207, 213, 221–2, 235, 236–7, 240, 242
Hunt, David 76, 87, 140, 151, 152, 154, 162, 176
Hunt, Jeremy 450, 483, 495
Hunt, Philip, Lord 329
Hunter, Anji 268
Hunter, Mark 386
Hurd, Douglas 189, 195, 200, 220
Hussain, Imran 491
Hussein, Saddam 319, 320, 322–3, 325

illness/death, voting and 93–8, 112
Independent Complaints and Grievance Scheme (ICGS) 469
Independent Group, The 445
Independent Inquiry into Child Sexual Abuse (2014) 405–10
Independent Parliamentary Standards Authority (IPSA) 359
Inside the Commons (BBC documentary) 403, 404
Intelligence and Security Committee (ISC) 463–5
Iraq 318, 319–27, 329–30, 342
Irvine, Arthur 120
Irvine, Derry 264
Irving, Charles 66, 122
Islamophobia 472–5
Israel–Gaza conflict (2023–) 494

Jack, Alister 448
Jenkin, Bernard and Anne 228, 230, 439
Jenkin, Patrick 168
Jennings, John 49, 50

INDEX

Jessel, Toby 171, 241
Johnson, Alan 332
Johnson, Boris 455–8, 461–4
   becomes PM 450, 451
   Blackford on 18
   Brexit and 426, 427
   Ghani and 473–4
   Pincher and 477–8
   as PM 471
   resignations 437, 478
   Spectator journalist 274
   three-line whip and 10
Johnson, Diana 337, 345, 350, 362–3
Johnson, Gareth 442
Johnson, James 55–6
Johnson, PC Susan 396
Johnson-Smith, Geoffrey 251, 252
Johnson, Walter 63, 91
Johnston, Russell 109
Jones, Alec 93
Jones, Fiona 306
Jones, George 126
Jones, Helen 358, 363
Jones, Lynne 235–6, 278, 281, 301, 305, 329, 336
Jones, Robert 227
Jopling, Michael 127, 138, 139, 167–8, 169, 170, 193–4, 405–6
Jowell, Tessa 268, 324
Judd, Frank 127

Kellett-Bowman, Elaine 123
Kennedy, Charles 231, 315, 317, 380, 390
Kennedy, Jane 268
Kerr, Russell 69
Khan, Sadiq 356–7, 424
King, Roger 170
King, Sir Mervyn 393
Kingham, Tess 277, 281
King's Speech 27–8, 490
Kinnock, Neil 67–70, 129–30, 259–61
   Cocks and 102–3, 259
   on Harrison 56, 98
   Maastricht and 220
   Major and 234
   on Mellish 41
   on Powell 262
   whips and 266, 497
Kirkhope, Timothy 31, 32, 196, 226, 230, 240, 242
Kirkwood, Archy 237
Knight, Greg 240, 242, 253, 393
Knight, Jill 89
Knight, Jim 324, 349, 351, 354
Kumar, Ashok 360
Kwarteng, Kwasi 483

Lait, Jacqui 255–7
Lamont, Norman 90, 197
Lavery, Ian 443, 444
Lawson, Nigel 82, 87, 189, 190
Leader of the House 100
Leadsom, Andrea 427, 432, 447
Leigh, Edward 239, 442
Leishman, Brian 493
Letwin, Oliver 436, 446, 449, 450, 456, 457
Levelling Up fund 499–500
Lever, Harold 50–51
Leveson Inquiry (2011–12) 384–5
Lewer, Andrew 21
Lewis, Brandon 437
Lewis, Julian 373, 381, 416, 463–5
Lib–Lab pact (1977–78) 107–10, 112
Liberal Democrats 239
Liberal Party 39, 114
Liddell, Helen 11, 264–5, 274, 284

Lidington, David 208, 224, 226, 248, 249–50, 441, 444–5, 447
Lightbown, David 211–17, 225–6, 230–31
   'burly bruiser' 210
   death 250
   EDMs and 222
   Hughes and 236
   Maastricht vote and 219, 242
   Ryder and 227
   TV interview 403
   and women as whips 255
Lilley, Peter 196, 253
line of a whip 8–9, 13, 45–6, 101
Lister, Edward 'Eddie' 177, 456
Litterick, Tom and Jane 97–8
Livingstone, Ken 262–3, 303, 336
Llewellyn, Ed 391, 392, 395
Lloyd, Peter 239
Lloyd, Tony 127, 259, 266
lobbies 229
lobbies, division 9, 81, 86, 94
Long-Bailey, Rebecca 491
Lord Chamberlain 27
Lord Commissioners 11, 19, 33–4, 358
Lord, Michael 241
Loyden, Eddie 89
Luce, Richard 30, 76, 123, 139–40
Lyon, Alex 93

Maastricht Treaty 210, 219–32, 235–8, 239–44, 256, 421, 435
McAvoy, Tommy 273, 274, 290, 326, 343, 345–51, 357, 362, 489–90
McBride, Willie John 227
McCarthy-Fry, Sarah 355
McCartney, Hugh 261
McCartney, Ian 261–2, 265, 266, 283–4
McCusker, Harold 117–18
McDonald, Oonagh 100
McDonnell, John 300, 336, 491
McDougall, Linda 306
McElhone, Frank 93
MacKay, Andrew 247
McKechin, Ann 320–21, 323, 325, 327, 343, 344
McKenna, Rosemary 304
Maclean, David 369, 370, 371, 420
Maclean, Murdo 112, 130, 198, 240, 241, 340
Macleod, Iain 49, 50–51
McLoughlin, Patrick xiv, 361, 366–9, 372, 377–81, 385–6, 390, 394, 422, 427
McNulty, Tony 277, 290
Macpherson, Nick 357
Magnus, Sir Laurie 474
Maguire, Frank and Philomena 63–4, 118–19, 120–21, 125
Mahon, Alice 321
Maitland, Olga 223
Major, John 219–32, 233–8, 239–44
   becomes PM 205
   Bruinvels and 172
   as Chancellor 189
   leadership bid 200
   Maastricht Treaty 210, 435
   on Le Marchant 143
   morality and 246, 248–9
   post-Maastricht 246
   resigns then re-elected 250
   Thatcher and 155, 176, 195
   and women as whips 255
Malone, Gerry 147, 158, 159, 163–4, 169, 175
Mandelson, Peter 267, 324
Le Marchant, Spencer 30, 74, 123, 143–5
Margesson, David 15, 159
Marlow, Tony 244
Marsden, Paul 311–18
Marshall-Andrews, Bob 285, 336

Martin, Joseph 158–9
Martin, Michael 356
Maskell, Rachael 493
Mason, Roy 113, 118
Mates, Michael 246
Mather, Carol 75–6, 146, 148–9, 153, 176
Matthewson, James 443
Maude, Francis 155, 198
May, Theresa 17–18, 439–42
    Brexit deal 434–7, 446, 447, 449–50
    Corbyn and 447
    as Home Secretary 405
    ICGS and 469
    as PM 425, 431
    resigns 450
    survives vote of no confidence 441
    Williamson and 427
Meadowcroft, Michael 57, 177, 233, 407, 408
Mellish, Bob 39–47, 52–3, 59–67, 81, 82–5, 89–90
Mellor, David 246
Members' Dining Room 42, 61, 145, 498
Members' Interest Committee (MIC) 251
Mercer, Johnny 468–9
Meyer, Anthony 191, 192
Mikardo, Ian 67
Miliband, Ed 353, 399, 423, 443
Miller, Millie 95
Milligan, Stephen 246–7
Milling, Amanda 437, 456
Mills, Iain 247
Milton, Anne 26–7, 28, 393, 426, 427–9, 431
Mitchell, Andrew 228, 242, 391–7, 403, 497
mobile phones 381–2
Modernisation Committee 284–5, 295–6, 374, 490
Molloy, William 93
Molyneaux, Jim 240
Moncrieff, Chris 4, 187
Montgomery, FM Bernard 'Monty' 75–6
Moore, John 155
More, Jasper 57
More, Sir Jasper 73
Morgan, Julie 277, 304, 322
Morgan, Nicky 393
Morris, Estelle 267–8
Morrison, Peter 117, 171, 193, 195, 198–9, 199, 409
Morton, Wendy 437, 468, 480–86, 495
Mudie, George 273, 275, 279, 332, 351
Mullan, Dr Kieran 29
Mullin, Chris 285, 330–31, 338, 346–7
Murphy, Jim 290, 294
Murphy, Paul 276

Naseby, Michael 238
Neave, Airey 126
Needham, Richard 170–71, 215
Nellist, Dave 260–61
Nelson, Nigel 213
Newmark, Brooks 383, 393–4, 501
Newton, Sarah 450
Newton, Tony 197
Nicholson, David 73
No lobby 9, 81, 229, 461
No Turning Back group 196, 199
Nolan, Michael 248
Nolan Principles 248
Norman, Archie 372
Norris, Steve 187, 248–9
Northern Bank 357
Nott, John 139
Nuttall, David 419, 421

Oaten, Mark 316–17, 387

Obama, Barack 398
O'Brien, Stephen 369–70
O'Malley, Brian 84
one-line whip 8, 45
O'Neill, Martin 349
Onslow, Cranley 194
Operation London Bridge (funeral plan) 481–2
Öpik, Lembit 314
Osborne, George 10, 313, 383, 384, 385, 388, 392, 393, 412, 426

Paedophile MP: How Cyril Smith Got Away With It, The (C4 documentary) 407
pairing 88–92, 121, 129, 131, 171, 240, 245, 273, 347, 437
Pairing Whip 21, 52–3, 79, 83, 85, 100, 117, 216, 262, 274, 370–71, 382, 387
Palmer, Angela 169
Parish, Neil 501
Parkhouse, Geoffrey 169
Parkinson, Cecil 4–5, 144–5, 199–200
Parkinson, Stephen 435
parliamentary private secretary (PPS) 67, 88
Parris, Matthew 56–7, 143, 144, 145, 167–8
Parry, Bob 241
'Partygate' 471, 475, 478
pastoral care 165–73, 306–7, 428, 495, 500, 501
Patel, Priti 471
Paterson, Owen 370, 471
Patten, Chris 73, 138, 184, 197, 205
Patten, John 205, 240
Peacock, Stephanie 445
Peart, Fred 86, 88
Pelham-Holles, Thomas 8
Pendry, Tom 85, 86, 87, 88, 90–91
Pickles, Eric 207, 209, 212–13, 500
Pidcock, Laura 436
Pincher, Chris 391, 431, 432, 434, 436, 467–9, 475–7, 501
Plaid Cymru 61–2, 111–13, 125, 237
'Plebgate' (2012) 395–7
'poll tax' 190, 192
Portcullis House (PCH) 296–7, 419
Portillo, Michael 73, 155, 239
Powell, Enoch 118, 379–81
Powell, Ray 262–5, 266, 267
Pratt, Garth and Jill 407–8
Prentice, Bridget 5, 268, 278, 308, 335
Prescott, John 286–7, 362–3
    Blair and 292, 324
    character 170, 315
    Drew and 277
    GLC and 299
    Higher Education Bill 331
    Prentice and 268
    protesting 55
Primarolo, Dawn 129
Prime Minister's Questions (PMQs) 220–21, 261, 293, 354, 368, 370, 387
principal private secretary (PrPS) 17–19, 21, 112, 495
Prior, Jim 87, 171, 215
Prisk, Mark 373
Private Eye 407, 408
Private Member's Bill (PMB) 185, 334, 490, 498
Procedure Committee 415–16
Proctor, Harvey 166–7, 213
Profumo, John 15
proxy voting 265–6, 461
Purnell, James 363
Pym, Francis 52–3, 141

Queen's Speech 27, 55, 112–13, 366–7, 386, 423, 491

R Group 419–24
Raab, Dominic 440
Radice, Giles and Lisanne 66

INDEX

Rammell, Bill 280, 294
Randall, John 379, 393, 395–6, 397
rebellions 66–7, 274, 299–305
    'cooling off' period 462
    on Europe 422–3, 434, 442
    first-time 327, 329
    Marsden and 331–6, 361–2, 389–90, 491–4
    numbers 371
    process for 387
    three-line whip 9, 59
    Villiers and 463
    see also Maastricht Treaty; Social Security Bill (1997/98)
Reckless, Mark 419, 423
Redmayne, Martin 404
Redwood, John 250, 442
Reece, Gordon 123
Rees, Merlyn 119
Rees-Mogg, Jacob 435, 440, 460, 484
Renton, Tim, *Chief Whip* xiv–xv, xvi, 7, 189–91, 193–5, 197–8, 199, 200–201
Richardson, Ian 183
Ridley, Nicholas 299
Rifkind, Malcolm 44–6, 78–9, 123, 197
Rippon, Geoffrey 87
Robathan, Andrew 373–4
Roberts, Gwilym 101–2
Robertson, George 275
Robinson, Geoffrey 83
Roe, Marion 155
Rooker, Jeff 98, 108–9
Rose, Paul 67
Rowland, PC Toby 397
royal whips 25–35
    'humble address' 31–2
    King's speech 27–8
    Lord Commissioners of His Majesty's Treasury 33–4
    'the message' 28–31
    peer review 34–5
    wands, parties and butterflies 25–7
Ryan, Joan 326, 445
Ryder, Richard 205–6
    back problem 236
    EDMs and 222
    on Foster 267
    Heseltine and 229
    Kirkwood and 237
    Lightbown and 227
    Maastricht and 220, 223, 230, 239, 242
    Major and 234, 240, 241, 251
    TV documentary and 403
Ryman, John 83

Sainsbury, Tim 34, 122, 137–8, 165–6, 171, 187, 365
Sanders, Adrian 388, 389
Savile, Jimmy 409
Scott, Norman 105
Scottish National Party (SNP) 112, 239, 490–91, 493–4
Sedgemore, Brian 278, 280
Sergeant, John 195
Serjeant-at-Arms 87, 92, 126
Shah, Naz 436
Shapps, Grant 481
Sheerman, Barry 56, 57, 260
Sheffield, HMS 140
Shepherd, Richard 244
Shit Lists 176–7, 384
Short, Clare 152, 329, 342
Short, Edward 16
Silkin, John 52
Silvester, Fred 161–2
Simon, Siôn 362
Simpson, Alan 260, 263–4, 279, 301, 302, 321–2, 329–30, 341, 348

Simpson, Kieran 275
Sims, Roger 45, 74–5
Skidmore, Chris 484
Skinner, Dennis 32, 69, 129, 148, 216, 260, 301
Slater, Harriet 52
Smith, Angela 289–90
Smith, Chris 325, 327
Smith, Cyril 105, 109, 185, 407–10
Smith, Jacqui 277, 279, 339–44, 350, 494
Smith, John 177, 235–6, 264, 289
Smith, Julian 431, 433–7, 440–43, 447–8, 467, 468, 482
Smith, Tim 247
Snape, Peter 64, 83, 84–5, 87, 97, 99–102, 130–31, 159, 299
social calendar 175–9
Social Democratic Party (SDP) 128, 138
Social Security Bill (1997/98) 278–81
Social Whip (Entertainment Whip) 12, 383
Socialist Campaign Group 275, 300–302, 321
Soubry, Anna 435, 445
South Africa 502
Spacey, Kevin 183
Speakership 85, 140–41
special advisers (SpAds) 20, 21, 360, 386, 455, 472–4, 490, 492, 499
Spelman, Caroline 450
Spencer, Mark 29–30, 455–8, 462–3, 472–6
    Blackford and 18
    dealing with complaints 470, 471
    dealing with leaks 20
    defeats as Comptroller 448
    Lewis on 464
    travel during Covid-19 459
    on Williamson 427
Spicer, Michael 87, 221, 222, 361, 371
Spriggs, Leslie 94
Squire, Rachel 241
Stallard, Albert 'Jock' 64, 113, 119
Standards and Privileges Committee 248, 252, 471
standing committees 14, 49, 84, 152, 432
Starmer, Sir Keir 34, 444, 461, 489, 491, 492, 494
stave, ceremonial white 25, 26, 32
Steel, David 106–10, 112, 126, 408, 409, 410
Stephenson, Andrew 448
Stewart, Bob 428
Stewart, Rory 450
Stone, Kathryn 471
Stone, Roy 340, 425, 432, 455, 458, 495–6
Stonehouse, John 59–61, 83–4
Story, Alex 468
Stradling Thomas, John 62, 85, 94, 127, 166
Strangers' Bar 74, 88, 314, 315, 317
Straw, Jack 55, 294, 322, 324, 331, 338
Street, Andy 383
Stuart, Graham 485–6
Stunell, Andrew 315–16
Sultana, Zarah 491
Sunak, Rishi xv, 480, 489
Sutcliffe, Gerry 32, 300, 303, 305–6, 307, 314, 322, 326, 365–6
Suttie, Alison 379–80
Swain, Tom 87
Swayne, Sir Desmond 12, 28, 31, 34, 399, 404
Swayner, Desmond 398
Sweeney, Walter 225–7, 228
'sweepers' and 'bogwatchers' 432
Swinson, Jo 436, 437
Syrian chemical weapons attacks (2013) 398–401

Tami, Mark 432
Taylor, Ann 130, 284, 286, 287, 489
Taylor, David 360
Taylor, John 457
Taylor, Teddy 244
Tebbit, Norman 148, 181, 193, 227, 228, 231, 405, 409

525

tellers 9, 22, 86, 94, 123, 241, 266, 326, 366, 433, 485
Terrorism Bill (2006) 338
Thatcher, Denis 115, 176
Thatcher, Margaret 77–9, 135–41
    becomes PM 115
    Brandreth and 252–3
    Brighton Grand Hotel bombing 148
    Callaghan and 88, 90–91, 123
    character 23
    Dobbs on 181–2
    Falklands War 138–40, 161
    first major defeat 178
    Garel-Jones and 184–5
    Hayman and 91
    on Lib–Lab pact 108
    Lister and 177
    loses leadership election 195–200
    Maastricht Treaty 221, 223, 227–8
    mace incident 87
    Morrison rumours and 409
    moves no-confidence motion 120, 123
    pairing and 93
    reshuffles 152, 189, 193
    views on 151
    Wakeham on 169
    Westland affair 147
    whips' dinner 175–6
Thomas, George 85, 120, 140
Thompson, Steve, *Whipping It Up* 344
Thornberry, Emily 338
Thorpe, Jeremy 105, 408
three-line whip 8–9, 10, 13, 45–6, 101, 244, 358, 373, 422, 491
Tipping, Paddy 266, 280, 283, 285, 286, 324, 326, 330
Today (R4) 21, 331
Tolhurst, Kelly 437
Treasurer *see* Deputy Chief Whip
Tribune Group 66–70, 84, 86–7, 113
Trickett, Jon 493
Truss, Liz 479–87
Tugendhat, Christopher 75
tuition fees, university 334, 389–90
Twinn, Ian 137–8, 199, 223, 243
two-line whip 8, 45
Tynan, Bill 327

Ulster Unionists 39, 108, 113, 114, 117–18, 125, 166, 237, 240
Umunna, Chuka 447
'upper deck' duty 96
Urquhart, Francis (fictional character) 181–7, 428

Vaizey, Ed 412
Vaughan, Gerard 229
Vice-Chamberlain 11, 25, 27–32, 314, 448
Vickers, Martin 400
Villiers, Theresa 463
Vine, Sarah 414
Viz magazine 153

Waddington, David 162, 189, 199, 500
Wainwright, Richard 109
Wakeham, John 146–9, 169, 175, 185–6, 199
Waldegrave, William 137, 197
Walker, Bill 227, 232, 240
Walker, Charles 4–5, 360–61, 381, 382, 416, 417, 421
Wall, Patrick 185
Wallace, Jim 196, 231, 387
Wallis, PC Keith 396
Walters, Alan 189
Walters, Simon 313
Warren, Victoria 18–19, 495
Watson, Tom 338, 342–3, 344, 354
Weapons of Mass Destruction (WMD) 320–21, 322
Weatherill, Bernard 'Jack' 71–8, 121, 127, 129, 140, 141, 194, 387

Weatherley, PC Gillian 396
Westminster's Secret Service (BBC documentary) 403, 404
Wheeler, Ted 407–8
whip, the 7–10
    bullying by whips 3, 4, 55, 314, 338
    'core' 10–13
    dealing with complaints 469–70
    'flock' 13–14, 115, 165–73, 256, 369
    history 7–8
    role of 8–10, 430
    suspending 342, 470, 471, 477, 491–2
    'The Whip' circular 8
Whips' Trips 12
White, Frank 119
White, Michael 169
Whitelaw, Willie 52, 123, 137, 160, 197, 403
Whittaker, Craig 479–82, 484–7
    on Brexiteers 435
    daily reports to the Queen 448–9
    on feedback 498
    Johnson and 456
    on Julian Smith 434
    pastoral care 501
    Spencer and 475–6
    on Trade Bill amendments 437
    on Williamson 429, 430
Whittingdale, John 222, 227–8
Widdecombe, Ann 153–4, 192, 217, 243, 368–9
Wigley, Dafydd 51, 61–2, 125, 237
Wilkinson, John 244
Willetts, David 251–2
Williams, Ben 386
Williams, Shirley 92
Williamson, Gavin 425, 426–30, 431–2, 433, 450–51, 482–3
Wilson, Alex 95
Wilson, Harold 39–40
    Callaghan and 84
    EEC and 68
    Harrison and 58
    Mellish and 62–3
    pairing and 53, 91
    resigns 82
    Short and 16
    sick MPs and 93–4
Wilson, Richard 344
Winter of Discontent (1978–9) 114
Winterton, Ann 229, 372
Winterton, Nicholas 223, 235, 241, 374, 406
Winterton, Rosie 397, 404, 414, 416, 443
Wise, Audrey 108–9, 278
Wollaston, Sarah 445
women, as whips 153, 255, 267–8, 437
Wood, Mike 336
Woolas, Phil 289
Wragg, William 499
Wright Committee 359, 377
Wright, Iain 339, 343

Yeo, Tim 246
Young, George 192–3, 398–9, 400–401, 406–7
    Cockerell and 404
    Heath and 194
    instilling discipline 76
    on MPs' private lives 163
    on pairing 88
    on Thatcher 195
    views on 397, 413